D1103796

For my parents, N. Wootton and A. C. Wootton

THE BIOLOGY
OF THE
STICKLEBACKS

For my parents, N. Wootton and A. C. Wootton

THE BIOLOGY
OF THE
STICKLEBACKS

R. J. WOOTTON

Department of Zoology,
University College of Wales,
Aberystwyth, Wales

1976

ACADEMIC PRESS
London   New York   San Francisco

A Subsidiary of Harcourt Brace Jovanovich, Publishers

387 pages

ACADEMIC PRESS INC. (LONDON) LTD.
24/28 Oval Road
London NW1

United States Edition published by
ACADEMIC PRESS INC.
111 Fifth Avenue
New York, New York 10003

QL
638
G27
W66

Copyright © 1976 by
ACADEMIC PRESS INC. (LONDON) LTD.

NMU LIBRARY

All Rights Reserved

No part of this book may be reproduced in any form by photostat, microfilm,
or any other means, without written permission from the publishers

Library of Congress Catalog Card Number: 76-22866
ISBN 0-12-763650-1

PRINTED IN GREAT BRITAIN AT
THE SPOTTISWOODE BALLANTYNE PRESS
BY WILLIAM CLOWES & SONS LIMITED
LONDON, COLCHESTER AND BECCLES

CONTENTS

PART I
THE BIOLOGY OF THE THREE-SPINED STICKLEBACK
(*GASTEROSTEUS ACULEATUS* L.) · 1

Part 2
THE OTHER GASTEROSTEIDS

PREFACE

The sticklebacks form a small family, Gasterosteidae, of that most diverse of vertebrate groups, the Teleostei, phylogenetically the most advanced of the bony fishes. The family contains only five genera, three of which contain just a single species each. For the two remaining genera, the situation is problematical with the debate on their taxonomy still proceeding, but a conservative view is that each genus contains two species. The living representatives of the family are:

Apeltes quadracus (Mitchill), the four-spined stickleback
Culaea inconstans (Kirtland), the brook stickleback
Spinachia spinachia (Linnaeus), the fifteen-spined or sea stickleback
Gasterosteus aculeatus Linnaeus, the three-spined stickleback
Gasterosteus wheatlandi Putnam, the black-spotted stickleback
Pungitius pungitius (Linnaeus), the nine-spined stickleback
Pungitius platygaster (Kessler), the Ukrainian stickleback.

One of these species, the three-spined stickleback (*Gasterosteus aculeatus*), has received more attention from zoologists than almost any other species of fish. This is not because this small fish supports an economically important commercial or sport fishery, but because it combines a fascinating biology with a hardiness that makes it an easy animal to keep and breed in the laboratory. Studies on the three-spined stickleback have made important contributions to ethology, evolutionary biology, vertebrate physiology and ecology. Accounts of these studies are scattered throughout the biological literature, but there have been few attempts to bring this information together in a coherent picture of the biology of the species. Part 1 of this book provides a description of the biology of *G. aculeatus*, while Part 2 considers the other sticklebacks and the evolutionary relationships within the family, and between the family and other teleosts.

The classification of *G. aculeatus* has been and continues to be a vexed problem (Chapter 14). The solution adopted here is conservative, no sub-species are recognised nor is the species split into two or more species. In describing the three morphological forms of *G. aculeatus*, the terms trachurus, leiurus and semiarmatus are used in a purely descriptive sense and are not intended to have any formal taxonomic significance and so they are not italicised. This cautious attitude to the taxonomic complexities of the three-spined stickleback does not represent the conviction that this is the correct solution to the problem, but the feeling that while relevant studies are still appearing in the literature, the situation is too fluid to justify any radical change in the classification of *G. aculeatus* from that generally used.

A significant proportion of Part 1 concerns the reproductive biology of *G. aculeatus*. This weighting reflects the bias that there has been in the research, there is far more information on this aspect of the biology of the stickleback than on topics such as growth, feeding, interactions with other species and population biology. Nevertheless, the information that is available on these subjects, in addition to its own intrinsic interest, provides a background into which the detailed analysis of the reproductive biology can be fitted.

Each chapter of the book is intended to be relatively self-contained with the restriction that they all make frequent reference to chapter 1 on the morphology and anatomy of the three-spined stickleback.

Aberystwyth   R. J. W.

ACKNOWLEDGMENTS

Several colleagues read sections of the manuscript and I thank Dr. K. Banister, Mrs. S. Cole Benjamin, Dr. R. Hinchliffe, Dr. M. Ireland, Dr. G. E. E. Moodie, Professor G. Rees·and Mr. A. Sutcliffe for their comments and help in improving the text. I would particularly like to thank Dr. W. Sinclair who read almost all the manuscript and spent a considerable amount of time trying to improve both the accuracy and clarity of my writing. In spite of all these efforts, mistakes and misinterpretations remain and these are my responsibility.

I would like to thank all those authors who sent me reprints, theses or other information on sticklebacks. The librarians at University College of Wales, especially Mrs. M. Edwards and Mrs. J. Harding, obtained innumerable inter-library loans for me, and were always helpful and patient no matter how obscure the reference I was trying to trace.

Mrs. A. Davies typed the manuscript quickly and accurately. Mrs. S. Hopkins typed the legends for the figures. Miss J. Allen helped with proof correction.

My wife, Maureen, read drafts, criticised, improved grammar, corrected spelling and generally found that giving birth to a book was a far more painful process than giving birth to twins. Without her help this book would never have been completed.

All the figures in the book were freshly drawn, but I would like to thank those publishers and authors who gave me permission to adapt copyright material.

Figs. 2, 3, 7a, 7b, 71, 77: Dr. K. Banister; Fig. 55: The Editor, *Evolution*; Fig. 25: Cambridge University Press; Figs. 8a, 8b, 8c: North Holland Publishing Co; Figs. 54, 61, 74: Reproduced by permission of Information Canada; Figs. 64, 67: Reproduced by permission of the National Research Council of Canada; Fig. 5e:

Fisheries Society of the British Isles; Figs. 27a, 27b, 29, 37a: Springer-Verlag, Heidelberg; Fig. 21: The Zoological Society of London and Prof. R. McN. Alexander; Figs. 13, 40, 43a, 48: Oxford University Press; Fig. 5e: Heinemann Educational Books Ltd. and Prof. G. M. Hughes; Figs. 74, 76: Masson et Cie; Fig. 27c: The Company of Biologists Ltd; Figs. 5d, 23, 26, 38, 46, 47, 51, 52, 63, 64: E. J. Brill, Leiden; Fig. 39: Paul Parey; Fig. 36: The Royal Society of London; Fig. 8d: Balliere and Tindall.

R. J. W.

Part 1

THE BIOLOGY OF THE THREE-SPINED STICKLEBACK
(*GASTEROSTEUS ACULEATUS* L.)

1. Morphology and Anatomy

At first glance the three-spined stickleback (*Gasterosteus aculeatus* L.) is a drab little fish. Only in the spring when the males in bright nuptial dress are performing their elaborate reproductive behaviour can the fascination and beauty of this small fish be immediately appreciated.

It is one of the smallest fish of northern waters; in exceptional circumstances it may reach an adult length of ten centimetres, but it is frequently only half this size. The laterally compressed body is spindle-shaped, tapering to a slender caudal peduncle which bears a truncate caudal fin (Fig. 1). Both the dorsal and anal fins are set well back along the body, with the insertion of the dorsal fin anterior to that of the anal fin. Inserted on the side of the body, the pectoral fins are broad and rounded, and for much of the time a stickleback swims gently by sculling along with these pectoral fins. In contrast, the pelvic fins each consist of just a spine and a single soft fin ray. In the pelvic and pectoral fins, the soft fin rays are simple but in the caudal, dorsal and anal fins, the soft rays are jointed and branched. The number of rays in these fins is somewhat variable for it is influenced by the environmental conditions in which the fish develop, but Table I gives the usual number of fin rays and spines, together with the ranges that have been observed (Nelson, 1971a).

In front of the dorsal fin are the three spines from which the fish takes its common name. Although the vast majority of three-spined sticklebacks justify that title, individuals with two or four dorsal spines turn up regularly in collections, and there are a few unusual populations in which all or a high proportion of individuals show a reduction in the number of dorsal spines (see Chapter 14). Each dorsal spine is separated from the others and the most posterior of the three is isolated from the dorsal fin. This posterior spine is by far the shortest of the three, less than half as long as the anterior two

3

spines. All three have a triangular fin membrane. The pelvic spines are slightly longer than the longest of the dorsal spines and both the dorsal and pelvic spines are serrated. All these spines can be erected and locked in the erect position; the mechanism for this is described in Chapter 5. A small spine which forms the anterior element of the anal fin completes the complement of spines.

Unlike the majority of teleost fishes, the stickleback lacks scales. Instead the body is protected by rows of bony plates or scutes. Along the back there is a row of usually six dorsal plates, although

TABLE I

Fins of *Gasterosteus aculeatus.* (After Banister, 1967 and Nelson, 1971a.)

Fin	Number of soft rays	Nature of soft rays	Number of spines
Pectoral	10	Simple	0
Pelvic	1	Simple	1
Anal	8–11 (rarely 6 or 7)	Branched and jointed	1
First dorsal	0		3 (rarely 2 or 4)
Second dorsal	10–14 (rarely 9)	Branched and jointed	0
Caudal	12	Branched and jointed	0

the number of these is not absolutely constant (Penczak, 1962, 1965). Along each of the flanks there is a row of lateral plates and variation in the number of these lateral plates provides one of the main themes in the study of the biology of the three-spined stickleback (Fig. 1).

On the basis of the number and arrangement of lateral plates, a stickleback can usually be assigned to one of three morphological forms or morphs. Correlated with the variation in number of lateral plates, there are variations in other morphological features, in physiology and in behaviour. The three forms are named trachurus, semiarmatus and leiurus (Münzing, 1959; Hagen, 1967).

Trachurus sticklebacks have a complete row of lateral plates stretching from just in front of the pectoral fin to the tail, the row containing thirty to thirty-five plates. The caudal peduncle is keeled, a morphological feature also found in fish such as tuna and mackeral that may enable the fish to turn rapidly in pursuit of elusive prey (Watts, cited in Marshall, 1971). Trachurus sticklebacks normally

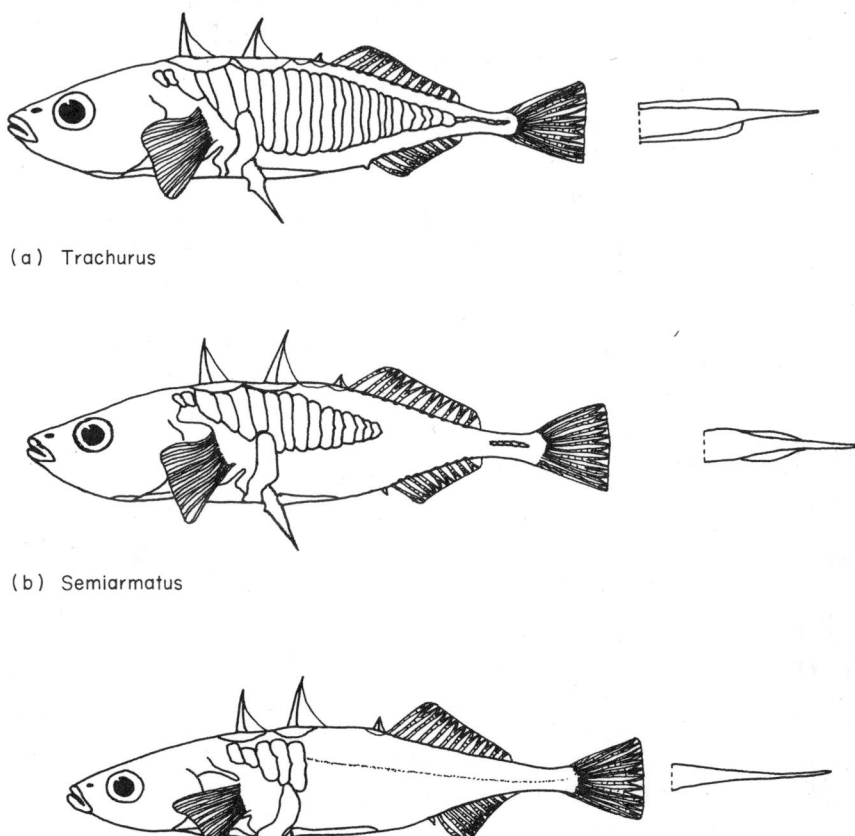

(a) Trachurus

(b) Semiarmatus

(c) Leiurus

Fig. 1. The three forms of *Gasterosteus aculeatus*, (a) trachurus, (b) semiarmatus and (c) leiurus. Lateral views show the extent of the row of lateral plates and the dorsal views show the extent of the keel on the caudal peduncle.

have silvery bodies although in the breeding season the males develop distinctive nuptial colours. Although landlocked populations of trachurus fish occur, most populations are anadromous; in spring they migrate into fresh or brackish water to breed and in the following autumn the young and any surviving adults migrate to the sea where they spend the winter. The possession of a complete row of lateral plates and a caudal keel is usually used as the criterion for identifying the trachurus form, but there is some variation in the degree of development of both the plates and the keel. In the Chignik River system in Alaska, the sticklebacks that had a complete row of lateral plates could be divided into two phenotypes. The estuarine phenotype had well-developed lateral plates and keel, whereas the lateral plates and keel of the lacustrine phenotype were noticeably less well developed (Narver, 1969). Some authors have restricted the term trachurus to completely plated sticklebacks that are anadromous, calling the completely plated sticklebacks that are permanently resident in fresh water the completely plated morph (Hagen and Gilbertson, 1972, 1973b); this problem is considered in more detail in Chapter 14.

The leiurus form, which in the older literature is also known as the gymnura form, has only a few lateral plates in the anterior region of the body. Usually there are between one and nine plates in a row, but in some populations there are individuals with no plates at all. The plateless form has been called hologymnura (Bertin, 1925). Leiurus sticklebacks lack a caudal keel. Outside the breeding season, they are olive brown with darker blotches. Leiurus populations are resident in fresh water throughout the year, so that at most the spring migration consists of a movement from deeper water into shallower water or from a main river into tributaries and backwaters. This restriction to fresh water is not absolute for in the southern part of its range in Europe the leiurus form penetrates into brackish water, while in northwestern Europe fish that morphologically fit into the leiurus category form a small proportion of the migratory stickleback populations (Munzing, 1959, 1963a).

The third form, semiarmatus, has a more variable number of lateral plates than the other two forms; the number can vary from eight or nine to thirty, that is covering the range between the leiurus and trachurus forms. There is invariably a gap in the row of lateral plates, so that they can be divided into an anterior and posterior series. Penczak (1961a) has shown that lateral plates can be regenerated, so that the gap in the row observed in semiarmatus sticklebacks does not represent a damaged area. A caudal keel is present. Recently Hay (1974) has argued that the criterion that distinguishes the semiarmatus form from the leirus form is not the presence of a caudal keel in the former, but the absence of a particular lateral plate in the latter. If the most anterior lateral plate is labelled A, and the succeeding plates B, C etc., the leiurus fish always lack plate I, which is invariably present in semiarmatus fish, whether or not they have a caudal keel. The generality of Hay's criterion has still to be determined. Both landlocked and anadromous populations of the semiarmatus form are known. Hagen and his co-workers in north-western America call sticklebacks that have a caudal keel, an incomplete row of lateral plates, and are permanent residents of fresh water, the partially-plated morph.

In a careful comparative study of the leiurus and trachurus populations that bred in a small river in southwest British Columbia (Canada), Hagen (1967) listed the characteristics of the two forms. In addition to the differences described above, the trachurus fish had more gill rakers than the leiurus fish, and furthermore the rakers were longer and finer than those of leiurus. This difference probably reflects a difference between the feeding ecology of the two forms, a point discussed in Chapter 4. Adult trachurus tended to be longer than adult leiurus sticklebacks but were more slender. There were also differences in the average number of anal and dorsal fin rays. Female trachurus sticklebacks produced more eggs per spawning than female leiurus sticklebacks (Table II).

Crosses between trachurus and leiurus fish yielded offspring that were morphologically intermediate between the two forms, the offspring fell within the semiarmatus range of lateral plates. These hybrids between trachurus and leiurus fish were restricted to a relatively small region of the river. In most situations it is likely that semiarmatus fish are produced in areas in which there is some interbreeding between the leiurus and trachurus components of the stickleback population, in such areas the semiarmatus form repre-sents an intergrade. This may not always be the case, for there are some populations in which all or a vast majority of the fish belong to the semiarmatus form (see Chapter 14). Although Bertin (1925) has suggested that the differences between the three forms were pro-duced by differences in the salinity and temperature regimes in which the fish developed, more recent studies show that the morphological differences reflect genetic differences. The eggs of trachurus x trachurus crosses yield trachurus offspring even if they are kept under identical environmental conditions to eggs of leiurus x leiurus crosses which yield leiurus offspring (Hagen, 1967). This topic is discussed in more detail in Chapter 14 along with a consideration of some unusual forms that do not fit neatly into the trachurus, leiurus and semiarmatus trichotomy.

In comparison with other fish of a similar size, the three-spined stickleback, and indeed the other sticklebacks, have sturdy skeletons (Benzie, 1965). A brief description of the skeletal anatomy of *G. aculeatus* is given here and more information is provided in Chapter 20 in the context of a discussion on the evolutionary relationships within the Gasterosteidae. More detailed accounts of the osteology of the three-spined stickleback are provided by Kampf (1962), Banister (1967), Nelson (1971a), Mural (1973), (Table III and Fig. 2).

The mouth of the stickleback is small and set obliquely so that the bottom jaw protrudes beyond the top jaw. Each half of the upper jaw consists of a pre-maxilla and a maxilla. The ascending process of the pre-maxilla lies on a rostral cartilage. Each half of the lower jaw

TABLE II

A comparison of the morphological characters of leiurus, trachurus and presumed hybrid sticklebacks (*Gasterosteus aculeatus*) from the Little Campbell River, British Columbia. Sample sizes are shown in brackets (from Hagen, 1967).

Character		Leiurus	Trachurus	Hybrid
Number of lateral plates	Mean	4.6	32.7	17.0
	SE	.040	.049	.263
	range	3–7	30–35	8–29
		(862)	(890)	(493)
Number of gill rakers	Mean	16.3	21.8	18.0
	SE	.052	.122	.183
	range	12–19	17–25	13–23
		(120)	(120)	(120)
Number of dorsal fin rays	Mean	11.0	12.0	11.8
	SE	.03	.02	.06
	range	9–13	9–14	10–14
		(456)	(465)	(382)
Number of anal fin rays	Mean	7.9	8.9	8.2
	SE	.08	.02	.04
	range	6–10	7–10	7–10
		(592)	(600)	(309)
Standard length at breeding (cm)	Mean	3.4	5.7	4.3
	SE	.03	.08	.09
		(472)	(468)	(200)
Body length: body depth	Mean	3.7	4.3	3.9
	SE	.04	.04	.05
		(50)	(50)	(50)
Number of mature eggs	Mean	105	241	190
		(40)	(40)	(40)

consists of a dentary, an articular which articulates with the quadrate to form the jaw articulation, and a small angular bone. Of these jaw bones, only the pre-maxillae and dentaries carry teeth, which are small but sharp. An unusual feature is that although the jaws are protusible, there are no jaw ligaments, that is the crossed ligaments between the ethmoid block and palatine and the pre-maxilla and maxilla. The mechanics of jaw protrusion are considered in Chapter 4. The suspension of the jaw from the neurocranium (brain case) is

TABLE III

Bones of the head region (syncranium) of *Gasterosteus aculeatus* (after Banister, 1967). Endochondral bones *in italics*. Dermal bones in normal print, toothed bones marked*.

| | **SYNCRANIUM** | |
| | *NEUROCRANIUM* | |
Olfactory region	Orbital region	Otic region
ethmoid	frontals	*autosphenotics*
lateral ethmoids	infraorbitals	*autopterotics*
vomer	dermosphenotics	*prootics*
nasals		*intercalaries*
		epiotics
		exoccipitals
		supraoccipital
		dermopterotics
		parietals
		posttemporals
		supra cleithra
		dermosupraoccipital
	Basicranial region	
	basioccipital	
	parasphenoid	

| | *BRANCHIOCRANIUM* | |
Oromandibular region	Hyoid region	Branchial region
autopalatines	*hyomandibulars*	*pharyngobranchials*
"*pterygoids*"	*symplectics*	2, (3–4), both plates
metapterygoids	*interhyals*	toothed
quadrates	*epihyals*	*epibranchials*
articulars	*ceratohyals*	1–4
premaxillae*	*upper* and *lower*	*ceratobranchials*
	hypohyals	1–5 (5 is toothed)
maxillae	*basihyal*	
dentaries*	operculars	*hypobranchials*
angulars	suboperculars	1–3
	preoperculars	*basibranchials*
	interoperculars	1–3
	branchiostegal rays	
	urohyal	

achieved through the suspensorium which consists of the hyomandibular, metapterygoid, sympletic, quadrate, the pterygoid and the autopalatine (Fig. 3). Two heads of the hyomandibular articulate with the brain case; one head fits into a cavity at the

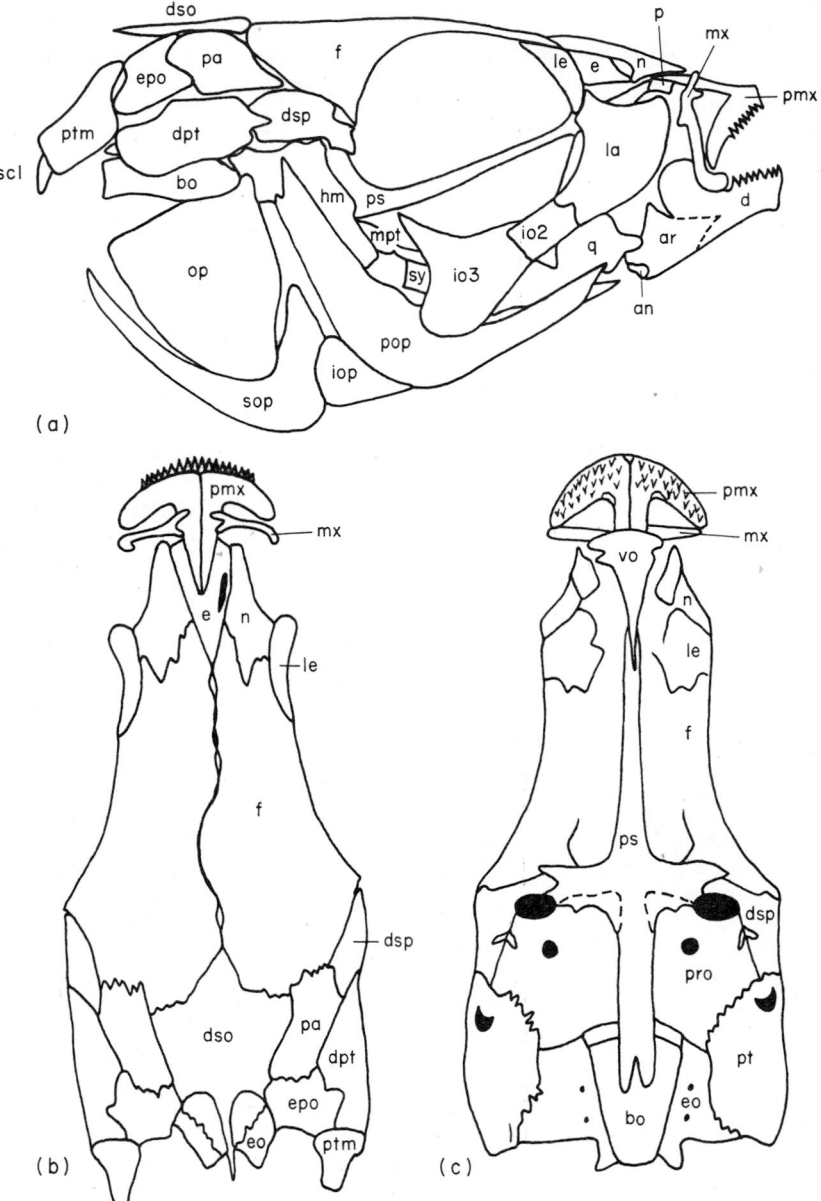

Fig. 2. Skull of *Gasterosteus aculeatus* (after Banister, 1967). (a) Lateral view; (b) dorsal view; (c) ventral view. Key to lettering: an, angular; ar, articular; bo, basioccipital; d, dentary; dpt, dermopterotic; dso, dermosupraoccipital; dsp, dermosphenotic; e, ethmoid; eo, exoccipital; epo, epiotic; f, frontal; hm, hyomandibular; io, infraorbital; iop, interopercular; la, lachrymal; le, lateral ethmoid; mpt, metapterygoid; mx, maxilla; n, nasal; op, opercular; p, autopalatine; pa, parietal; pmx, premaxilla; pop, preopercular; pro, prootic; ps, parasphenoid; pt, autopterotic; ptm, posttemporal; q, quadrate; sop, subopercular; sy, symplectic; vo, vomer.

junction of the autosphenotic and prootic bones and the other head fits into a depression in the ventral face of the autopterotic bone (a third head articulates with the operculum forming a link between the jaw and opercular regions).

The roof of the skull is formed principally by the nasals, frontals, parietals and the dermosupraoccipital (Fig. 2b) and these bones are strongly sculptured. A ventral view of the skull is shown in Fig. 2c; there are no palatine teeth. A feature of the skull is the large size of the eye orbits. The dorsal border of the orbit is formed by the frontal bone, the anterior border by the lateral ethmoid, the

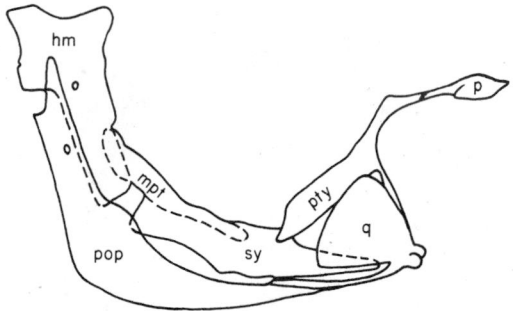

Fig. 3. Suspensorium of *Gasterosteus aculeatus* (after Banister, 1967). Key to lettering; hm, hyomandibular; mpt, metapterygoid; p, autopalatine; pop, preopercular; pty, pterygoid (= endopterygoid + ectopterygoid); q, quadrate; sy, symplectic.

lachrymal (1st infraorbital) and the second and third infraorbitals, but the posterior border is unusual because infraorbitals are missing, and instead the posterior wall of the orbit is formed by a descending process from the frontal, an ascending process from the parasphenoid and a process of the autosphenoid. A spike on the dermosphenotic points towards a spike on the third infraorbital (Fig. 2a).

On each side the gills are protected by a bony opercular flap; the bones of the opercular region are the opercular, subopercular, interopercular and preopercular. The gills are the site where the de-oxygentated blood is recharged with oxygen which diffuses into the blood from the surrounding water. There are five branchial arches, but only four of these carry gills. Typically each arch consists of a dorsal element, the epibranchial, and a ventral element, the ceratobranchial. These elements are augmented by a pharyngo-branchial which lies dorsal to the epibranchial, and a hypobranchial and basibranchial which lie ventral to the ceratobranchial. In the stickleback epibranchials occur in arches one to four, cerato-branchials in arches one to five, while the hypobranchials and basibranchials are found in arches one to three with a small cartilaginous basibranchial associated with arch four. There is a pharyngobranchial in arch two, but those of arches three and four are fused to form a toothed plate (Fig. 4). On their inner margins, the gill arches bear projections, the gill rakers, while on the outer

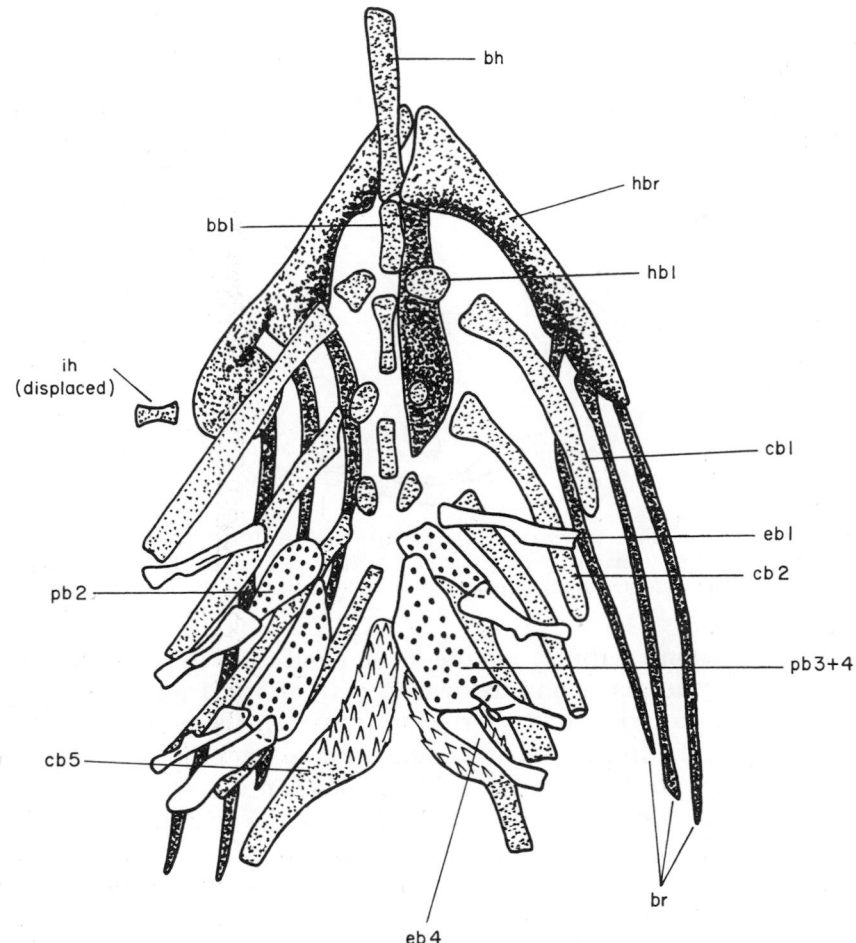

Fig. 4. Dorsal view of branchial skeleton of *Gasterosteus aculeatus* (after Banister, 1967). Key to lettering; bb, basibranchial; bh, basihyal; br, branchiostegal rays; cb, ceratobranchial; eb, epibranchial; hb, hypobranchial; hbr, hyoid bar; ih, interhyal; pb, pharyngobranchial.

margin are gill rays which stiffen the gill filaments. These filaments bear secondary lamellae which serve to increase the surface area of the gills exposed to water and so provide a greater area over which oxygen diffusion can take place. The two sides of a secondary lamella have an epithelium of flattened, interdigitating cells, with pillar cells

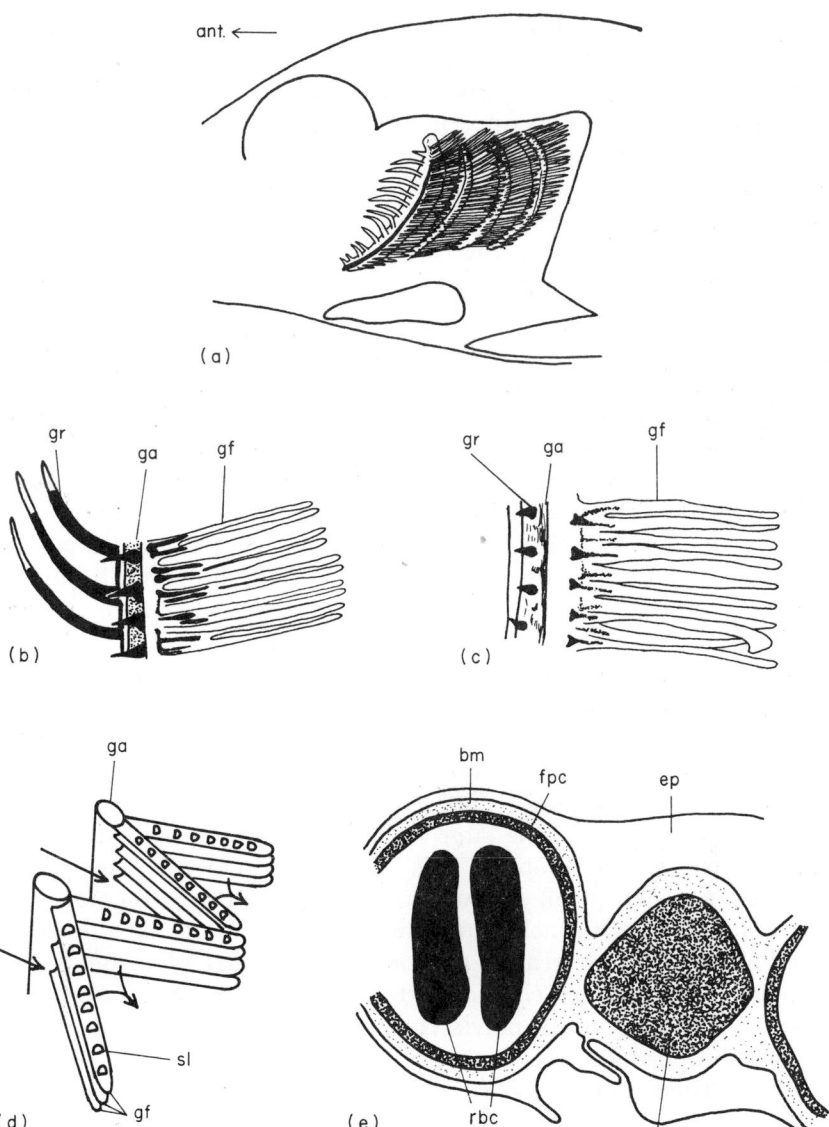

Fig. 5. The gills of *Gasterosteus aculeatus*. (a) Lateral view of branchial region with operculum removed; (b) segment of first gill arch showing long gill rakers on this arch; (c) segment of third gill arch showing short gill rakers; (d) schematic diagram of the arrangement of the gill filaments showing secondary lamellae and the direction of water flow across the filaments (after Bijtel, 1949, and Hughes, 1963); (e) schematic diagram of a transverse section through a secondary lamella showing arrangement of pillar cell (after Matthiessen and Brafield, 1973). Key to lettering: bm, basement membrane; ep, epithelial cell; fpc, flange of pillar cell; ga, gill arch; gf, gill filament; gr, gill raker; pc, pillar cell; rbc, red blood corpuscle; sl, secondary lamella. Headed arrows show direction of water flow over filaments.

separating the two sides. Flanges of these pillar cells line the blood spaces in the lamella (Fig. 5). This arrangement means that the distance that oxygen has to diffuse from water to blood is very short. Chloride cells, which are concerned with osmoregulation (Chapter 8), are concentrated on the filaments and at the bases of the lamellae, but are rarely found on the secondary lamellae themselves (Matthiessen and Brafield, 1973).

The occipital condyle, the skull component of the articulation between the skull and the vertebral column, is formed solely by the basioccipital bone, with the other bones in the region of the occiput, the exoccipitals and the supraoccipital not contributing to the condyle. Although there are usually thirty-two vertebrae, this number may range from twenty-nine to thirty-three. In the normal complement, fourteen are precaudal or abdominal vertebrae and eighteen caudal vertebrae, so that the first haemal arch is usually found on the fifteenth vertebrae. Fusions between adjoining vertebrae occur in some individuals, possibly because of suboptimal conditions during ontogeny (Coad, 1974). Epipleural ribs are commonly found on the first thirteen vertebrae and pleural ribs on the third to fourteenth vertebrae (Fig. 6).

Modified elements of the vertebrae form the skeletal elements that support the caudal fin. Two hypurals, partly fused, but which nevertheless can be clearly distinguished, are derived from the haemal arches, and dorsal to the hypurals are one, or occasionally two, epurals (Fig. 14) (Huxley, 1859).

Since the pectoral fin is large it is not surprising that the pectoral skeleton is well developed (Fig. 7a). The skeleton for each fin consists of a cleithrum, scapula, coracoid and ectocoracoid, with a posttemporal and supracleithrum linking the pectoral skeleton to the skull. All but the uppermost pectoral fin rays articulate on the four actinosts (radials) which lie just posterior to the scapula and coracoid. Although each pelvic fin consists of just one spine and one fin ray, the pelvic skeleton is sturdy, if simple, in structure (Fig. 7b). It is not fused with any part of the pectoral skeleton. Each half of the pelvic skeleton consists of a sculptured ascending process which is partially overlapped by the anterior lateral plates and a ventral plate which has an anterior and a posterior process. The ventral plates of the halves interdigitate in the ventral mid-line and together form a strong bony plate covering the ventral fore-belly (Fig. 7c).

Kampf (1962) and Anker (1974) have described the muscles of the head region and Hoogland (1951) the muscles involved in the erection and depression of the spines, but the muscle system of the stickleback has attracted little attention probably because the fish is too small to

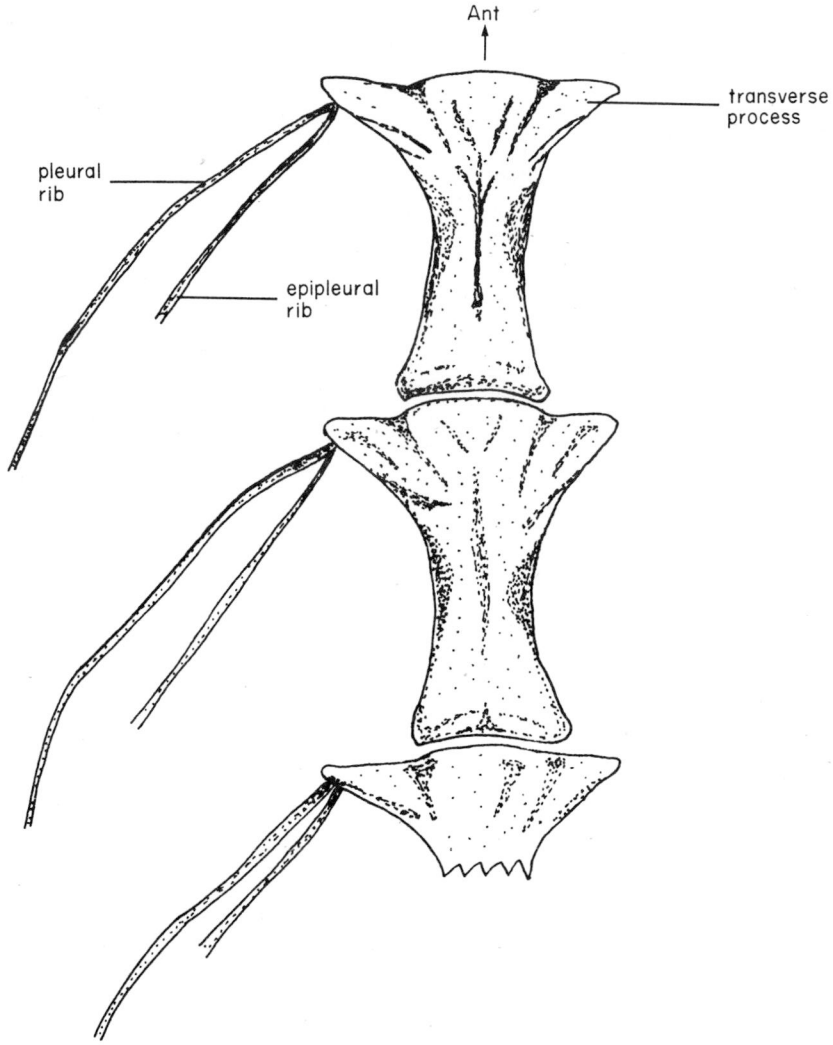

Fig. 6. Ventral view of two pre-caudal vertebrae of *Gasterosteus aculeatus* (ribs on one side have been removed).

provide good material for experimental studies on muscles. Titschack (1922) found that in the breeding season the muscles associated with the pectoral fins of the male fish enlarged, a change that is correlated with the reproductive behaviour of the male stickleback (Chapter 10).

Muscular activity is coordinated by the central nervous system, which consists of the brain and spinal cord, and the associated

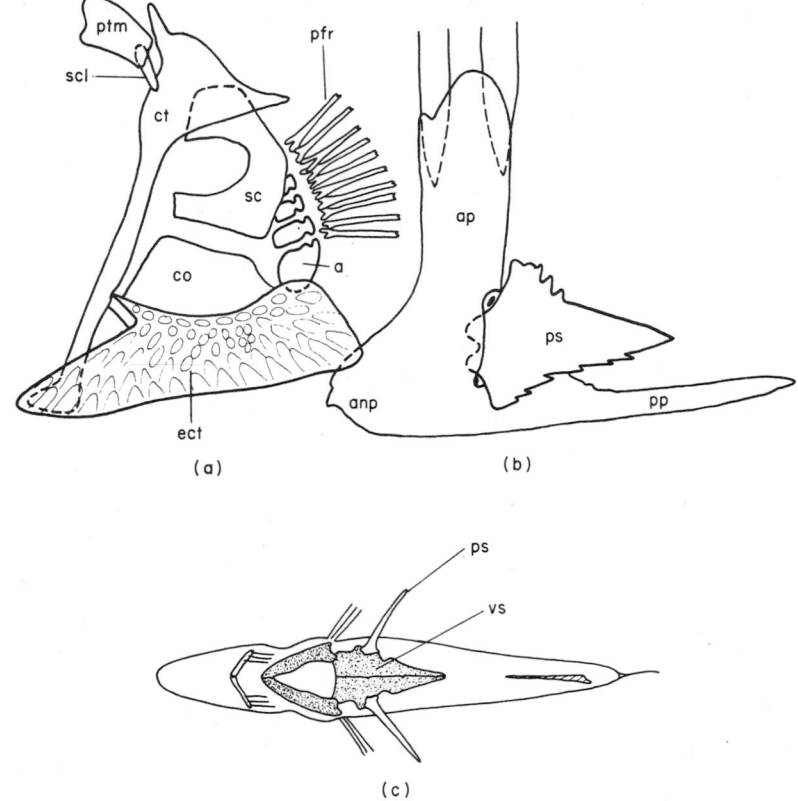

Fig. 7. Pectoral and pelvic skeletons of *Gasterosteus aculeatus*. (a) Lateral view of pectoral skeleton and (b) lateral view of pelvic skeleton (after Banister, 1967); (c) ventral view of fish showing ventral shield formed by the pelvic skeleton. Key to lettering: a, actinost; ap, ascending process of pelvic skeleton; anp, anterior process of pelvic skeleton; co, coracoid; ct, cleithrum; ect, ectocoracoid; pfr, pectoral fin rays; pp, posterior process of pelvic skeleton; ps, pelvic spine; ptm, posttemporal; sc, scapula; scl, supracleithrum; vs, ventral shield.

autonomic nervous system. The brain can be divided into three sections, the fore-brain (prosencephalon), the mid-brain (mesencephalon) and the hind-brain (rhombencephalon). The fore-brain is subdivided into the telencephalon and the diencephalon (Fig. 8).

In a discussion of the structure of the telencephalon of the stickleback, or indeed any other teleost fish, a difficulty arises because the teleost telencephalon develops from the embryonic state in a completely different way from the telencephalon of mammals and other tetrapods. This makes it difficult to label parts of the teleost telencephalon as though they correspond to equivalent structures in the tetrapod brain. As in other vertebrates, the stickleback telencephalon is derived from the anterior of the embryonic neural tube, but in the stickleback and other teleosts, the telencephalon thickens by an eversion of the lateral plates of the neural tube. This eversion results in the roof plate being attached on the

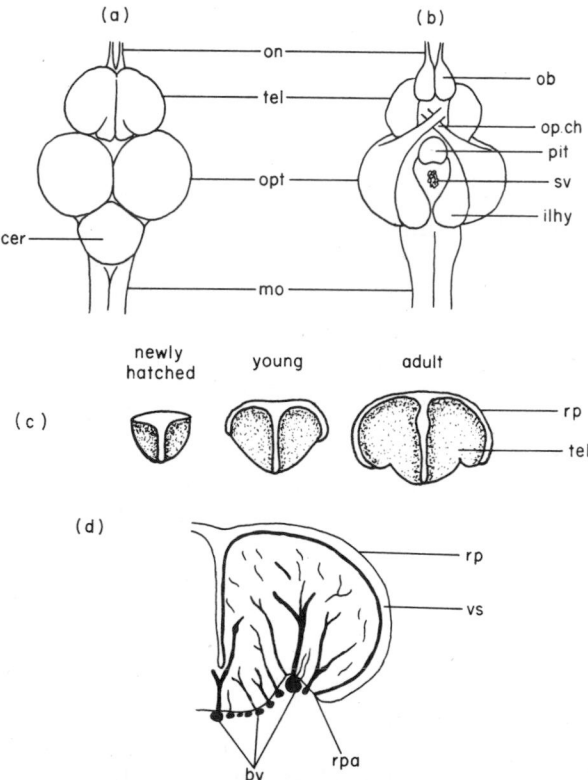

Fig. 8. The brain of *Gasterosteus aculeatus*. (a) Dorsal view; (b) ventral view; (c) ontogeny of brain showing thickening of telencephalon by evagination; (d) transverse section through the telencephalon showing extent of roof plate and the reduced meningeal surface. (a), (b) and (c) after Nieuwenhuys (1959); (d) after Segaar and Nieuwenhuys (1963). Key to lettering: bv, blood vessels; cer, cerebellum; ilhy, inferior lobe of the hypothalamus; mo, medulla oblongata; ob, olfactory bulb, on, olfactory nerve; opch, optic chiasma; opt, optic tectum; pit, pituitary; rp, roof plate; rpa, attachment of roof plate; sv, saccus vasculosus; tel, telencephalon; vs, ventricular space.

ventrolateral side of the telencephalon and not merely covering the roof (Fig. 8c). A further consequence of this lateral extension of the roof plate is that the meningeal surface of the telencephalon is confined to a small basal area, but it is only through this meningeal surface that blood vessels enter and leave the telencephalon (Fig. 8d).

Paired olfactory bulbs, which receive axons from the sensory cells of the nasal organs, lie on the anterior ventral surface of the telencephalon, but the bulk of this portion of the fore-brain is made up of paired hemispheres. In these hemispheres two regions are distinguished, the ventral area of the telencephalon which forms the ventromedial region of the hemispheres, and the dorsal area of the telencephalon which occupies the dorsolateral regions of the hemispheres. Although all the groups of cells (nuclei) in the ventral area receive nerve fibres from the olfactory bulbs, only a portion of the dorsal area is connected with the bulbs. The major connections for the dorsal area are with regions of the diencephalon, particularly the thalamus and hypothalamus. These connections include both afferent and efferent fibres so that the dorsal region both receives and sends nervous impulses to the diencephalon. There is also a connection between the ventral area of the telencephalon and the thalamus. In the posterior region of the telencephalon, there is a commisure, the anterior commisure, which connects the two hemispheres of the telencephalon. Behind this commisure there is a region, the praeoptic nucleus, which sends nerve fibres to the hypothalamus and pituitary organ. Scattered through the praeoptic nuclei are neurosecretory cells whose neurosecretions are liberated into the bloodstream in the neurohypophysial region of the pituitary organ (Nieuwenhuys, 1959; Segaar and Nieuwenhuys, 1963). Removal of the telencephalon did not cause any differences in the general behaviour of the stickleback, nor in its ability to distinguish colours (Nolte, 1933), but effects on reproductive behaviour of lesions to the telencephalon have been observed and are discussed in Chapter 13.

The diencephalon consists of the epithalamus, the thalamus and the hypothalamus. Two elements comprise the epithalamus, the pineal complex and the paired habenular ganglia, which receive nerve fibres from the pineal complex, the telencephalon and from the praeoptic nuclei. The thalamus is connected both to the telencephalon and to the mid- and hind-brain, as well as with the hypothalamus. Several features indicate the importance of the hypothalamus which forms the floor of the diencephalon. The first is the intimate contact between the hypothalamus and the pituitary gland; the hypothalamus sends fibres, including neurosecretory fibres, into the pituitary where they form the neurohypophysis (Dodd and Kerr, 1963). Secondly the hypothalamus receives fibres from the telencephalon and from the hind-brain and sends fibres to the telencephalon, the hind-brain, the thalamus, the optic tectum and the cerebellum. Unfortunately, the small size of the stickleback has so far prevented the study of this part of the diencephalon by electrical stimulation, although Schönherr (1955) has studied the effects of lesions of the hypothalamus on the reproductive behaviour of the male stickleback. Just behind the hypothalamus the saccus vasculosus protrudes through the floor of the diencephalon. It is formed from ependymal cells, the epithelial cells that line the ventricle, but its function is not known (Benjamin, 1974c).

The mid-brain consists of the optic tectum which forms the roof of the third ventricle of the brain, and the tegmentum which forms the floor of the ventricle. Vision is a most important sense for the stickleback, so it is not surprising that the tectal lobes are large. Each lobe receives the fibres of the optic nerve on the opposite (contralateral) side of the head, so that the right eye projects onto the left tectal hemisphere and the left eye onto the right hemisphere; the crossing-over of the optic nerves forms the optic chiasma (Fig. 8b). After the removal of the roof of the mid-brain, a stickleback was blind, but did not show disturbed swimming (Baudelot, 1864, cited in Healy, 1957).

Behind the mid-brain lies the cerebellum, whose function is probably the coordination and regulation of movement, and the maintenance of equilibrium. Some very early work on the function of the cerebellum found that its removal did not cause any drastic changes in the behaviour of the stickleback (Baudelot, 1864, cited in Healy, 1957), but this study needs to be replicated using more modern techniques. The medulla oblongata is the most posterior region of the brain and it merges into the spinal cord so that the border between the two is indistinct. At the posterior end of the spinal cord there is a neuroendocrine organ, the urohypophysis, whose function is uncertain though it may be involved in osmoregulation.

Information about the external environment is fed into the central nervous system through the sense organs, and in the stickleback vision seems to be the dominant sense, with the retinal surface accounting for 3.5 per cent of the total surface area of the body (Beukema, 1968). Behavioural studies have shown that sticklebacks have colour vision with peaks of sensitivity to light of 510 and 594 nm for females and 502 and 594 for males (Cronly-Dillon and Sharma, 1968). Meesters (1940) had already shown that sticklebacks have good form vision, for example they readily discriminate between a square and triangle.

The olfactory epithelium makes up only 0.4 per cent of the total body surface so that the stickleback is classed as a microsmatic species (Teichmann, 1954). There is a single nasal opening on either side of the snout and each opening leads into a small olfactory cavity in which the olfactory epithelium shows only two folds. Water is inhaled and expelled from the cavity by pressure changes occurring in normal respiration (Bannister, 1965). Sticklebacks detect their food by sight, and smell seems to play no role in the finding of food (Pipping, 1926). Food is tested by the taste receptors in the buccal cavity and pharynx (Glaser, 1966); the structure and ultrastructure of these taste receptors are described by Campos (1969) and Whitear (1971b).

Information about mechanical disturbance in the water around fishes is obtained by the sense organs of the lateral line system, but in the stickleback the extent of the lateral line system is reduced, especially in the head region. The labyrinth or ear has a common embryological origin with the lateral line system but has become completely isolated from the external environment. It detects angular and linear acceleration and so provides the information required if the fish is to maintain its equilibrium. The labyrinth can also act as a sound detector, but the importance of sound for the stickleback has not been studied, although some authors have suggested that the pelvic spines might be used as stridulatory organs. The otoliths of the labyrinth, small calcareous masses, are used to age sticklebacks for they show annual growth rings (Chapter 3).

In addition to these sensory systems, there is a general cutaneous sensory component which supplies the skin of the stickleback with receptor fibres for tactile and temperature stimuli and perhaps painful stimuli. These nerve fibres come to free endings in the epidermis (Whitear, 1971a).

Neural activity results in rapid changes in the state of the animal, but longer term changes such as the onset of sexual maturity are mediated by the endocrine system in which the transfer of information depends on chemical substances, hormones, which circulate in the blood system. In most, if not all, vertebrates, the principal endocrine organ is the pituitary gland, which, through its hormones modulates the activity of other endocrine organs, and which because of its close association with the hypothalamus provides the main link between the central nervous system and the endocrine system.

In the stickleback, the pituitary is a small organ which lies under the hypothalamus, behind the optic chiasma and just in front of the saccus vasculosus. It is joined to the brain by thin strands of tissue anteriorly and posteriorly. The fine structure of the stickleback pituitary has received considerable attention (Bock, 1928; van Mullem, 1959; Follenius, 1968c; Leatherland, 1970a, b; Benjamin, 1973, 1974a). It is a complex organ made up of two components which have different embryological origins, the neurohypophysis and the adenohypophysis. The neurohypophysis is essentially an extension of the floor of the diencephalon and is the site where the neuro-secretory cells of the diencephalon release their hormonal products into the blood stream (Dodd and Kerr, 1963). Some of the nerve fibres in the neurohypophysis were found to accumulate γ-amino-butyric acid (GABA) which is thought to be a neurotransmitter (Follenius, 1972b). It is possible that these fibres may play a role in the control of the glandular cells of the pituitary. There is consider-able interdigitation of the neurohypophysis with the adeno-hypophysis although they have distinct origins. Nerve fibres which

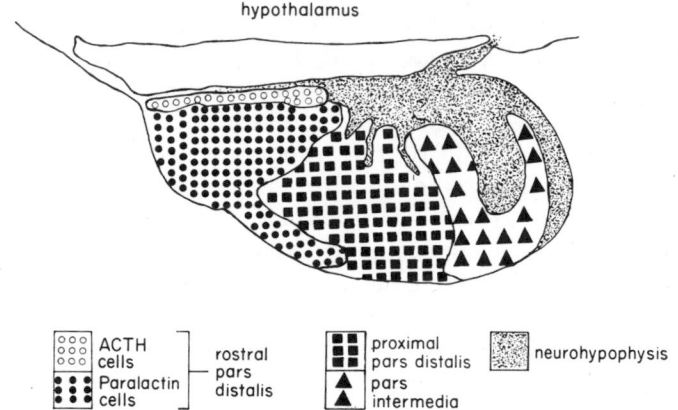

Fig. 9. Schematic diagram of sagittal section through the pituitary of *Gasterosteus aculeatus*. Based on section stained with alcian blue-PAS-orange G from a leiurus female in breeding condition.

selectively accumulated nor-adrenalin and dopamine have been demonstrated in the pars intermedia of the adenohypophysis (Follenius, 1968a, 1971). Although there has been relatively little study on the function of the neurosecretions from the neuro-hypophysis they may be implicated in osmoregulation (Chapter 8).

The adenohypophysis derives from an ectodermal pouch which pushes dorsally from the embryonic mouth to make contact with the neurohypophysis. By convention the adenohypophysis is divided into three regions, the rostral pars distalis, the proximal pars distalis and the pars intermedia (Fig. 9). In the rostral pars distalis are cells which produce the hormone paralactin, the fish equivalent of prolactin, and cells which produce adrenocorticotropic hormone (ACTH) which probably controls the activity of the interrenals, the teleost equivalent of the tetrapod adrenal cortex. In the proximal pars distalis, three types of cell have been identified, the somatotropes which produce growth hormone (SH), the thyrotropes which produce thyroid-stimulating hormone (TSH), and the gonadotropes which produce gonadotropic hormone (GTH). The somatotropes were found to accumulate nor-adrenalin, but the functional significance of this is not clear (Follenius, 1967). Two cell types have been identified in the pars intermedia. One of these cells is probably where the melanocyte-stimulating hormone is produced (Follenius and Dubois, 1974). Melanophores are cells which contain the black pigment, melanin, and they occur in the skin of the stickleback. The function of the other cell type of the pars intermedia is not known as yet. Detailed descriptions of the ultrastructure of the cells of the adenohypophysis are available for both the leiurus and trachurus forms (Benjamin, 1974a; Leatherland, 1970a, b).

One of the target organs of a pituitary hormone is the interrenal gland, which is a paired organ for each half is contained within the head kidney on either side of the body (see below). Although the bulk of the head kidney is made up of haemopoetic and lymphatic tissue, the interrenal consists of a layer of tissue several cells thick, which lines a blood space in the head kidney. In the stickleback there is only a single cardinal vein, usually that on the right-hand side. This vein penetrates the head kidney and the interrenal tissue lines a portion of the cardinal vein. In the head kidney on the left-hand side the interrenal tissue lines a smaller venous space. The head kidney is innervated by the second cervical ganglia of the autonomic nervous system, and within the interrenal tissue there is a rich plexus of nerve fibres (Stanworth, 1953). Cells of the interrenal can synthesise the steroid hormones typical of the adrenal cortex of the tetrapods. ACTH secreted by the corticotrope cells of the rostral pars distalis of the pituitary controls, at least partially, the activity of the interrenal. When trachurus fish were injected with ACTH during the winter, there was a decrease in the size of the corticotropes but an increase in the size of the nuclei of interrenal cells together with other signs that the interrenal cells had been stimulated. Other effects of the injections were the development of a green skin coloration and a decrease in the rate of growth in length relative to fish that were given control injections of saline (Leatherland and Lam, 1971). Injections of ACTH also stimulated the interrenals of leiurus fish but did not produce histologically detectable effects on the corticotrope cells of the pituitary, although treatment with the drug metopirone produced changes in both the corticotropes and the interrenal cells (Benjamin, 1973; Benjamin and Ireland, 1974).

The kidneys of the stickleback are paired, although the two halves fuse posteriorly. They lie just under the vertebral column and each half consists of a trunk portion which is joined by a strand of tissue to a head kidney in which the interrenal cells occur. Only the trunk portion is concerned with the production of urine (Chapter 8) and, in the sexually mature male, a glue used for sticking the nest together

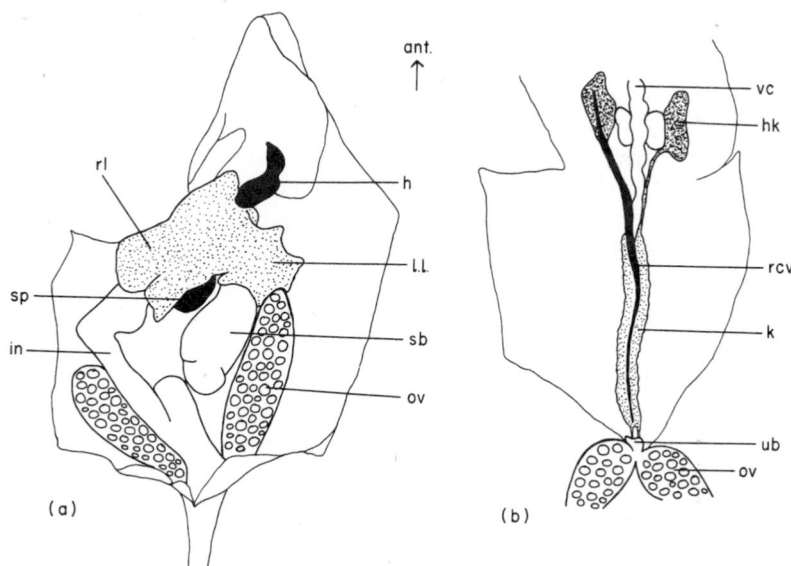

Fig. 10. Internal organs of female *Gasterosteus aculeatus*. (a) Body cavity opened and alimentary canal displaced to one side; (b) digestive organs and swim bladder removed. Key to lettering: h, heart; hk, head kidney; in, intestine; ll, left lobe of liver; ov, ovary; rcv, right cardinal vein; rl, right lobe of liver; sp, spleen; sb, swim bladder; ub, urinary bladder; vc, vertebral column.

is also produced in the trunk portion of the kidneys (Chapter 10). Small endocrine glands, the corpuscles of Stannius, lie at the surface of the kidneys (Wendelaar Bonga and Grevan, 1975). Also lying in the abdominal cavity are the gonads, paired ovaries in the female and paired testes in the male. The gonads are target organs for the hormone(s) produced by the gonadotropic cells of the proximal pars distalis of the pituitary.

Another target organ for a hormone from the pituitary is the thyroid tissue which is found in the pharyngeal region ventral to the oesophagus. Activity of the thyroid cells is modulated by the TSH produced by the thyrotropes of the proximal pars distalis.

In the stickleback, the alimentary canal consists of an oesophagus, stomach and a short, straight intestine and rectum. Associated with the alimentary canal is a bilobed liver, a gall bladder, pancreatic tissue and a spleen. Fat bodies may be distributed along the length of the intestine from just behind the stomach, but particularly towards the end of the intestine.

A swim bladder lies in the dorsal region of the abdominal cavity. In newly hatched fish this swim bladder is connected to the alimentary canal and, a few days after hatching, the young fish swims to the surface and gulps in air to fill the swim bladder. Soon after the bladder has been filled it loses its connection with the alimentary canal and so becomes isolated from the external environment; that is the stickleback is a physoclist fish. For a fish to maintain neutral buoyancy in the water and so not have to work to maintain a particular depth, the volume of gas in the swim bladder must remain constant as the fish changes its depth in the water. In physoclist fish such as the stickleback, that cannot alter the pressure of gas in the bladder by burping or swallowing air, this pressure variation is achieved by the secretion or reabsorption of gas through specially adapted areas of the swim bladder wall. In the stickleback the swim bladder is divided into anterior and posterior portions with the two separated by a diaphragm. The anterior portion is the secretory bladder and associated with this is the rete mirabile of blood capillaries typical of the secretory region of the swim bladder of teleosts. In the posterior portion of the bladder, gas is reabsorbed (Fänge, 1953).

The skin of the stickleback is covered with a thin extra-cellular external coating layer called the cuticle. This layer, which is probably a muco-polysaccharide, is thought to be produced by the epidermal cells. Also in the skin there are goblet cells that produce mucus, cells which have a similar ultrastructure to the chloride cells of the gills, and some chemosensory cells (Whitear, 1970, 1971b). Pigment cells such as melanophores (black pigment), xanthophores (yellow pigment), erythrophores (red pigment) and guanophores (silver) are also scattered throughout the skin (Titschack, 1922; Bock, 1930; Burton, 1975).

In the chapters that follow, many of the organs which have been briefly described in this chapter will be considered in more detail in the context of their function in the life of the stickleback.

2. Distribution

As a family, the Gasterosteids are restricted to the temperate and sub-polar zones of the northern hemisphere. The three-spined stickleback is found between about 35°N and 70°N in Europe, parts of Asia and North America, but is absent from Africa. On all three continents, it is present in fresh, brackish and salt water, although restricted to the coastal waters of seas and oceans. A further restriction on its distribution is that it is not found in steep, fast-flowing streams and so is rare or absent in mountainous areas. The three-spined stickleback is most common in the slow-flowing backwaters and tributaries of rivers and in ditches, dykes, sheltered bays and harbours. It is also common in lakes and ponds where there are areas of emergent or submerged, rooted vegetation.

Good descriptions of the distribution of the three-spined stickleback in Europe are provided by Bertin (1925), Berg (1949) and Münzing (1959, 1963a). It was Bertin who pointed out that the stickleback is most common in flat, low-lying areas such as eastern England, Holland and Belgium. The most noticeable feature of the distribution in Europe is that the trachurus form is restricted to the northern regions and the Black Sea, whereas the leiurus form occurs throughout western Europe but has a predominantly southern distribution (Fig. 11). Leiurus is absent from the rivers of the Black Sea. Intergrades between trachurus and leiurus, the semiarmatus form, are found particularly in the North Sea and the western and north-western Baltic where the main distribution zones of leiurus and trachurus overlap.

In northern Europe, trachurus has an almost continuous distribution along the coast of Novaya Zemla, through the White Sea to the northern and western coast of Norway. Pure trachurus populations also occur in the coastal waters of Iceland and along the northern and eastern coasts of Scotland. South of this, in the

NMU LIBRARY

southern North Sea, mixed populations of trachurus and semiarmatus and a very small proportion of leiurus occur.

Although Münzing (1963a) considered that there was a pure
trachurus population along the Baltic coast of Poland and the Baltic
states of the U.S.S.R., the situation is complicated in eastern Europe
by the presence of populations of the trachurus and semiarmatus
forms that are resident in fresh water throughout the year and so

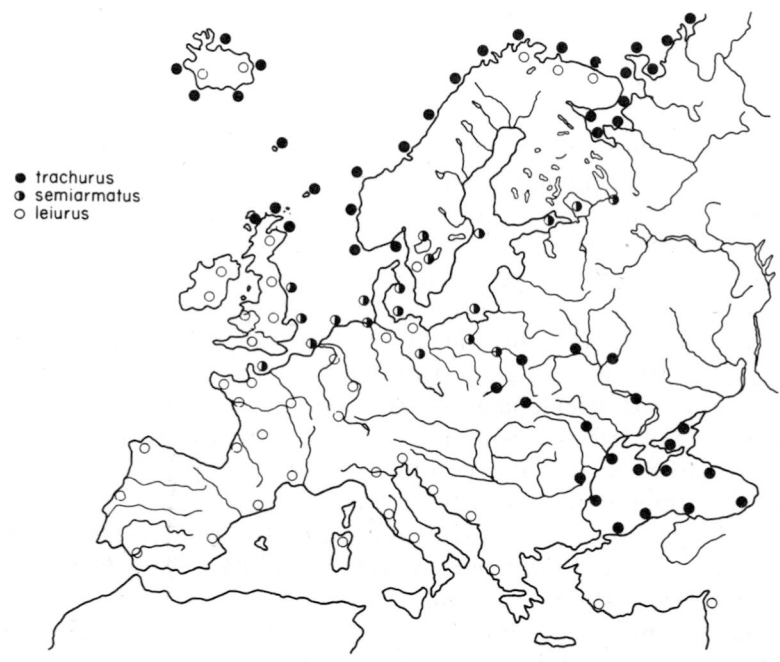

- trachurus
- semiarmatus
- leiurus

Fig. 11. European distribution of *Gasterosteus aculeatus*.

occupy a habitat that in most of western Europe is occupied by
populations of the leiurus form (Penczak, 1965, 1966). A somewhat
comparable situation is also found on the Atlantic and Pacific coasts
of North America and the significance of these populations is
considered in Chapter 14.

Only the trachurus form is present in the Black Sea, probably
extending along almost the entire coastline including the Sea of
Azov. Sticklebacks have been reported in the delta of the Danube but
not further inland. There are also records for the Dneister and
Dneiper which drain into the Black Sea, though Berg (1949) reported

NMU LIBRARY

that there are no recent records from the Dneister. Sticklebacks occur in the lower reaches of the Don and Kuban, but they are absent from the Caspian Sea, the Volga and the Aral Sea.

Two lakes adjacent to the Black Sea have stickleback populations characterised by a reduction in the number of lateral plates. One such population occurs in Lake Techirghiol close to the Rumanian coast of the Black Sea. This lake has a very high salinity (80–100‰) and was separated from the Black Sea only about a hundred years ago. The stickleback population consists of a mixture of completely plated and partially plated forms (Bacescu and Mayer, 1956; Münzing, 1963a). Lake Iznik is a fresh water lake in north-western Turkey; its stickleback population consists entirely of partially plated form. The phenotype of the Iznik stickleback is stable, with usually seven anterior lateral plates and six caudal lateral plates (Münzing, 1962a, 1963a). This uniformity of the phenotype is in marked contrast to the variability of the semiarmatus intergrade. Populations that show a strong mode for seven anterior lateral plates have been found in North America, usually in lakes where predatory fish are an important component of the fauna; unfortunately it is not known whether the Lake Iznik sticklebacks are heavily predated by piscivorous fish (see also Chapters 5 and 14). Since the leiurus form is absent from the Black Sea area, these partially plated forms cannot be trachurus x leiurus intergrades, but must have evolved independently of the semiarmatus form of western Europe.

In southern Europe, south of the English Channel, only the leiurus form living in fresh or brackish water is found. The southern limit for leiurus runs from the south of Spain to the south of Sardinia and through southern Italy to the south of Naples. Sticklebacks are absent from Sicily, but are found along the eastern coast of the Adriatic. Some of these southern leiurus populations are characterised by having all or a high proportion of individuals that lack any lateral plates. This naked leiurus form was recognised as the hologymnura form by Bertin (1925). Several populations in North America that have few or no lateral plates have also been described (see below).

Although restricted primarily to water of low salinity, the leiurus form is rarely found far from the coast. Its maximum inland penetration in Europe is probably not more than 700 km; it is found as far down the Rhine as Basel. Although not found, for example, in the coastal waters of the Mediterranean, the relatively high salinity tolerance of the leiurus form outside the breeding season suggests that it has achieved its modern distribution in Europe by movements along the western and southern coasts. Leiurus populations are also found in Ireland, Britain and Iceland and, although its distribution tends to be southerly, in Scandinavia.

The European distribution of the stickleback suggested to Bertin (1925) that the stickleback was genetically homogenous throughout Europe and that the morphological variation was a result of differences in the environmental factors of salinity and temperature in which the fish developed. According to this hypothesis, the leiurus form developed in fresh water and at relatively high temperatures, the trachurus form developed in salt water at relatively low temperatures and the semiarmatus form in areas intermediate in both salinity and temperature. This thesis has now proved to be untenable; the distinct phenotypes of the three forms reflect distinct genotypes (Heuts, 1947a; Münzing, 1963a; Hagen, 1967). Heuts showed that along the western coast of Europe, the stickleback populations can show two distinct modes of lateral plates. In the extreme north only monomorphic trachurus populations which overwinter in the sea are present, but further south both high plated and low plated populations occur, the high plated populations overwintering in the sea, and the low plated populations remaining in fresh water. In the south of the range, the populations are again monomorphic but now it is the low plated leiurus form restricted to fresh and brackish waters and not overwintering in the sea (Fig. 11), although in these warmer southern areas the leiurus form is better able to tolerate high salinities than in cold northerly waters (Heuts, 1945; Gutz, 1970).

The present day distribution of the stickleback in Europe has been interpreted as a result of the Pleistocene glaciations (Münzing, 1963a, 1972). This theory argues that during the Riss-Würm interglacial period, there were two geographical races. The trachurus race occupied a northern, circumpolar distribution, whilst the leiurus race had a more southerly distribution. With the onset of the Würm glaciation, the trachurus form was forced southwards and may have come into contact with northerly elements of the leiurus race. The ability of the trachurus form to tolerate low water temperatures probably enabled it to survive the cold periods relatively close to the ice-caps. As the Würm glaciation retreated, the range of the trachurus form expanded. From an area in the northern North Sea it spread into the western Baltic and the southern North Sea as these areas became submerged. With the submergence of the land connection between Britain and the continent of Europe and the increasing warmth of the more northerly regions, leiurus populations spread northwards, coming into contact with the trachurus form in the area of the southern North Sea and western Baltic. This meeting gave rise to the intergradation that resulted in the semiarmatus form providing an important component of stickleback populations in this area of western Europe.

An interpretation of the modern distribution in the eastern Baltic and eastern Europe has proved more difficult. Münzing (1963a) suggested that the most likely origin of these populations was from fish that had moved south westwards from the White Sea, through the Onega Ice Lake, across a system of ice-dammed lakes into the Baltic Ice Lake. Only when the land connection between Denmark and Sweden became submerged could the eastern Baltic be invaded from the west by stickleback populations from the western Baltic and North Sea. Münzing's interpretation was questioned by Penczak (1965) who argued that the eastern Baltic was invaded by mixed trachurus, semiarmatus and leiurus populations from Germany moving both along the coast and through the rivers. More recently Münzing (1972) suggested that eastern Europe was colonised by trachurus populations moving north westwards from the Black Sea region, while leiurus populations moved into the area along the coastal plain from western Europe. The region where these two colonisations met in the area between the Oder and Elbe Rivers is characterised by fresh water populations that include leiurus, trachurus and semiarmatus (Paepke, 1970).

Two plausible suggestions on the origin of the pure trachurus populations of the Black Sea were given by Münzing (1963a). The first of these was that there was a southerly invasion by trachurus populations from the Baltic but, since in his more recent paper (1972) he derives the eastern European trachurus populations from the Black Sea populations, this first suggestion has been abandoned. The second suggestion was that populations of trachurus survived the glaciation in southwest refugium (the Pontic glacial refuge) and the Black Sea populations are derived from this refugial population. No trace of trachurus is found in the eastern Mediterranean, presumably because the water temperatures are too high, or became too high during the post glacial period. It would be interesting to compare the morphology of the Black Sea trachurus sticklebacks with that of trachurus sticklebacks from eastern and western Europe making use of far more characters than simply the number of lateral plates. Such a multi-variate study might indicate the affinities between the three groups.

Another distributional problem is posed by the northerly, land-locked leiurus populations. Such populations are found in Iceland, Greenland and Scandinavia. One possibility is that these populations were established during temporary northwards extensions of populations that consisted of a mixture of the three forms, with the leiurus form being able to establish itself permanently in fresh water. These northerly extensions could have occurred during the warmer periods of the post-glacial period. An alternative explanation is that these leiurus populations were all derived independently from pure trachurus populations by a reduction in the body armour in land-locked populations (Münzing, 1963a).

There has been only one recorded population of sticklebacks in Africa; a leiurus population existed near Algiers (Bertin, 1925). It was doubted whether this was an indigenous population and thirty years later no trace of it could be found (Heuts, 1956).

Three-spined sticklebacks are absent from the Siberian coast of the Arctic Ocean and from the rivers that drain into that coastline. After this extensive gap, the species reappears in the Bering Straits and from there is found southwards along the Pacific coast of the U.S.S.R., Manchuria, and as far south as the east coast of Korea at Fusan (36° 6′ N). It also occurs in Japan, where on the Sea of Japan coastline it reaches Hamada (35° 44′ N), while on the Pacific coastline it reaches Chosi at a similar latitude, but there are records even further south than this, both on the island of Honshu and even as far south as Nagasaki City on the island of Kyushu (32° 44′ N) (Okada, 1959/1960; Amaoka and Haruta, 1972). The descriptions suggest that the trachurus form is the commonest stickleback in Japan, but the leiurus and semiarmatus forms are also present (Igarishi, 1970b).

At the moment there is insufficient evidence to indicate whether the distributional pattern in Asia shares a common feature with the pattern in Europe where the leiurus form tends to have a southerly distribution whilst the trachurus form has a northerly distribution. But, as in Europe, the stickleback in Asia does not penetrate deep into the continent.

In the north Pacific, sticklebacks occur on St. Lawrence Island in the Bering Straits and on the Kurile Islands. These populations are thought to be exclusively trachurus. On the Aleutian Islands stickle-backs are widely distributed. Both the anadromous trachurus form and the fresh water leiurus form are present (Valdez and Helm, 1971).

On the North American continent, the three-spined stickleback occurs on both the Pacific and Atlantic coastlines (Fig. 12). The distributional pattern in North America seems to be basically comparable to the situation in Europe. The anadromous trachurus form has the more northerly distribution, whilst the fresh water leiurus form extends furthest to the south, although it does occur in the north as well. Leiurus populations were found in Bare and Karluk

Lakes on Kodiak Island, Alsaka (Greenbank and Nelson, 1959) and in the Chignik River system, Alaska (Narver, 1969). No three-spined sticklebacks occur on the northern coastline of the North American continent, so the circum-polar distribution is interrupted along both the Eurasian and American coastlines of the Arctic Ocean (Hagen and McPhail, 1970; Scott and Crossman, 1973).

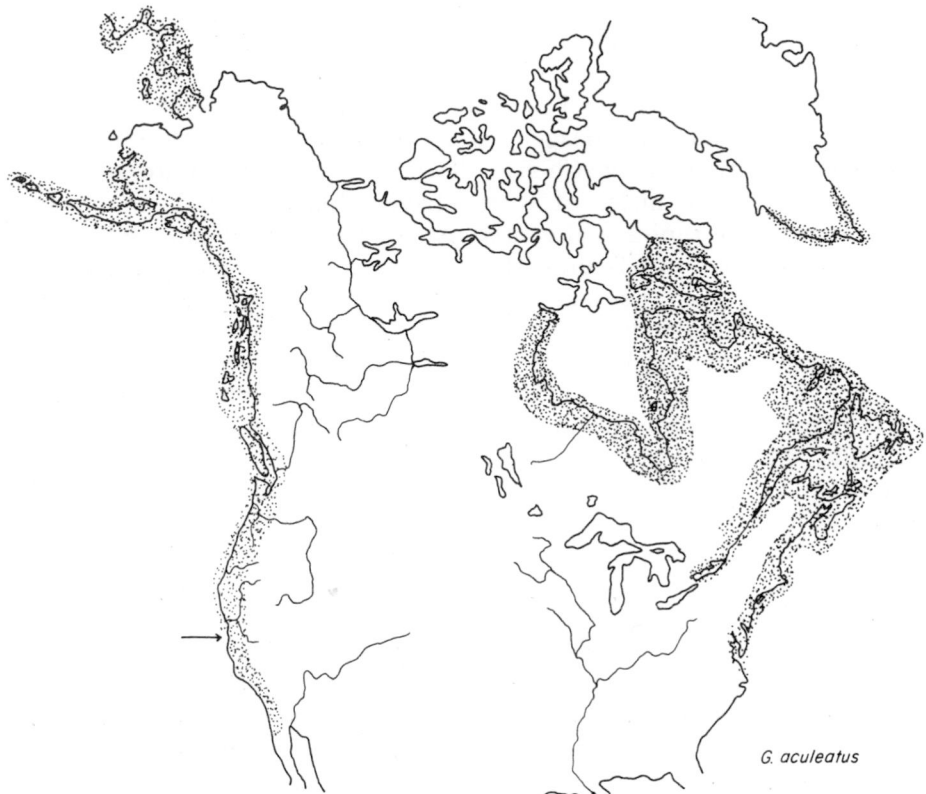

Fig. 12. North American distribution of *Gasterosteus aculeatus*. Arrow marks southern limit of the trachurus form on the Pacific coast.

Along the Pacific coastline the species is restricted, with few exceptions, to the coastal regions and rivers that flow into the Pacific. The southern limit of the trachurus form is the San Lorenzo River in the north of Monterey Bay, California (37° N), while the southern limit of the leiurus form is in Baja California at El Rosario (approx. 32° N) (Miller and Hubbs, 1969). Sticklebacks are found in the Mohave River which drains into the interior rather than towards the Pacific, but these were introduced accidently in the past thirty to forty years. These leiurus populations in southern California frequently consist of plateless individuals, a situation that parallels the situation in southern Europe. The plateless form of southern California has been described as a distinct sub-species *Gasterosteus aculeatus williamsoni* and the plated leiurus form described as *G. aculeatus microcephalus* (see discussion in Chapter 14).

The Pacific coast of North America is notable for the phenotypic variation in the stickleback populations. In addition to the plateless forms of southern California, there are also plateless forms as far north as Texada Island and the Queen Charlotte Islands off the coast of British Columbia (Hagen and McPhail, 1970; Moodie and Reimchen, 1973). In the Chehalis River in Washington State, there is a stickleback the males of which have a black nuptial coloration rather than the typical red venter and blue eyes (McPhail, 1969). On the Queen Charlotte Islands, there is an unusually large stickleback found in one of the lakes as well as populations with a high proportion of plateless individuals or individuals with reduced pelvic skeletons (Moodie, 1972a, b; Moodie and Reimchen, 1973). Many of the lakes of the region have polymorphic populations consisting of various proportions of individuals that fall into the leiurus, the semiarmatus and the trachurus ranges of number of lateral plates. These populations are resident in fresh water throughout the year (Hagen and Gilbertson, 1972). The significance of this phenotypic variation is discussed in more detail in Chapter 14.

Along the Atlantic seaboard of North America, the three-spined stickleback ranges from Hudson Strait, Baffin Island to as far south as New York and possibly as far south as Chesapeake Bay or Cape Hatteras; this southern limit does not seem to be well defined. The fresh water populations on Baffin Island are composed of the leiurus form, but the trachurus form has been taken in the sea north of Baffin Island (McPhail, personal communication). In the Ottawa Valley and Lake Ontario, landlocked populations of the trachurus form occur, and in other lakes in the region the populations are polymorphic, a situation comparable to that for some populations in the Pacific northwest (Garside and Hamor, 1973; Coad and Power, 1974).

Sticklebacks occur in Greenland on both the east and west coasts probably as far north as 70° N. These Greenland populations include some leiurus populations that are permanent residents of fresh water (Münzing, 1963a).

This survey of the world distribution pattern of the three-spined stickleback suggests that three factors are important in determining the pattern. The first of these factors is history, for the events of the Pleistocene with the alternately advancing and retreating glaciations seem to have imposed particular patterns on the distribution of the stickleback that could not have been deduced from a consideration of its physiological tolerances alone. The two environmental factors that seem to have been important are salinity and temperature.

Chapter 8 discusses the salinity tolerance of the three-spined stickleback. Although both the trachurus and leiurus forms are euryhaline, the leiurus form has a lower tolerance of salinity especially in cold water or during the breeding season.

There have been relatively few studies on the thermal tolerances of the stickleback though it is usually regarded as a eurythermal fish. Heuts (1947b) found that the mean length of survival of leiurus fish kept at 25° to 28°C was inversely related to the number of lateral plates. Fish with fewer lateral plates survived for a longer period of time at these high water temperatures. During the same study Heuts showed that the eggs of trachurus and leiurus fish were adapted to different, narrowly restricted bands of salinity and temperature. Even within the leiurus form there is evidence that the more southerly populations are adapted to a higher temperature regime than northerly populations. This was found to be true of the eggs as well as the adults (Heuts, 1956). Jordan and Garside (1972) investigated the upper lethal temperature of three-spined sticklebacks taken from the harbour of Halifax, Nova Scotia. Unfortunately they do not give any information on which form the fish belonged to, though presumably they came from a population that was either entirely trachurus or a trachurus and semiarmatus mixture. The upper lethal temperature depended on the temperature at which the fish had been acclimated and on the salinity of the water. Fish were most tolerant of high temperatures when in a salinity of 12‰ which is about isotonic with the blood of the stickleback. When fish were in either fresh water or 30‰ sea water, the upper lethal temperature was correspondingly lower. The minimum upper lethal temperature noted in the experiments was 21.6°C for fish kept at 10°C in 30‰ sea water, while upper lethal temperatures of over 28°C were noted for sticklebacks kept at 10° and 20°C in 12‰ sea water. The salinity in which the fish had been kept prior to the measurement of the upper lethal temperature did not seem to have a significant effect on the upper lethal temperature. Nevertheless there is some interaction between the thermal and salinity tolerances of the stickleback. Experiments at controlled temperatures and salinities showed that at low temperature, the ability of the leiurus form to survive in high salinities was reduced, while at high temperature, outside the breeding season, the anadromous trachurus form was unable to survive in water containing less than 5‰, salt. During the breeding season, the trachurus form was able to tolerate fresh water even when the temperature was 20°C (Heuts, 1945; Gutz, 1970).

Experiments of the type performed by Jordan and Garside would be even more valuable if performed on populations of trachurus, semiarmatus and leiurus fish from a variety of localities so that a comprehensive picture of the salinity and temperature tolerances of the three forms could be built up. Similar studies on the lower lethal temperature would be useful in indicating whether the absence of sticklebacks from the Arctic Ocean coastline of Eurasia and America and from the heart of these continents is because of the extremely low winter temperatures in these regions. It would also be interesting to compare the temperature tolerances of leiurus fish with those of landlocked trachurus fish to see whether the failure of the leiurus form to penetrate as far as the trachurus form into eastern Europe and eastern America is because it is less able to tolerate the cold, continental winters.

3. Development and Growth

After the elaborate courtship behaviour of the stickleback described in Chapter 12 ends in success, the male guards and tends a nest containing the fertilised eggs. From these eggs the recruits to the next generation of sticklebacks are drawn. Although some eggs may be eaten or die from various causes before they hatch, others will develop, hatch and take up an independent life. A few of these will grow to become sexually mature adults able to initiate another round of reproductive activity. The development of the eggs takes place in the male's nest, and the male only abandons his parental care when the young fish are active and free-swimming. These young fish leave the vicinity of the nest and join schools of young sticklebacks. In the first two weeks when the eggs and young are most vunerable to predation, they are protected by the male, so the survival rate in this period is probably higher in the stickleback than in fish that lack parental care.

When they are laid, the eggs stick together in a mass surrounded by mucus. They vary in diameter from about 1.1 to 1.8 mm and an egg weighs about 0.002 g fresh or 0.0003(4) g when dried. Most of the eggs are spherical but some distorted eggs are usually present in an egg mass. The colour of a mass of eggs can vary from almost colourless through a straw colour to slightly orange. The same female kept on the same food can produce egg masses of different colour, though those laid later in the spawning period are sometimes more coloured than those produced early in the period (Vrat, 1949; Wootton, 1973b).

A vitelline membrane or chorion forms the outer covering of the egg. This membrane is pierced by a small, funnel-shaped pore, the micropyle, and it is through the micropyle that a sperm passes to fertilise the egg. Yolk, which contains numerous oil droplets, makes up the bulk of the egg, with the cytoplasm forming a thin coat around the yolk. In this cytoplasm there are cortical alveoli which probably contain a muco-polysaccharide. Before the egg is fertilised, it is flaccid, with the vitelline membrane closely applied to the cytoplasm (Thomopoulos, 1953).

Ten minutes or so after the eggs have been laid, they become hard and stiff and firmly attached to each other. A male is unwilling to fertilise such hard eggs (van Iersel, 1953), but eggs have been artificially fertilised up to three hours after they were laid (Thomopoulos, 1953).

At fertilisation, a single sperm makes its way through the micropyle into the egg. Immediately after, the cortical alveoli start to disappear and the vitelline membrane separates from the surface of the egg, so that a perivitelline space is formed between the egg and the vitelline membrane. The egg becomes turgid. These changes probably depend on the release of colloidal substances from the cortical alveoli which, because they cannot pass out of the egg through the vitelline membrane, set up an osmotic gradient across the membrane so that water passes through the membrane into the egg. This water cannot enter the cytoplasm of the egg and it accumulates in the perivitelline space. Another consequence of fertilisation is that the entry of any more sperm is blocked. These post-fertilisation changes were also induced by pricking a fresh, unfertilised egg with a fine glass needle, but this artificial activation of the egg did not lead to the development of an embryo (Thomopoulos, 1953; Yamamoto, 1961).

The rate at which the egg develops after fertilisation depends on the water temperature and the times quoted in the following description apply to eggs kept at 18 to 19°C (Swarup, 1958a) (Fig. 13).

About thirty minutes after fertilisation, waves of contraction cause the accumulation of the egg cytoplasm at one of the poles of the egg, the animal pole. This process of accumulation lasts for about seventy-five minutes and results in the formation of a cap of cytoplasm at the animal pole, this cap is called the blastodermic disc. A couple of hours after fertilisation, the blastodermic disc begins to cleave giving rise first to a two cell stage and then a four cell stage. The yolk is not affected by these divisions. The cell division continues and after another four hours has produced a mass of cells, the blastoderm, sitting on the yolk at the animal pole of the egg. This mass of cells has a convex base lying in a hollow in the yolk. Between the cells and the yolk, a syncytial layer is formed as cell nuclei divide, but cell membranes fail to form between the divided nuclei.

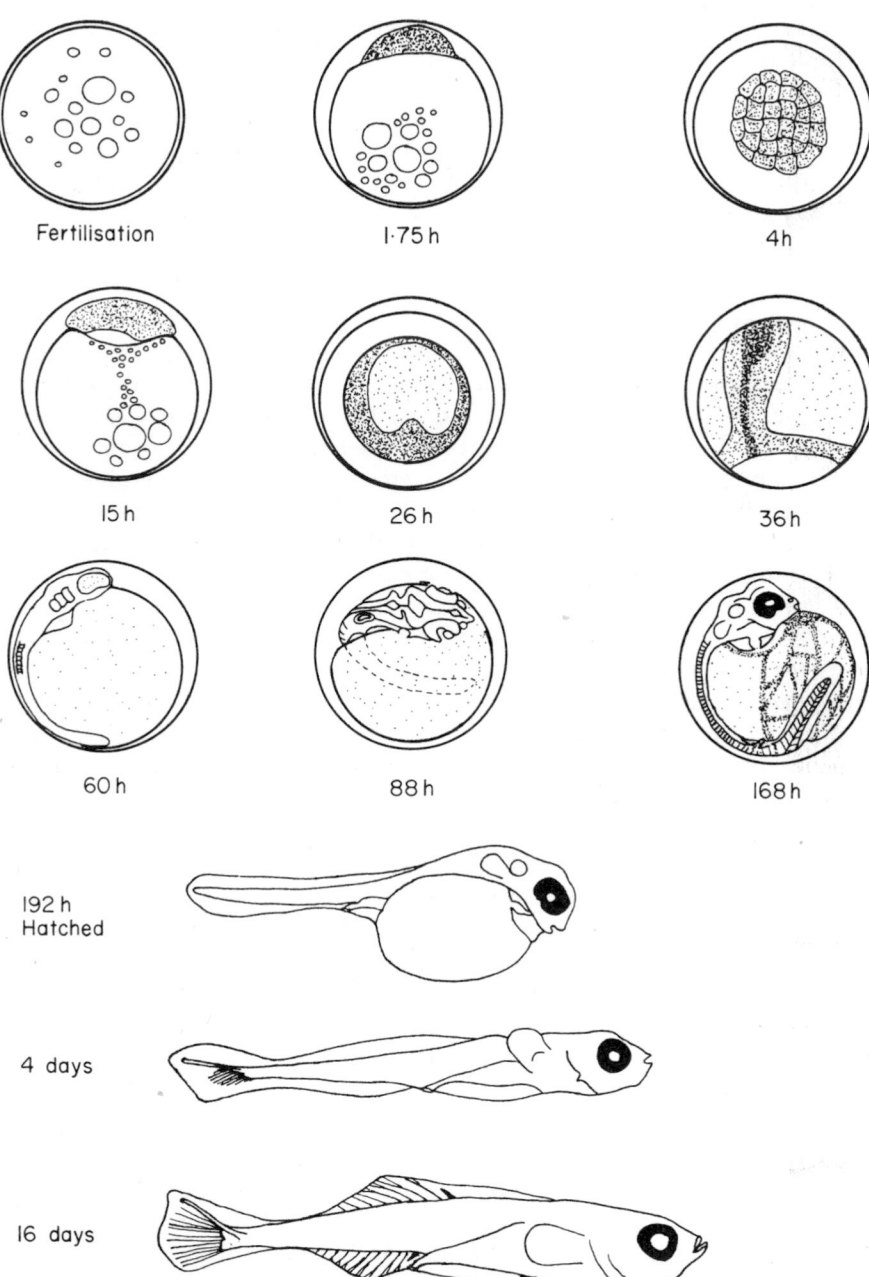

Fig. 13. Development of the embryo of *Gasterosteus aculeatus* at 18–19°C (after Swarup, 1958b). Post-fertilisation times in hours; post-hatching times in days.

This syncytial layer, the periblast, forms an interface between the cells of the blastoderm and the yolk.

Cells around the periphery of the blastoderm remain in contact with the periblast, but the central cells of the base of the blastoderm become detached from the periblast and a subgerminal space is formed. Twenty-two hours after fertilisation, cells at the edge of a thicker sector of the blastoderm start to invaginate where the edge of the blastoderm meets the yolk. Invagination spreads laterally around the edge of the blastoderm, but the invaginated layer does not spread into the subgerminal space, and so it forms a thickened ring, the germ ring, round the margin of the blastoderm. This germ ring moves over the yolk towards the equator of the egg, while behind the germ ring the blastoderm covers an increasing area of the egg's surface. Part of the blastoderm, lying anterior to the place on the margin of the blastoderm where invagination began, assumes a triangular shape with the apex of the triangle pointing towards the animal pole of the egg. This is the embryonic shield and it is in the shield that the thickening of the embryonic axis appears.

The blastoderm continues to spread over the yolk and the germ ring passes the equator so that its circumference now starts to decrease. At this time, some thirty-six hours after fertilisation, the embryonic shield looses its triangular shape and becomes elongated. Eventually the blastoderm almost entirely covers the yolk, and in the anterior of the embryonic axis the presumptive brain can be seen to be subdivided into fore, mid and hind brain areas. The blastoderm now completely covers the yolk. Optic lobes, destined to give rise to the eyes, appear as lateral outgrowths from the fore-brain. Invaginated parts of the embryo converge towards the embryonic axis, and this, allied with the development of the central nervous system, causes a thickening of the embryo so that it protrudes from the surface of the egg. Somites, or muscle blocks, first appear sixty hours after fertilisation, with six or seven pairs of somites appearing in the middle of the embryo. The optic lobes, which developed first into optic vesicles with the formation of a central cavity, become differentiated into optic cups, and the eye lenses form. A longitudinal groove in the dorsomedial region of the brain deepens to form the brain ventricles, and the otic capsules can be seen lateral to the hind-brain. Just behind and ventral to the brain a pericardium, the coelomic cavity which contains the heart, appears although the heart still cannot be seen. The number of somites increases, and Kupffer's vesicle appears at the posterior end of the body.

Eighty-eight hours after fertilisation, the brain continues to differentiate. All three ventricles are visible while, anterior to the fore-brain, the olfactory lobes differentiate. The otic capsules contain otoliths. Posterior to the brain, in an enlarging pericardium, the heart can be seen beating, and it is in communication with the blood spaces of the yolk sac. A tail develops posterior to where the germ ring finally closed over the yolk, and occasional muscular beats of the tail start to occur some 106 hours after fertilisation. The pigment of the eyes becomes prominent and the ventricles of the brain start to be roofed over; the mid-brain ventricle is the first one to be closed.

Next the heart becomes visibly differentiated into a sinus venosus, atrium and ventricle and beats vigorously, red blood corpuscles can be seen in the blood. Gill slits appear about 130 hours after fertilisation. The head of the embryo is fully formed about 160 hours after fertilisation as the last ventricle of the brain, that of the fore-brain, closes over. The pericardium and heart continue to increase in size and the heart becomes bent upon itself into the S-shape characteristic of the heart of fishes. Blood from the tail runs into blood capillaries on the entire surface of the yolk. From these capillaries, the blood collects in blood islands in front of the head, and from these passes into the heart.

The mouth now forms and the eye cup completely surrounds the lens. Pectoral fins, the rudiments of which had appeared some 144 hours after fertilisation, vibrate. A tail fin is visible as the tail beats rapidly. As these tail beats increase in strength, the pectoral fins vibrate more and more rapidly, the head of the embryo pushes against the vitelline membrane and the membrane finally ruptures just in front of the head. Tail movements free the embryo from the egg and the larval fish is hatched.

At a temperature between 18 and 19°C hatching takes place about eight days after fertilisation. Newly hatched larvae vary in length from 3 to 5 mm, with the yolk sac still protuberant so that the embryo is perched on a ball of yolk. The hind gut opens just behind the yolk sac. The mouth is open at hatching according to Swarup (1958a) and closed according to Vrat (1949). A fin fold runs along both the dorsal and ventral mid-lines, linking with the tail fin. The eyes are large.

The newly hatched larvae are active, swimming by a rapid beating of the tail and vibrations of the pectoral fins. After each bout of swimming, a larva sinks to bottom, and rolls over on its side because of the round yolk sac underneath the embryo (Vrat, 1949).

Even when a larva is lying on the bottom, the pectoral fins move continually. The skeleton of each pectoral fin appears when the embryo is about 3mm long as a cartilaginous plate which differentiates into the scapula and coracoid, and into the actinosts (see Chapter 1). By the time the fry is about 11 mm long, the dermal bones of the pectoral skeleton, the cleithrum and ectocoracoid, have become associated with the scapula and coracoid and these latter begin to ossify (Swinnerton, 1905).

In the day after hatching, the larval fish grows by about a millimetre, absorbing half its yolk. The head straightens out, obliterating a mesencephalic flexure and allowing the pericardium and heart to unfold. Over the next four days, all the yolk is used up. The jaws develop and the mouth can be opened and shut. A swim-bladder appears above the alimentary canal and to fill this swim-bladder the larval fish has to swim to the surface to gulp air; later the connection between the swim-bladder and alimentary canal is lost. Also at about this time, the opercula covering the gills develop.

In the next eighteen days, the young fish looses its larval characteristics and assumes an adult-like shape and a length of about 11 mm. The fin-fold, which earlier had been continuous, breaks up into the dorsal, caudal and anal fins. Fin rays appear in the caudal fin and then in the dorsal and anal fins after they have become separate. The pelvic spines develop first, then the small anal and third dorsal spines and finally the long first and second dorsal spines (Swarup, 1958a).

Of particular interest is the development of the skeletal elements that support the tail fin, for one of the characters that distinguishes *Gasterosteus* from the other genera in the stickleback family is the presence of a deep split in the hypural plate (Chapter 20). When the larval stickleback is about 7 mm long, the posterior end of the notochord is bent upwards at an angle to the axis of the body and terminates in the upper corner of the tail fin. At the point where the notochord bends up, a bony ring develops, and below this ring there is a cartilaginous plate. Behind and above this plate, there is another cartilaginous plate on the underside of the notochord. As the larvae grows, these cartilaginous plates enlarge and start to ossify, while the bony ring extends further back to form the base of the posterior plate. Above the bony ring, two other cartilages develop which eventually ossify to form the epurals. With the complete ossification of the two cartilaginous plates, and their partial fusion, the characteristic hypural plate of *Gasterosteus* is formed (Huxley, 1859) (Fig. 14).

Fig. 14. Development of caudal skeleton of *Gasterosteus aculeatus* (after Huxley, 1859). (a) Tail of fish 8 mm long; (b) 11 mm long; (c) half grown; (d) fully grown. Key to lettering: cfr, caudal fin rays; e, epural; ea, anterior epural apophysis; ep, posterior epural apophysis; h, hypural plate; ha, anterior hypural apophysis; hp, posterior apophysis; lc, centrum of last normal vertebra; n, notochord; u, urostyle.

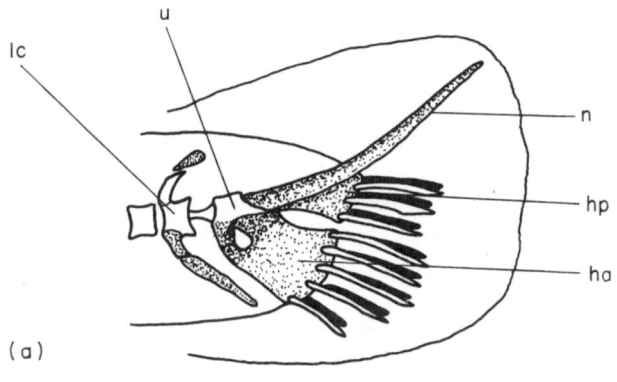

(a)

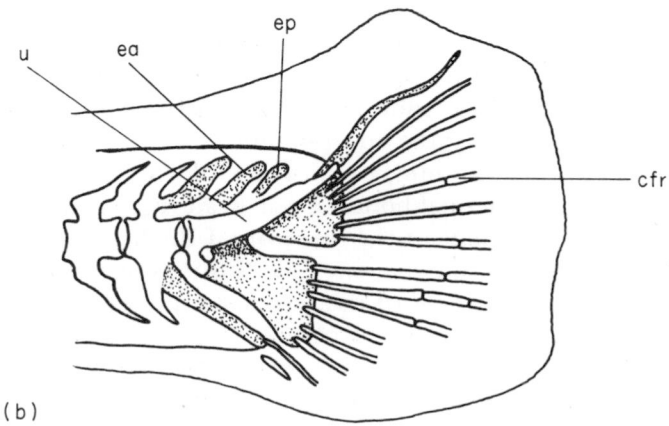

(b)

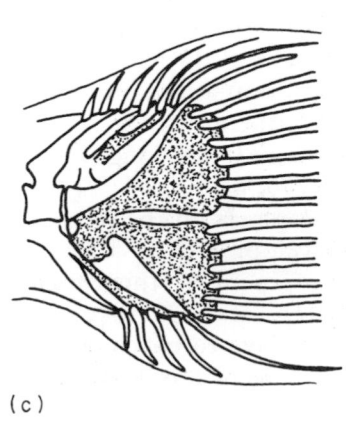

(c)

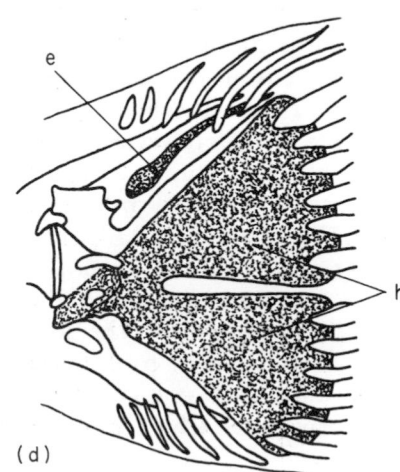

(d)

The development of the skeleton of the head region begins about five days after the egg is fertilised (Swinnerton, 1902; de Beer, 1937). On the fifth day, the notochord is the only representative of the skeleton of the head region, but between the sixth and seventh day, when the embryo is about 4 mm long, cartilaginous elements which are destined to form parts of the brain case, the jaw suspension and the branchial skeleton become visible. Between the eighth and eleventh day after fertilisation, the elaboration of the brain case (the chondrocranium), the otic capsules and the occipital arch at the posterior margin of the brain case continues. The hyomandibular and sympletic elements of the jaw suspension are represented by a single cartilage but the symplectic region of the cartilage already shows the elongation so characteristic of the sympletic bone of the Gasterosteidae (Chapter 20). The dermal bones of the head region start to make their appearance at this stage with dentaries, maxillae and opercula becoming visible. Larval fish 6-9 mm long, that is about eleven days after fertilisation, still do not show any development of bone in the cartilaginous brain case, but this soon assumes virtually the adult condition in its morphology. In larval fish longer than 11 mm, ossification of the chondrocranium progresses and all the dermal bones of the head region are present. A feature of the development of the skeleton of the head region is that those elements concerned with the jaw suspension and the oper-culum, and in the attachment of the associated muscles, develop at a relatively faster rate than the rest of the head skeleton. The young fish is ready to take up independent existence soon after hatching and can leave the vicinity of the male's nest as a self-sufficient individual.

The last of the morphological features characteristic of the adult stickleback to develop are the lateral plates. These do not start to appear until the fish is about 13 mm long, and in the trachurus form the lateral row is not complete until the fish is almost 30 mm long. The size of larva at which the plates first appear and the age at which the row is complete varies from population to population, but young fish cannot reliably be assigned to either the trachurus, the semiar-matus or the leiurus form until the fish is at least 30 mm long (Heuts, 1947a; Hagen and McPhail, 1970; Igarishi, 1970a, b).

The timing of these developmental events depends on the tempera-ture of the water in which the eggs are developing (Fig. 15). The lower the temperature the longer the development of the embryo takes. At 8°C, eggs took forty days to hatch, at 12°C they took twenty days, and at 25°C they took only six days to hatch (Heuts, 1956). Embryos which developed abnormally were produced when freshly fertilised eggs were subjected to very high (33°C) or very low (0°C) temperature for between one and a half to three hours (Swarup, 1958b, 1959e, f, g). Amongst the abnormalities produced by this treatment were triploid sticklebacks. These were fish with a chromosome number of 63, whereas the normal diploid number of chromosomes for the three-spined stickleback is 42 (Swarup, 1956,

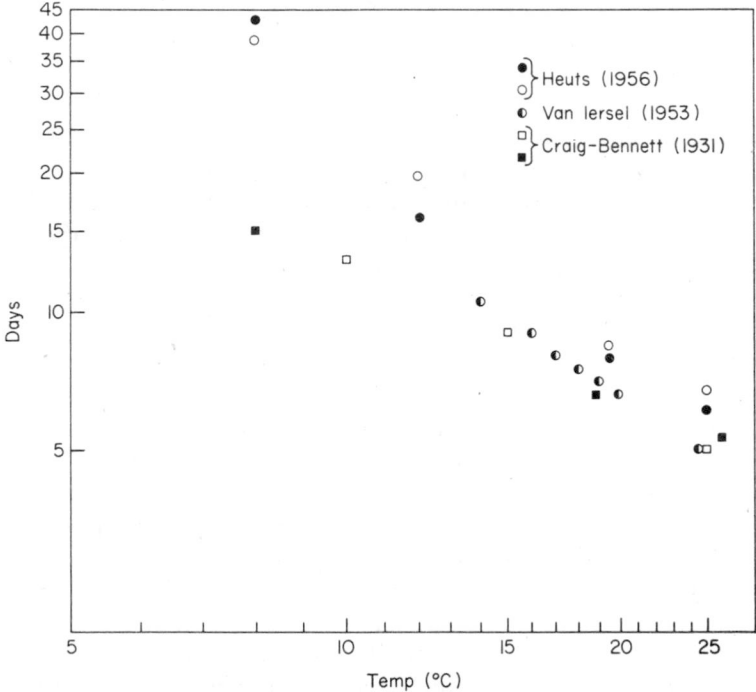

Fig. 15. Effect of temperature on time taken for eggs of *Gasterosteus aculeatus* to hatch.

1959a). The triploid fish developed and grew at the same rate as normal, diploid sticklebacks, but they had slightly different body proportions, for the trunk was relatively shorter and the tail relatively longer than normal. The cells of the triploid sticklebacks were larger than normal, but the body organs were the same size as normal which meant that the organs of the triploids contained fewer cells (Swarup, 1959b).

For the first twelve days or so after fertilisation, the developing fish depends on its yolk for nutrients and energy. The calorific value, that is the energy content of the eggs at fertilisation, is about 5400 calories per g dry weight (22.6 kJ). Each egg weighs approximately

0.0003 g dry weight, so that the embryo starts with about 1.62
calories to support it until it is able to feed. The rate of energy
expenditure by the embryo could be measured by the rate of oxygen
consumption, but as yet there are no published data on this aspect of
stickleback development. Some idea of the changes in metabolic rate
of the embryos can be obtained by noting the changes in the rate at
which the male fans the nest. Fanning is the behaviour by which the
male drives a current of water over the eggs and so ventilates them
(Chapter 13). The rate of fanning reaches a peak shortly before the
young hatch (van Iersel, 1953).

After the yolk is exhausted, the young fish starts to feed on
infusoria, the larval stages of copepods and other small food items
(Chapter 4). The initial growth rate is such that the fish can attain a
length of about 17 mm within thirty days of hatching (van Mullem,
1967). In the laboratory, with the temperature maintained at about
20°C and a good supply of food, the stickleback can grow to sexual
maturity in as little as four months. By this time the fish can be as
long as 45 mm and weigh over a gram.

In natural populations such a rapid growth and maturation is never
achieved. Variations in food supply, the changes in the day length,
the changes in water temperature may all influence the rate at which
the fish grows, although a systematic study of the effects and
interactions of these factors has still to be done. There have been
several studies on the growth of sticklebacks in natural populations,
but in the absence of concomitant experimental studies, they have
not yielded any clear indications of the factors that restrict the
growth rate.

In addition to the study of the feeding habits of the leiurus
sticklebacks in the River Birket, described in Chapter 4, their growth
was also analysed (Jones and Hynes, 1950). The River Birket is
slow-flowing, muddy, and in summer there is considerable emergent
and submergent vegetation. Water temperatures vary from just above
freezing in winter with the stream rarely freezing over, to over 18°C
in the summer. There is an abundant invertebrate fauna, with small
crustacea such as ostracods, copepods and cladocerans; chironomids;
oligochaetes and molluscs. In spite of this apparently favourable
environment, the growth of the sticklebacks in the Birket is amongst
the slowest yet recorded (Fig. 16).

Breeding in the Birket took place in April and May, so that young
were present in samples taken in May, June and July. These young
fish had a mean length of 15 mm, which suggests that they had
grown at a rate comparable to that of young fish in laboratory
conditions (van Mullem, 1967). At the end of their first year of life,

the Birket fish had a mean length of 42.7 mm, at the end of their second year 45.6 mm and at the end of the third year 51.4 mm. There was, then, a considerable slowing up in the growth rate when the fish became mature.

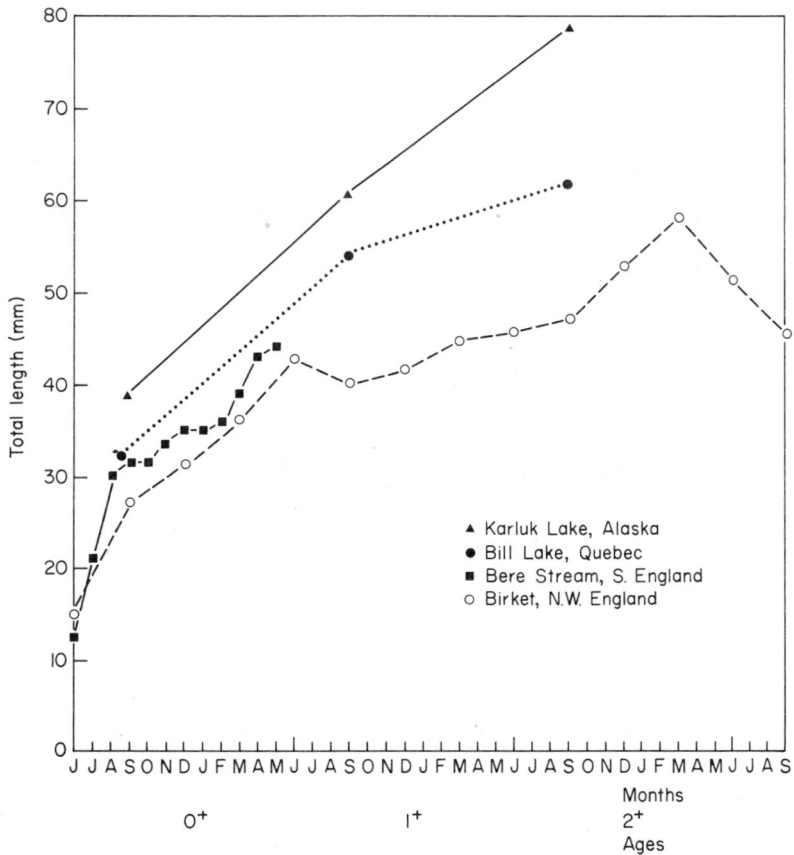

Fig. 16. Growth in length of *Gasterosteus aculeatus* from Karluk Lake, Alaska (Greenbank and Nelson, 1959); Bill Lake (Coad and Power, 1973b); Bere Stream (Mann, 1971); and Birket River (Jones and Hynes, 1950).

A similar pattern of growth was shown by the semiarmatus sticklebacks of Priddy Pool, a small pond in the southwest of England (Pennycuick, 1971a). Priddy Pool is at a height of 270 m in the Mendip Hills whose limestone ensures that the water is hard. The pool has an exposed position and often freezes over in winter. In summer, the water becomes overgrown with horsetail, *Equisetum fluviatile*, which dies back in the autumn. The growth in length of the Priddy Pool sticklebacks was described by the equation:

$$L = 41.7t^{0.288}$$

where L is the length of the fish in millimetres, and t is the age of the fish in years, the date of birth being taken as June 1st. Although the use of an equation of this form is useful in some circumstances, it obscures the fluctuations in the growth rate which occur in natural populations and so draws attention away from a study of the factors that induce these variations. The sticklebacks of Priddy Pool and the Birket had similar life spans, with a maximum age of about three and a half years.

This is in marked contrast to sticklebacks living in a hard water stream in southern England (Mann, 1971). These fish had a slightly higher growth rate reaching a length of about 45.0 mm after one year, but few fish lived longer than a year and none lived to be two years old.

Leiurus sticklebacks living in two lakes on Kodiak Island, Alaska, had far higher growth rates than those reported above (Greenbank and Nelson, 1959). In Bare Lake, the smaller of the two lakes, breeding took place in May and June and by the September when the fish were sixteen months old they averaged about 52 mm in total length. Only a few fish survived a further year and these reached a length of between 54 and 73 mm. In Karluk Lake, breeding was slightly later than in Bare Lake, but even so by the end of the first summer of life, the fish had reached an average length of nearly 40 mm. At the end of their second summer, they were about 60 mm long, and at the end of the third summer the surviving fish ranged in length from 72 to 79 mm. The maximum life span in both lakes seemed to be two and a quarter years.

A similar life span has been reported for sticklebacks in populations in eastern Canada. Bill Lake and Matamek Lake are in the Matamek River system in Quebec. In Bill Lake, the population is predominantly made up of the semiarmatus form, with a significant proportion of the trachurus form but no leiurus fish, and the Matamek Lake population consists entirely of the semiarmatus form (Coad and Power, 1974). The growth rate in both these populations was comparable to that of the fish in Bare Lake, Alaska (Fig. 16) (Coad and Power, 1973b).

All the patterns of growth so far described are those of populations that are resident in fresh water throughout the year. The growth pattern of an anadromous population that bred on the Island of Tholen in the Netherlands was analysed by van Mullem and van der Vlugt (1964). This population was a mixture of trachurus and semiarmatus fish. Collections of fish were made throughout the year in four distinct habitats: the sea, the "boezems" (which are tidal drainage basins connected by sluices to the sea and into which water is pumped from the canals), the central channels of the canals along which the fish had to migrate, and the fourth habitat consisted of the ditches in which breeding took place. The four habitats in which collections were made form the pathway of the annual migrations. In the spring, the fish moved from the sea into the boezems, they then made their way into the canals and along them into the ditches, and in the autumn the migration was in the opposite direction.

Fish were caught in the ditches between May and October, and these fish fell into two distinct size classes. Those over 42 mm long were the breeding adults, while the fish that in June were less than 30 mm long were the young born that year. Most of the large fish had disappeared from the ditches by the end of July, while the young-of-the-year persisted until September, with the larger fish of this group tending to move out into the canals before the smaller fish. In the deep channels of the canals, fish were caught at two periods in the year, in March and April, and between July and late autumn. Fish were taken in the boezems and the sea from September through to April. In the ditches, the young sticklebacks reached a mean length of 30 mm with a maximum length that rarely exceeded 40 mm. Fish between 35 and 55 mm were found in the canals during the autumn migration, whilst in the boezems the average length of fish in September was 40 mm, but 60 mm by the following April. In the autumn, fish taken in the sea had a mean length of around 48 mm but by the following spring they were around 60 mm in total length (Fig. 17).

The evidence from the length measurements and the pattern of movement of the fish through the waterways suggested that the adults died after spawning and so had a maximum life span of a year and a few months, the fish maturing after their first winter in the sea.

Although most of these studies have analysed the growth of the sticklebacks in terms of length, an increase in the length of the fish usually implies that there has been an increase in the weight of the fish. The increase in weight of the sticklebacks in Priddy Pool was described by the equation:

$$W = 0.514t^{0.79}$$

where W is the weight of the fish in grams and t is the age of the fish in years. The equation predicts that at one year of age, the fish would weigh an average of 0.514 g, two year old fish would average 0.888 g, and three year olds 1.224 g (Pennycuick, 1971a). A faster increase in weight was achieved by sticklebacks in a hard water stream in southern England, for they weighed 0.86 g on average at

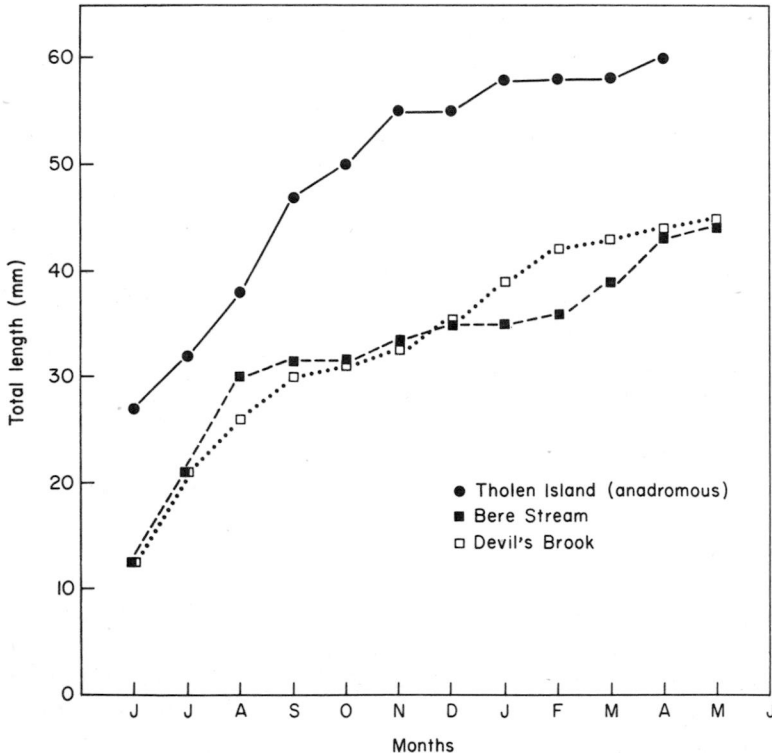

Fig. 17. Growth in length in three annual populations of *Gasterosteus aculeatus*. Tholen Island population anadromous (van Mullem and van der Vlught, 1964), Bere Stream and Devil's Brook populations permanently resident in fresh water (Mann, 1971).

one year old, but these fish did not survive much past their first birthday (Mann, 1971) (Fig. 18).

The relationship between the weight and the length of fishes is usually described by the equation:

$$W = aL^n$$

where W is weight, L is length and a and n are constants. If the fish maintains the same shape throughout its growth, then $n = 3$, so the equation can be written:

$$W = aL^3$$

and the constant a can be used as an indicator of the condition of the fish, that is:

$$a = W/L^3 = \text{Condition Factor.}$$

It is probably rare for the shape of a fish to remain constant

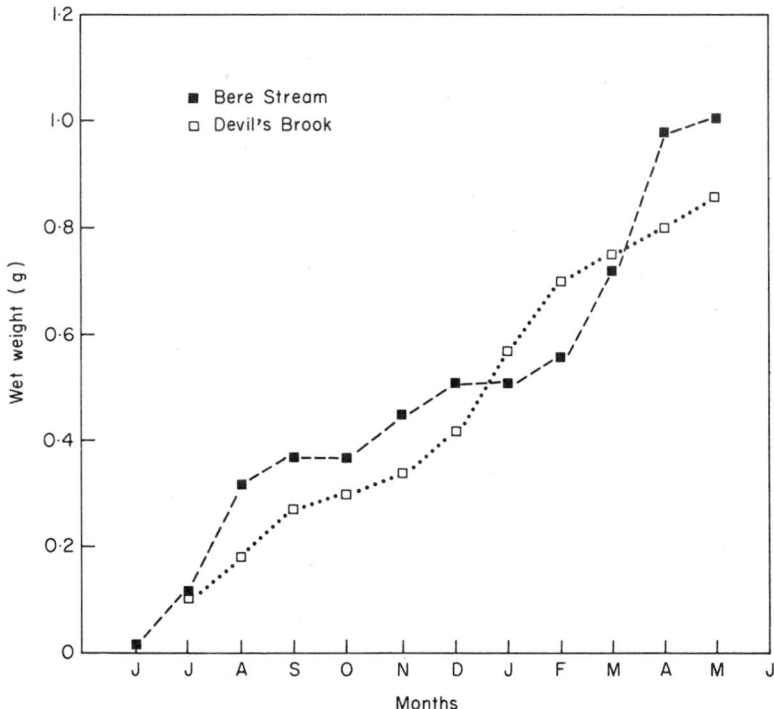

Fig. 18. Growth in weight of *Gasterosteus aculeatus* in two streams in southern England (Mann, 1971).

throughout its growth, and n has been found to vary between 2.5 and 4.0 for various species (Le Cren, 1951).

A graph of the form $W = aL^n$ for three-spined sticklebacks from the River Rheidol in West Wales is shown in Fig. 19. A linear realationship between length and weight is given by:

$$\log W = \log a + n \log L$$

which indicates that a plot of the logarithm of weight against the logarithm of length yields a straight line whose slope is n. The data from Fig. 19 are plotted in this form in Fig. 20.

For the sticklebacks of Priddy Pool and those of the Rheidol, n

was found to be close to 3.0. The condition factor of the fish in Priddy Pool showed a significant seasonal variation. It tended to fall during the winter, and the fall was more rapid in a cold winter, but increased in the spring. The sharp drop in the condition factor in

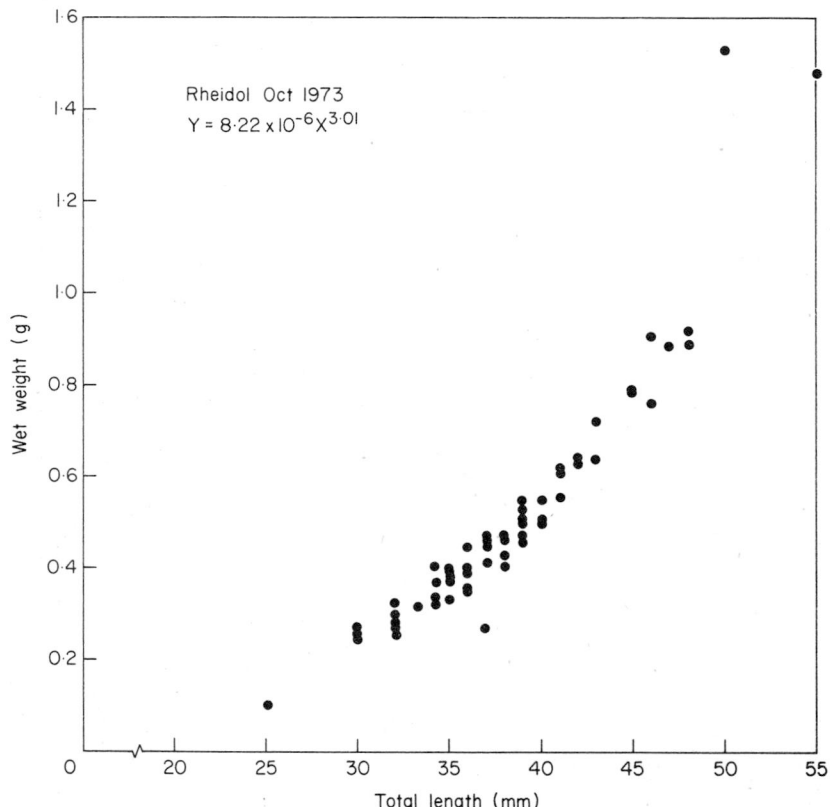

Fig. 19. Arithmetic plot of the relationship between weight and length of *Gasterosteus aculeatus* from the Rheidol. Y, weight; X, length.

May, presumably because the fish were spawning, was followed by a slow rise until the autumn (Pennycuick, 1971a).

Growth patterns in the stickleback vary both within populations and between populations, but the factors responsible for these variations are largely unanalysed.

In many populations there is a sexual dimorphism in size, for females of a given age tend to be larger than males of an equivalent age (van Mullem and van der Vlugt, 1964), so that variations in the proportion of females in a population may cause that population to show changes in the pattern of growth. The incidence and intensity of parasitism also affects the growth of sticklebacks so that variations in the parasitic infestation either within a population or between

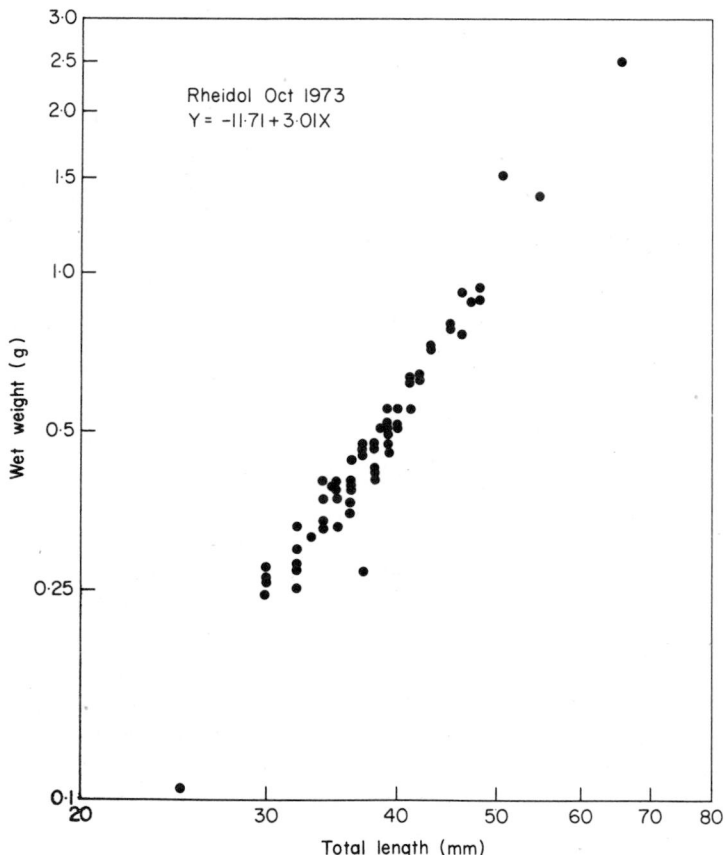

Fig. 20. Logarithmic plot of the relationship between weight and length of *Gasterosteus aculeatus* from the Rheidol. Y, log$_e$ (weight); X, log$_e$ (length).

populations will probably be reflected in changes in the growth rate (see Chapter 5).

There is some evidence that the trachurus form has a faster growth rate than the leiurus form. In the Littl' Campbell River in southwest British Columbia, breeding trachurus adults that had overwintered in the sea were significantly longer than breeding leiurus adults that had been resident in the river throughout the year (Hagen, 1967).

Trachurus sticklebacks in a brackish water quarry on Easdale Island in Scotland reached a total length of almost 50 mm after one year and had an average length of about 85 mm when three years old (Jones and Hynes, 1950). But other studies have indicated that in mixed populations along the coast of Europe, the trachurus, semiarmatus and leiurus forms did not differ in size (Heuts, 1947a; Münzing, 1959; van Mullem and van der Vlugt, 1964). The leiurus populations in two Alaskan lakes had comparable growth rates to the trachurus and semiarmatus populations in two lakes in Quebec (Greenbank and Nelson, 1959; Coad and Power, 1973b). This contradictory evidence indicates that only controlled experiments on the growth of the three forms will indicate whether differences in growth rate depend on genetic differences or depend primarily on environmental differences. Other factors whose effects on growth require experimental analysis are variations in the food supply both in quantitative and in qualitative terms, variations in temperature, photoperiod and salinity, all of which probably influence the growth rate of sticklebacks.

A feature of the growth patterns of stickleback populations is the variation in the maximum life span of the sticklebacks from population to population. This variation has led to considerable debate about the maximum life span of the three-spined stickleback. Information on the subject has come from two sources, reports on the life span of fish kept in the laboratory and analyses of the probable ages of fish in natural populations. In a well-maintained aquarium, both leiurus and trachurus sticklebacks have lived for more than three years with perhaps a maximum age span of five years (Bock, 1928; Wunder, 1928, 1930), but of course ages reached in the protected world of the aquarium probably bear little relationship to ages reached under natural conditions.

Normally two methods are available for ageing fish from natural populations. The first depends on some structure such as a scale or a bone which lays down annual rings in a manner reminiscent of the annual rings of a tree trunk. Scales, opercular bones and the calcareous ear otoliths have all been used to age fish of various species (Frost and Brown, 1967; Le Cren, 1947), but in the stickleback the only structures that reliably show annual rings are the ear otoliths. The second method of ageing fish is the use of frequency distributions of the lengths of the fish in the population. If the breeding season is relatively short, so that fish are recruited into the population in a series of waves, each wave being separated by about a year, then each age class should form a relatively distinct peak in a frequency distribution of the lengths of the fish. The number of peaks in such a distribution gives the number of age classes. Both methods can be used together, but the use of ear otoliths has the grave disadvantage that the fish must be killed before the otoliths can be removed, whereas data on the frequency distribution of lengths can be collected from live fish. Otoliths are often taken from a relatively few fish in order to confirm the ageing scheme obtained from the length data.

On the basis of the frequency distribution of lengths, Bertin (1925) concluded that the three-spined stickleback normally has a maximum life span of just over a year and dies after spawning, although in a few populations animals may live for a further year. The sticklebacks in a stream in southern England had a life span of just over a year (Mann, 1971) as did sticklebacks from the Belgium coast (Heuts, 1947a). On the basis of the length of the fish at maturity and histological features of the gonads, Graig-Bennett (1931) argued that in the leiurus population which he studied in Cambridge, England, some fish did not breed until they were two years old and that the maximum life span was over three years. From observations on trachurus fish kept in the laboratory, Wunder (1928, 1930) concluded that yearling fish did not breed, a conclusion that was supported by later analyses of mixed populations of trachurus and semiarmatus fish both in the North Sea and in the Baltic. The fish did not become mature until two years after hatching; the second summer of their life was spent in the sea rather than on the breeding grounds (Münzing, 1959; Aneer, 1973). In contrast to this, Leiner (1931a) found that yearling trachurus fish would breed and still live for over three years in an aquarium. A study of a mixed population of sticklebacks from the coast of the Netherlands indicated that the fish had a life span of just over a year, with the adults dying after breeding. This conclusion was strengthened by the observation that no large fish were found in the population during the autumn migration from the breeding sites to the sea (van Mullem and van der Vlugt, 1964).

In most of these studies the ages of the fish were deduced from the frequency distribution of their lengths, but in some populations this may not be a reliable technique. When the growth rate of the adult fish is very slow, the variations in length within an age class may be sufficient to mask the variations between age classes. In such a population, the frequency distribution usually shows only two modes, the one representing the young-of-the-year, and the other representing the adult fish (Leiner, 1931a; Jones and Hynes, 1950). Another complication is that in certain conditions there may be more than one wave of breeding in a year. A population of leiurus fish at Vaasen in the Netherlands had two reproductive periods in a year which were separated by two months. The first period was in spring and the second in late summer, so that the frequency distribution of the lengths of the fish born that year was multi-modal (van Mullem, 1967). In such situations the fish must be aged on the basis of the growth rings in the ear otoliths.

A scheme for ageing sticklebacks from their otoliths was devised by Jones and Hynes (1950). The largest of the three ear otoliths, the sagitta, is always used. An otolith can be classified as $S-$, S, $S+$, $2S$, $2S+$, $3S$, $3S+$ or $4S$. S refers to the transparent ring which is laid down during June and early July, throughout the rest of the year an opaque ring is laid down. An $S-$ otolith lacks any transparent ring, and so must be from a fish in the first month or so of its life. An S otolith has one transparent ring which forms the edge of the otolith, and indicates a fish in the first summer of its life, and an $S+$ otolith has one transparent ring with an opaque ring forming the edge so must come from a fish still in its first year. Fish that are in the first year of their life are often referred to as $0+$ fish. Fish whose otoliths have two transparent rings, $2S$ and $2S+$, are in the second year of life, that is they are in the $1+$ age class. When the otoliths have three transparent rings, $3S$ and $3S+$, the fish are in the third year of life and so belong to the $2+$ age class and so on. Although this scheme for ageing sticklebacks from their ear otoliths was devised for use on fish from the River Birket, it has been applied to fish from Priddy Pool, from lakes in Alaska, and Quebec and from the Baltic Sea. Unfortunately, the otoliths from fish from some migratory populations have been found unsuitable for ageing the fish (Münzing, 1959).

In the River Birket, the sticklebacks had a maximum life span of nearly four years, and most fish first bred in their second summer of life when they were about a year old (Jones and Hynes, 1950). The sticklebacks in Priddy Pool had a similar life span (Pennycuick, 1971a). The leiurus populations of Bare Lake and Karluk Lake in Alaska bred first at the age of one year and had a maximum life span of two and a quarter years. A similar life history was shown by the trachurus and semiarmatus populations of two lakes in Quebec (Coad and Power, 1973b). In mixed trachurus and semiarmatus populations in the Baltic Sea, the fish did not breed until two years old and some fish lived to be four years old (Aneer, 1973).

For both migratory and non-migratory populations, the maximum life span seems to vary from just over a year to almost four years, and the age at first breeding from a year to two years. The factors that cause these interpopulation variations and the adaptive significance of such variations remains unknown. Sticklebacks do not become mature until they are about 40 mm in length (Craig-Bennett, 1931; Baggerman, 1957) so that the age at which breeding first takes place will depend on the rate of growth of the sticklebacks. If the critical length is not reached in the summer that follows the summer of the fish's birth, then breeding will not take place until the fish is two years old. In many populations the aftermath of spawning is that all or most of the adults die (van Mullem and ver der Vlugt, 1964; Hagen, 1967; Mann, 1971). In these populations the life span will be determined by the age at which the fish mature.

The rate at which sticklebacks grow will depend on the rate at which they consume food, a topic considered in Chapter 4, and the efficiency with which they convert the food into stickleback flesh. Growth efficiency can be defined in several ways, but one of the most useful definitions is:

$$\frac{\text{growth of fish} \times 100}{\text{amount of food consumed to give that growth}}.$$

In this expression it is usual to express both the growth of the fish and the amount of food consumed in terms of energy, so that the growth efficiency is measured as:

$$\frac{\text{energy equivalent of growth} \times 100}{\text{energy equivalent of the food consumed to give that growth}}$$

with the energy equivalents expressed as calories or joules. Using this expression, Walkey and Meakins (1970) estimated that sticklebacks whose weight ranged from 0.732 to 1.156 g and which were feeding on *Tubifex* had growth efficiencies that ranged from 2.46 to 9.90 per cent with a mean value of 6.08 per cent. A similar range of growth efficiencies was observed when sticklebacks kept at three different temperatures were fed on *Tubifex*. At 7°C, the mean efficiency was 5.9 per cent, at 12.5°C the mean was 9.6 per cent and at 20°C the mean efficiency was 11.3 per cent (Cole, unpublished).

These results indicate that, when food is in sufficient supply, for every 100 calories of food consumed, between 6 and 12 calories are incorporated in the form of growth of the stickleback. These results applied to fish above about 0.20 g, and it is possible that smaller fish have somewhat different growth efficiencies, but no measurements are available. If it is assumed that the growth efficiencies given above can be applied to sticklebacks of all sizes and that sufficient food is always available, a crude estimate of the cost of producing an adult stickleback can be made. Stickleback flesh has a calorific value of approximately 4500 to 4700 cal per g dry weight, and the dry weight of a stickleback is about a quarter of its fresh wet weight

(Walkey and Meakins, 1970; Wootton, 1974a). An adult stickleback with a wet weight of one gram has a dry weight of about 0.250 g and so an energy content of about 1150 calories. Each calorie of stickleback flesh costs between 100/6 and 100/12 calories of food consumed, so that the cost of producing the one gram of stickleback is between 9500 and 19,000 calories. Since the food of the stickleback has a calorific value of the order of 5000 calories per gram dry weight, the dry weight of food consumed is around 1.9 to 3.8 g, and if the food contains about eighty per cent water, then the wet weight of food consumed is between 9.6 to 19.2 g. This calculation does not include the costs of egg or sperm production which must be met when the stickleback becomes sexually mature. Krokhin (1970) estimated that it took 15 g of zoo-plankton to produce a gram of stickleback, though he did not specify the assumptions he made to obtain this estimate.

Although these figures are crude, they indicate that it is feasible to calculate the energy requirements of a population of sticklebacks, and as similar figures become available for other species of fish that coexist with the stickleback, it will become possible to compare the relative importance of the species in terms of the energy demands they make on the environment. These demands will depend not only on the growth of the individual fish but also on the numerical abundance of the fish. Estimates of the abundance of sticklebacks are relatively difficult to make because it is such a small fish. In Lake Dal'neye, a lake with an area of 136 ha, the population of sticklebacks was estimated to be 2.5 million, with the total population of the lake divided up into several sub-populations each containing 100–200,000 fish (Krokhin, 1970). In a small stream in southern England, a density of four sticklebacks per square metre was observed (Mann, 1971) while in a backwater of the River Rheidol in West Wales that had an area of about 300 m^2, the stickleback population was estimated to vary from 1000 to 5000 fish. These abundances indicate that an area supporting a population of sticklebacks must produce of the order of 10–100 g of food suitable for the stickleback from a square metre each year.

4. Feeding and Digestion

Three-spined sticklebacks are predominantly carnivorous fish, hunting for their prey by sight. Although their small size restricts the range of potential prey, when kept in captivity they display a catholic choice of food items. They will take items such as tubificid and enchytraeid worms from the bottom of an aquarium, they will chase and seize swimming zoo-plankters such as *Daphnia* and *Cyclops* and they will take food floating on the surface such as commercial, dried fish food. Other food items they will readily take include fish eggs, including stickleback eggs, frozen brine-shrimp (*Artemia*) and minced meat. Newly hatched fry can be fed with infusoria, and then on the larval stages of small crustaceans such as the nauplii of brine-shrimp.

Do sticklebacks show this wide choice of food items when feeding in natural environments? Though many authors have described the stomach contents of sticklebacks caught in the wild (Saunders, 1914; Blegvad, 1917; Markley, 1940; Hartley, 1948 and Hagen, 1967), the most thorough study is that of Hynes (1950). He analysed the feeding habits of a population of leiurus sticklebacks living in the Birket, a small stream on the Wirral Peninsular in northwest England. Each month throughout a year he examined the stomach contents of a sample of fish, so that not only was a picture built up of the spectrum of food items taken by the sticklebacks, but the seasonal changes in the diet could also be described. The fish took a wide range of food items (Table IV), copepods, cladocerans and other crustaceans, oligochaetes, and the larvae and pupae of chironomids (a dipteran insect) were the most important foodstuffs. Although most of the diet was animal in origin, the Birket sticklebacks did eat some plant material including diatoms and other algae and higher plant matter, but this vegetable matter formed only a small proportion of the stomach contents. An earlier study of sticklebacks living in a

TABLE IV

Seasonal variations in the diet of the three-spined stickleback (*Gasterosteus aculeatus*) from two sites in England. Figures give the percentage composition of the food. Data from Birket River from Hynes (1950) and for Monkton Pool from Walkey (1967).

	Jan	Feb	Mar	Apr	May	June	July	Aug	Sept	Oct	Nov	Dec
(1) Birket River												
CRUSTACEA												
Cladocera	0.7	5.3	11.3	6.0	20.5	33.4	39.2	3.5	1.6	9.2	0.8	0.2
Copepoda	11.6	20.1	27.8	23.4	14.0	10.5	27.9	38.2	11.9	25.0	6.5	15.0
Ostracoda	0.6	0.6	3.5	0.9	3.4	2.4	0.8	10.5	6.7	4.1	4.2	5.0
Asellus	7.4	6.2	—	13.0	6.3	7.8	6.7	11.4	19.6	12.7	15.2	19.0
INSECTA												
Chironomid larvae	18.8	11.5	17.1	20.0	14.5	23.7	15.6	23.4	21.8	8.7	18.7	15.9
Chironomid pupae	0.6	0.7	14.5	18.5	15.7	2.5	1.3	1.9	0.5	3.7	0.3	0.5
Trichoptera larvae	0.7	1.5	14.2	1.8	—	0.9	—	—	0.2	—	—	—
Other diptera	9.7	2.4	1.2	0.3	5.8	—	1.5	—	2.0	0.7	0.3	3.7
Terrestrial insects	1.6	0.2	1.7	2.0	4.4	0.1	—	—	3.7	1.8	9.7	5.7
Mollusca	15.7	2.3	1.3	0.8	0.7	3.0	0.9	0.3	2.3	9.1	23.8	12.3
Oligochaeta	13.3	39.6	3.9	1.2	0.9	—	—	—	1.0	5.1	2.5	16.9
Fish eggs and larvae	—	—	—	8.1	3.5	1.7	—	—	—	—	—	—
PLANT												
Algae	0.1	0.1	0.1	—	0.7	7.6	2.9	9.4	22.4	6.2	0.8	0.1
Higher plants	2.4	3.8	1.2	1.9	2.1	0.4	0.3	—	0.4	2.0	9.9	1.7
Unidentified	13.1	1.8	—	0.6	1.1	—	—	—	3.8	4.2	5.7	3.2

(2) Monkton Pool

CRUSTACEA												
Cladocera	20.1	15.3	10.0	17.3	31.0	8.3	2.1	2.3	1.0	4.3	5.2	2.5
Copepoda	21.1	17.4	22.4	8.3	1.0	3.2	3.1	6.1	38.7	39.9	39.5	13.1
Ostracoda	23.7	6.1	10.8	2.1	0.5	7.0	27.5	20.3	14.6	13.1	16.9	13.4
Asellus	–	2.9	1.6	–	–	–	–	–	–	–	–	–
Gammarus	–	–	3.2	–	2.0	–	2.6	–	–	–	–	2.0
INSECTA												
Ephemeroptera	4.6	–	–	–	–	–	–	2.4	–	–	–	–
Sialis	–	–	1.6	1.7	–	–	–	–	–	–	–	–
Chironomid larvae	24.0	55.5	48.5	34.6	12.1	40.3	26.3	12.0	8.0	11.0	24.9	18.0
Chironomid pupae	–	–	–	28.8	44.6	22.6	2.0	5.6	–	–	–	–
Chironomid adults	–	–	–	–	–	–	–	–	11.2	6.5	4.5	2.0
Trichoptera	–	1.4	–	–	1.7	0.8	–	–	–	0.4	–	–
Hemiptera	–	–	–	–	–	7.1	22.8	31.7	19.8	1.9	–	–
Mollusca	–	–	–	–	1.2	1.6	8.7	14.4	3.4	16.1	10.2	6.9
Oligochaeta	–	0.4	1.8	0.4	2.9	–	–	0.3	3.0	3.8	–	–
Fish eggs and larvae	–	–	–	–	0.5	6.3	2.6	0.9	–	–	–	–
Plant material	0.6	0.2	–	0.4	0.5	1.6	0.7	0.9	–	0.6	4.5	38.5
Unidentified	5.9	0.8	–	6.4	2.0	1.2	1.6	3.1	0.3	2.4	4.3	3.6

pond near Cambridge found that the stomachs of large fish were full of *Nitzschia sigmoidea*, a diatom (Saunders, 1914), but this seems to have been a somewhat exceptional situation.

The sticklebacks in the Birket study showed distinct seasonal variations in their diet (Table IV). Cladocerans were most important in early summer while copepods were important in all but the mid-winter months. Chironomid larvae also formed a significant portion of the food taken throughout the year. Only in winter, when items such as cladocerans and copepods became less important did molluscs, terrestrial invertebrates and higher plant tissue become important. This switch probably reflects a decline in the abundance of the small crustaceans during the winter months rather than a switch in the food preferences of the fish, though the feeding behaviour of the fish may change as the temperature of the water changes. Algae, mostly elongate diatoms, formed a peak in the diet in September, but only fish in large schools fed on algae to any extent, perhaps because the high density of fish in schools meant that the preferred food items were scarce and so the fish were forced to feed on the diatoms.

A quantitative analysis of the data indicated that there was a slight decrease in the amount of food eaten during the winter. In March, just before the start of the stickleback's breeding season, fifteen per cent of the fish had empty stomachs, but the fish that were feeding had fuller stomachs than fish in winter. Once breeding started, fewer fish had empty stomachs and there was evidence that the amount of food eaten increased. This is not surprising for breeding imposes high demands for energy on both the males and the females. There is a weakness in Hynes' quantitative analysis of food consumption for it did not take into consideration the effect of temperature on the rate at which food passes through the digestive system of the stickleback, an effect which significantly influences the amount of food consumed (see below).

Sticklebacks living in an isolated pond in the northeast of England showed rather similar seasonal variations in their diet to those shown by the Birket sticklebacks. Chironomid larvae and pupae, cladocerans and copepods were again the principal prey items (Walkey, 1967) (Table IV).

Leiurus sticklebacks living in lakes take a similar range of food items to sticklebacks living in streams and ponds. In Lake Windermere in northwest England, cladocerans and copepods formed the main food of the sticklebacks, though chironomid larvae and aquatic oligochaetes were also important (Hynes, 1950). Copepods, cladocerans and chironomid larvae and pupae were the principal food of leiurus sticklebacks in Bare Lake and Karluk Lake on Kodiak Island, Alaska (Greenback and Nelson, 1959). Sticklebacks were introduced into Lac Leman (Lake Geneva) in 1872 and it is claimed that they have contributed to the decline in the population of coregonid fishes in the lake because of their predation on coregonid eggs (Laurent, 1972).

A few studies have compared the diets of leiurus and trachurus sticklebacks. Hynes (1950), in addition to his study of the leiurus sticklebacks of the Birket, also examined the stomach contents of trachurus fish caught in brackish water in a quarry on Easdale Island, in Scotland. These large fish, ranging in length from 38 to 96 mm, were feeding predominantly on higher crustacea especially *Gammarus*. Copepods and chironomids formed a small proportion of the diet, and cladocerans were not found at all. Sticklebacks collected in *Zostera* (eel grass) beds in brackish water in Denmark had a similar diet, with higher crustacea such as young gammarids, other amphipods and isopods forming the most important component (Blegvad, 1917). The young fish fed on copepods and to a lesser extent on cladocerans, and in the Easdale sticklebacks it was only the smaller fish that were feeding on copepods. Perhaps more significant than this comparison between leiurus and trachurus fish from different habitats, is the data of Hagen (1967) on the diets of leiurus and trachurus fish breeding in the same stream in south western British Columbia. The leiurus fish took mainly organisms that were associated with the bed of the stream, especially coleopteran and zygopteran larvae and *Musculium* (a fresh water lammelibranch), whereas the trachurus fish fed more on surface or swimming organisms such as cladocerans and *Palaemonetes* (a decapod crustacean). Chironomids were an important component of the diet of the trachurus fish but not of the leiurus fish. Associated with this difference in the diets of the two forms was a difference in the number and morphology of the gill rakers. The trachurus form had a higher average number of rakers and they were longer and finer than those of the leiurus form (Chapter 1). This difference may indicate that the trachurus form is better adapted to feeding on planktonic organisms while leiurus is better adapted to feeding on benthic organisms. Whether this difference in gill rakers is maintained throughout the distribution of trachurus and leiurus is still unclear.

As the stickleback grows in size a wider range of organisms become potential prey. Abdel'-Malek (1968) studied the diet of larval trachurus sticklebacks in the White Sea in northern U.S.S.R. Young fish that still had small yolk sacs fed largely on the nauplii stage of copepods, but as the fish grew larger and began to swim more proficiently they tended to switch to feeding on the copepodid stages of copepods especially those of *Harpacticus uniremis*. With further growth the range of food items taken increased so that young fish of 15 mm or more in length were including in their diet many of the food organisms taken by adult sticklebacks. For these young fish, the main prey was adult *H. uniremis* and other adult copepods, but chironomid larvae, higher crustaceans and annelids were occasionally eaten. In the Birket, the young leiurus fish fed mostly on copepods, cladocerans and chironomid larvae, but the larger fish included higher crustaceans, caddis fly larvae and chironomid pupae in their diet (Hynes, 1950).

The wide range of prey species taken by the three-spined stickle-back makes it inevitable that it will take food items sought by other species of fish. If the supply of food is not sufficient to meet the demands of all the species of fish present, then there will be competition for food between the stickleback and the other species that have a similar diet. In the Birket, the three-spined stickleback took the same range of prey organisms and in the same proportions as the nine-spined stickleback (*Pungitius pungitius*). In the breeding season these two species have different habitat preferences, for *P. pungitius* nests amongst weed, whereas the three-spined stickleback prefers to nest in more open areas, and this difference may help to reduce the intensity of any competition for food between the two species. In contrast to the close similarity between the diets of the two species of stickleback in the Birket, the roach (*Rutilus rutilus*) living in the same stream showed relatively little overlap in diet with the sticklebacks. The cyprinid fish fed largely on molluscs and vegetable matter which included both higher plant material such as grasses, and diatoms and a little filamentous algae (Hynes, 1950).

A study of the feeding relations of a number of species of fish in the River Endrick in Scotland showed that the three-spined stickle-backs had a diet that overlapped with the other species. This overlap was particularly marked with the loach (*Nemacheilus barbatula*), and to a lesser but still significant degree with the fry of the trout (*Salmo trutta*) and the salmon (*Salmo salar*). If food was ever in short supply it seemed inevitable that these species would be in competition for the available food. A fifth species present in the River Endrick, the minnow (*Phoxinus phoxinus*) which like the roach is a cyprinid, seemed to partially avoid the possibility of competing for food with the other four species for a significant portion of its diet consisted of algae. This was also taken by the stickleback but not in great amounts (Maitland, 1965).

In a hard water stream in southern England, the three-spined stickleback and the minnow were found to have very similar diets (Mann and Orr, 1969). The two species were usually found in the slacker waters of the stream so the similarity of diet probably reflects a similarity of habitat.

Competition for food between the three-spined stickleback and the fry of the Pacific salmon (*Oncorhynchus* spp.) has economic implications, for these salmon support important commercial fisheries both in North America and in the U.S.S.R. Both in Alaska and the Kamchatka area of the U.S.S.R., the lakes contain large numbers of sticklebacks and the young of sockeye (or red) salmon *Oncorhynchus nerka*. The young sockeye spend the first year of their life in fresh water before migrating to the sea.

Sockeye fry and sticklebacks in the Wood River Lakes of western Alaska exploited a similar range of food organisms, and this overlap in diets occurred in fish from the open waters of the lakes as well as in those from the littoral zone (Rogers, 1968). In the littoral zone, the food of both species consisted mainly of small crustaceans, such as copepods and cladocerans, and of insects, in particular the larvae and pupae of chironomids. Although the two species took the same range of food items, there was a difference in the relative importance of the items in their diets, a difference which indicated that the sticklebacks tended to take more food off the bottom, whereas the sockeye fry fed more off the surface of the water. The sticklebacks made greater use of the larvae of chironomids, molluscs, algae and stickleback eggs while the sockeye fry diet included winged insects and collembolans which had obviously fallen into the water. In open water both species relied mainly on zooplankton, though the sockeye tended to take more cladocerans such as *Daphnia* and *Bosmina* while the sticklebacks took more copepods. Zooplankters accounted for over ninety per cent of the food of sticklebacks in open water, but the sockeye fry from the open water included insects, particularly winged insects, in their food. These insects formed nineteen per cent of the sockeye diet. The sockeye fry had more food items in their stomachs than did sticklebacks of a comparable size, the salmon seemed to be eating about two and a half times the amount of food of the sticklebacks.

Rogers' (1968) study did not indicate whether food in the lake system was ever in such short supply that competition between the species became sufficiently intense to influence the growth or survival of the fish. The similarity in the diets of the sockeye and stickleback makes this a real possibility (see Chapter 6).

Russian studies on the relationship between the three-spined stickleback and the sockeye salmon have provided estimates on the quantities of zooplankton consumed by sticklebacks and sockeye salmon in Lake Dal'neye (Krokhin, 1970). The estimates suggest that when sticklebacks were abundant they accounted for a third of the total consumption of zooplankton by fishes, but at other times they accounted for only five or ten per cent of the total consumption. Such gross estimates do not indicate how efficient the stickleback is at discovering and capturing food or what factors influence the success of the stickleback as a predator.

A stickleback detects its prey visually, the importance of vision and the unimportance of olfaction means that the sticklebacks feed little, if at all, at night. A stickleback can detect a single *Tubifex* worm against a plain surface at a distance of up to 30 cm, and up to 15 cm, the probability that the fish will detect the worm is one hundred per cent (Beukema, 1968). Sticklebacks in a pond were observed to attack a corixid, *Vermicorixa nigrolineata*, and the sticklebacks attacked a much greater proportion of the corixids whose colour made them more conspicuous against the substrate (Popham, 1966). Although smell plays no role in the detection of food (Pipping, 1926), the taste of the prey is relevant because there are taste receptors (Glaser, 1966). The majority of these taste receptors are in the pharynx and buccal cavity, but there are some on the lips and in the oesophagus (Campos, 1969). Frequently sticklebacks will mouth a piece of food repeatedly sucking it into the mouth then spitting it out, until it is finally swallowed or rejected.

When feeding on food such as a *Tubifex* worm which is lying on the bottom, the stickleback approaches the ground, tilting its body from the horizontal and fixing the prey with its eyes. After this fixation, the fish usually makes a rapid sideways twist and a snapping movement as it grasps the prey (Tugendhat, 1960a). Prey are swallowed without being chewed, although the repeated mouthing described above may help to break up the food, especially as the teeth of the stickleback are sharp even though small.

As it goes to seize a prey, a stickleback protrudes its jaws. An analysis of films of sticklebacks feeding has shown the mechanisms by which this protrusion is achieved. Initially the mouth is closed and the pre-maxilla bone is retracted, but when the mouth opens to grasp the prey the pre-maxilla is protruded and even after the prey has been taken and the mouth closed the pre-maxilla remains protruded. Two mechanisms operate to cause this protrusion. Firstly, as the mouth opens the ventral ends of the maxillae swing anteriorly for they are connected to the coronoid process of the lower jaw. The pre-maxillae swing with the maxillae but this presses the rostral cartilage against the ethmoid cartilage and so the pre-maxillae are protruded. Secondly, as the mouth opens, the articular-maxillary ligament becomes taut. Tension in this ligament rotates the maxilla about its long axis moving the pre-maxillary condyle of the maxilla forward. The pad of tissue which connects the pre-maxillary condyles is also connected to the rostral cartilage so that rotation of the maxilla causes protrusion of the pre-maxilla (Fig. 21) (Alexander, 1967).

What advantages does the stickleback gain from this ability to protrude the jaws? When the fish is taking food, protrusion moves the mouth suddenly nearer the food item, so the chances that the prey will escape are reduced. Protrusion also makes it easier for the fish to take food from the bottom, for the fish does not have to take up such an oblique stance. There are also advantages when the fish closes its mouth. With the jaws protruded, the mouth can be closed more quickly because the angle through which the jaws must be adducted is reduced. In addition, a greater volume of water can be sucked into the mouth as well. A further advantage is that if food is held between the jaws before being swallowed, protrusion makes it possible for the fish to hold the food straight, pointing towards the gullet and this may make swallowing easier (Alexander, 1967).

As the mouth is closed, the floor of the buccal cavity is depressed and the brachiostegals are spread, so that the food is presumably sucked into the mouth by the expansion of the buccal and opercular cavities. Food passes from the buccal cavity into the pharynx, and from there into the oesophagus. The alimentary canal of the stickleback consists of the oesophagus which leads to a true stomach, an uncoiled anterior intestine and a rectum or posterior intestine. A pyloric sphincter guards the opening of the stomach into the anterior intestine, and there is an ileo-rectal valve between the anterior intestine and the rectum. In all, the gut is about the same length as the body cavity (Hale, 1965).

Histologically, the gut of the stickleback is relatively simple (Hale, 1965).

The stratified epithelium of the oesophagus consists of saccular mucus-secreting cells and undifferentiated polyhedral cells. These polyhedral cells cover the tops and occur in the troughs of the longitudinal folds of the oesophageal mucosa while the mucus-secreting cells line the sides of the folds. A layer of connective tissue lies below the epithelial layer, the fibres of the connective tissue are randomly arranged and there are a few, isolated, striated muscle fibres amongst the connective tissue. Under the layer of connective tissue there is a relatively thick layer of striated muscle. Most of the

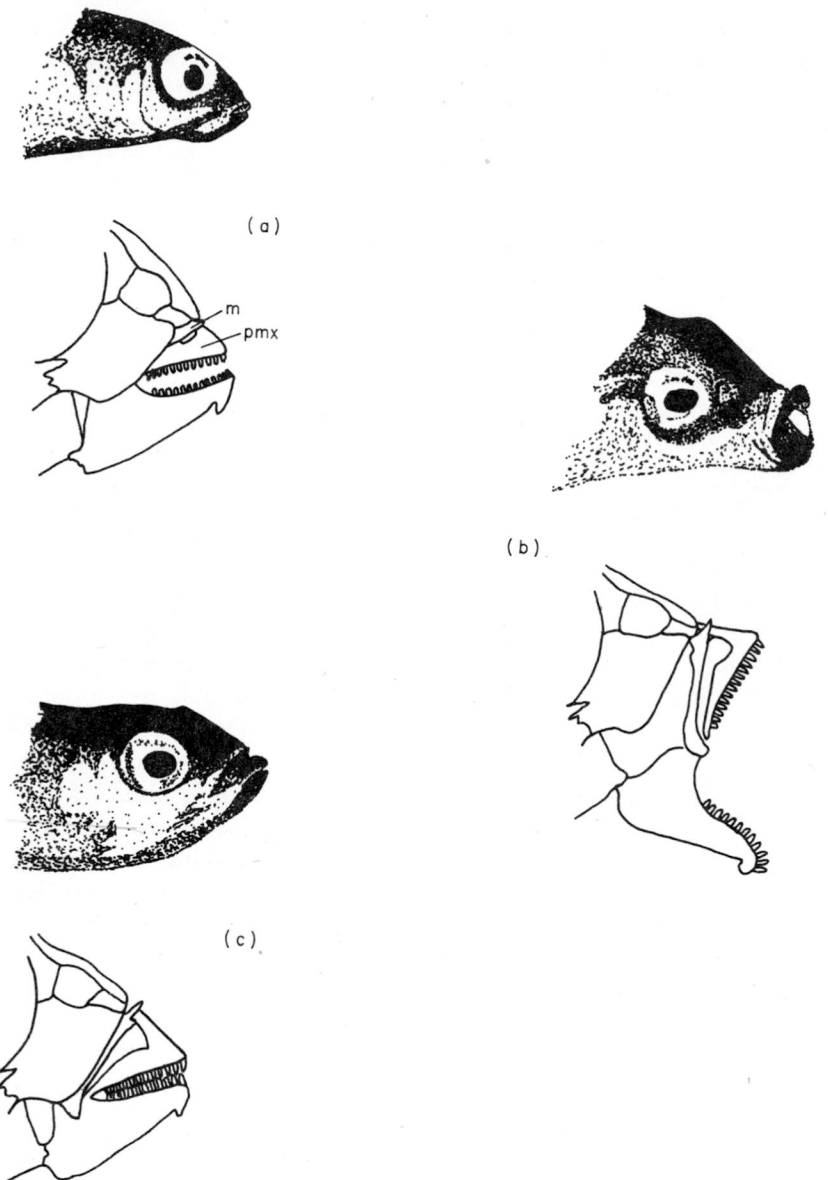

Fig. 21. Jaw protrusion of *Gasterosteus aculeatus*. (a) Mouth closed, jaws retracted; (b) mouth open, jaws protruded; (c) mouth closed, jaws protruded (after Alexander, 1967). Key to lettering: m, maxilla; pmx, pre-maxilla.

muscle fibres run circularly around the oesophagus, though in a few places there are bundles of fibres which run longitudinally, the length of the oesophagus. These longitudinal fibres lie internally to the circular muscle coat. Towards the posterior of the oesophagus, the stratified epithelium is replaced by a simple columnar epithelium, which is also characteristic of the stomach. At the junction of the oesophagus and stomach, a sphincter is formed by a thickening of both the sub-epithelial connective tissue layer and the circular muscle layer. Gastric glands occur in the front half of the stomach. These glands are lined by only one type of secretory cell, and in each gland there is a short neck region of six to ten cells with a gradual change from the superficial columnar epithelium to the secretory type of epithelium. The glands project into the sub-epithelial connective tissue layer, which is increased in thickness in this region of the stomach. The muscle of the stomach consists of an internal layer of circular muscle and an external layer of longitudinal muscle. In the most anterior region of the stomach the muscle is striated, but in the rest of the stomach the striated muscle is replaced by smooth muscle. The posterior or pyloric region of the stomach contains no gastric glands, but the muscle layers are about three times as thick as in the glandular part of the stomach. A pyloric sphincter controls the junction between the stomach and the dilated anterior region of the intestine; it prevents the return of food to the stomach. Another valve, formed by the thickening of the sub-epithelial connective tissue and the circular muscle layer, divides the anterior two-thirds of the intestine from the rectum and prevents an anterior movement of faecal material. Histologically, there is no difference between the anterior intestine and the rectum. The intestinal epithelium consists of columnar absorbing cells with a striated free border, mucus-secreting cells, lymphocytes and small granular leucocytes. Outside the epithelial layer is the connective tissue layer, then a layer of circular muscle and a layer of longitudinal muscle. In the intestine, the circular muscle layer is about three times the width of the longitudinal muscle layer. The epithelial folds of the intestine are arranged in a herring-bone pattern.

Other organs associated with alimentary canal are the liver, the gall-bladder and the pancreas. The liver has two lobes, with the right lobe much larger than the left. This right lobe curves around the stomach and reaches past the pyloric region. The large polyhedral liver cells surround the blood sinusoids which run randomly between the cells throughout the liver. Enclosed between the right lobe of the liver and the stomach, the gall-bladder opens into the intestine through the bile duct which enters the intestine just behind the pylorus. Pancreatic tissue is spread diffusely around the mesenteric blood vessels, and the pancreatic ducts open into the intestine in the same region as the bile duct. The endocrine component of the pancreas, a large Islet of Langerhans, lies in a mass of pancreatic tissue which occurs in an angle of the gut at the pyloric sphincter. Cells of the Islet of Langerhans presumably produce insulin (Hale, 1965; Baron, 1934).

The chemistry of digestion in the stickleback has received little attention. In fish that had been fed two hours previously, the gastric juice was distinctly acid, with a pH between 2.5 and 5.5. This indicates that the gland cells of the stomach produce hydrochloric acid. Bile from the gall-bladder was slightly alkaline with a pH between 7.0 and 8.0 (Hale, 1965).

Both the amount and the rate at which sticklebacks consume food depend on several factors which include the size of the stickleback, its hunger, the palatability of the prey and the temperature of the water. The influence of these factors will only be significant if the density of prey organisms is suffcient for this not to be the limiting factor in determining the food consumption.

Beukema (1968) found that when sticklebacks were provided with *Tubifex* worms for eight hours a day, they consumed between nine and seventeen per cent of their own wet body weight of *Tubifex* per day. In this experiment the food was not provided every day and over a three month period the average daily consumption was estimated at about four or five per cent of the fish's body weight per day. On this food level, there was no noticable increase in the weight of the fish although two females did become sexually mature and spawned two or three times. A relationship between the weight of the fish and the weight of *Tubifex* consumed daily is shown in Fig. 22. In this experiment, the weight of food consumed was not directly proportional to the weight of the fish for the larger fish ate proportionally less than the small fish. In mathematical terms:

$$FC = aW^b \quad (b < 1.0)$$

where FC is the weight of food consumed and W is the weight of the fish, a and b are constants (Cole, unpublished).

During their period of sexual maturity, female sticklebacks have high levels of food consumption and may eat a third of their body weight of *Tubifex* in one day. The relationships between food consumption and spawning are considered in more detail in Chapter 9.

The influence of hunger on food consumption by the stickleback
has been analysed in some detail. Tugendhat (1960a) studied the
effect of periods of food deprivation of one hour, a day, two days,
and three days on the feeding behaviour of fish exposed to high
densities of *Tubifex* for an hour. An initiated feeding response was
recorded when the fish visually fixated a worm, and a completed
response when the fish both fixated and grasped the worm. Increased

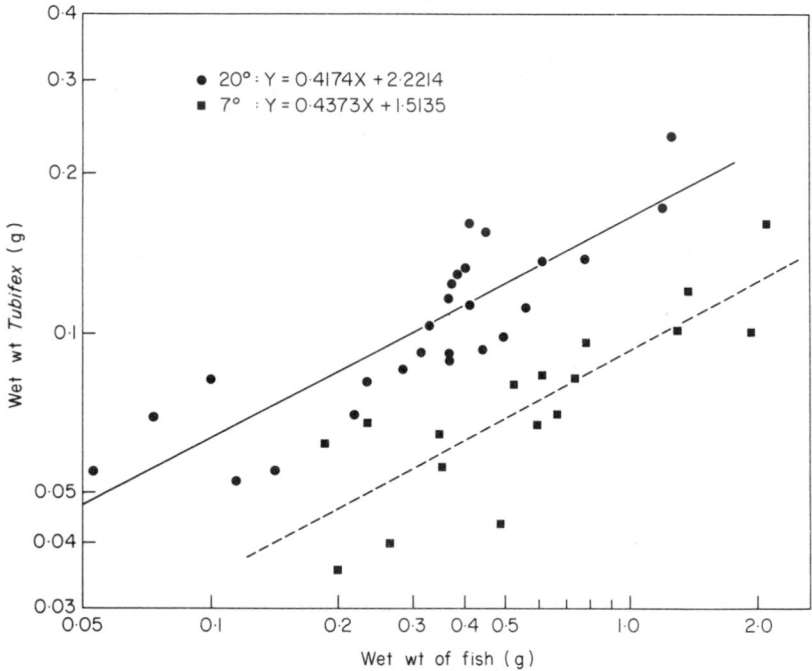

Fig. 22. Logarithmic plot of the relationship between wet wt of *Tubifex* consumed per day
and the wet wt of *Gasterosteus aculeatus* at 20°C and 7°C. Y, log$_e$ (wt *Tubiflex*); X, log$_e$
(wt fish).

periods of food deprivation led to an increase in the total number of
completed responses made during the hour, although the total
number of initiated responses did not increase significantly. Fish
which had experienced the longer periods of food deprivation tended
to complete more initiated responses than fish on short deprivation.
The average duration of a feeding response, whether complete or
incomplete was longer in fish on the shorter deprivations. These fish
made fewer completed responses but took longer on average to
complete each response with the result that although the fish on the
long deprivation periods completed more feeding responses they did
not spend a greater amount of the hour feeding. In the hour the fish

usually spent between twenty-one and twenty-two minutes making feeding responses.

These effects of increased deprivation on feeding behaviour were reversed during the course of a feeding session, that is as the stomach of the fish filled with food. As the hour long feeding session progressed, the number of completed responses declined, although the number of initiated feeding response did not decline. The average duration of a feeding response increased during a feeding session but the total time spent feeding did not change. Because of the interactions between the variables that determined feeding rate, the frequency of completed responses did not decline at a constant rate throughout the hour that food was available. After an initial decline at a constant rate, a decline that was most rapid in fish that had experienced the longest periods of food deprivation, there was a slight recovery in the frequency of completions, then a further slow decline (Fig. 23).

The conclusion that hunger did not influence the total time spent feeding, but increased the rate at which the fish fed is compatible with finding that hunger did not influence the total daily consumption of sticklebacks but did influence the pattern of food consumption during the day (Beukema, 1968). Fish that had experienced longer periods of food deprivation consumed a much higher proportion of their total daily consumption within the first hour or so of feeding than fish that had a short period of food deprivation.

When sticklebacks were made to hunt for single *Tubifex* worms in a maze-like system, several aspects of the fish's behaviour were changed as a result of a period of food deprivation (Beukema, 1968). An increase in the length of the period of food deprivation increased the rate at which the fish visited areas in which food was likely to be found. There was also an increase in the probability that once the prey was detected it would be grasped and an increase in the probability that the prey would be eaten.

Since most of the effects of hunger on feeding behaviour disappear relatively soon after the fish starts feeding, they are probably mediated through the degree of fullness of the stomach. The daily feeding pattern of sticklebacks also reflects the importance of the degree of fullness of the stomach as an influence on the pattern of food consumption. In the morning, as the level of light increases, the stickleback begins to feed, and in the first hour, if sufficient food is available, eats up to seventy per cent of its daily food consumption. This initial intake of food fills up the stomach and subsequent food consumption will depend on the rate of evacuation from the stomach.

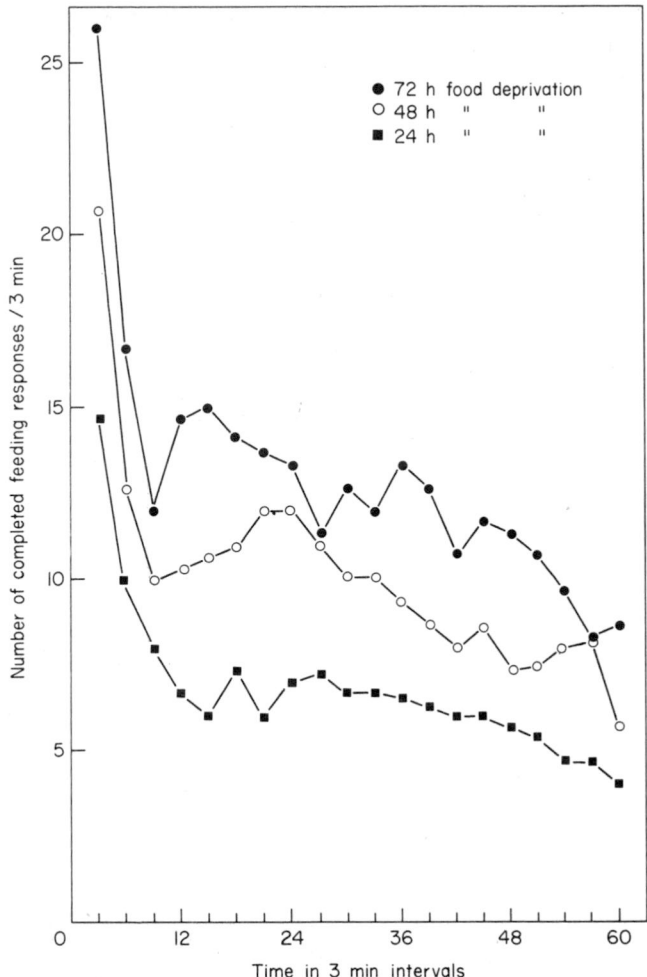

Fig. 23. Pattern of feeding by *Gasterosteus aculeatus* on *Tubifex* after periods of food deprivation (after Tugendhat, 1960a).

Some of the ways in which hunger altered the feeding behaviour of sticklebacks such as the increase in the ratio of completed responses to initiated responses and the decrease in the average time spent on a feeding response also occurred when fish received an electric shock during a feeding session (Tugendhat, 1960b). In this situation there is a conflict between the tendency of the fish to feed and the tendency to flee from the shock and the resolution of the conflict involves an increase in the intensity with which the fish feeds.

Prey organisms differ in palatability, and this has consequences for the feeding behaviour of the stickleback. When a prey organism was taken by a stickleback, the searching behaviour of the stickleback changed so that the fish tended to increase the intensity of its searching in the area where food had been found. But when a prey organism was rejected, the fish tended to move directly from the area and reduced the initial intensity of its search (Thomas, 1974). In some situations, sticklebacks find *Enchytraeus* worms more palatable than *Tubifex* worms. The presence of *Enchytraeus* caused an increase in the rate at which prey were discovered but a reduction in the rate at which *Tubifex* were taken compared with the situation in which only *Tubifex* was present. It was as though the stickleback was inhibited from taking the *Tubifex* by the expectation of finding a more palatable item, the *Enchytraeus* worm (Beukema, 1968).

The rate at which the stickleback consumes food depends on the rate at which the contents of the stomach are evacuated into the intestine, for only as space becomes available in the stomach can more food be taken in. The rate at which the stomach is evacuated is approximately proportional to the amount of food remaining in the stomach, so that following a meal the weight of food in the stomach declines exponentially (Cole, unpublished). At low temperatures the contents of the stomach are evacuated more slowly, so that as the temperature of the water falls, the time taken to reach a given degree of evacuation becomes longer. At $18-20°C$, stomach evacuation was completed in one night, but at $11-12°C$ it took more than sixteen hours before the stomach was empty (Beukema, 1968). The effect at lower temperatures is even more marked (Fig. 24).

The experiments on the effect of hunger, electric shocks, the palatability of the prey and the temperature of the water on food consumption were all carried out in artifical conditions, so the relevance of the conclusions to the feeding behaviour of fish in natural environments has still to be clarified.

One aspect of the feeding behaviour of sticklebacks that has been observed both in laboratory experiments and in the field, is that the sight of one stickleback feeding tends to attract other sticklebacks to the same area. A rapid build up in the number of sticklebacks around a food source can occur (Keenlyside, 1955; Black and Wootton, 1970).

Food consumed by the stickleback represents its income, the income that must cover both the nutritional and energy requirements of the fish. Of this income a portion is lost almost immediately in the form of faeces. Sticklebacks fed on *Tubifex* lost between five and thirteen per cent of the energy content of the food in the form of faeces (Wootton and Evans, 1976). Energy is also lost in the nitrogeneous substances that are excreted in the urine, but this loss is probably only a few per cent of the energy content of the food consumed. A portion of the energy is expended in the digestion, transportation and deposition of the food materials, and during the

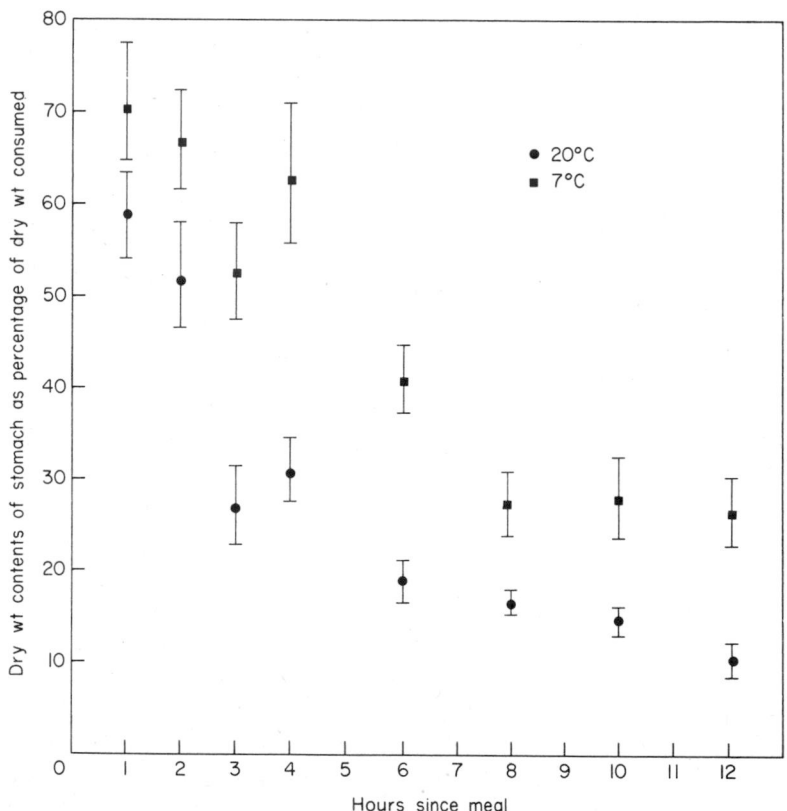

Fig. 24. Evacuation of stomach contents of *Gasterosteus aculeatus* at 20°C and 7°C. Groups of sticklebacks were sacrificed at intervals after feeding on *Tubifex* for 15 mins.

deamination of proteins. The energy that still remains is available to do useful physiological work, this includes the basic metabolic processes characteristic of living organisms, the work associated with muscular activity, growth and the production of eggs or sperm for reproduction (Davis and Warren, 1971). The mechanisms which control the partitioning of energy between these various requirements remain undescribed, though the energy costs of growth and egg production are considered in Chapters 3 and 9, respectively.

Since the energy in the food is made available by the oxidation of food, the rate of energy expenditure is related to the oxygen consumption by the fish. The rate of oxygen consumption depends on the weight of the fish, and the relationship takes the form:

$$R = aW^b$$

where R is the rate of oxygen onsumption and W is the weight of the fish, and a and b are constants. The rate of oxygen consumption per unit weight of fish is given by:

$$\frac{R}{W} = \frac{aW^b}{W}$$

or

$$\frac{R}{W} = aW^{b'}$$

where $b' = b - 1$. The linear form of these two equations are given by:

$$\log R = \log a + b \log W$$

and

$$\log R = \log a + b' \log W$$

(Walkey and Meakins, 1970; Lewis, Walkey and Dartnall, 1972).

Large sticklebacks whose average weight was 4.5 g from Lake Dal'neye consumed oxygen at a rate that varied from 0.127 to 0.365 mg oxygen per g wet weight per hour (Krokhin, 1957).

The rate of oxygen consumption varies with the activity of the stickleback (Walkey and Meakins, 1970), the rate of food consumption (Taylor, unpublished) and the water temperature (Meakins, 1975). High levels of activity, high rates of food consumption and high temperatures are all associated with high rates of oxygen consumption, but the interrelationships between these four factors have still to be quantified.

These and other gaps in the data on the food consumption and rate of energy expenditure of the stickleback reflect the situation that although there is considerable qualitative information on the food and feeding of the stickleback, much more accurate, quantitative information is required before the role of the stickleback as a predator can be fully assessed.

5. Parasites and Predators

In the chapters on growth and feeding (Chapters 3 and 4), the stickleback appears as predator, converting the flesh of its prey into stickleback flesh, but in turn it is exploited as a source of energy and nutrients by parasites and predators. The influence of this exploitation by parasites and predators on the biology of the stickleback is analysed as another step in placing the stickleback in its ecological context.

A surprising aspect of the role of the stickleback as a host to parasites, is the number of parasitic species that take advantage of this opportunity. In the U.S.S.R. about fifty different parasitic species have been found in or on the stickleback, though of course any one fish is host to only a fraction of this number of species. Fifteen of the species are ecto-parasites living on the external surface of the fish, while thirty-two species are endo-parasites living within the host in such places as the alimentary canal, the urinary bladder and the body cavity. A list of the parasites is shown in Table V which shows that six phyla are represented (Bykhovskaya-Pavlovskaya *et al.*, 1964). Britain is an island with an impoverished fauna, but nevertheless forty species of parasites have been recorded from the three-spined stickleback, and again six phyla are represented (Chappell and Owen, 1969; Kennedy, 1974).

For many of these parasites the stickleback is the definitive host, the parasites become sexually mature on or in the stickleback. But for some of the parasites the stickleback is only an intermediate host and the parasite does not become sexually mature until the stickleback is eaten by the parasite's definitive host. The completion of the life history of many of the endoparasites depends on particular links in the food web in which the stickleback is meshed. *Neoechinorynchus rutili* is an acanthocephalan that reaches sexual maturity in the alimentary canal of the stickleback, but the stickleback becomes

TABLE V

Parasites recorded from *Gasterosteus aculeatus*

Fungi

Saprolegnia parasitica Coker. In nostrils. North America (e).
Saprolegnia sp. Caudal peduncle. North America (e).

Protozoa

1. FLAGELLATA

Cryptobia branchialis (Chen, 1956). Ectoparasite on gills. U.S.S.R. (a).
Costia necatrix (Henneguy, 1884). Ectoparasite on gills. North America (e).
Hexamita salmonis (Moore, 1923). Endoparasite in the intestine. North America (e).

2. SPOROZOA

Eimeria gasterostei (Thelohan, 1890). Endoparasite in the liver. U.S.S.R. (a), North America (c).
Myxidium gasterostei Noble, 1943. Endoparasite in the gall bladder. U.S.S.R. (a), North America (e).
Sphaerospora elegans Thelohan, 1892. Endoparasite in the kidney tubules and urinary bladder. U.S.S.R. (a), U.K. (d), North America (e).
Myxobilatus gasterostei (Parisi, 1912). Endoparasite in kidney tubules and urinary bladder. U.S.S.R. (a), North America (e).
M. medius (Thelohan, 1892). Endoparasite in the kidney tubules. U.S.S.R. (a).
Glugea anomala (Moniez, 1887). Endoparasite in connective tissue. U.S.S.R. (a), U.K. (d), North America (c).
Dermocystidium gasterostei Elkan, 1962. Endoparasite in skin. U.K. (d).
Henneguya sp. U.K. (d).
Ceratomyxa sp. Endoparasite in intestine. North America (e).
Thelohania baueri. Parasite of eggs. U.S.S.R. (f).

3. CILIATA

Hemiophrys branchiarum (Weinrich, 1925). Ectoparasite on gills and skin. U.S.S.R. (a).
Trichodina gracilis Polyanskii, 1955. Ectoparasite on gills and skin. U.S.S.R. (a).
T. domerguei (Wallengren, 1897). Ectoparasite on gills and skin. U.S.S.R. (a), U.K. (d), North America (e).
T. domerguei f. *latispina* Dogel', 1940. Ectoparasite on gills, skin and fins. U.S.S.R. (a).
T. reticulata Hirschmann and Partsch, 1955 (= *T. megamicronucleata*). Ectoparasite on skin. U.K. (d).
T. tenuidens Faure-Fremiet, 1943. Ectoparasite. U.K. (d), North America (e).
Ichthyophthirius multifiliis Fouquet, 1876. Endoparasite of skin. Commonly known as "white-spot" or "ich". U.S.S.R. (a), U.K. (d), North America (c).
Trichophrya intermedia Prost, 1952. Ectoparasite on gills. U.S.S.R. (a).
Glossatella amoebae (Grenfell, 1887). Ectoparasite on gills and skin. U.S.S.R. (a).
Apiosoma (= *Glossatella*) sp. North America (e).
Epistylis lwoffi Faure-Fremiet. Ectoparasite on gills and body surface, frequently attached to the bases of *Apiosoma*. North America (e).

TABLE V—*continued*

Platyhelminthes

1. MONOGENEA (All ectoparasites)

Gyrodactylus arcuatus Bykhovskii, 1933. Gills and fins. U.S.S.R. (a), U.K. (d).

G. bychowskyi Sproston, 1946. On Gills. U.S.S.R. (a).

G. rarus Wegener, 1909. On fins. U.S.S.R. (a), U.K. (d).

G. elegans Nordmann, 1832. On gills and fins. U.K. (d).

G. pungitii (Malmberg, 1956). U.K. (d).

G. alexanderi Mizelle and Kritsky, 1967. On skin. North America (e).

G. avalonia Hanek and Threlfall, 1969. On fins. North America (b).

G. canadensis Hanek and Threlfall, 1969. On gills. North America (b).

G. lairdi Hanek and Threlfall, 1969. On fins. North America (b).

G. memorialis Hanek and Threlfall, 1969. On fins. North America (b).

G. terranovae Hanek and Threlfall, 1969. On fins. North America (b).

2. DIGENEA

Brachyphallus crenatus (Rudolphi, 1802). Endoparasite in alimentary canal. U.S.S.R. (a), North America (c).

Lecithaster gibbosus (Rudolphi, 1802). Endoparasite in intestine. U.S.S.R. (a), North America (c).

L. salmonis Yamaguti, 1934. Endoparasite in the intestine. North America (e).

Podocotyle atomon (Rudolphi, 1802). Endoparasite in the intestine. Mostly in fish taken from the sea. U.S.S.R. (a).

P. reflexa (Creplin, 1925). Endoparasite in intestine. Mostly in fish taken from the sea. U.S.S.R. (a).

Cotylurus pileatus (Rudolphi, 1802). Endoparasite in wall of swim bladder and other organs. Stickleback is the intermediate host, definitive host is a gull. U.S.S.R. (a).

Diplostomum spathaceum (Rudolphi, 1819). Endoparasite in lens capsule of the eye. Stickleback is intermediate host, definitive host is a bird. U.S.S.R. (a), U.K. (d), North America (e).

D. gasterostei Williams, 1966. Endoparasite in pigmented layer of eye. Stickleback is an intermediate host, definitive host is a bird. U.K. (d).

D. scudderi (Olivier). Endoparasite in the eye between retina and choroid. Stickleback is the intermediate host, definitive host is a bird. North America (e).

Bunodera luciopercae (Müller, 1776). Endoparasite in intestine. U.K. (d).

B. mediovitellata Zimbaluk and Roytman. Endoparasite in the intestine. *North America (e)*.

Crepidostomum farionis (Müller, 1784). Endoparasite in intestine. North America (b).

C. cooperi Hopkins, 1931. North America (b).

Crepidostomum sp. U.K. (d).

Phyllodistomum folium (Olfers, 1816). Endoparasite in the urinary bladder. U.K. (d).

Derogenes viricus (Müller, 1784). Endoparasite in alimentary canal. North America (b).

Nanophyetus salmincola Chapin, 1926. Stickleback is an intermediate host, definitive host is a carnivorous mammal. North America (c).

TABLE V—*continued*

Posthodipolostomum   minimum   (MacCallum,   1926).   Stickleback   is   an intermediate host, definitive host is a bird. North America (c).

P. cuticola Nordmann, 1832. Endoparasite in skin and fins. Stickleback is intermediate host, a heron is the definitive host. U.S.S.R. (a).

Tylodelphys clavata (Nordmann, 1832) (= *Diplostomum clavatum*). Endo-parasite in the humour of the eye. Stickleback is an intermediate host. U.K. (d).

Apatemon gracilis (Rudolphi, 1802). Endoparasite in intestine. Stickleback is an intermediate host, definitive host is a bird. North America (e).

3. CESTODA

Triaenophorus nodulus (Pallas, 1781). Endoparasite, encysted plerocercoids in the liver. Stickleback is an intermediate host, definitive host is a piscivorous fish. U.S.S.R. (a).

Bothriocephalus scorpii (Müller, 1776). Endoparasite. Stickleback is an intermediate host, definitive host is a piscivorous marine fish. U.S.S.R. (a).

B. claviceps (Goeze, 1782). Endoparasite in intestine. U.K. (d), North America (c).

Diphyllobothrium dendriticum (Nitzsch, 1824). Endoparasite in body cavity and viscera as a plerocercoid. Stickleback is an intermediate host, definitive host is a gull or tern. U.S.S.R. (a), U.K. (d).

D. norvegicum Vik, 1957. Endoparasite, encysted plerocercoid in stomach, intestine and liver. Stickleback is an intermediate host which must be eaten by a second intermediate host, a trout or char. Definitive hosts include birds, men and cats. U.S.S.R. (a), U.K. (d).

Schistocephalus solidus (Müller, 1776). Endoparasite, plerocercoids in body cavity. Stickleback is an intermediate host, definitive host is a bird. U.S.S.R. (a), U.K. (d), North America (c).

Proteocephalus cernuae (Gmelin, 1790). Endoparasite in intestine. U.S.S.R. (a), North America (c).

P. filicollis (Rudolphi, 1802). Endoparasite in intestine. U.S.S.R. (a), U.K. (d).

P. pugitensis Hoff and Hoff, 1929. North America (c).

Eubothrium crassum (Bloch, 1779). Endoparasite in intestine U.K. (d).

Cyathocephalus truncatus (Pallas, 1781). Endoparasite in intestine. North America (e).

Aschelminthes

1. NEMATODA

Raphidascaris acus (Bloch, 1779). Endoparasite, encysted in liver, body cavity, intestinal walls and gonads. Stickleback is an intermediate host, definitive host is a piscivorous fish. U.S.S.R. (a), North America (c).

R. cristata (Linstow, 1872). Endoparasite. Stickleback is an intermediate host. U.K. (d).

Cystidicola farionis Fischer, 1798. Endoparasite in swim bladder. U.S.S.R. (a), North America (c).

Camallanus lucustris (Zoega, 1776). Endoparasite in intestine. U.S.S.R. (a).

C. truncatus (Rudolphi, 1814). Endoparasite in intestine. U.S.S.R. (a).

Eustrongylides sp. Endoparasite in musculature or body cavity. Stickleback is an intermediate host, definitive host is a bird. North America (c).

TABLE V—*continued*

2. ACANTHOCEPHALA

Neoechinorhynchus rutili (Müller, 1780). Endoparasite in the intestine. U.S.S.R. (a), U.K. (d), North America (c).
Pseudoechinorhynchus clavula = (?) *Acanthocephalus clavula* = *Echinorhynchus clavula* (Dujardin, 1845). Endoparasite in intestine. U.S.S.R. (a), U.K. (d).
Metechinorhynchus salmonis (Müller, 1780). Endoparasite in the intestine. U.S.S.R. (a).
Acanthocephalus lucii (Müller, 1776). Endoparasite in the intestine. U.S.S.R. (a), North America (c).
Pomphorhynchus laevis (Müller, 1776). Endoparasite in the intestine. U.S.S.R. (a), U.K. (d).
Corynosoma semerme (Forssell, 1904). Endoparasite. Stickleback is an intermediate host, definitive host is a marine mammal or occasionally a piscivorous fish. U.S.S.R. (a).
C. strumosum (Rudolphi, 1802). Endoparasite in coelome, musculature and internal organs. Stickleback is an intermediate host, definitive host is a marine mammal or occasionally a piscivorous fish. U.S.S.R. (a).

Annelida

1. HIRUNDINEA (leeches)
Piscicola geometra (L. 1761). Endoparasite. U.S.S.R. (a).

Arthropoda

1. CRUSTACEA
(i) Copepoda
Ergasilus auritus Markevich, 1940. Ectoparasite on gills and fins. U.S.S.R. (a), North America (c).
E. turgidus Fraser, 1920. Ectoparasite. North America (c).
Thersitina gasterostei (Pagenstechner, 1861). Ectoparasite, on the internal surface of the operculum. U.S.S.R. (a), U.K. (d), North America (c).
Caligus lacustris Steenstrup and Lutken, 1861. U.S.S.R. (a), North America (c).
G. clemensi Parker and Margolis. Ectoparasite on fins. North America (e).
Lernaea esocina Burmeister, 1833. Ectoparasite on skin and gills, U.S.S.R. (a).
L. cyprinacea L. 1758. Ectoparasite on skin. U.K. (d).
Salmincola sp. North America (c).

(ii) Branchiura
Argulus foliaceus (L. 1758). Ectoparasite on skin and gills. U.S.S.R. (a), U.K. (d).
A. canadensis Wilson, 1916. Ectoparasite. North America (b).

Mollusca
Unionidae gen. sp. Ectoparasite of gills, larvae (glochidiae of fresh water mussels). U.S.S.R. (a), U.K. (d), North America (g).

Sources. (a) Bykhovskaya-Pavolovskaya *et al.*, 1964. (b) Hanek and Threlfall, 1969b, c. (c) Hoffman, 1967. (d) Kennedy, 1974. (e) Lester, 1974. (f) Voronin, 1974. (g) Wiles, 1975.

infested by eating ostracods which are infested with the larvae of *N. rutili* (Walkey, 1967). *Schistocephalus solidus* is a cestode that becomes sexually mature in the intestine of birds but which has an immature stage, the plerocercoid, that lives in the body cavity of the stickleback, so an infested stickleback must be eaten by a bird before *S. solidus* can complete its life cycle. The stickleback becomes infested with *S. solidus* by eating copepods such as *Cyclops* which are infested with the procercoid stage of the parasite (Hopkins and Smyth, 1951; Clarke, 1954). Sticklebacks can also become infested with the cestode, *Proteocephalus filicollis*, by eating infested *Cyclops*, but in this case the stickleback is the definitive host and the cestode becomes sexually mature in the stickleback (Hopkins, 1959).

Two measures are frequently used to quantify the degree of parasitism in a population of sticklebacks. The incidence of infestation is the percentage of fish that are carrying the parasite, while the intensity of infestation is the average number of parasites per infested fish. Both the incidence and intensity of infestation can vary seasonally, and with the size or sex of the fish, or the age structure of the fish population.

Sticklebacks living in a pond in Yorkshire were infested by eight species of parasite (Chappell, 1969a, b). A protozoan ectoparasite, the ciliate *Trichodina megamicronucleata* (?), occurred on all the fish. The other ectoparasite was the monogenean (Platyhelminthes), *Gyrodactylus rarus*, which was found on the fins, the skin and occasionally on the gill filaments of infested fish. Two parasitic species live within the eyes of the fish, *Diplostomum gasterostei* and *D. spathaceum*. These are digeneans (Platyhelminthes) for whom the stickleback is an intermediate host and fish-eating birds the definitive host. The metacercariae of *D. gasterostei* were found in the pigmented layers of the retina, whilst those of *D. spathaceum* lived in the outer layers of the lens capsule. Another digenean, *Phyllodistomum folium*, lived in the urinary bladder of the fish, but unlike *Diplostomum*, *P. folium* becomes sexually mature in the stickleback. Two cestodes (Platyhelminthes) parasitised the sticklebacks. Adults and plerocercoids of *Proteocephalus filicollis* lived in the intestine of the fish and plerocercoids of *Schistocephalus solidus* lived in the body cavity. *Neoechinorynchus rutili* (?), an acanthocephalan, lived in the intestine and rectum. In fish that harboured both *P. filicollis* and *N. rutili* (?) in the alimentary canal, the cestode tended to be found in the anterior region of the intestine and the acanthocephalan in the posterior region of the intestine (Chappell, 1969c). *N. rutilus* normally becomes sexually mature in the stickleback, but no sexually mature individuals were found in this population of sticklebacks. Although some fish were infested by all eight species, the average number of parasite species per fish ranged from 5.8 in January to 3.3 in August. Small fish, those less than 30 mm in length, had significantly fewer species parasitic on them than did the larger fish.

TABLE VI

Incidence and intensity of parasitic infestation of *Gasterosteus aculeatus* in a Yorkshire pool (Chappell, 1969a).

Parasite	Sept	Nov	Jan	Mar	May/ June	Aug
(i) Percentage of fish infested (Incidence of infestation)						
Trichodina sp	100	100	100	100	100	100
Gyrodactylus rarus	93	79	99	100	82	0.8
Phyllodistomum folium	34	49	48	48	45	55
Diplostomum gasterostei	97	99	97	88	95	41
D. spathaceum	97	98	97	95	92	98
Proteocephalus filicollis	40	41	35	28	41	12
adults	18	20	16	15	23	5
plerocercoids	26	26	28	22	29	6
Schistocephalus solidus	1	31	15	18	55	16
Neoechinorynchus rutili	7	11	22	13	4	7
Number of fish in sample	100	100	91	99	91	120
(ii) Mean number of worms per infested fish (intensity of infestation)						
Gyrodactylus rarus	6.7	6.1	11.5	23.4	6.2	2.0
Phyllodistomum folium	1.8	1.8	1.9	1.9	2.1	3.1
Diplostomum gasterostei	4.5	4.9	3.8	3.3	4.7	5.6
D. spathaceum	5.9	4.7	4.9	4.5	4.0	12.6
Proteocephalus filicollis	1.5	1.5	2.4	2.4	4.5	1.3
adults	1.4	1.3	1.6	1.8	4.2	1.3
plerocercoids	1.3	1.4	1.8	1.7	3.0	1.1
Schistocephalus solidus	1.0	1.4	1.2	1.1	1.6	1.1
Neoechinorynchus rutili	1.6	1.1	1.4	1.9	1.5	1.0

The frequency distribution of the lengths of the fish indicated that there were two age classes, the 0^+ fish and the 1^+ fish (see Chapter 3), and in August the population was dominated by the 0^+ fish that had been born that summer, and so had been exposed to the possibility of parasitic infestation for a relatively short time. This was reflected in the incidence of some of the parasites (Table VI), most notably the ectoparasite *Gyrodactylus rarus* and *Diplostomum gasterostei*. Throughout most of the year almost all the fish carried these two parasites, but in August the incidence of *G. rarus* fell to one per cent, and the incidence of *D. gasterostei* fell to forty-one per cent. The incidence of *S. solidus* was low in August and September and reached a peak in May and June when fifty-five per cent of the population was infected. *N. rutilis* (?) had a low incidence from May and June through to September but then increased so that in January twenty-two per cent of the population of sticklebacks carried *N. rutilis*.

Neither the incidence nor the intensity of parasitic infestation was significantly different in male and female fish, but the size of the fish was an important factor. The incidence and intensity of the infestation by *G. rarus* increased with the size of the fish except that the largest fish, those over 5 cm long, had a reduced incidence and intensity. A similar effect of size was shown in the infestation by *Proteocephalus filicollis*. The incidence of *Phyllodistomum folium*, *Diplostomum gasterostei* and *S. solidus* all increased with the size of the fish, and the intensity of infestation by *P. folium*, *P. gasterostei* and *D. spathaceum* also increased with the size of the fish. But the intensity of infestation by *S. solidus* and *N. rutili* at first increased with the size of the fish, but then decreased in the larger fish. Overall, the larger fish had more species of parasites and a greater total number of parasites irrespective of species per fish.

Sticklebacks living in Priddy Pool in the Mendip Hills in southwest England carried three endoparasitic species; *S. solidus, D. gasterostei* and the acanthocephalan *Acanthocephalus* (=*Echinorynchus*) *clavula* (Pennycuik, 1971a, b, c).

The incidence of *S. solidus* was very high, for eighty-eight per cent of the fish sampled were harbouring this cestode. Although there was a tendency for the incidence and intensity of the infestation to increase in summer and autumn, this seasonal variation was much less than the variation between successive years. The seasonal variation in the incidence and intensity of the infestation by *D. gasterostei* was more pronounced. There was an increase in summer and autumn and a decrease in early spring. Overall, fifty-six per cent of the fish sampled were infested with *D. gasterostei*, and although the average intensity was 9.4 metacercariae per fish, one fish carried 443. The incidence of *A. clavula*, a parasite of the gut of the fish, was lower, with 31.5 per cent of all fish infected. Unlike *S. solidus* and *D. gasterostei*, this acanthocephalan becomes sexually mature in the stickleback. Both the incidence and the intensity of the infestation tended to increase in the autumn and decrease in the spring.

Male and female sticklebacks in Priddy Pool did not differ in either the incidence or the intensity of their parasitic infestation, although the weights of *S. solidus* in female fish tended to be higher than in male fish. Few fish less than 25 mm in length carried *S. solidus*, but then there was a rapid increase in the incidence of infestation with the length of the fish, so that about ninety per cent of fish that were between 40 and 65 mm in length harboured *S. solidus*. The intensity of the infestation increased more steadily with the length of the fish, but both the incidence and intensity of infection decreased in fish longer than 65 mm. There were few sticklebacks in which the weight of the cestode was greater than the weight of the fish, and few in which the total weight of the fish plus the *S. solidus* it contained exceeded three grams. No fish less than 30 mm in length carried *A. clavula*, but both the incidence and intensity of infestation increased with the length of the fish, reaching a maximum in fish between 60 and 65 mm long, but then decreasing sharply. The incidence and intensity of infestation with *D. gasterostei* increased with the length of the fish reaching a maximum in fish longer than 70 mm.

The factors which cause these variations in the incidence and intensity of a parasitic infestation are complex and not well understood. Part of this complexity arises from the complexity of the life histories of the parasites. Fish become infested with *S. solidus* by eating infested copepods, so the rate of infestation will depend on the degree of infestation in the copepod population and the rate of feeding on the copepods. In turn, the degree of infestation in the copepod population will depend on the abundance of birds that are carrying the sexually mature *S. solidus*, which will depend on the rate at which the birds are feeding on sticklebacks. There is no evidence that the plerocercoids of *S. solidus* die once inside the stickleback so an infestation is accumulative until the stickleback is eaten by a bird, the definitive host of the cestode, or dies from other causes. *Diplostomum* also has fish-eating birds as the definitive host, and again there is no evidence that the metacercariae die while in the stickleback unless their host is inconsiderate enough to die. Sticklebacks become infested with *Diplostomum* by cercariae which penetrate the skin of the fish. The cercariae are released from infested water snails such as *Limnaea pereger*, but such large numbers of cercariae are released by a single snail that only a low incidence in a snail population is probably sufficient to maintain a significant incidence of *Diplostomum* in a stickleback population. A fall in the incidence of infestation by these two parasites must be a result of either the death of infested sticklebacks, or the entry into the fish population of uninfested individuals such as occurs during the breeding season when the young-of-the year are entering the population. In contrast, the cestode *Proteocephalus filicollis*, and the acantho-cephalans *Neoechinorynchus rutili* and *Acanthocephalus clavula*, become sexually mature in the stickleback and can die while in the fish and be passed out. Hopkins (1959) estimated that about one per cent of the population of *P. filicollis* in a population of sticklebacks was lost every day. Although these three species of parasite mature in the stickleback, the fish can only become infested by eating an inter-mediate host. For *P. filicollis* the intermediate host is *Cyclops*, a copepod, for *N. rutili* the intermediate host is probably an ostracod while the intermediate host of *A. clavula* is the isopod crustacean, *Asellus* (Berrie, 1960; Walkey, 1967; Chappell, 1969a, b; Pennycuick, 1971b, c).

The simpler life history shown by the ectoparasite *Gyrodactylus alexanderi*, a monogenean (Platyhelminthes), has allowed a quan-titative analysis of some of the factors that influence the population size of *G. alexanderi* on sticklebacks (Lester and Adams, 1974a, b). The parasite reproduced on the fish, producing two daughters within seven days of attachment to the host. This reproduction tended to increase the number of parasites on the host, but the increase was opposed by the mortality of the parasite on the host and because the stickleback shed a mucoid layer, a "cuticle", and some of the parasites were carried away from the fish on this cuticle (Lester, 1972). Once away from the fish, the parasites died within two days unless they were successful in re-infesting their host or another fish. Some of the shed parasites were eaten by the sticklebacks. Once a fish had recovered from an infection, there was a period of about two weeks when the stickleback was relatively immune from re-infec-tion. The shedding response of the stickleback is probably the main factor that prevents the build-up of a lethal number of *G. alexanderi* on most sticklebacks. If a stickleback dies as a result of a high level of infestation, the parasites lose a host and are themselves much more likely to die, so the shedding response may enable the host and parasite to coexist for a longer period of time than would otherwise be the case. The mechanism did not always operate successfully, for if the population of *G. alexanderi* on a fish increased above 150, the fish usually died within two weeks, by which time the number of parasites had reached 300 to 400.

There are a few observations which indicate that infestations by parasites can sometimes cause severe mortality in stickleback popula-tions. Threlfall (1968) records mass deaths of sticklebacks living in Ocean Pond, Newfoundland. The fish were heavily infested with *S. solidus* and *Argulus canadensis*, a branchiurian ectoparasite commonly called the fish louse. They were also infested with

Crepidostomum farionis, a digenean (Platyhelminthes) found in the gall-bladder and *Thersitina gasterostei*, a copepod found on the gills. Threfall suggested that the deaths were caused by the "stresses" produced by the combination of heavy infestations of *S. solidus* and *A. canadensis*. A population of sticklebacks in a loch in Scotland was severely depleted by an infestation by the ciliate *Ichthyophthirius* (white-spot or "ich"). This infestation almost completely destroyed the yearling age class (0^+), and caused severe mortality amongst older fish (Hopkins, 1959). In Priddy Pool, dead sticklebacks contained heavier *S. solidus* than living fish and were in poorer condition. Some dead fish were found to contain over 100 metacerceriae of *D. gasterostei* (Pennycuick, 1971a).

Even if they do not cause the death of the stickleback, parasites can have severe sub-lethal effects. A comparison of infested and uninfested sticklebacks in Priddy Pool showed that the parasites had an inhibitory effect on the growth of the fish. Of the three endoparasitic species present, *S. solidus* had the most severe effects. Fish infested with the cestode weighed less than uninfested fish of the same length, and grew at a slower rate. Growth in weight was inhibited more than growth in length. Infestation with *D. gasterostei* also adversely affected the growth of the sticklebacks, but *A. clavula* had no deleterious effects that were detected. Since this acanthocephalan becomes sexually mature in the stickleback, it is advantageous for it not to have too severe effects on its host. *S. solidus* and *D. gasterostei* complete their life cycle in a bird so it is to their advantage if they weaken the stickleback sufficiently to make it an easy prey for a fish-eating bird (Pennycuick, 1971a).

A surprisingly high proportion of the stickleback population in Priddy Pool did not breed, probably because heavy infestations with *S. solidus* either delayed or completely prevented sexual maturation in the females and perhaps in the males too (Pennycuick, 1971a). Arme and Owen (1967) obtained histological evidence that heavy infestations of *S. solidus* interfered with the breeding of female sticklebacks. The eggs of infested females showed delayed formation of the yolk (delayed vitellogenesis), and after the breeding season the ovaries of the infested females contained many pre-ovulatory *corpora atretica* which indicated that the females had failed to spawn (see Chapter 9). During a breeding season the ovaries of females infested with *S. solidus* were significantly smaller than those of uninfested fish, indeed the ovaries of the infested females were smaller than would be expected in females that were soon to spawn. After the breeding season, the ovaries of the infested females were larger than those of uninfested fish, more evidence that spawning had been inhibited (Meakins, 1974). The pituitary glands of infested females did not differ histologically from those of uninfested fish, an observation which has been interpreted as evidence that the inhibition of egg maturation in the presence of S. solidus is not a result of interference with the hormonal control of oogenesis. This interpretation is strengthened by the observation that spermatogenesis in infested males was normal (Arme and Owen, 1967), though neither of these observations eliminates the possibility that the presence of S. solidus interferes with the production of gonadal hormones directly rather than interfering with the production of gonadotropic hormones by the pituitary (Chapter 9). But it is more likely that the effect of S. solidus is a consequence of the nutritional demands that this parasite makes on its host. Infested females cannot consume sufficient food to support the parasitic burden and at the same time meet the costs of egg production (Meakins, 1974). The inverse relationship between the relative weight of the liver of the fish and the intensity of the infestation provided further evidence that the presence of S. solidus can impose considerable nutritional demands on the stickleback (Arme and Owen, 1967).

A large plerecercoid of S. solidus can weigh over 0.6 g, and as many as 106 small plerocercoids have been taken from one fish. Since few sticklebacks reach a weight of more than three grams, the presence of plerocercoids in the body cavity often causes severe deformities. Heavily infested fish have grossly distended bodies, and the heart and liver may be displaced anteriorly (Fig. 25) (Arme and Owen, 1967).

The presence of S. solidus also has significant metabolic consequences. Two studies showed that infested fish had significantly higher oxygen consumption than uninfested fish, a difference that was accentuated when the fish were forced to swim at increasing speeds (Lester, 1971; Walkey and Meakins, 1970). Parasitised sticklebacks were more efficient at converting the food they consumed into an increase in weight than uninfested fish, but were less efficient at converting the food into stickleback flesh. The improvement in overall growth efficiency was attributed to the greater efficiency of the parasite in its energy transformations when compared with the fish. The decreased efficiency in synthesising stickleback flesh provides an explanation for the effect of S. solidus infestations on the growth of sticklebacks. When groups of twelve infested and twelve uninfested fish were left for thirty days without food, none of the parasitised fish survived for more than the thirty days, but seven out of the twelve uninfested fish were still alive (Walkey and Meakins, 1970). These results provide further evidence that infestation by S.

solidus imposes a considerable strain on a stickleback and makes it
less likely that the fish could survive periods when food was in short
supply. A heavy infestation coupled with a shortage of food might
well cause considerable mortality in a population of sticklebacks.

Infestations of parasites may also have deleterious effects on the
behaviour of the fish. The distortion of body shape caused by *S.
solidus* infestation affects the swimming ability of the fish. Swimming is restricted to that produced by the pectoral fins or the short

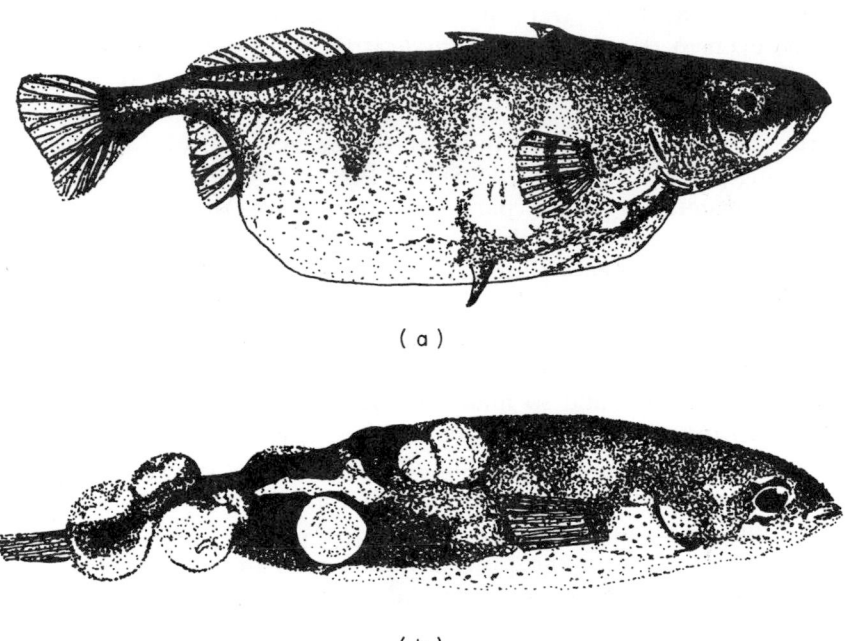

(a)

(b)

Fig. 25. Distortion of body shape of *Gasterosteus aculeatus* by (a) *Schistocephalus solidus*
plerocercoids and (b) *Glugea anomala* cysts (after Arme and Owen, 1967).

post-anal region of the body, the fish swims slowly occasionally
sinking to the bottom, although if scared it is capable of rapid
swimming over short distances (Arme and Owen, 1967). In hot
weather, infested fish were seen swimming slowly near the surface of
the water whereas the uninfested fish were in deeper water (Lester,
1971). The effect of *S. solidus* on the swimming behaviour of the
stickleback makes the fish more vulnerable to capture by a piscivorous bird, which is the definitive host of the cestode.

Males heavily infested with *S. solidus* attempted to build nests
during the breeding season but failed to complete them. It is not

clear whether this was because the males could not produce the glue from the kidneys which binds the nest together (Chapter 10) or whether the distorted shape of the fish made it mechanically impossible for them to complete the nests (Arme and Owen, 1967). Heavily infested females were usually unresponsive to the male's courtship, but even when they did respond the distension of the body make it impossible for a female to enter a nest without destroying it. The numerous pre-ovulatory *corpora atretica* in the ovaries of infested females at the end of the breeding season suggested that they were unable to spawn. Normal females will spawn even in the absence of a male if they are very ripe, so that the failure of infested females to spawn is abnormal. It is not clear whether the inhibition of spawning is because of a physiological disturbance or because the bulk of the parasites physically prevents spawning (Arme and Owen, 1967).

The effects of other parasitic species on the metabolism or behaviour of the stickleback has not received much attention, perhaps because their visible effects are less obvious than those of *S. solidus*. Possibly the cysts of *Glugea anomala* impede normal swimming and respiratory movements (Fig. 25). The presence of the metacerceriae of *Diplostomum* sp. in the eye may interfere with the vision of the fish, and so make the stickleback more susceptible to predation by the birds which are the definitive hosts of the digenean.

Nevertheless, although sticklebacks may be severely affected by parasites, many can carry a burden of parasites and still survive, grow and reproduce, but a stickleback that is eaten by a predator is irreversibly lost from the population. The main predators of adult sticklebacks are fish-eating birds and mammals and large carnivorous fish. Eggs and larvae have a wider range of potential predators because of their relatively small size. Predation, especially that by other species of fish, has probably been one of the most important selective forces shaping the evolution of the three-spined stickleback (Chapter 14).

That predation by fish-eating birds can be important can be gauged from the life histories of parasites such as *S. solidus* and *Diplostomum* spp. which only become sexually mature in the alimentary canal of birds. The eggs of the parasites pass out with the faeces of the bird, and in the case of *S. solidus* the first intermediate host is a copepod while for *Diplostomum* sp. the first intermediate host is a water snail. For these complex life cycles to be completed, and for these parasites to be as widely distributed and abundant as they are, birds must frequently be eating infected sticklebacks.

There is behavioural evidence that birds are significant predators on sticklebacks, for sticklebacks show a marked fright response to a dark object about the size of a bird moving above them (Phillips, 1962; Huntingford, 1974).

Amongst the bird species that are known to include sticklebacks in their diet are the heron (*Ardea cinerea*), the black-headed gull (*Larus ridibundus*) and terns (*Sterna paradisea* and *S. hirundo*) (Owen, 1960, Creutz, 1963; Lemmetyinen, 1973). Five out of six species of diving duck living on Lake Myvatn in Iceland included sticklebacks in their diet, and the merganser (*Mergus serrator*) was feeding almost exclusively on sticklebacks (Bengston, 1971). Penczak (1968) has also shown that mergansers feed on sticklebacks. The quantitative effects of this bird predation on stickleback populations are not known, but in a situation such as Lake Myvatn are likely to be considerable.

Fish-eating mammals also take sticklebacks. Mink (*Mustela vison*) occasionally have sticklebacks in their stomachs, but never as a major part of their diet (Gerell, 1968). The European otter (*Lutra lutra*) also takes sticklebacks, but they form only a relatively small portion of its diet (Harris, 1968).

Probably the most important predators on sticklebacks are piscivorous fish, and sticklebacks themselves are significant predators of their own eggs and larvae. During the breeding season, the stomachs of adult males and females frequently contain stickleback eggs (Hynes, 1950). The phenomena of nest raiding by territorial males on the nests of neighbouring males is considered in Chapter 13, but in some cases the activity of these raiding males attracts groups of other non-territorial fish to the scene and any eggs in the nest are quickly eaten (Black and Wootton, 1970). When a female spawns her eggs away from the nest of a male, they are rapidly eaten, either by the female or by other sticklebacks. In Lake Wapato in Washington State, fifty-two per cent of the sticklebacks examined had stickleback eggs in their stomachs. The majority of the eggs were uneyed which indicates that either they were unfertilised eggs or they had been eaten only a short time after fertilisation. Males over 41 mm in length were the heaviest predators on the eggs (Semler, 1971).

Other species of fish also eat the eggs and larvae of sticklebacks. An interesting and evolutionary significant example of such predation was analysed by McPhail (1969). In the Chehalis River system in Washington State, a fish endemic to the system, the western mudminnow (*Novumbra hubbsi*), feeds on the eggs and particularly the larvae of the stickleback. This predation seems to have been the main selective pressure that has led to the evolution of an unusual three-spined stickleback. This stickleback is unusual because the male does not develop the red throat and blue eyes characteristic of the typical breeding male, instead in the breeding season the male becomes black. The larvae of this "black" stickle-back behaved differently from the larvae of the normal stickleback when attacked by *N. hubbsi*. "Black" larvae started to take evasive action before the *N. hubbsi* got close enough to strike. This evasive action consisted of a series of rapid darts which usually took the larvae to the surface where they remained motionless. Larvae of normal sticklebacks usually took evasive action only after the *N. hubbsi* had started to strike and, if they evaded this initial strike, they stayed motionless for only a short period and then swam slowly away. The predator struck again as the larvae swam away. These behavioural differences between the larvae meant that *N. hubbsi* was more successful at taking the larvae of normal sticklebacks than those of "black" sticklebacks. The evolutionary implications of this situation in the Chehalis River are considered in more detail in Chapter 14.

Some large invertebrates also prey upon the eggs and larvae. In a lake on the Queen Charlotte Islands off the Pacific coast of Canada, a leech (*Haemopis marmorata*) was a predator of the eggs of stickle-backs. An experiment showed that 94 eggs was the average intake by a leech at one feeding (Moodie, 1972a). Large predatory aquatic insects such as *Dytiscus* and dragonfly nymphs are also likely to take the larvae, but the importance of these as predators is unknown (Benzie, 1965).

Adult sticklebacks are eaten by large predatory fish. In Europe, the pike (*Esox lucius*), the trout (*Salmo trutta*) and the perch (*Perca fluviatilis*) are typical of such predators, while in North America the pike, the squawfish (*Ptychocheilus oregonensis*), the cutthroat trout (*Salmo clarki*), the rainbow trout (*Salmo gairdneri*) and chars (*Salvelinus malma* and *S. alpinus*) are known to include sticklebacks in their diet (Hagen and Gilbertson, 1972). Several physical characteristics of the stickleback seem to be involved in restricting the effectiveness of these predatory fish. Such features include the length and stoutness of the dorsal and ventral spines, the number of lateral plates, the size of the fish and the intensity of the breeding colours.

An important property of the spines of the stickleback is that they can be locked in the erect position, not simply held erect by muscular contraction, so fatigue or even the death of the fish does not lead to the depression of the spines. A feature of the locking mechanism is that the spines cannot be pushed down, so that pressure exerted on the spines, for example by the jaws of a predator, does not cause the spines to collapse. The locking mechanism depends on the structure of the bony basal plate and the base of the spine which articulates with the basal plate, and also on the position of the ligaments that bind the spine to the plate. The spines have both an erector and depressor muscle, but to lower the spines both the depressor and erector muscles are required. In the dorsal spines, the ligaments hold the erect spine in such a position that the spine is held by three points of contact with the basal plate. A contraction of the depressor muscle alone merely increases the contact between the spine and the plate, but a coordinated contraction of both the depressor and erector muscles guides the spine clear of the points of contact with the plate. The locking mechanism of the ventral spines is similar although some of the structural details differ (Hoogland, 1951).

There is both experimental evidence and evidence from natural populations that shows the importance of the spines as a defence against predation.

The experimental evidence comes from studies in which pike and perch were used as predators and the prey fish were three-spined sticklebacks, nine-spined sticklebacks (*Pungitius pungitius*) whose spines are shorter than those of the three-spined stickleback, and species which lack any spines, the minnow (*Phoxinus phoxinus*), the roach (*Rutilus rutilus*), the rudd (*Scardinius erythrophthalmus*) and the Crucian carp (*Carassius carassius*) (Hoogland *et al.*, 1957).

When three-spined and nine-spined sticklebacks and minnows were present together, a perch preferred to take the minnows first, then the nine-spined sticklebacks and to avoid the three-spined sticklebacks until most of the other prey fish had been taken. If the prey were given one at a time, the perch still preferred minnows and rejected or avoided the three-spined sticklebacks. The results for the pike were similar although its method of hunting the prey was different from that of the perch. When all three prey species were together, then the pike took the minnows before the sticklebacks, and of the two species of stickleback it was the three-spined stickleback that the pike avoided most. If the sticklebacks had their spines cut off, the despined sticklebacks were taken at about the same rate as the species which naturally lacked spines. This result provides direct evidence of the importance of the spines as a defence against predators. Although the short spines of the nine-spined stickleback provided some protection relative to fish species that lacked spines, the long, stout spines of the three-spined stickleback were even more effective. This difference between the two species of stickleback seems to have important implications, for a number of the behavioural and ecological differences between the two can be related to the differences in the protection provided by their spines (see also Chapter 16).

A BBC film, "The Making of a Natural History Film", showed vividly the difficulty that a pike had when trying to swallow a three-spined stickleback with erect spines. The pike repeatedly grasped the stickleback but then spat it out again. Even after the stickleback had been grasped it could be seen lying in the gape of pike, while the pike tried to manoeuvre it into a position from which it could be swallowed (Fig. 26). The experiments described above provided evidence that once either a pike or a perch had tried to seize a three-spined stickleback then the predator tended to avoid sticklebacks, presumably because of the negative conditioning induced by the first encounter. There is an interesting parallel between the spines of the stickleback and the spines of an ectoparasite of the stickleback, *Argulus*. The spines on *Argulus* seem to make it difficult for the stickleback to swallow this parasite, just as the spines on the stickleback make *it* difficult for a predatory fish to swallow. This common solution to the biological problem of how to reduce the chances of being eaten conjures up a Breughelian picture of a stickleback spitting out an *Argulus* while being spat out of a pike.

A study of natural populations of the three-spined stickleback along the west coast of North America showed that there was a positive correlation between the length of the dorsal and pelvic spines and the commonness of predatory species, spines were longer in populations that coexisted with large populations of predatory fish (Hagen and Gilbertson, 1972). At the other extreme, a few populations are known in which the ventral spines and the associated pelvic skeleton is missing in a high proportion of individuals in the population. Such populations tend to occur where predators are scarce or absent (Hagen and McPhail, 1970).

Spines provide only a relative and not an absolute defence against predators. Pike living in Lake Windermere included sticklebacks in their diet (Frost, 1954). In pike less than 400 mm in length, minnows formed a larger proportion of the diet than did sticklebacks, but in larger pike the proportion of sticklebacks eaten exceeded the proportion of minnows although the latter were more abundant in the lake. In contrast to this, pike living in lakes in Ireland studied by Healy (1956) also included sticklebacks in their diet, but in this case it was the smaller pike, those between 200 and 450 mm, that were feeding most heavily on sticklebacks. In these lakes there were no minnows. Brown trout (*Salmo trutta*) living in

Llyn Alaw, Anglesey (North Wales), also included sticklebacks in their diet, but only trout above 300 mm in length were eating sticklebacks, and they formed the most important component of the diet only for trout longer than 430 mm (Hunt and Jones, 1972). The experimental evidence for the importance of spines as a defence

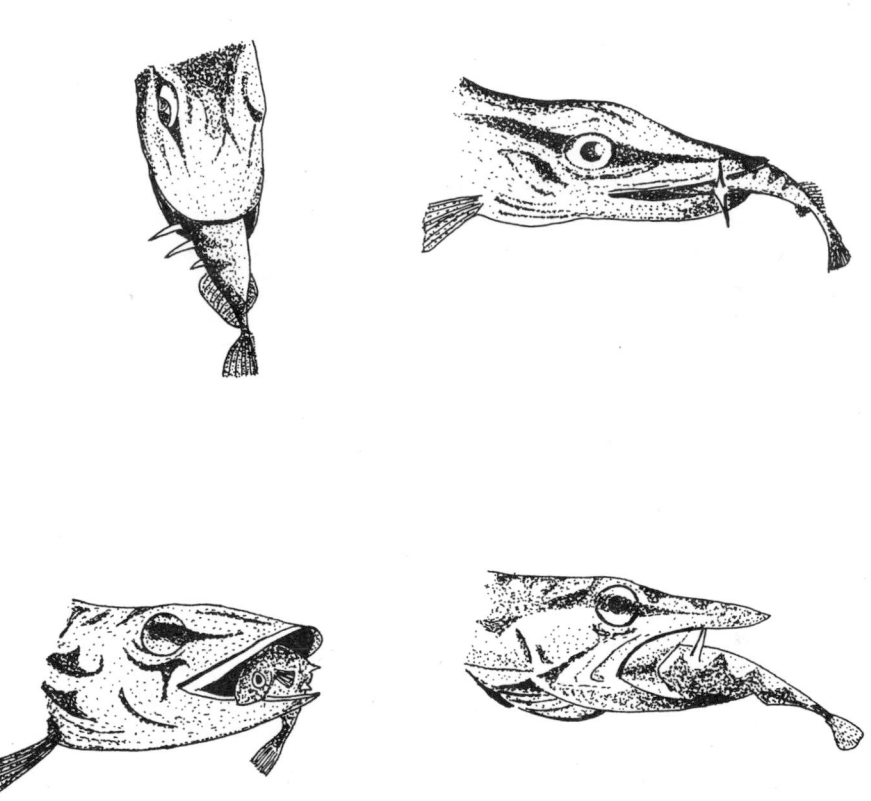

Fig. 26. Pike (*Esox lucius*) attempting to swallow a three-spined stickleback (*Gasterosteus aculeatus*) (after Hoogland *et al.*, 1957).

against predation was obtained using predators that were between 150 and 250 mm long, and it seems likely that predators larger than this are much less inconvenienced by the spines, presumably because larger fish have a larger gape.

The lateral plates of the stickleback may act as armour protecting the flanks of the body. If this is so, the trachurus and semiarmatus forms would seem to be better protected from damage by predators than the leiurus form. Lea (1968) obtained some evidence that trachurus fish suffered less damage after being seized by a predator than did leiurus fish, but there is relatively little experimental evidence on the protective function of the plates. Landlocked populations of the trachurus form in the Pacific northwest often coexist with predators such as cutthroat trout and squawfish, but so do populations of leiurus and semiarmatus fish. The one relationship between plate number and predation that has been documented is unexpected. Those populations of leiurus fish that coexist with predators tend to have a modal frequency of seven lateral plates, whereas in populations not associated with predatory fish, the proportion of sticklebacks with seven plates is usually very low or zero (see Fig. 55, Chap. 14). This correlation between plate number and predation may not be related to the degree of protection given by the plates but to some behavioural trait of fish with seven plates that makes them less susceptible to predation (Hagen and Gilbertson, 1973a). Indeed this behavioural trait may be exhibited even before the lateral plates have developed (Moodie, 1972a, b). Although an experimental analysis has demonstrated that differential predation on fish such that those with seven plates was taken by the predator at a lower frequency than expected on the basis of their abundance, the experiments were not always consistent nor did they clarify what property of the seven-plated fish it was that enabled them to escape predation (Moodie *et al.*, 1973).

Large fish are likely to be at less risk from predators than smaller fish, for there will be a more restricted number of predators of a sufficient size to take the larger fish. In Mayer Lake on the Queen Charlotte Islands in British Columbia, an unusually large race of sticklebacks occurs (Moodie, 1972a, b). The streams that feed the lake are free of predatory fish and these streams contain leiurus fish of the normal size, but the lake contains two species of piscivorous fish, the cutthroat trout and the prickly sculpin (*Cottus asper*). These fish feed extensively on the stickleback, and it is probable that this predation has been the main selection pressure in the evolution of this unusual population of sticklebacks.

The breeding colours of the male stickleback seem to have two functions, to attract females and to intimidate rival males. But colours which make the male conspicuous to other sticklebacks are also going to make him conspicuous to predators. If the main form of predation on the stickleback population is the eating of eggs by other sticklebacks, then there is no conflict for a fully developed breeding coloration will serve to attract mates and to intimidate predators. But if the main predator is not a conspecific, then fish which develop the full male breeding colours may gain an advantage in attracting females but at the expense of becoming more conspicuous to predators.

In the Chehalis River system the eggs and young of the stickleback are eaten by the western mudminnow (*Novumbra hubbsi*), and associated with the presence of this predator is a population of sticklebacks in which the breeding colours of the male are black not the usual red throat and blue eyes. When one of these "black" sticklebacks is disturbed, the black breeding colours fade to an even more drab colour. Experiments showed that the mudminnow was preferentially attracted to the normal male stickleback compared with the male "black" stickleback, so the mudminnow is more likely to find the nest of a normal stickleback than the nest of a "black" stickleback. This unusual breeding coloration seems to have evolved to make the breeding male less conspicuous to the predator (McPhail, 1969).

The large sticklebacks of Mayer Lake also tend to be dark coloured and the typical red coloration of the breeding male is often absent. Fish that did have red throats were more likely to be eaten by trout than the drab males (Moodie, 1972a, b).

In Lake Wapato, the males are polymorphic for breeding colours. About fourteen per cent of breeding males show the full red coloration, but others occur with a silver throat and belly or drab ventral coloration, or a completely black ventral surface. Females tended to prefer to spawn in the nests of normal red males, and it is probable that the red males were more successful at guarding their nests from the raids of other males. But these red males would also be more conspicuous to the rainbow trout which feed heavily on the stickleback in Lake Wapato (Semler, 1971).

The evolutionary consequences of predation on stickleback populations are considered in more detail in Chapter 14, but the evidence suggests that predation by fish has been a most important selective force.

Allied to the morphological adaptations that serve to reduce predation by piscivorous fishes, the stickleback also shows behavioural adaptations that serve the same function.

On detecting a predatory fish such as a pike, a stickleback stops its normal activity, sinks a little in the water and fixes the predator with its eyes. At this point, the stickleback may approach towards the predator for a short distance before backing away. This investigatory phase may lead to the stickleback keeping its distance from the predator or taking cover in weed. But if the predator is relatively close the stickleback attempts to escape. The type of escape behaviour shown depends on distance of the stickleback from the predator. If the predator is relatively distant, the stickleback backs away, while still visually fixating the predator, but if the predator, is not so distant, the stickleback swims away smoothly using its body muscles rather than relying on the sculling with the pectoral fins that is so characteristic of an undisturbed stickleback. With the predator even closer, the stickleback escapes with a slow jerky swimming, and if the predator approaches yet closer the stickleback jumps away and then swims off rapidly. Up to a point, the closer the stickleback is to a predator the faster is its pectoral fin and opercular beat, but if the predator is very close, the stickleback freezes rather than attempting to jump away, its pectoral fins stop beating while the opercular beat slows up. The closer the stickleback is to a predator the more likely it is that the spines will be raised, and if the stickleback is seized, the spines are locked in the erect position and the stickleback remains motionless in the predator's jaws (Hoogland, *et al.*, 1957; Benzie, 1965). A recent analysis of the behaviour of sticklebacks in the presence of a pike has suggested that the behaviour can partly be interpreted in terms of a "precaution–investigation" factor and a "boldness–timidity" factor (Huntingford, 1974).

Previous experience with a predator modifies the behaviour of a stickleback on subsequent exposures to that predator. Experienced fish responded to the presence of a predator at a greater distance than naive sticklebacks, the reaction distance increased from about 19 cm to 39 cm. The experienced sticklebacks were more likely to retreat into weed, and less likely to approach the predator before taking fright than naive fish. Another factor that influenced the behaviour of the stickleback to a predator was the length of time that the stickleback had been in the presence of its father after hatching. Sticklebacks whose father was removed when the eggs hatched, so-called "orphan" fish, were more easily frightened in their first encounter with a predator than normal fish. In contrast, sticklebacks that had been in the presence of their father for an unusually long period after hatching, "over-fathered" fish, were less responsive to predators than normal fish. These differences tended to disappear once the sticklebacks had had experience with a predator (Benzie, 1965).

A comparison of the three-spined and nine-spined stickleback indicated that in the presence of a predator or in an unfamiliar environment, the three-spined stickleback was bolder, less likely to hide in weed and less likely to show precautionary behaviour. So, although the three-spined stickleback's spines are more effective as an anti-predator device than those of the nine-spined stickleback, the former's behaviour probably puts it more at risk (see also Chapter 16) (Benzie, 1965).

Huntingford (1974) found that sticklebacks that were relatively bold in the presence of a pike or in an unfamiliar environment also tended to be more aggressive towards conspecifics during the breeding season. The more aggressive males in the breeding season tend to be more successful in courting females and in guarding their nests from raiding males (van den Assem, 1967 described in Chapter 13), so boldness is not so biologically inappropriate as it might seem at first sight.

There is one report which indicates that the boldness of three-spined sticklebacks in the presence of a predator can reach almost suicidal proportions. Bartmann (1973) has recorded a cleaning symbiosis between sticklebacks and pike in a large aquarium. Sticklebacks were seen taking what were presumably ectoparasites from the skin of the pike, not only from the flanks of the pike but from around its mouth. The pike were well fed, and satiated pike will not snap at sticklebacks, so perhaps the sticklebacks had not experienced the pike as a predator, but merely as a surface from which food could be obtained. In view of the high frequency with which sticklebacks appear in the diet of pike in natural populations, it would seem unlikely that this cleaning symbiosis is more than an artefact of the aquarium. A much more plausible cleaning symbiosis involving the four-spined stickleback, *Apeltes quadracus*, is described in Chapter 18.

So far, the behaviour of individual sticklebacks to the presence of a predator has been considered, but outside of the breeding season sticklebacks tend to live in schools. When alarmed or disturbed the sticklebacks in a school tend to pack closer together, whereas when they are undisturbed or searching for food the school becomes less cohesive (Keenlyside, 1955; Symons, 1971). Although conclusive evidence is lacking, many authors have suggested that schooling behaviour of this type tends to reduce the intensity of predation on the schooling fish and experimental evidence in favour of this hypothesis is slowly gathering (Brock and Riffenburgh, 1960; St. Neill and Cullen, 1974).

During the breeding season, the aggressive defence of their nests by the males reduces the incidence of cannibalism by other sticklebacks on the eggs and larval fish (van den Assem, 1967; Semler, 1971).

Of the three major groups of predators on the three-spined stickleback, fish, birds and mammals, fish have probably been the most important, in the sense that predation by fish has significantly influenced the evolution of the stickleback, a topic that will be taken up again in Chapter 14. As yet, there are no quantitative data on the rate of mortality caused by predation, or on the relative importance of piscivorous fish, birds and mammals as mortality factors in stickleback populations.

6. Economic and Applied Biology

Although its biology has received considerable attention, in economic terms the stickleback is of slight importance for it supports neither a significant commercial fishery nor a sport fishery except that pursued by small boys with jam jars and dip nets. In some aspects of its biology, the stickleback may be directly harmful to economic interests, but the evidence suggests that on balance the stickleback's contribution has been more beneficial than harmful.

The harmful effects of the presence of the stickleback, if they exist, stem from its voraciousness and pugnacity. It has been claimed that the stickleback is an important predator of the eggs and larvae of fish that are either commercially or recreationally important. A stickleback was observed to eat 74 dace (*Leuciscus leuciscus*) larvae in a single day (Regan, 1911), and Laurent (1972) has claimed that stickleback predation on the eggs of coregonid fishes was a contributory factor in the decline of the latter in Lac Leman. But detailed analyses of the food of the stickleback indicate that while it is a significant predator on its own eggs, it is probably not an important predator of the eggs or young of fish such as salmon and trout (see Chapter 4). Such detailed analyses did indicate that it might be a significant competitor for food with the young stages of salmonid fishes (Maitland, 1965; Rogers, 1968), although studies by Rogers (1973) and Krogius (1973) have suggested that when food is short it is the stickleback rather than the salmonid that suffers from the consequent competition.

In Lake Aleknagik of the Wood River system, Alaska, juvenile sockeye salmon (*Oncorhynchus nerka*) and the three-spined stickleback are the most abundant fish in the littoral region of the lake. Rogers (1973) found that there was no significant correlation between the catches of sockeye fry in one year and the catch of three-spined sticklebacks (or any other species of fish present) in that or the following year. This indicates that the numerical abundance of the sockeye juveniles was not related to the abundance of stickle-backs. The mean length of sticklebacks in the second year of their life was, at the start of the summer, negatively correlated with abundance of sockeye fry in the previous year. Apparently, the growth rate of sticklebacks in their first year was adversely affected when sockeye fry were particularly abundant. This inhibitory influence of the sockeye fry on the sticklebacks may have been mediated by competition for food, although there is no direct evidence that this was so. The growth of the sockeye fry was primarily determined by climatic factors, particularly those that affected the date on which the ice cover on the lake broke up.

Lake Dal'neye in the U.S.S.R. also contains sticklebacks and sockeye salmon. A decline in the abundance of sockeye salmon in the lake was followed by an increase in the abundance of stickle-backs, but subsequently the abundance of both the salmon and the stickleback has declined. During this decline the lake became less fertile because the fall in the numbers of sockeye salmon meant that the lake received a smaller injection of nutrients such as phosphate from the decomposing bodies of the adult sockeye that die after spawning (Krogius, 1973).

A beneficial effect of the presence of a population of sticklebacks together with a population of game fish such as salmon or trout is that if the game fish grow large enough to become piscivorous, then they exploit the stickleback population for food. Sticklebacks frequently form an important part of the diet of such predators (see Chapter 5).

Man has also exploited sticklebacks to a minor extent. Regan (1911) has described how sticklebacks were fished during the autumn in the Baltic. They were caught either with seine nets, or they were attracted with torchlight at night and scooped up with hand nets. The sticklebacks were boiled down for the oil and the residue used for manure. They have also been used as food for animals such as ducks and, in the arctic, fed to sledge dogs.

Because it is a hardy fish, easy to keep in the laboratory in large numbers, the stickleback has often been used as an experimental animal for studies on the effect of water pollution on fish life (Jones, 1964).

In west Wales, the hills are scarred with the spoil heaps of old mines that were worked for silver, zinc, lead and copper, while rivers such as the Rheidol and Ystwyth were polluted by the salts of these heavy metals. In a series of experiments Jones (1935, 1938, 1939) investigated the toxicity of salts of lead, zinc and copper to the three-spined stickleback. All three metals were highly toxic, with copper the most poisonous. Sticklebacks could survive for only 192 hours in a 0.02 p.p.m. concentration of copper as the nitrate salt, and for 160 hours in a 0.03 p.p.m. concentration as the sulphate salt. In lead as the nitrate salt at a concentration of 0.1 p.p.m. Pb, they survived for 336 hours, while in zinc sulphate at a concentration of 0.03 p.p.m. Zn they survived for 204 hours. The toxicity of these heavy metals was less when calcium salts were added to the water which suggests that in areas with hard water, pollution by heavy metals is likely to be less severe than in soft water regions such as west Wales.

When the toxicity of a series of metals was tested, again using the three-spined stickleback as the test fish, the ascending order of toxicity was given by:

Sr Ca Na Ba Mg K Mn Co Cr Ni Au Zn Cd Pb Al Cu Hg Ag

when concentrations were expressed as mg of metal per litre, and by:

Na Ca Sr Mg Ba K Mn Co Cr Ni Zn Al Au Cd Pb Cu Hg Ag

when expressed as molar concentration (Jones, 1939). Thus, lead, copper, mercury and silver were the most toxic heavy metals to the stickleback and all four metals are likely to be significant pollutants of water in industrial areas.

When a stickleback was placed in water containing a toxic heavy metal such as zinc or copper, the fish showed an increase in the rate of opercular movement, indicating an increase in the rate of gill ventilation. This higher rate of ventilation persisted for some time before the rate declined abruptly and ventilation ceased altogether. The fish's rate of oxygen consumption also initially increased, but then it declined steadily, this decline starting long before any decline in ventilation rate. *Post-mortem* analysis revealed that the gills were covered with a layer of coagulated mucus which may have prevented oxygen diffusion from the water into the fish's blood so that it died from asphyxiation (Jones, 1947a). Heavy metals also cause structural changes to the gills which may be another factor causing the death of the stickleback. In toxic solutions of zinc in soft water, the epithelial cells of the gill filaments (cf. Fig. 5) tended to detach from the basement membrane and slough off. If the stickleback was removed from the solution and survived, the gill filaments recovered their normal appearance after about nine days. Even in solutions of zinc in hard water that were not toxic, there were significant changes in the ultrastructure of the gills, and chloride cells appeared on the secondary lamellae where they are normally absent (Matthiessen and Brafield, 1973).

Given that solutions of heavy metals are highly toxic to the stickleback, can the fish detect when it has moved into water containing heavy metals? Three-spined sticklebacks were found to detect water containing lead nitrate. Curiously, the sticklebacks tended to move into a lead nitrate solution of 0.04N although this was toxic, but toxic solutions, ranging in concentration from 0.004N to 0.00002N, were avoided (0.00002N is approximately 2 mg Pb/l). Nine-spined sticklebacks avoided water containing zinc sulphate at concentrations as low as 0.0003N, but copper salts were detected only at high concentration (0.1N) and they seemed to interfere with the stickleback's ability to detect the presence of other toxic substances subsequently. So, although the ascending order of toxicity of heavy metals is:

Zn Pb Cu Hg

the ability of the stickleback to detect the heavy metals is ordered:

Cu Zn Hg Pb

(Jones, 1947b, 1948).

The three-spined stickleback has also been used to study the effects of other pollutants such as cyanides, sulphides and chloroform which are respiratory depressants (Jones, 1947a, b, 1948). These substances were toxic, causing a decline in the rate of oxygen consumption; but the rate of opercular movement declined in parallel to the rate of oxygen consumption and the gills retained a healthy appearance not becoming clogged with mucus.

Ammonia is another important pollutant of water, and this is also toxic to sticklebacks. For sticklebacks in fresh water at 15°C, the 96 hour median tolerance limit was 2.1 mg NH_4OH/l. The toxicity of the ammonia depended on the salinity and temperature of the water, the fish were more resistant to ammonia poisoning at higher salinities and at lower temperatures (Hazel et al., 1971). Sticklebacks avoided ammonia solutions more concentrated than 0.01N (350 mg NH_4OH/l), but moved into solutions of 0.001N and 0.0001N, though these were toxic (Jones, 1948).

The effect of the pH of water on fish is another aspect of water quality that has been investigated using sticklebacks as test animals. Water whose pH had been lowered to below 5.0 by the addition of hydrochloric acid was toxic to the fish, an observation which may account for the toxicity of some iron salts such as ferric chloride which hydrolyse yielding acidic solutions (Jones, 1939). Sticklebacks avoided water that had a pH of less than 5.6 or greater than 11.4, but since the pH scale is logarithmic, it is clear that the stickleback tolerates water with a wide range of hydrogen ion concentrations (Jones, 1948).

A frequent property of water of poor quality is a low oxygen content, a consequence of pollution by organic materials such as raw sewage. The minimum oxygen concentration at which sticklebacks can exist is about 0.25 to 0.50 p.p.m. (Jones, 1964), but Lewis *et al.* (1972) have presented some evidence to suggest that the nine-spined stickleback is better able to tolerate water that has a low oxygen content than the three-spined stickleback. The former is more likely to be found in stagnant, densely weeded streams than the latter species. When exposed to de-oxygenated water, three-spined sticklebacks showed a rapid increase in the rate of opercular movement from the normal rate of about 120 movements per min. up to about 240 per min., but then the rate declined to very low levels as the fish asphyxiated (Jones, 1947a). If a three-spined stickleback swam into a region of low oxygen content, it did not appear to detect the abnormality until respiratory distress developed. Then the fish's agitated movements sometimes took it out of the region of low oxygen concentration. At low temperatures the respiratory distress developed slowly, even at oxygen concentrations as low as 0.3 mg/l of oxygen, but at 20°C the response was rapid at oxygen concentrations below 2 mg/l (Jones, 1952). In this context it is interesting to note that when the male stickleback is fanning his nest containing eggs during the parental phase of his reproductive cycle, he responds to changes in the quality of the water in the nest by changes in the amount of fanning he performs. The changes in quality probably involve changes in the oxygen and carbon dioxide content of the water (see Chapter 13).

One of the advantages of using the three-spined stickleback as a test animal in investigations on water quality is that much is known about the biology of the species so that the results of an investigation can be evaluated in the light of this information. A disadvantage is that the family Gasterosteidae is not closely related to teleost families that include economically important species, so that results obtained using the stickleback will have to be interpreted with care before they can be applied in the context of the economically significant species.

7. The Reproductive Cycle: An Introduction

Of all aspects of the biology of the three-spined stickleback, it is the reproductive behaviour that has received most attention. Observations on the breeding behaviour of sticklebacks formed one of the cornerstones in the development of ethological theory, a development that revolutionised the study of animal behaviour (Tinbergen, 1951), while important modifications of this theory are still being made as a result of further analyses of this behaviour. To a lesser extent, studies on the physiology of reproduction in the stickleback have contributed to an understanding of the causal factors implicated in the control of reproduction in teleost fishes.

Before a consideration of the reproductive biology of the male and female separately, this short chapter provides a summary of the sequence of events during the reproductive cycle and so provides the background for a more detailed analysis of the breeding biology of the two sexes. The reproductive cycle can be divided into two phases, the breeding season which lasts for two or three months in the spring or summer, and a non-reproductive phase that lasts for the rest of the year. During this non-reproductive phase males and females are difficult to distinguish either in morphology or in behaviour, but during the breeding season there is marked sexual dimorphism.

Outside the breeding season, the stickleback lives in schools, though these schools are not the highly polarised groups that occur in pelagic fish such as herring (*Clupea harengus* L.). In a school of sticklebacks, most individuals tend to be doing the same thing at the same time but the spacing and orientation of the fish relative to each other varies considerably. The school is maintained because individual sticklebacks respond to the presence of other fish by staying close to them. Experiments on this schooling behaviour showed that a single stickleback preferred to join a large group of sticklebacks rather than a small group. A small stickleback preferred to join a group of large sticklebacks rather than a group of the same number of small sticklebacks, although in most schooling species all the fish in a school tend to be about the same size. An individual three-spined stickleback preferred to join a group of conspecifics rather than a group of bitterlings (*Rhodeus amarus* L.), but failed to show a consistent preference for groups of conspecifics over groups of the nine-spined stickleback or groups of roach (*Leusciscus rutilus* L.) (Keenlyside, 1955; Symons, 1971).

Schools of sticklebacks tended to disperse the longer the fish had been without food, though when a fish found food and adopted the typical head-down feeding posture, the other fish rapidly joined the individual that had found food (Chapter 4). A disturbance caused the fish in a school to aggregate closer together and to adopt a more polarised orientation relative to each other as they swam rapidly away from the source of disturbance (Keenlyside, 1955). Even during the breeding season, when the males are territorial, they will leave their territories and swim away from the source of disturbance, usually swimming towards the deeper water where there are schools of females. The rapid, smooth swimming that characterises a stickleback swimming away from a source of disturbance is in marked contrast to the swimming of an undisturbed fish whose movements consist of a series of jerky forward movements as the stickleback sculls itself along with its pectoral fins then stops abruptly.

Both during and outside the breeding season, sticklebacks show various behaviours whose function is not clear, but which are loosely termed "comfort" movements. Occasionally a stickleback will rub the side of its body against a hard surface. When this chafing is done against a horizontal surface, the fish takes up a position with its side parallel to the surface and then makes a series of strong tail beats so that at each tail beat the side of the body, especially in the opercular region, is pushed against the surface. This action may dislodge ecto-parasites from the body surface, but it also attracts the attention of other sticklebacks perhaps because it stirs up the substrate and so uncovers food items. Another "comfort" movement that is frequently seen is yawning, the stickleback arches its back, erects its spines and opens its mouth wide. Two other stretching movements are also performed. In S-bending, the fish adopts a sigmoid posture with the head turned to one side and the tail to the other, usually the spines are erected as the fish bends. Tail-bending is similar but only the tail is bent away from the long axis of the fish (Morris, 1958). The frequency of yawning was found to be positively correlated with S-bending and tail-bending, which suggests that these three behaviours share a common causal factor (Tugendhat, 1960a). During an experiment in which sticklebacks received an electric shock in the area of the tank where they fed, Tugendhat (1960b) found that the fish showed "comfort" movements most frequently during the transition between retreating from and advancing back towards the feeding area.

In spring, a migration of sticklebacks into the breeding grounds marks the start of the breeding season. This spring migration is most obvious in those sticklebacks that have overwintered in the sea, but even those fish that have spent the winter resident in fresh water tend to move from deeper water into shallow ditches and back-waters. Craig-Bennett (1931) has described such movements by sticklebacks living in the River Cam at Cambridge. On the breeding grounds, the females remain in schools, but the males take on their breeding colours and start to defend territories, with each territory holding only one male. A male develops a red throat and fore-belly, the irises of the eyes become blue and the back often becomes greenish. Although the females do not develop such a conspicuous breeding coloration, some authors have noted that during the breeding season, the females develop contrasting concentrations of dark pigment as spots and a metallic glitter on the opercula and abdomen (Penczak, 1965). During courtship, the dark patterns on the female's body become more pronounced.

Within his territory, the male builds a nest on the substrate. This nest is constructed out of vegetation and sand grains glued together with a mucus secretion of the kidneys. The male continually defends this nest and his territory from other males, and will also chase off other species of fish that get too close to the nest. When he has completed the nest, this completion being signalled by the male creeping through the nest forming a tunnel with an entrance and an exit, he is ready to court females.

Gravid females move out of the schools into the territories of the males. When a male approaches either directly or in a series of zigzags, the female adopts a head-up posture, and moves towards the male, who usually returns to the nest and performs nest-directed activities such as fanning or glueing. While the male is at the nest, the female maintains the head-up posture and remains still. The male leaves the nest and returns to the female in a series of zigzags, on reaching the female he turns abruptly and swims in a straight line back to the nest. If the female follows the male, he leads her down to the nest and shows the nest entrance. The male lies on his side and points his snout towards the opening of the nest tunnel and moves rapidly to and fro. A female ready to spawn will push her way into the nest until only her caudal peduncle and tail stick out of the entrance. Now the male quivers, rapidly but gently butting the anal region and flanks of the female. After a few bouts of quivering, the female raises her tail and spawns the eggs. After depositing the eggs, she leaves the nest by the exit, and the male creeps through the nest releasing sperm over the eggs, a high proportion of the eggs are usually fertilised.

Immediately after the fertilisation, the male is very aggressive and drives the spawned-out female away. Nor is he yet willing to court and mate with another gravid female. First he pushes the eggs deep into the nest and eventually fastens them firmly to the bottom of the nest. Each clutch of eggs is flattened, so that successive clutches are partly stacked on top of each other like tiles. Repairs to the nest, which is often damaged as the distended, gravid female forces her way in, are also carried out at this stage so that the nest is prepared to receive another female. About an hour after fertilisation, the male is ready to court another female, and he will fertilise up to seven clutches before he stops courting altogether. After spawning, the female returns to the school, where she feeds voraciously as another batch of eggs matures.

With eggs in his nest, the male now assumes a parental role. Fanning, which was already a component of nest-directed behaviour, now becomes the predominant activity. With this behaviour he ventilates the eggs by driving a stream of fresh water through the nest. The amount of time spent fanning increases until just before the eggs hatch, but once the eggs hatch there is a relatively rapid decline in fanning. Once the eggs have hatched, the male tears the nest to pieces until in some cases the nest pit is cleared of vegetation. For a few days, the male retrieves young that stray from the nest, he sucks the errant larva into his mouth and spits it out into the nest pit. But as the young become more active, fill their swim bladders and become agile swimmers, he can no longer retrieve them and the young disperse from around the nest site. During the parental phase, the male tends to become much darker in colour, a change which presumably makes the male less conspicuous to potential predators of both him and his eggs. There is also a decline in the aggressiveness of the male with a tendency for the area defended to decrease. After the young hatch, the aggressiveness of the male increases, but this does not necessarily lead to an increase in territory size if adjacent males are able to defend their territories successfully.

A few days after the young disperse the male may build another nest, although this need not always be in the original territory, and so the cycle is started again. It has been estimated that a male may build up to five nests in a breeding season, although there is no information whether a male in a natural population can reach this total. The females will also produce several clutches during the breeding season, the number depending on the size of the female and the food supply. In the breeding system of the three-spined stickleback, parental care by the male is combined with relatively high egg production by the female. A limitation of the system is that there are long periods of time when a male is not willing to fertilise gravid females for protection of the eggs is given priority over the fertilisation of more eggs. In the four-spined stickleback, *Apeltes quadracus*, this limitation is less severe (see Chapter 18).

Although the reproductive behaviour of the three-spined stickleback is complex, males and females that had been reared in isolation from the time they hatched until they became mature, showed qualitatively normal aggressive, sexual and parental behaviour (Cullen, 1960).

The reproductive behaviour of leiurus, trachurus and semiarmatus fish is qualitatively similar, but there may be more subtle quantitative differences in the behaviour of fish from different populations. There is some evidence that males from populations on the east coast of North America are more aggressive than males taken from an English population (Wilz, 1973), but insufficient research has been done on this subject to assess the importance of such interpopulation differences.

There has been one report of a population of sticklebacks in which hermaphroditic individuals were present (Greenbank and Nelson, 1959) which if it had proved true would have opened up the possibility of research on the implications of such hermaphroditism for the reproductive behaviour of the fish. Stenger (1963) showed that the apparent hermaphroditism was a result of the mis-identification of internal organs by the investigators rather than an aberration of the sticklebacks.

At the end of the breeding season, there is often a high mortality and, as described in Chapter 3, in some populations no adults survive to reach a second breeding period. Those adults that do survive, together with the young born that year, migrate back to their winter habitat during the autumn. For some populations this implies a movement from fresh or brackish water into the sea.

8. Migration and Osmotic Regulation

For those sticklebacks that over-winter in fresh water, the spring migration to the breeding areas, if it occurs at all, consists only of a movement from deeper water into shallower water, or a movement from a main river system into tributaries and backwaters. But for the sticklebacks that over-winter in the sea, the migration involves a movement from a salt water environment into a brackish or fresh water environment. This change in the osmotic and ionic character-istics of the external medium means that a migrating fish must undergo a physiological adaptation which will enable it to live in the new environment. In autumn, when the surviving adults and young return to the sea, the adaptation must be reversed. This raises the problem of what form the adaptation takes, and how the adaptation is regulated so that the fish is in the appropriate physiological state at the appropriate time. Migrations to and from breeding areas such as those undertaken by the stickleback pose other problems for the biologist. What factors initiate and maintain the migration; how does the fish orientate itself during the migration; and what factors terminate the migration? Another set of problems emerges when an attempt is made to determine the function of the migration. What advantages does the animal gain from over-wintering in one area but breeding in another? This problem is particularly acute when posed for an animal such as the stickleback in which some populations migrate while others do not, yet all seem to be successful and often coexist within the same river system.

Although the biannual migrations of the stickleback usually go unremarked, occasionally the numbers of fish moving are sufficient to attract attention. A classical example of such an occasion is cited by Regan (1911), quoting a report by Pennant in 1776:

> Once in seven or eight years amazing shoals appear in the Welland and come up the river in the form of a vast column. The quantity is so great

that they are used to manure the land, and trials have been made to get oil from them. A notion may be had of this vast shoal by saying that a man employed by the farmer to take them has got for a considerable time four shillings a day by selling them at a halfpenny a bushel.

The man was collecting ninety-six bushels a day! In April 1909, a similar phenomenon occurred in the region of Whittlesey, when vast hordes of sticklebacks were seen in the canals and rivers of the neighbourhood. Both the Welland and Whittlesey are in the fen district of eastern England.

In a discussion of the timing of the spring migration, Baggerman (1957) mentions that during the war year of 1943, the collection of sticklebacks by the Dutch for use in the production of fish meal and as food for ducks became commercially important on February 11 and the fishing lasted to the middle of April, with the largest captures made between February 20 and March 10. A later study on the migration of a stickleback population of the island of Tholen in the Netherlands found that the spring migration started around the middle of March (van Mullem and van der Vlught, 1964). Although a few fish may be found in sluices of the sea dykes as early as January, the main migration in the Netherlands takes place in February, March and April. In eastern England, the migration takes place in April and May (Craig-Bennett, 1931), and the same is true for the north German populations (Leiner, 1930, 1931a). In Japan, the spring migration of sticklebacks takes place from mid-February until the end of March (Ikeda, 1933). A detailed description of the migration of the trachurus form comes from Hagen's (1967) study of the stickleback populations of a small river in southwestern British Columbia. A small number of trachurus moved into the spawning area in the middle of May, but the bulk of the fish did not arrive until a month later.

In autumn, the young fish and any surviving adults move back to the sea. In late autumn, sticklebacks were sufficiently abundant in the Baltic Sea to support a fishery (Regan, 1911). The movement into the sea takes place in September and October in the Netherlands, although the fish are moving seawards even earlier than this (Baggerman, 1957; van Mullem and van der Vlught, 1964). Populations in Germany move seawards in August and September (Leiner, 1930, 1931a), while in British Columbia, Hagen (1967) found that there was a rapid disappearance of trachurus fish from the breeding grounds in late August and early September.

All these populations share the characteristic that the movement onto the breeding ground takes place at a time when the hours of daylight and the water temperature are increasing, while the seaward migration takes place when daylengths and the water temperature are decreasing. This suggests that a changing photoperiod or changing water temperature may provide the cue or cues that initiate migrations. Studies on the reproductive cycles of other vertebrates suggest that hormones produced by the pituitary gland (Chapter 1) will mediate the influence of photoperiod or water temperature on migration, and that the release of the pituitary hormones will be controlled by the hypothalamic region of the brain (Chapter 1). The same factors that stimulate the stickleback to migrate are also likely to initiate the physiological adaptations that must be made for the fish to move between salt and fresh water.

When a stickleback is in salt water, its blood and other body fluids are hypotonic to the external medium. They have both a lower concentration of inorganic ions and a lower osmotic pressure than sea water, so although surrounded by water, the fish tends to lose water and gain inorganic ions from the external environment. The fish must have mechanisms that conserve water and excrete inorganic ions. In freshwater the situation is reversed, now the internal fluids of the fish are hypertonic to the external medium, and the osmotic and concentration gradient favours a flow of water into the fish and a loss of inorganic ions from the fish. (Table VII). In both salt and freshwater the stickleback must have mechanisms that maintain the osmolarity and ionic composition of the internal fluids constant. The two organs most immediately concerned with the regulation of the osmotic and ionic composition of the body fluids are the kidneys and the gills.

The paired kidneys of the stickleback lie under the vertebral column, each member of the pair consists of a trunk region and a head region. This head region contains lymphoid, haematopoietic and interrenal tissue and so is not directly concerned with osmo- and ionic regulation, although some of the hormones produced by the interrenals may be involved in the control of the organs directly involved in the regulation. The trunk portion is the region whose primary function is the regulation of water and ionic balance. Posteriorly, the two halves of the trunk kidney fuse, but anteriorly each half is separate and connected by a slender thread of tissue to the head kidney. Clusters of ten to twenty renal corpuscles are distributed throughout the trunk kidney, and a small artery runs to each cluster supplying the corpuscle with a short arteriole. The functional unit of the kidney, the nephron, consists of a renal corpuscle which comprises of Bowman's capsule and the associated glomerulus, and a nephronic duct which is made up of a short neck segment, a first and second proximal segment and a collecting tubule.

All the collecting tubules which originate from a cluster of renal corpuscles fuse and open into a branch of the ureter. Each kidney has a ureter which runs ventrally through the trunk kidney and opens into the urinary bladder which voids the urine via a small duct at the urinary papilla (Wendelaar Bonga, 1973a).

The glomerulus of a renal corpuscle is a tangle of blood capillaries which lies cupped in and almost surrounded by Bowman's capsule.

TABLE VII

Osmotic and ionic characteristics of blood serum of *Gasterosteus aculeatus.*

System	Osmotic value	Na$^+$	Ionic composition K$^+$	Cl$^-$	Source
Trachurus in sea water (winter)	344 mosmol/ kg water	172 meq/l	5.5 meq/l	140 meq/l	Lam, 1968
Trachurus in sea water (spring)	339 mosmol/ kg water				Lam and Hoar, 1967
Trachurus in sea water (spring)	340 mosM				Lange and Fugelli, 1965
Trachurus in fresh water (spring)	290 mosM				Lange and Fugelli, 1965
Leiurus and trachurus at 10°C in					
(a) salt water FPD = 1.90	FPD = 0.65				
(b) salt water FPD = 0.60	FPD = 0.62				Koch and Heuts, 1943
(c) fresh water	FPD = 0.60				

Sea water: FPD = 1.906, approx. 1000 mosmol, contains 470 mM/kg water Na$^+$, 10 mM/kg water K$^+$ and 550 mM/kg water Cl$^-$.
Fresh water: FPD negligible, approx. 1 mosmol, contains 0.30 mM/kg water Na$^+$, 0.06 mM/kg water K$^+$ and 0.20 mM/kg water Cl$^-$.
FPD is freezing point depression in °C.

Blood enters the glomerulus via an afferent arteriole and leaves it by an efferent arteriole. Associated with arteries and arterioles are the juxtaglomerular cells. These cells are thought to contain renin, a hormone that may be implicated in the regulation of water and ion balance, but whose role in the stickleback is still uncertain. Bowman's capsule is the closed end of the nephron duct so the lumen of Bowman's capsule is continuous with the duct. The parietal epithelium of the capsule is not in contact with the glomerulus and consists of a layer of flattened cells resting on a basement membrane.

But the visceral epithelium of the capsule has an intimate connection with the blood capillaries. Fluids filter through the walls of the capillaries and through the visceral epithelium into the lumen of the capsule and from there into the duct of the nephron. Not surprisingly, the cells of the capillary wall and the visceral epithelium show some interesting structural modifications. The endothelial cells of the capillary wall have fenestrations, parts of the cell which lack cytoplasm and consist only of a membrane. Also associated with the endothelial cells are mesangial cells, whose function is uncertain but they may help to support the glomerulus. A basement membrane separates the cells of the capillary wall from the cells of the visceral epithelium of the capsule. This visceral layer consists of podocytes, so called because these cells have foot-like cytoplasmic processes separated by membranes (Fig. 27) (Wendelaar Bonga, 1973a).

A short neck region which leads out of the capsule is a transitional zone between the flattened cells of the capsule and the more columnar cells of the first proximal segment. Some of the neck cells have cilia which may help the flow of the filtrate down the duct, but unlike the cells of the rest of the tubule they lack a brush border. The first proximal segment of the tubule is relatively short, and consists of columnar cells. These have a well developed brush border that consists of numerous microvilli projecting into the lumen of the tubule, while the basal end of the cell has a basal labyrinth, a system of branched membranes enclosing spaces which communicate with the exterior through small pores in the outer cell membrane. The mitochondria of the cells are strongly associated with this basal labyrinth. Histochemical evidence suggests that this first proximal segment modifies the glomerular filtrate by reabsorbing macromolecules such as carbohydrates and low molecular weight proteins from the filtrate. The cells of the second proximal segment of the tubule also have a brush border and a well developed basal labyrinth, while the cells of the epithelium of the collecting ducts and ureter lack a brush border but the basal labyrinth remains well developed. This suggests that these cells, as well as those in the proximal segment, can modify the glomerular filtrate by reabsorbing or in some cases secreting inorganic ions (Fig. 28) (Mourier, 1970; Wendelaar Bonga, 1973a; Wendelaar Bonga and Veenhuis, 1974).

In all vertebrates, the kidney is concerned with water and ion balance, but at first sight a more surprising site for the regulation of the ionic composition of body fluids is the gills. Because of their primary function as the site at which the blood is oxygenated, it is essential that the gills present a very large surface area to the surrounding water, but this means that a large surface area is exposed

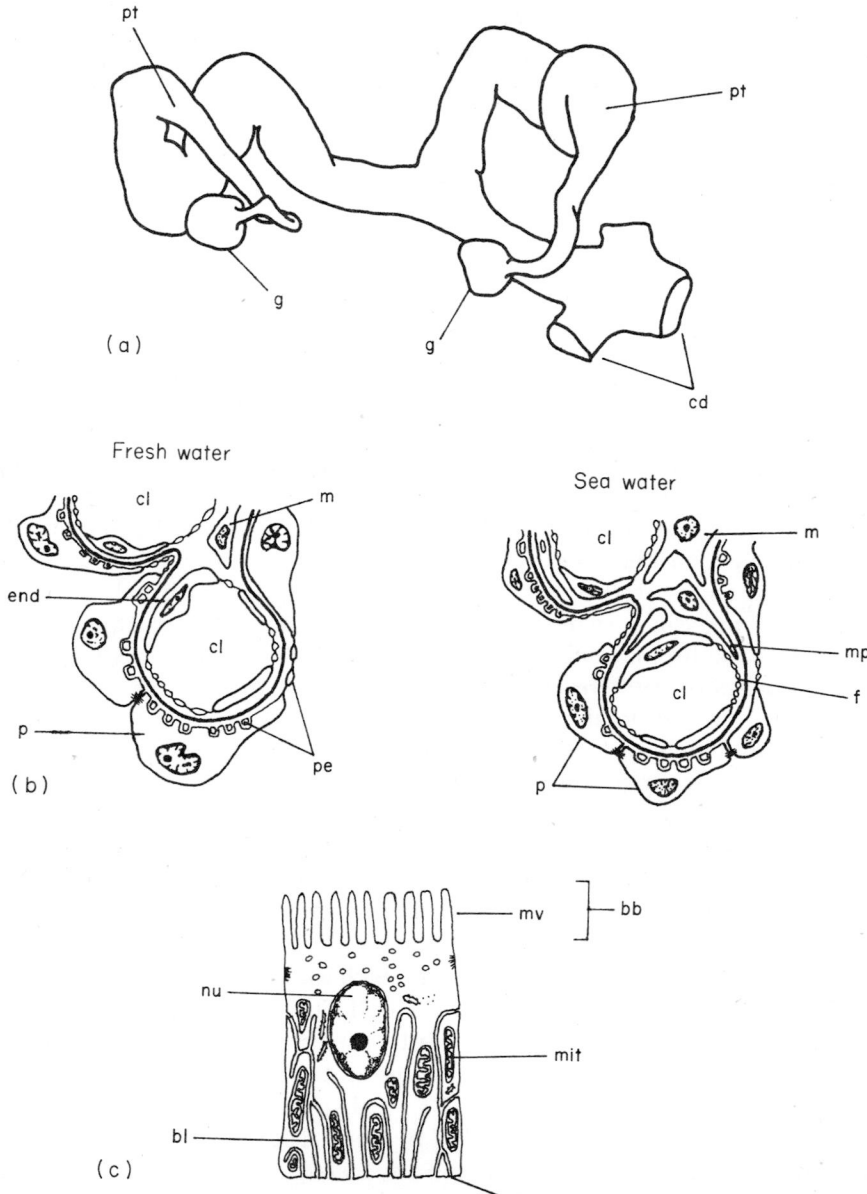

Fig. 27. The kidney of *Gasterosteus aculeatus*. (a) Kidney tubule (after Mourier, 1970); (b) schematic diagrams of the glomerulus in fresh and sea water (after Wendalaar Bonga, 1973a); (c) schematic diagram of a cell of the second proximal segment (after Wendalaar Bonga and Veenhuis, 1974). Key to lettering: bb, brush border, bl, basal labyrinth; cd, collecting ducts; cl, lumen of capillary; end, endothelial cell; f, fenestrations; g, glomerulus; m, mesangial cell; mit, mitochondrion; mp, cytoplasmic process of mesangial cell; mv, microvillus; nu, nucleus; p, podocyte; pe, pedicels; po, pore; pt, proximal tubule.

through which water and inorganic ions can pass. There is some evidence that the flux of water between the fish and the external medium is mainly across the gills, and not the rest of the body surface (Evans, 1969). In the epithelium of the gill filaments

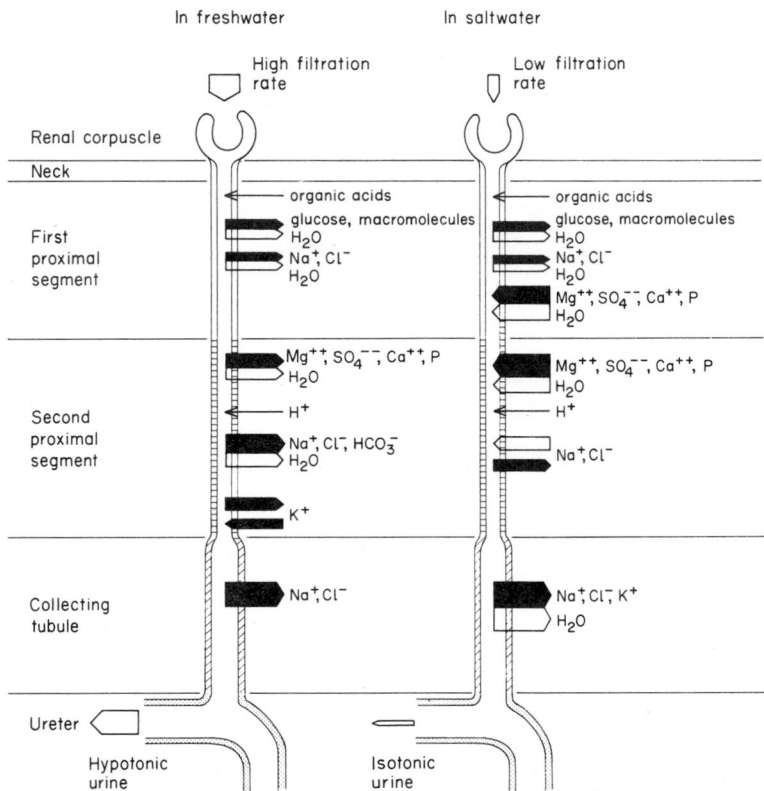

Fig. 28. Modification of glomerular filtrate by kidney tubule of a euryhaline fish in fresh and sea water (after Hickman and Trump, 1969). Solid arrows indicate active processes that require the expenditure of energy; open arrows indicate passive processes; width of arrows approximately proportional to the rate of movement.

(Chapter 1), there are chloride cells which can secrete or take up monovalent ions such as sodium and chloride. These cells are characterised by an abundance of mitochondria and a well developed smooth endoplasmic reticulum which in each cell connects with the exterior at a pit that lies at the apex of the cell. A chloride cell secretes mucus into the apical pit (Fig. 29) (Biether, 1970; Matthiessen and Brafield, 1973). Another probable site of ion and water exchange is the intestinal epithelium.

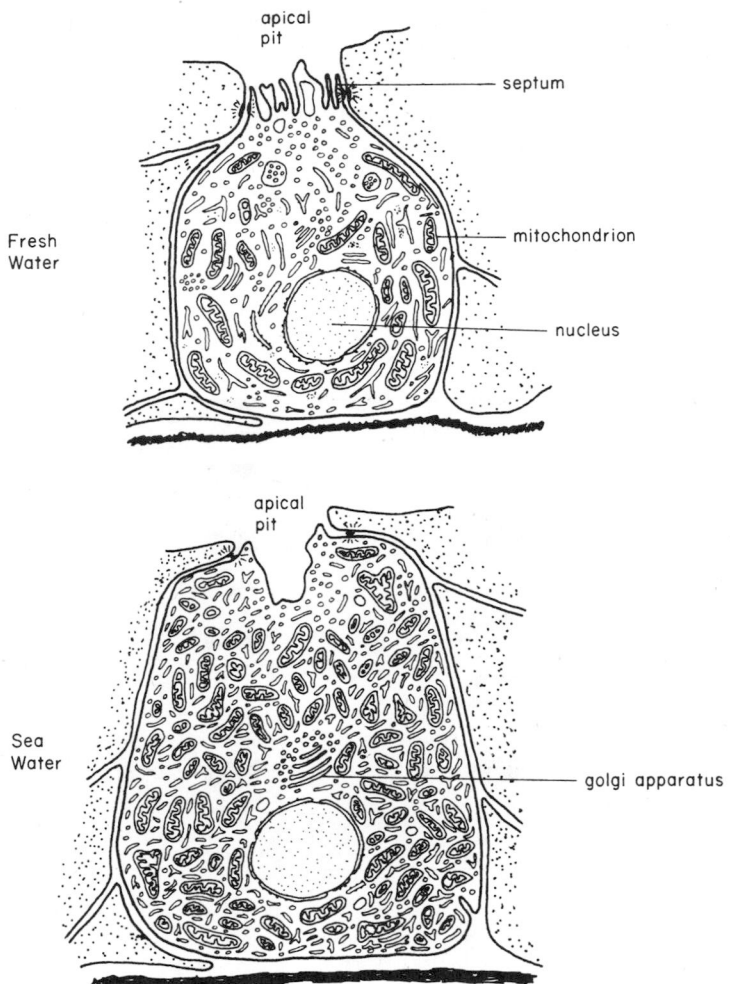

Fig. 29. Schematic diagram of chloride cells of *Gasterosteus aculeatus* in fresh and sea water (after Biether, 1970).

The sites of water and ion exchange between the external medium and the body fluids of the stickleback when the fish is in sea and fresh water are shown in Fig. 30. In sea water the stickleback looses water across the gills and the body surface, and the fish makes good this water loss by drinking salt water (Mullins, 1950). The excess salts taken in across the gills, the body surface and in the drinking water are eliminated in the faeces, by the kidneys and through the chloride cells of the gills. In fresh water, water enters the stickleback through the gills and body surface and inorganic ions are lost. The excess water is eliminated in the urine, while monovalent ions are taken up from the external medium by the chloride cells, and reabsorbed from the glomerular filtrate by the cells of the kidney tubules.

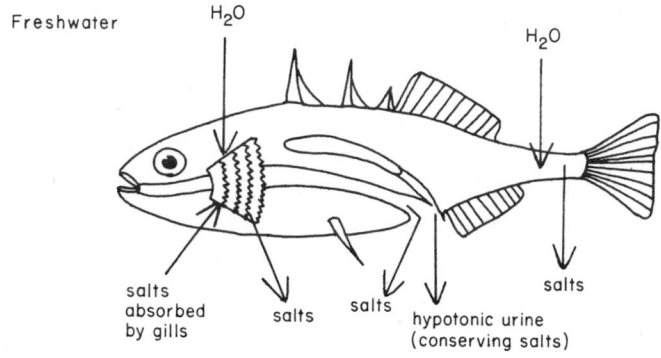

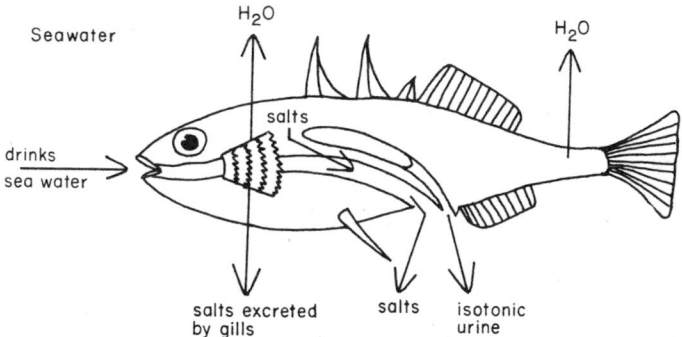

Fig. 30. Movement of water and salts between fish and the external medium in fresh and sea water.

What happens when a stickleback is transferred between water of differing salinities? When trachurus and semiarmatus fish were moved from water of low salinity into sea water, they showed an increase in oxygen consumption, which indicated that work was being done by the fish to maintain the osmotic and ionic characteristics of the body fluids, the regulation was an active process requiring the expenditure of energy. Leiurus fish did not show an increase in oxygen consumption, instead there was an increase in the height of the pool of free amino acids, an increase which helped the fish to adjust to the increase in osmotic pressure of the external medium passively, without the expenditure of energy (Gutz, 1970). Although this study indicates that there are important differences in the way in which leiurus and trachurus fish adapt to a change in salinity, most of the studies have used trachurus fish, for it is a normal feature of the life cycle of this form that it moves between the sea and fresh or brackish water.

The appearance of the chloride cells of the gills changed when sticklebacks were transferred from fresh water to sea water. In fresh water, the apical portion of the chloride cell had fingers of cytoplasm which pushed into the apical pit forming septa that divided up the pit. These septa increased the surface area of the apical cell membrane, and so presumably increase the surface area through which the monovalent ions can be taken up from the external medium and so counterbalance the loss of ions that the fish suffers in fresh water. The monovalent ions are transported against a concentration gradient, a process that requires the expenditure of energy. In sea water, the apical pit lacked the septa and was just a simple pit, the endoplasmic reticulum was more developed and the mitochondria acounted for a larger proportion of the cell volume than in fresh water. When the fish is in salt water, the chloride cell must secrete excess monovalent ions such as sodium and chloride out into the external environment, again against a concentration gradient. The abundant mitochondria bear witness that the activity of the chloride cell requires the expenditure of energy. In both fresh and sea water the apical pit contained a mucoid layer that was rich in both sodium and chloride ions (Biether, 1970) (Fig. 29).

In fresh water sticklebacks were less permeable to water than in sea water, and since most movement of water across the body surface probably takes place across the gills, this indicates that the gill surface becomes less permeable to water (Evans, 1969).

Since the kidney is an organ whose primary function is urine production, it is an organ likely to show significant changes when fish move between water of differing salinities. In fresh water, large quantities of water must be eliminated, but with as little as possible loss of osmotically active material, while in sea water the elimination of salts and the retention of water are the primary concerns.

Wendelaar Bonga (1973a) compared the kidneys of trachurus sticklebacks kept in fresh water with those of trachurus fish kept in sea water. Although the diameter of the renal corpuscles did not differ, the diameter of the glomeruli of fish in fresh water was slightly larger than those of fish from sea water. In fresh water, the podocytes of the visceral epithelium of Bowman's capsule had larger nuclei and contained secretory granules which were absent in the podocytes of the sea water fish. Mesangial cells were far more common in the fish from sea water. In these fish, cytoplasmic processes of the mesangial cells tended to infiltrate between the endothelial cells of the capillary wall and the basement membrane, and so these processes may form a barrier to the passage of filtrate from the blood capillary into the lumen of Bowman's capsule (Fig. 27b). Juxtaglomerular cells were also far more common in fish from sea water than in fish from fresh water. The epithelial cells of the nephron tubules and ureters were taller and had larger nuclei in the fish from fresh water. They also had better developed basal labyrinths and a greater proportion of the total cell volume consisted of mitochondria. These structural differences suggest that the tubules are far more active in ion transport when the fish is in fresh water than in salt water. Although there are no detailed studies on the composition of the filtrate in different segments of the nephron tubule, comparison with other species of fish suggests the scheme shown in Fig. 28. In fresh water, the ducts reabsorb sufficient inorganic ions from the filtrate to make the urine hypotonic to the blood plasma. Trachurus fish transferred to fresh water from sea water in spring produced, within twenty-fours, urine that had an osmolality of 164 mosmol per kg water although the osmolality of the blood was 315 mosmol per kg water (Lam and Hoar, 1967). In sea water, although there is some modification of the filtrate, notably by the secretion of divalent ions such as magnesium and sulphate into the filtrate, the urine is isotonic with the body fluids (Hickman and Trump, 1969; Wandelaar Bonga, 1973a).

At least three other tissues show changes when sticklebacks move between water of different salinities. The saccus vasculosus is a thin walled, folded sac that grows out of the floor of the third ventricle just behind the pituitary (Chapter 1). One possible function of the saccus vasculosus is that it regulates the osmotic or ionic concentration of the cerebro-spinal fluid. Ultrastructural changes in the coronet cells of the saccus vasculosus followed the transfer of leiurus fish from fresh water to seventy per cent sea water, although the functional significance of these changes is not known (Benjamin, 1974c). A transfer of sticklebacks from fresh water to sea water caused a depletion in the neurosecretory granules of the praeoptic nuclei and tracts of the fore-brain and the neurohypophysis (Chapter 1) which suggests that factors released by these regions of the brain may play a part in osmo-regulation (Fridberg and Olsson, 1959). There was an increase in the size of the interrenal cells and the nuclei of the interrenal cells when leiurus fish were transferred from fresh water into seventy per cent sea water (Benjamin and Ireland, 1974). The significance of this change in the interrenal cells is not clear, though it may imply that the interrenals play a role in osmo-regulation, it may also simply signify that the animals were being "stressed" by being placed in the salt water.

So far all the mechanisms for osmo- and ionic regulation have been involved with the regulation of the body fluids, that is extracellular fluids. But there is evidence that regulation of the intracellular fluids is also possible. If there are changes in the osmolarity of the extra-cellular fluids, the cells can maintain an iso-osmotic relation-ship with the extra-cellular fluids without being damaged. This is achieved not by the movement of inorganic ions between the cell and the extra-cellular fluid, but by an adjustment in the number of small molecular weight organic compounds in particular amino acids and trimethylamine within the cell (Lange and Fugelli, 1965).

The ability of the stickleback to osmo-regulate depends on which form it belongs to, the temperature of the water and the degree of sexual maturity (Gueylard, 1924; Koch and Heuts, 1943; Gutz, 1970).

Although able to tolerate a wide range of salinities, the leiurus form has a narrower range than the trachurus form, and even within a leiurus population the fish with the higher numbers of lateral plates tend to have a better tolerance of high salinities (Heuts, 1947b). Leiurus sticklebacks rely, at least partly, on a passive process to osmo-regulate in sea water making use of the pool of free amino acids. But this mechanism is not effective at very low temperatures (4°C), and so leiurus is excluded from salt water at low temperatures. Trachurus and semiarmatus fish use an active process to regulate in sea water and so tolerate high salinities even at low temperatures (Gutz, 1970).

Seasonal changes in the ability of both the trachurus and leiurus forms to osmo-regulate were described as early as 1943 (Koch and Heuts, 1943). In spring, when the fish were sexually mature, they were less tolerant of high salinities than they were outside the breeding season. This decline in tolerance was most noticeable in leiurus fish, which outside the breeding season could survive in solutions of 45 parts per thousand salt (sea water is about 35 parts per thousand), but sexually mature individuals were unable to tolerate normal sea water. Trachurus fish showed a similar, but less marked, decline. During the breeding season, the fish were physio-logically better adapted to live in water of comparatively low salinities. In autumn, migratory trachurus fish lose the ability to tolerate water of low salinity (Lam and Hoar, 1967).

These seasonal changes in the ability of sticklebacks to tolerate water of low or high salinity provoked a search for the factors that cause the changes, and investigations into the relationship between the changes in osmo-regulation and migratory behaviour of the stickleback.

Sexually immature leiurus fish in fresh water and fed food that contained desiccated thyroid tissue showed a marked drop in the concentration of chloride ions in the blood, but there was no unusual mortality. If the fish were in sea water, the treatment with thyroid tissue led to a marked rise in the chloride content of the blood and many of the fish died. This experiment showed that feeding the fish with a preparation of a known endocrine gland, the thyroid (Chapter 1), led to a change in the ability of the fish to regulate the chloride content of the blood (Koch and Heuts, 1942). This implicates a hormone produced by the thyroid, thyroxine, in osmo-regulation and so perhaps in migration, but as yet there is no evidence that there are changes in the activity of the thyroid that correlate with the migratory cycle of the stickleback (Koch, 1968). However, young trachurus sticklebacks kept in fresh water for more than a month did develop hypertrophied thyroids (Hamada, 1975).

Thyroxine had other effects on the stickleback which implicate this hormone in the regulation of body fluids. It caused a lowering in the pool of free amino acids and the water content of the muscle tissue, and an increase in the rate of oxygen consumption. Trachurus and semiarmatus fish were more sensitive to thyroxine than leiurus fish (Gutz, 1970).

Evidence that thyroxine might also be implicated in the control of migration comes from studies on the behaviour of sticklebacks in a salinity gradient (Baggerman, 1957). The experimental fish chose a salinity out of a graded series of salinities. If a fish spent most of its time in fresh water, it was scored as showing a fresh water preference, and a fish that spent most of its time in regions of high salinity was scored as showing a preference for salt water. The salinity preferences of both trachurus and leiurus fish changed over a year. In late winter and spring, adult fish preferred freshwater, but they switched to preference for salt water towards the end of the breeding season. Young-of-the-year showed a preference for salt water as soon as two months after hatching. The effect of a rise in temperature on salinity preference depended on the time of the year. In late autumn and early winter, a rise in temperature from 5°C to 14°C had no effect on the prevailing preference for salt water. A similar rise in temperature in late winter induced a change to a preference for fresh water within one to three days. The effect of a rise in temperature depends on the physiological state of the fish which varies over the year, and the refractoriness towards a rise in temperature during early winter may serve to inhibit migration at a biologically inappropriate time.

A change to a fresh water preference was associated with the onset of maturity, but even gonadectomised fish, if kept under conditions of light and temperature that would induce maturity in intact fish, showed the change from a preference for salt water to fresh water. This suggests that hormones produced by the gonads are not responsible for the change in salinity preference, although they may modify the timing of the change in salinity preference. Treatment of fish with exogeneous gonadotropins, an attempt to simulate the output of the gonad-stimulating hormones by the pituitary, did result in a slight increase in preference for fresh water, but this effect was only noted some weeks after the hormone treatment. This result suggests that any effect of gonadotropins is indirect. In contrast to these results, the effects of treating the fish with a thyroid hormone, thyroxine, and the thyroid inhibitor, thiourea, were clear cut. Thyroxine induced a preference for fresh water in both intact and gonadectomised fish, and this effect was hardly influenced by external conditions. When given to a fish showing a preference for fresh water, thiourea induced a preference for salt water. The effect of thyroxine or thiourea on the salinity preference could be detected within three to five days.

These studies implicate the thyroid gland in the causation of migration and the physiological changes that accompany migration. A possible hypothesis is that in spring the increasing day lengths and water temperature induce an increase in the activity of the pituitary gland, which produces both gonadotropic and thyrotropic hormones. The increased output of thyrotropin stimulates the thyroid to increase its output of thyroxine, which leads to a decrease in the ability of the fish living in salt water to regulate the ionic composition of their body fluids and to a change in their salinity preference so that the fish will move down a salinity gradient towards fresh water. Increased thyroxine levels may also induce heightened locomotor activity which may well be essential for successful migration. With the decreasing days lengths and water temperature of late summer and early autumn, pituitary activity will decline and the thyroid become less active. The fish will now have an increased ability to tolerate a hypertonic external medium and show a behavioural preference for salt water. Seaward migration would be downstream and so would not require enhanced locomotor activity, indeed it could well be a largely passive process.

Much of this scheme is conjectural and requires further experimental evidence. It is necessary to compare the behaviour and physiology of leiurus fish which do not migrate over long distances with that of anadromous trachurus and semiarmatus fish. The work of Gutz (1970) has suggested that the basic mechanisms of osmoregulation may be different in migratory and non-migratory forms, and that the forms may differ in their sensitivity to the effects of thyroxine. In particular the effect of thyroxine on the ability of trachurus and semiarmatus forms to regulate the ionic composition of their body fluids requires clarification.

There are seasonal changes in the histological appearance of cells in the pituitary of trachurus fish which are presumed to produce thyrotropic hormone (Leatherland, 1970b). These changes indicated that the thyrotropes were active in fish undergoing rapid growth and were maximally developed in spring fish collected in the sea prior to migration into fresh water. Leatherland suggested that the thyroid was only indirectly involved in ionic regulation and migration through its influence on metabolism. He drew this conclusion on the basis of work on other species of fish and these studies may not be directly relevant to the stickleback. Nevertheless, this does suggest that the hypothesis may over-emphasise the direct role of the pituitary-thyroid axis in migration and so adds weight to the proviso already made that much of the hypothesis remains to be rigorously tested.

A brief observation indicates that gonadal hormones may play a role in initiating or maintaining the spring migration. Male fish injected with testosterone, a male gonadal hormone, showed increased amounts of "fluttering". This "fluttering" is a continuous swimming up and down the sides of an aquarium which has been interpreted, though without clear supporting evidence, as migratory movement (van Iersel, 1953).

Yet this is only part of the story. Trachurus sticklebacks that normally migrate to the sea in autumn show very poor survival if kept in water of low ionic concentration during autumn and early winter (Fig. 31), but in spring they tolerate these conditions perfectly well. In late summer and autumn, trachurus fish undergo a physiological change which makes them unable to survive long periods in fresh water, while in spring a change takes place that enables the fish to survive and reproduce in water of low salinity.

A hormone that has been implicated in the ability of cyprinodont fish to survive in fresh water is paralactin, the teleost equivalent of the mammalian pituitary hormone, prolactin (Ball, 1969). In mammals prolactin induces lactation, its equivalent in some amphibians plays a causal role in the migration of the young, but in fish paralactin seems to be primarily active in regulating the ability of some species to survive in the hypotonic environment of fresh water. It may also be implicated in the control of parental behaviour in fish, a point which is taken up in Chapter 13.

Good experimental evidence that paralactin is an important factor in the ability of the anadromous trachurus form to tolerate fresh

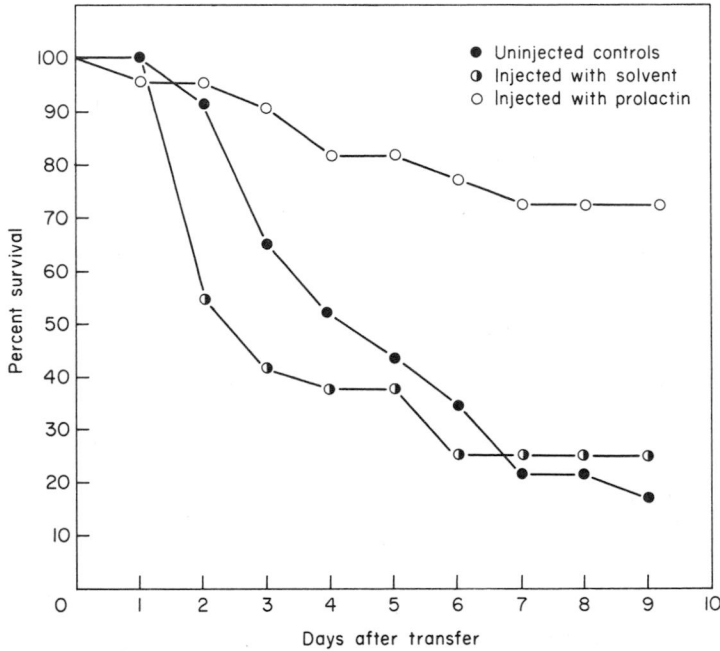

Fig. 31. Effect of prolactin on the survival of *Gasterosteus aculeatus* form trachurus when transferred from sea water to fresh water in autumn (after Lam and Leatherland, 1969a).

water during spring and summer has been obtained by Lam and his co-workers (Lam, 1972). Injection of ovine prolactin significantly reduced the mortality of trachurus sticklebacks transferred from sea water to fresh water during early winter and kept on a regime of short days and long nights (eight hours light, sixteen hours dark) (Lam and Leatherland, 1969a). Prolactin injections even reduced significantly the mortality rate of trachurus fish that were transferred from sea water to deionised water. The injections were most effective if given a day or two days before the fish were transferred and in doses of more than 1 μg per g wet weight of fish (Leatherland and Lam, 1969a). This range of dosages is similar to the range that was found to be effective in stimulating a parental behaviour known as fanning in mature male sticklebacks, a study described in Chapter 13 (Molenda and Fiedler, 1971). The latency of one or two days for the effect of prolactin is somewhat comparable to the latency of about three days for the effect of thyroxine on salinity preference.

Other hormones were also tested for their effects on reducing the mortality rate of trachurus fish in deionised water. The mammalian pituitary hormones follicle stimulating hormone (FSH), luteinising hormone (LH), thyroid stimulating hormone (TSH), growth hormone (GH), and the neurohypophysial hormones vasopressin and arginine vasotocin did not reduce mortality nor did the interrenal steroid hormone, cortisol. Adrenocorticotrophic hormone (ACTH), a hormone which stimulates the release of adrenal cortex, or, in teleosts, interrenal steroids, did reduce the rate of mortality, but not to such an extent as prolactin (Lam and Leatherland, 1970). Although cortisol was ineffective, the fact that ACTH has an effect and that other workers have found that steroids, especially cortisol, influence the movements of the sodium ion in some species of fish (Henderson et al., 1970) suggests that hormones of the pituitary-interrenal axis may play a role in the control of osmo-regulation in the stickleback, perhaps acting synergistically with paralactin.

Trachurus fish transferred from sea water to fresh water in early winter showed a significant drop in the osmolality of their blood plasma. Injections of prolactin before the transfer reduced this drop in plasma osmolality. After the transfer to fresh water, the blood plasma of fish not receiving prolactin showed a drop in the concentrations of sodium, potassium and chloride ions. Fish that received prolactin still showed a drop in the concentration of potassium in the plasma, but prolactin significantly reduced the rapid fall in the plasma levels of sodium and chloride. Fish injected with prolactin were able to excrete highly hypoosmotic urine, a physiological adaptation to life in fresh water. When the transfer experiment was repeated in spring, even fish not receiving prolactin showed the same changes in plasma and urine osmolalities which were shown by the winter fish injected with prolactin (Lam and Hoar, 1967; Lam, 1968). This suggests that in anadromous trachurus fish there is a seasonal variation in paralactin secretion so that when the fish migrate into fresh water there is an increased output of paralactin by the pituitary. When fish caught in the autumn were put on a photoperiod of sixteen hours of light and eight hours of dark per day, light conditions that simulate spring and summer day lengths, they developed the ability to produce hypoosmotic urine on transfer to fresh water (Hoar, 1965).

Two likely target organs for the action of paralactin are the kidneys and the gills. Prolactin injections given to trachurus fish in early winter led to structural changes in the kidney. After transfer from sea to fresh water, the fish injected with prolactin showed an increase in glomerular size, although the Bowman's capsules did not show any increase in size. These changes mimic, to a certain extent, the changes in kidney structure observed when untreated fish were transferred from sea water to fresh water in spring. The changes in the kidney suggest that prolactin increases the glomerular filtration rate (Ogawa, 1968; Lam and Leatherland, 1969b). The changes in kidney structure which take place when fish are transferred from sea water to fresh water in spring occur within six to nine days of the transfer, but the changes took place within three days when the fish were injected with prolactin during the transfer (Wendelaar Bonga, 1973b). Prolactin injections reduced the net loss of both sodium and chloride ions from the head region of trachurus fish kept in fresh water, this loss was presumably occurring mostly through the gills (Lam, 1969a, b, c). Although prolactin had no effect on the histology of the gills of fish kept in sea water after the injections, after the fish were transferred to fresh water those treated with prolactin had a higher density of mucus cells on the gills than fish that did not receive prolactin. A thick layer of mucus on the gills may help to reduce the rate of loss of ions through the gills (Leatherland and Lam, 1969b). There is, then, experimental evidence that both the kidneys and the gills are target organs for paralactin.

There is some histological evidence that supports the suggestion that anadromous trachurus sticklebacks show seasonal variations in paralactin production. Marked changes in the proportion of the pituitary taken up by paralactin cells and changes in the ultrastructure of the cells indicated that these cells were most active during spring and least active during early winter. The pituitary cells presumed to produce ACTH showed no changes in ultrastructure but the size of the cells was greatest in fish in spring (Leatherland, 1970a). In contrast to this, the paralactin cells of leiurus sticklebacks that are resident in fresh water throughout the year did not show such a marked change between winter and spring. The cells were probably active throughout the year (Benjamin, 1974a, b).

A hypothetical scheme for the role of paralactin in the migratory cycle of trachurus fish can now be developed. In autumn, the decreasing daylengths and water temperature cause a decrease in the activity of the pituitary and so a decrease in the production of paralactin. The fish loses its ability to osmo-regulate in fresh water. At the same time a reduction in the activity of the thyroid may be improving the ability of the fish to osmo-regulate in salt water, and there is a change in the salinity preference of the fish. This situation remains throughout the winter. In spring, the increase in daylength and the increase in water temperature induce an increase in the activity of the pituitary and so an increase in paralactin production and greater activity of the thyroid. Higher levels of paralactin enable the fish to osmo-regulate in water of low salinity, whilst the higher levels of thyroid hormone may reduce the ability of the fish to stay in salt water, and also induce a preference for fresh water. Increased levels of ACTH and gonadotropin either directly or by stimulating the release of interrenal steroids and gonadal hormones perhaps augment the tolerance of the fish for water of low salinity.

There are many unanswered questions associated with this scheme. Does paralactin have any effects on the behaviour of the fish comparable to those induced by thyroxine? What, if any, is the role of the ACTH and the hormones of the interrenals? The urohypophysis, a neurosecretory organ of the posterior spinal cord, has been implicated in osmo-regulation but its role remains conjectural (Ireland, 1969), as does that of the saccus vasculosus and the neurosecretory parts of the brain. Some anadromous fish stop feeding when they move into fresh water, a typical example is the salmon, and this has been interpreted as a method of reducing the amount of water swallowed by the fish during a period when a major physiological problem is the tendency for the internal environment of the fish to become excessively diluted. Do trachurus sticklebacks reduce their feeding when they move from sea water to fresh water, because such a reduction would have important consequences for their reproductive biology (Chapter 9)?

In contrast to the relatively extensive studies on the osmotic problems associated with migration, and on the factors that initiate migration, there is virtually no information on the factors that bring the spring migration to an end. Some clues on the factors that may be involved come from studies on the type of habitat in which sticklebacks prefer to build their nests during the breeding season (see also Chapter 11). In one such study a comparison was made between trachurus and leiurus fish. Leiurus males preferred to nest amongst *Oenanthe* plants whereas trachurus males preferred to nest amongst *Elodea*. When given a choice, the leiurus males built their nests on a mud substrate but the trachurus males built on sand (there do not seem to be any sticklebacks that prefer to build on rock). Trachurus males spent more time riding a current of water than leiurus males, who preferred to stay in still water, although both nested in still water. Even the quality of the water was a relevant factor, for trachurus males showed a preference for clear water while leiurus males preferred water discoloured by organic material. The way in which these preferences were determined probably ruled out the possibility that these preferences were the result of short term pre-experimental learning (Hagen, 1967).

These findings suggest two plausible mechanisms by which these preferences could be determined. The fish may be genetically programmed to react to certain environmental conditions such as vegetation, substrate or water quality by ending their migration and initiating breeding activities. Alternatively, the fish may learn the qualities of their breeding areas in the few weeks or months that they spend in the area as young before the autumn migration. These two mechanisms are not mutually exclusive and could operate to reinforce each other and so ensure that the fish select the appropriate breeding areas. The relative importance of these two mechanisms could probably be tested by keeping trachurus and leiurus fish under the same conditions from birth and then testing their preferences when they are sexually mature.

The presence of fish already breeding may also be a cue that terminates the migration.

There is a small piece of evidence that fish may return to the area of their birth in order to breed. After the breeding grounds of a population of anadromous trachurus fish had been extensively fished during one summer, the following year relatively few fish bred in the same area. This drop in the population may have been a result of the destruction of eggs and fry during the fishing (Hagen, 1967). But it still remains to be shown unambiguously that sticklebacks do return to the stream of their birth to breed.

Finally, the question has to be posed, what is the adaptive significance of the migration of the trachurus sticklebacks? Since leiurus sticklebacks do not make extensive migrations between fresh and salt water, such migrations cannot be essential for the success of the stickleback. In general the functional significance of migrations is poorly understood. Even in a thorough review on fish migrations, little space is devoted to the topic (Harden Jones, 1968). This is a true reflection of the current state of knowledge of the problem. The most plausible explanation is that by possessing this behavioural polyphenism such that a segment of the stickleback population of an area migrates to the sea where it feeds and overwinters, while the other segment of the population remains in the river system, the population exploits a wider range of habitats than if all the population either migrated or remained as residents. The energy costs that must be met by the migrating fish both in swimming and in making the physiological adjustments to the changes in the salinity of the water are probably relatively small when expressed as a proportion of the energy expenditure during the entire life history, and so are more than compensated by the new habitat that becomes available for exploitation. Certainly both the migratory and non-migratory forms are widely distributed and abundant.

To ensure the integrity and necessary adaptations of the two forms, a restriction in the gene flow between the two forms would seem to be necessary. The extent to which this restriction is achieved, and the mechanisms involved are discussed in Chapter 14.

9. Reproduction: The Female

In comparison with the male, the female three-spined stickleback has the less spectacular role in reproduction. Her role is the production of eggs and the spawning of those eggs in the appropriate place, the nest of a male. Not surprisingly then, the reproductive biology of the female has attracted less attention than that of the male. Nevertheless, a considerable body of relevant information is available, in some respects more than is available for other species of fish.

Sticklebacks less than 9 mm long have gonads that cannot be characterised as male or female. In this undifferentiated period, the germ cells which are destined to give rise to the eggs or sperm are enclosed in a pair of genital ridges. These ridges lie beneath the pronephric (head kidney) ducts and are distinctly marked off from surrounding tissue. The genital ridges take the shape of definitive ovaries in female larvae about 9 mm long. At this stage the paired ovaries are about 1 mm long, but the oviduct is incomplete. As the fish grows, the ovaries lengthen, the oviducts from each ovary fuse posteriorly and this common oviduct opens into the cloaca (Swarup, 1958c). The wall of the ovary has three layers, the outermost of these is the peritoneum, an epithelial layer that is continuous with the lining of the body cavity. Internal to the peritoneum, there is a thick layer of connective tissue, while the innermost layer is formed by the germinal epithelium. It is this germinal epithelium that gives rise to the ova. The lumen of the ovary is continuous with the oviduct. As the ovary enlarges with the growth of the fish, the ovarian lumen is invaded by evaginations of the ovarian wall which form transverse lamellae and in these lamellae the developing oocytes are embedded (Craig-Bennett, 1931; Stanworth, 1953).

In vertebrates such as fish, the development of the ova can be divided into fairly distinct stages and this is true of the stickleback.

Initially, the germ cells or oogonia divide by normal mitotic division to give rise to oocytes. The oocytes enlarge, and each has a distinct nucleus which contains numerous nucleoli arranged around the nuclear membrane. Each oocyte becomes surrounded by layers of cells. The most external of these layers is the theca, which is several cells thick and is formed by fibroblasts that migrate from the connective tissue layer. Internal to this is the follicular epithelium or granulosa layer, a single layer of cells derived from the germinal epithelium. Immediately external to the plasma membrane of the oocyte there develops the vitelline membrane, a layer that looks nearly structureless but which may have transverse striations. This vitelline membrane may also be called the oolema, the zona pellucida or the chorion. At about the same time as the vitelline membrane appears, the nucleoli in the nucleus of the oocyte disperse. The appearance of yolk is the next prominent event in the maturation of the oocyte. Initially, yolk formation or vitellogenesis is associated with vacuoles which first appear in the perifery of the cytoplasm, but which eventually fill all the cytoplasm. It is at this time that the thecal and follicular layers become very distinct. Yolk formation then continues in the cytoplasm and the mature ovum filled with a great mass of extra-vesicular yolk surrounded by a thin layer of cytoplasm is formed. The meiotic divisions of the nucleus which reduce the chromosome number from the diploid to the haploid condition, that is from forty-two to twenty-one, is believed to take place at spawning (Stanworth, 1953; Tromp-Blom, 1959).

Not all the oocytes develop at the same rate so that, just prior to the first spawning, the ovary contains oocytes in almost all stages of development. A typical time scale for oocyte maturation would be that oogonial division takes place in the breeding season or, in an under-yearling female, when the fish is about 15–20 mm long; the enlargement of the oocyte and arrangement of nucleoli around the nuclear membrane takes place during late summer, with the appearance of vacuoles associated with yolk formation in the autumn and early winter. The final rapid deposition of yolk and thickening of the vitelline membrane does not take place until the spring. Immediately after the first spawning, mature ova are absent from the ovary for these have been spawned, but most stages of the oocyte are still present with the early developmental stages predominating (Stanworth, 1953; Tromp-Blom, 1959). During the period of oocyte maturation, the ovary forms an increasing proportion of the total body weight of the female. In late summer and early autumn, the ovaries account for about two per cent of the total body weight, but in early winter this value has reached about four per cent. In the

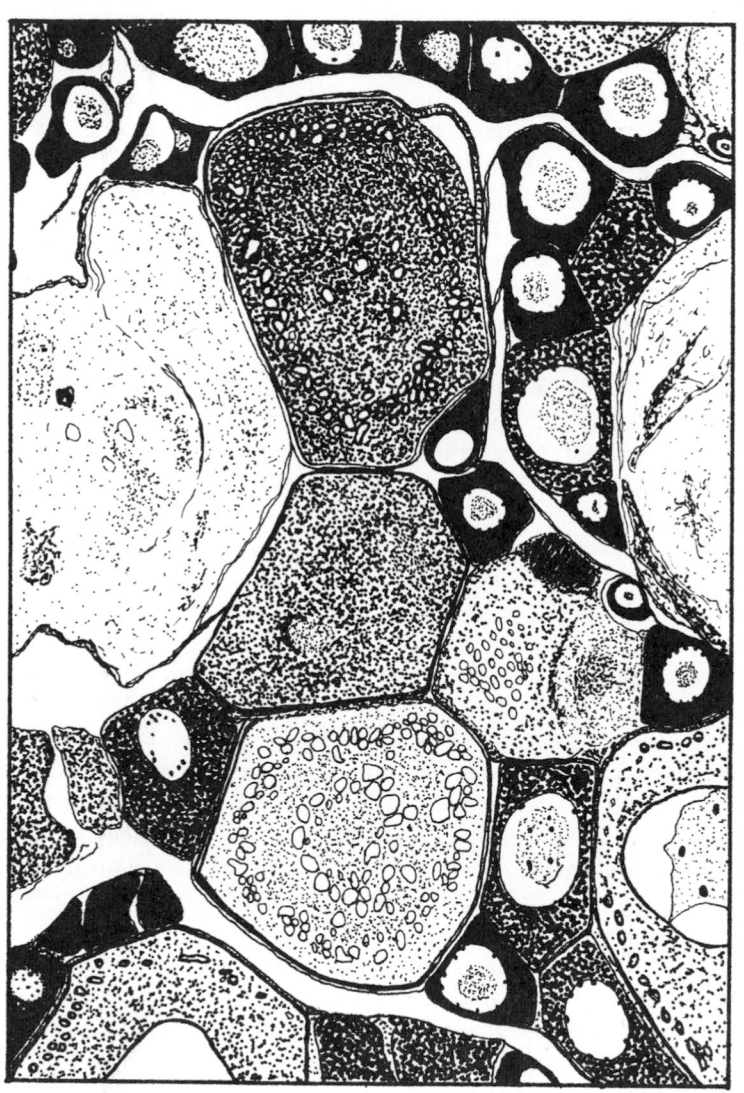

(a)

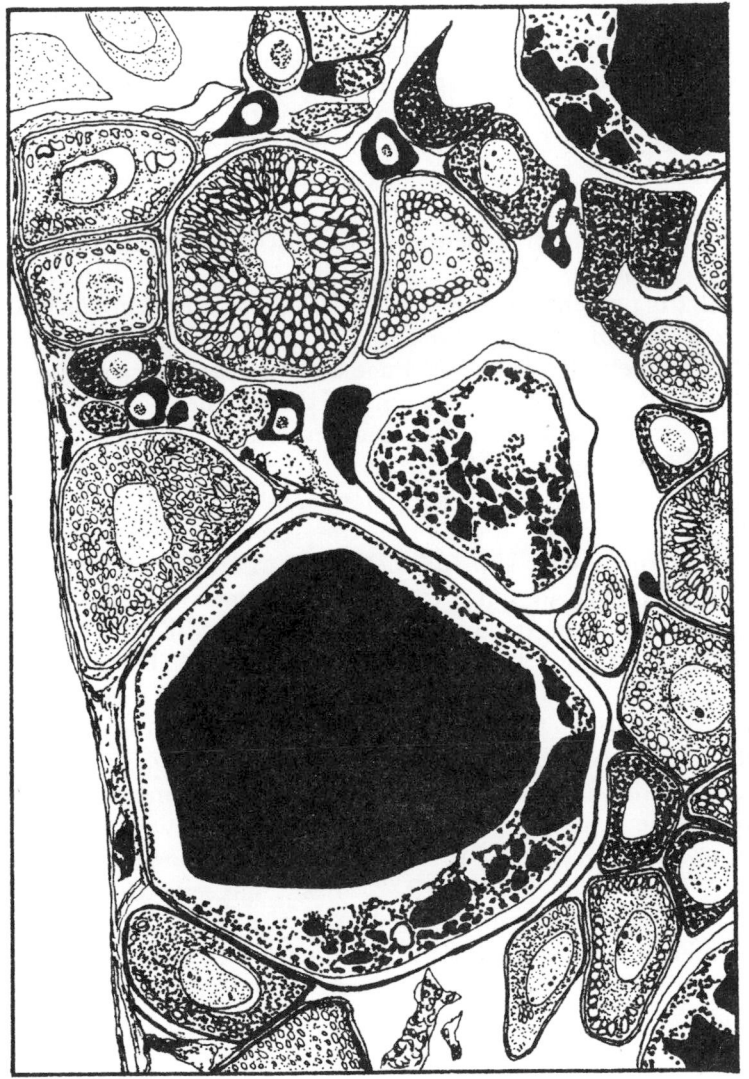

(b)

Fig. 32. Drawing of histological sections of ovaries of female *Gasterosteus aculeatus* that were sacrificed in January. (a) Female kept under natural day-lengths, note that no oocytes have developed past the vesicular yolk stage and that earlier developmental stages predominate; (b) female kept under constant illumination for 6 weeks, ovaries contain yolk-filled oocytes.

breeding season the ovaries account for between eight and thirty per cent of the total body weight depending on how recently the female has spawned (Meakins, 1974; Evans and Wootton, unpublished). Accompanying these changes in the ovaries there are also changes in the liver. In the period between August and December, the liver forms about five per cent of the total body weight and has a relatively high percentage of dry matter. At this time, the bulk of the glycogen reserves of the female are in the liver. During the spawning period, the liver forms about four per cent of the total body weight and has a much lower percentage of dry matter while the ovaries now contain the bulk of the glycogen. In the post-breeding period, the glycogen content of the ovaries falls abruptly, while that of the liver increases, but the percentage of dry material in the liver remains low, so that percentage of glycogen in the dry matter of the liver is a maximum at a time when the percentage of dry matter of the liver is a minimum. The total glycogen content of the female is a maximum in the period between August and December, and a minimum during the spawning period (Immers, 1953).

What factors control the development and maturation of the ovaries and their oocytes and so set the stage for the onset of breeding during the spring and summer? For an animal such as the stickleback which lives in temperate and sub-arctic regions, three factors immediately spring to mind as likely to control the onset of breeding. These factors are temperature, light and food. The physical factors of temperature and light show distinct seasonal changes and it is likely that the biotic factor of food supply also changes seasonally.

An early study by Craig-Bennett (1931) had suggested that temperature was the most important external factor controlling the maturation of the gonads, but Eekhoudt (1946) showed that the photoperiod was probably more significant. In a long series of experiments, Baggerman (1957, 1972) has analysed the relative importance of photoperiod and temperature. Unusually in this type of study, a behavioural rather than a histological criterion of sexual maturity was used. Mature females were those that showed egg laying.

On the basis of her experiments, Baggerman considered that there were four phases in the development of sexual maturity. Phase 0 was found only in juvenile fish which were usually less than 22 mm long, that is in young fish in the June and July after their birth. Fish in phase 0 did not mature when kept under constant conditions of sixteen hours of light per day (afterwards referred to as 16L 8D) and 20°C even though kept in these conditions for almost a year. In contrast to this, fish in phase 1 would mature if kept on a regime of

16L 8D and at 20°C, but fish in phase 1 could be sub-divided into two groups. Fish in phase 1a showed an acceleration in the rate of gonadal maturation when kept under a photoperiod of eight hours of light and sixteen hours of dark (8L 16D) and at low temperature (4°C), whereas fish in phase 1b showed no such response. All fish in phase 1 could be kept sexually immature by maintaining them on a constant regime of 8L 16D and 20°C. Phase 2 fish became mature on a regime of 8L 16D and 20°C, as well as on 16L 8D and 20°C.

When females were caught in the wild between November and May and exposed to 16L 8D and 20°C, they all matured. The time taken to reach maturity decreased from about thirty one days for November fish to two days for May fish. If females caught between November and early January were kept at 8L 16D and 20°C, very few became mature. After January, the percentage of females maturing under the conditions of short daylength and high water temperature increased rapidly, and all the females caught in March matured under these conditions. Wild-caught fish matured more rapidly when kept at 16L 8D rather than 8L 16D. These data on wild-caught fish taken together with the data on fish reared in the laboratory suggest that under natural conditions phase 0 lasts from when the young hatch until late July, phase 1 from August through until late winter or early spring and phase 2 from early spring until the start of the breeding season.

For females in phases 1b and 2, an increase in daylength increased the rate of gonadal maturation at both high and low temperatures. Baggerman thought that light of an intensity less than about 300 lux might be less effective, although light of a higher intensity had no additional accelerating effect on maturation. However, light of an intensity as low as 5 lux induced normal gonadal maturation (McInerney and Evans, 1970), who also showed that the effect of light was relatively independent of its wavelength. Fish that were illuminated by purple, blue, green or red light showed similar rates of gonadal development.

There is evidence that it is not the total amount of light that is important, but its distribution within the day (Baggerman, 1969, 1972). Normally, when a light regime of 8L 16D was imposed on fish in the autumn, none matured. But when the eight hours of light was split into two components, a period that lasted six hours, then a period of darkness, then another period of two hours of light, certain sequences allowed a high proportion of the fish to mature. A sequence of 6L-8D-2L-8D allowed seventy-eight per cent of the fish to mature. Sequences of 6L-6D-2L-10D and 6L-11D-2L-5D were also relatively successful. A photoperiod of 16L 32D has the same ratio of light to dark as 8L 16D, but was in practice almost as effective as 16L 8D in inducing sexual maturation. The causal mechanism that mediates these effects of photoperiod is not understood.

The effect of temperature on the rate of sexual maturation depended on the phase the fish was in. At long daylengths, higher temperatures accelerated the rate of maturation, but at short daylengths such acceleration occurred only if the fish were in phase 2. If the fish were in either phase 1b or phase 2, then long daylengths permitted gonadal maturation even at temperatures as low at 5°C. This may be important in allowing fish to breed in areas where even in spring and early summer the water temperatures are low. Clearly then, for most of the year, long daylengths are both a necessary and, except at very low water temperatures, a sufficient external condition for gonadal maturation.

There are three exceptions to this rule. In phase 0, neither high temperatures nor long daylengths are able to induce sexual maturation, but fish are only in phase 0 for a short period at the start of their life and the phase does not recur. Fish could be brought out of phase 0 by keeping them at 16L 8D at low temperatures or at 8L 16D and 20°C. The second exception is that females are refractory to the effects of long daylengths for about a month and a half after the end of the breeding season. This refractory period may be a mechanism to prevent a premature maturation of the gonads in a period when natural daylengths are long and water temperatures still high. The third exception is for fish in phase 1a. These fish do become mature at long daylengths and high water temperatures, but may also become mature if kept for a period on a short daylength (8L 16D) and at a low temperature (4°C) and then on a short daylength and a high temperature (20°C). In other words, for fish in phase 1a, a combination of short daylengths and low temperatures stimulates sexual maturation. In natural conditions, fish are in phase 1a at the start of winter, so that the environmental conditions will be just those that prepare the fish for sexual maturation.

Because in the majority of her studies Baggerman used a behavioural criterion of sexual maturity the histological equivalents of the four phases are undefined and indeed there may not be clear histological equivalents for these phases. Schneider (1969) obtained histological evidence that a combination of long daylengths and high temperatures stimulated maturation of the oocytes, while a combination of short daylengths and high temperature caused a cessation of ovarian development in females that had been collected between October and January. At both long and short daylengths, low temperature allowed slight ovarian development. Perhaps plausible histological equivalents to the phases defined by Baggerman are that phase 0 is the initial period of oogonial division and formation of the oocytes; phase 1 probably corresponds to the period of growth of the oocytes, the definition of thecal and follicular layers, and the vacuole formation that marks the initial stage of yolk formation; whilst phase 2 represents the period of intra-vesicular and extra-vesicular yolk formation and the final maturation of the oocyte. Fish that were kept from October for almost a year at 8L 16D and 20°C, did not mature and their ovaries contained no oocytes that had passed the stage of vesicle formation. This suggests that it is the process of vitellogenesis that is stimulated by long daylengths (Baggerman, 1972) (Fig. 32).

Under favourable conditions of long daylengths, high temperatures and adequate supplies of food, sticklebacks can mature within four or five months of hatching. In the seasonal climate of the northern temperate zone, a period of short daylengths, low temperatures and perhaps in some cases inadequate food supplies is interposed between the hatching of the young and their sexual maturation. The timing of maturation in such a zone depends, as shown above, on the interaction between external environmental factors and internal changes in the fish. This raises the question of the pathway by which changes in external factors such as daylength and temperature influence the status of the gonads.

By virtue of its close relationship to the central nervous system which will detect the changes in the external environment and the probability that the ovaries are a target organ for one or more of its hormones, the pituitary is in a central position to mediate the effects of external factors on gonadal maturation.

This possibility was investigated by Ahsan and Hoar (1963). They maintained fish at 8L 16D. Under these conditions no females became mature, or reached the stage at which their ovaries contained many large oocytes. Other fish held under the same conditions were injected with various hormones. The hormone most effective in inducing further gonadal maturation was the mammalian gonadotropin, luteinising hormone (LH). Another mammalian gonadotropin, follicle stimulating hormone (FSH), was not effective in inducing gonadal maturation. A crude extract of salmon pituitaries also caused some gonadal stimulation but less than the purified mammalian LH. None of the treatments induced full sexual maturation with the females laying eggs, and it is not clear whether this merely reflects a difference between mammalian pituitary gonadotropins and piscine gonadotropin or that factors in addition to gonadotropin are required to induce complete sexual maturation.

These results suggest, at least tentatively, that under long daylengths the pituitary is more active in producing gonadotropin and this gonadotropin stimulates the ovary to complete its maturation. Studies on other species of fish suggest that gonadotropin is essential if yolk formation is to occur in the oocytes (Hoar, 1969). The early stages of ovarian maturation do not seem to depend on gonadotropin, at least at the levels that are required to stimulate vitellogenesis. The mechanism by which a short daylength combined with low temperature can also stimulate sexual maturation so that females treated in this way can mature under conditions of short daylengths and high temperatures remains obscure. Studies on the ultrastructure of the stickleback pituitary have indicated that the cells that are thought to produce gonadotropin are maximally active during the spawning period, which is a stage when yolk formation is occurring most rapidly (Leatherland, 1970b; Benjamin, 1974a).

Two other external factors have also been implicated as factors controlling ovarian maturation, food supply and crowding; but neither of these factors has received the attention paid to the effects of light and temperature. When groups of females were kept at different food levels, those receiving the lowest food ration produced fewest mature females. Those females on the lowest food ration that matured did so at a smaller size than females at the higher food levels (Wootton, 1973a). Crowding of females inhibited ovarian maturation, but it was not clear whether this was an effect of crowding *per se* or that when crowded some females received insufficient food (Schneider, 1969).

Thus the onset of breeding in the female depends primarily on the photoperiod, permissive temperatures and an adequate food supply, which interact with changes internal to the female, to ensure that breeding in the natural environment takes place in spring and summer.

During the breeding season, which lasts two or three months, the female stickleback is capable of producing several clutches of eggs. The duration of the breeding phase and the number of spawnings depends partly on the external factors of light, temperature and food supply, and partly on factors intrinsic to the female.

Females kept at 16L 8D and 20°C had a breeding season that lasted sixty days on average, during which time up to fifteen clutches were produced. At 8L 16D and 20°C the breeding period lasted only six and a half days on average during which only a mean of two clutches were produced. The effect of this short daylength depended to some extent on when it was imposed. If it was not imposed until after the first spawning, the breeding period lasted eleven days on average and a mean of three clutches were produced (Baggerman, 1957). These results are significant in the analysis of the causal mechanisms of ovarian maturation, for they imply that even at the start of the breeding season, only a portion of the oocytes have entered phase 2 and can mature at 8L 16D and 20°C, a conclusion supported by the histological evidence that at the start of the breeding season oocytes at all stages of maturation are present in the ovary (Tromp-Blom, 1959). But in natural environments, the day-lengths increase steadily during the spring and although the temperature may show marked variation there will be an upward trend, so that changes in these two factors are not likely to be significant in determining the length of the breeding season. However, in the brook stickleback *Culaea inconstans* breeding is inhibited once the water temperature gets above 19 or 20°C (see Chapter 17).

Variations in food supply also influence the number of spawnings, the length of time between spawnings and the weight of the female during the breeding season. Females that were fed on *ad libitum* ration until they had started spawning and were then given no more food produced at most only one more clutch of eggs. The lower the food ration a female received during the breeding season, the fewer times she spawned and the longer the interval between successive spawnings (Wootton, 1973a and unpublished).

Even given favourable environmental conditions of long day-lengths, high temperatures and adequate food supplies, the breeding season comes to an end. Since the external factors remain suitable, this termination of the breeding season must be a result of changes internal to the female. One possibility is that the supply of oocytes which can mature becomes exhausted, or perhaps the cells in the pituitary which produce gonadotropin stop producing the hormone. As yet no adequate explanation has been given for the ending of the breeding season when external factors remain favourable. Under constant, favourable, environmental conditions there is an alternation of breeding and non-breeding phases, so that after a refractory period of about one and a half months that occurs immediately after a breeding phase, the female responds to the favourable conditions by once more becoming sexually mature. When females were kept constantly at 16L 8D and 20°C, the non-reproductive period lasted an average of 168 days (Baggerman, 1957).

With the onset of the breeding season, a female starts a series of cycles each of which ends with a spawning. The period between successive spawnings can be called the inter-spawning interval (ISI).

During this interval there are changes in the histology of the ovaries, the behaviour of the female and the weight of the female. Each of these changes will be considered in turn.

Immediately after spawning, the ovaries of the female contain no mature eggs, but apart from this there are oocytes in all stages of maturation present with a preponderance of the early maturational stages. Over the next few days, the later maturational stages become more prominent and eventually mature eggs are present (Tromp-Blom, 1959). Until the eggs are spawned the external genital aperture is closed by a transparent membrane which isolates the ovarian cavity from the external environment. The lumen of the ovary contains a fluid in which the eggs are bathed, the ionic composition of this fluid is somewhat similar to that of the blood serum (Table VI) (Thomopoulos, 1953). Not all the oocytes that develop are spawned. In some, the vitelline membrane breaks down and the oocyte is invaded by the follicular cells which phagocytose the yolk and cytoplasm of the oocyte. Such structures are known as preovulatory *corpora lutea* or *corpora atretica*. The follicular and thecal cells left after the egg has been ovulated form the postovulatory *corpora lutea*. Ovulation, that is the release of the eggs into the ovarian lumen, takes place shortly before spawning (Stanworth, 1953).

A female with mature eggs must spawn these eggs in the nest of a male if the eggs are to be fertilised rather than eaten. This means that the female must respond to the courtship of the male. A female that is ready to spawn tends to wander away from the school of females and juveniles into the area where the males hold territories. The female responds to the approach of a male by adopting a head-up posture and orientating towards the male, a movement graphically described as weather-vaning (Sevenster, 1973). This posture and movement makes the female's silver belly, which is distended with eggs, prominent. When the male leads back to the nest the female follows, keeping behind and slightly above the male. If she is ready to spawn, she pushes her way into the nest after the male has shown the nest entrance. Once the female is in the nest, the male induces her to spawn by quivering, butting the female gently but repeatedly on the flanks. Once a female is in a male's nest, she can be induced to spawn even in the absence of the male by nudging her flanks gently with a glass rod (Tinbergen, 1951). At spawning, the female holds her tail raised and slightly to one side, and it can be seen quivering slightly. Immediately after spawning, the female wriggles out of the nest and leaves the male's territory, frequently being driven out by the attacks of the male. A ripe female rarely spends more than a minute or so in the male's nest, though longer periods do occur.

In natural circumstances the female rejoins the group of females after spawning, but under experimental conditions a cycle of responsiveness to a courting male during the inter-spawning interval can be demonstrated. Such a cycle was shown when females were kept isolated during the inter-spawning interval except for short periods each day when they were exposed to a strongly courting male. For a few hours after spawning, some females responded to the approach of the male by adopting a head-up posture and a few even followed the male back to his nest. Not all females were this responsive and some showed no courtship behaviour after spawning, especially when the male was relatively aggressive towards them. Towards the middle of the inter-spawning interval, very few females showed any courtship responses at all when the male approached but they often fled and were attacked by the male. As the inter-spawning interval progressed, elements of the female's courtship behaviour reappeared. First just the head-up posture and slight following occurred. But eventually some females followed the male down to the nest and nosed or attempted to nose into the nest. At this stage, the nosing was either so badly orientated that the female did not get her snout in the nest entrance, or she withdrew after nosing a short way into the nest. In a few cases, the female entered the nest but emerged without spawning, but within an hour or so of this stage, the female spawned successfully (Baggerman, 1964; Wootton, 1974a, b). If a female is very ripe, she may go straight to the nest when she sees a male fanning or creeping through the nest, and will enter the nest without the nest entrance being shown by the male. The presence of the female in the nest then induces the male to start quivering and spawning takes place although part of the normal courtship sequence described in Chapter 12 has been by-passed.

In the absence of mature males, a ripe female eventually spawns the eggs without stimulation by the male. When this happens, the eggs are eaten either by the female herself or by other fish.

One of the male characteristics which seems to be important for the female is the red of his nuptial coloration. Evidence for this comes from two types of study, mate preference tests and measurements of the colour sensitivity of the female.

In mate preference tests, a ripe female is given the choice of courting and, in some experiments, mating with one of two males. The female has to make a choice between the males which differ in the degree of development of the red throat and belly. Such tests indicate that the female tends to select the male with the brightest breeding colours. In his study of the sticklebacks of the Chehalis River system (see also Chapters 5 and 14), McPhail (1969) found that given a choice between a normal male with the typical red throat and a "black" male, normal females and even females from the "black" stickleback population preferred the normal, red male. Similarly, Semler (1971) found that in preference tests using males from the polymorphic population in Lake Wapato (see Chapters 5 and 14), the females preferred the males with the best developed breeding colours.

In order to measure the sensitivity of sticklebacks to various colours, their spectral sensitivity, Cronly-Dillon and Sharma (1968) made use of the optomotor response of the fish. When the fish are kept in a circular container and a pattern of vertical stripes is displayed on the walls of the container, the fish will swim around the container when the striped pattern rotates. The fish follow the stripes trying to maintain a constant position relative to the stripes. Interference filters were used to produce stripes of different colours and neutral density filters used to alter the intensity of illumination until the fish no longer showed the optomotor response because they could not see the stripes. Females were most sensitive to light of wavelengths 510 nm and 594 nm. The males had sensitivity peaks at 502 nm and 594 nm. These peaks were stable throughout the year, but during the spawning period the threshold for a response to light of the red peak at 594 nm was lower for females than males. In the spawning period, the females are more sensitive to the red end of the spectrum than are males, a difference that disappears during the winter.

Although colour is important, it is not essential for successful courtship. When fish were kept under monochromatic light, they still mated (Leiner, 1931a), while the evolution of forms such as the "black" stickleback of the Chehalis River and the polymorphic males of Lake Wapato indicates that males that lack any red colour can successfully court females.

In addition to the behavioural changes shown by the female during the inter-spawning interval, there are marked changes in weight (Fig. 33). Immediately prior to a spawning, a female weighed between fifteen and twenty-five per cent more than she did immediately after the previous spawning. This gain in weight was lost when the eggs were spawned. The changes in weight seen during the inter-spawning interval were a reflection of changes in weight of the ovaries not changes in weight of the somatic tissue of the fish. With an adequate food supply, the changes in weight of the ovaries were not reflected in changes in the weight of the somatic tissue. After a spawning, the ovaries formed eight to nine per cent of the total body weight, and just prior to a spawning they formed more than twenty per cent of the total body weight. The increase in weight of the ovaries represented an increase in both the water content and dry matter content of the ovaries. At the time of spawning, the ovaries became hydrated so that the dry matter represented about 17.6 per cent of

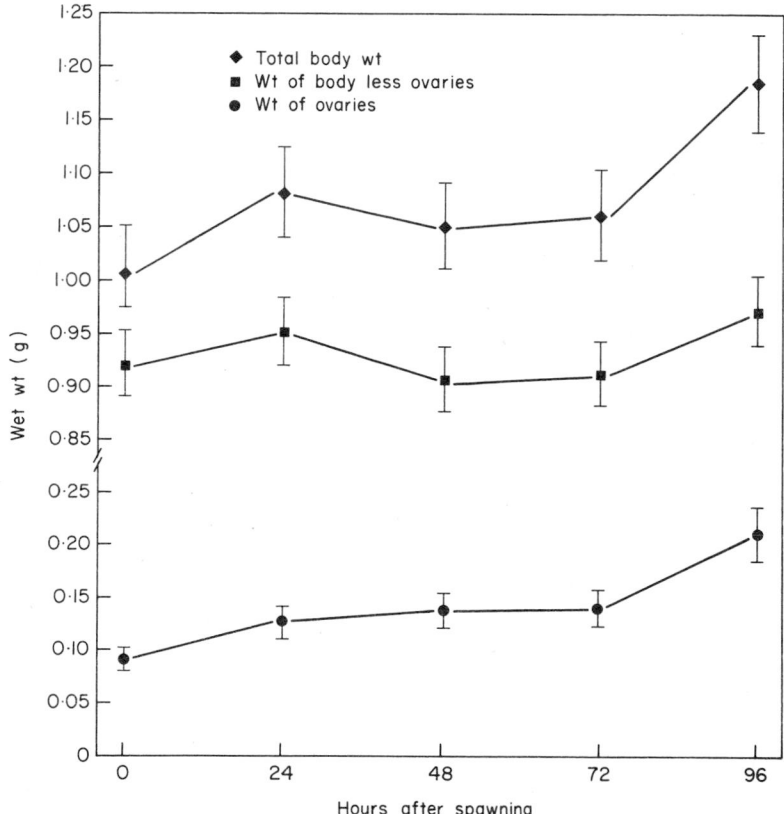

Fig. 33. Changes in wet wt of intact body, body without ovaries and the ovaries of female *Gasterosteus aculeatus* in the 96 hr after spawning. Means have been adjusted by covariance analysis on logarithmically transformed data to refer to a female of 47 mm total length (see Wootton, 1974a).

the ovaries' weight, but this increased to 20 per cent or more by the middle of the inter-spawning interval. No significant change in the calorific value of the ovarian material could be measured, but the calorific value of the somatic tissue did change, being a minimum at the time of spawning and a maximum about halfway through the inter-spawning interval. This change in the calorific value of the somatic tissue suggests that there was an export of relatively high energy substances into the ovaries as the weight of the ovaries increased. This cost of producing eggs was also reflected in the observation that the condition of the female measured as W/L^3 (see Chapter 3) was inversely related to the weight of eggs produced relative to the weight of the female. Egg production imposes a strain on the female that is reflected in both calorific changes and changes in the condition of the female (Wootton, 1974a).

In an experiment in which females were fed on minced beef, they made a net gain of energy at a rate of about two calories per hour during the inter-spawning interval. This gain was primarily the growth of the ovaries, and so was lost when the eggs were spawned. When females were fed on *Tubifex* worms *ad libitum*, the conversion of food to eggs was about thirty per cent efficient, that is:

$$\frac{(\text{calorific value of eggs produced} \times 100)}{(\text{calorific value of food consumed})} = 30.$$

Since a portion of the food consumed was lost as faeces, the conversion of food assimilated into eggs spawned was even more efficient.

The length of the inter-spawning interval depends partly on the rate at which food is supplied, but about sixty hours is the shortest yet observed, with three, four and five days being the most common. Beukema (1968) reported that in the week before spawning, the food consumption of female was much higher than average, but that on the day of spawning and for a few days after, food consumption was reduced. Certainly in the twenty-four hours before spawning, food consumption is reduced, but this is not always true of the day after spawning (Fig. 34). The weight changes of females during the inter-spawning interval showed two patterns. Some females gained weight rapidly even over the first half of the period, but other females gained little or even lost weight over the first day or two, and then gained weight very rapidly up to spawning. This variation in the rate of weight gain may reflect individual differences in the rate of food consumption, or it may indicate that some females had to make good the drain of high energy substances incurred during egg production.

Unfortunately little is known of the causal factors that control the changes that take place during the inter-spawning interval, or how the events are synchronised so that the female shows the correct courtship response at a time when the eggs have been ovulated and are ready to be spawned. Studies on other species of fish have indicated that gonadotropin produced by the pituitary is essential if vitellogenesis, ovulation and the hydration of the ovaries are to occur (Barr, 1968; Liley, 1969), but the role of estrogens produced by the ovaries is less clear, and other steroid hormones produced by the interrenals may also play a role.

How many eggs will a female stickleback produce during a breeding season? This will be the product of the number of

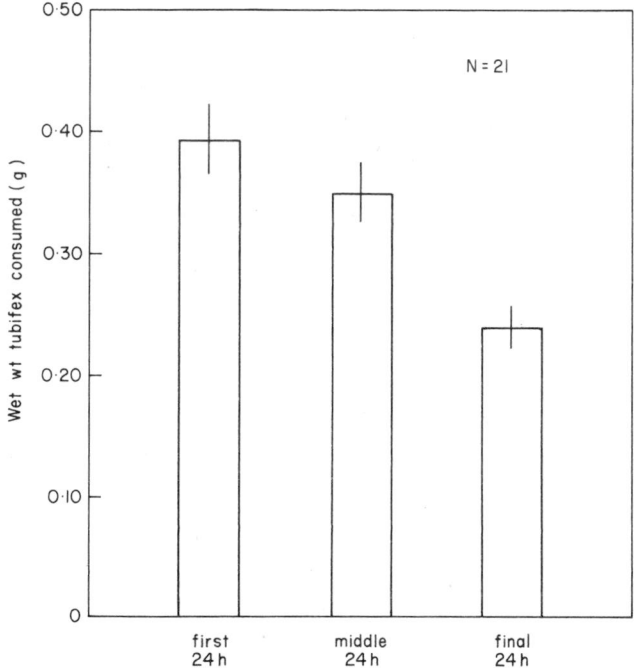

Fig. 34. Consumption of *Tubifex* by female *Gasterosteus aculeatus* during the interval between successive spawnings. Mean wt consumed ± 1 standard error.

spawnings and the average number of eggs produced per spawning. Both these items depend on the size of the female, bigger fish produce more eggs per spawning and also spawn more times during the breeding season as long as the food supply is adequate (Wooton, 1973a). The number of eggs laid at a spawning varies from twenty to thirty for small fish weighing around 0.40 g, which is the minimum size at which females become mature, to three or four hundred eggs for large females weighing three grams or more. Females from the population of unusually large sticklebacks living in Mayer Lake on the Queen Charlotte Islands (see Chapters 5 and 14) produced an average of 257 eggs per spawning (Moodie, 1972b). The relationship between egg production per spawning and the size of the fish can be described by the relationships:

$$EP = aL^b$$

or

$$\log EP = \log a + b \log L$$

and

$$EP = c + dW$$

where EP is egg production measured either as the number of eggs or the weight of the eggs, L is the length of the fish, W is the weight of the fish and a, b, c and d are constants.

Hagen (1967) measured the lengths and number of eggs produced by leiurus, trachurus and semiarmatus females from the Little Campbell River in British Columbia. From his data, the relationship between standard length measured in millimetres and number of eggs produced was:

$$EP = aL^{2.43}.$$

The value of the constant a was different for the leiurus, trachurus and semiarmatus forms, so that for females of length 50 mm, a leiurus female would be expected to produce 133 eggs, a trachurus female 163 eggs and a semiarmatus female 154 eggs per spawning. This may indicate that there is a genetic difference affecting egg-production of the three forms, but because the trachurus form over-wintered in the sea, and all three forms occupied slightly different habitats in the river, the differences may simply reflect these environmental differences. A group of leiurus females kept in the laboratory under controlled temperature and light conditions and fed about 0.20 g of minced beef per day, yielded a relationship between length and number of eggs produced per spawning of:

$$EP = aL^{3.32}.$$

The females varied in length from 41 to 74 mm, while the minimum number of eggs produced was 40 and the maximum was 295 (Fig. 35) (Wootton, 1973b).

The relationship between the length of the female and the number of eggs produced depends on the more fundamental relationship between the weight of the female and egg production. That this is the more fundamental relationship can be shown by restricting the food supply to the female during the breeding season. As the female loses weight, her egg production per spawning also declines although

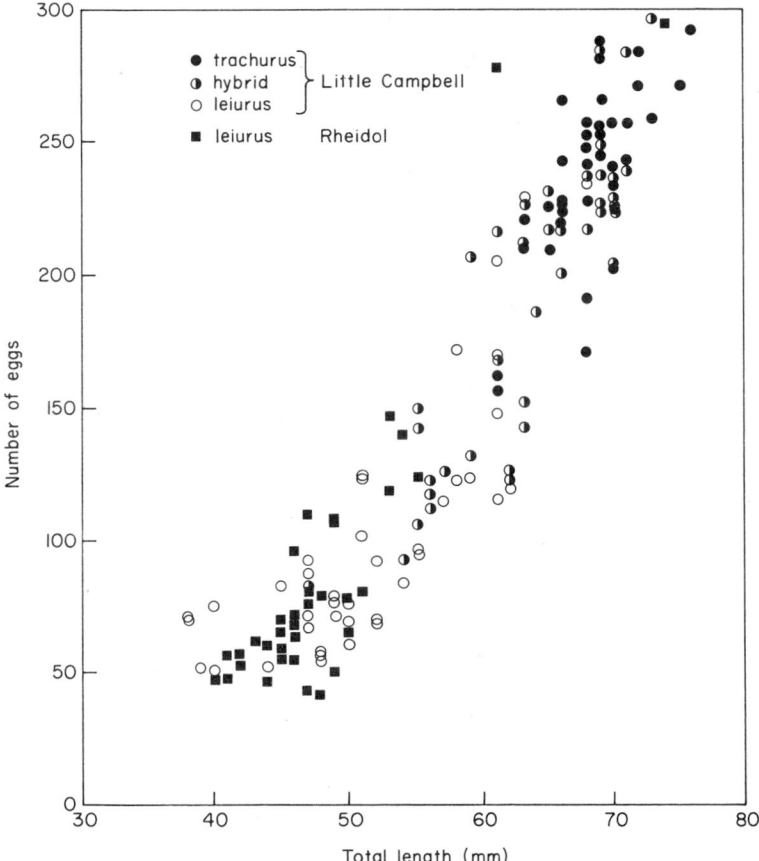

Fig. 35. Relationship between number of eggs produced per spawning and total length for female *Gasterosteus aculeatus* from Little Campbell River (after Hagen, 1967) and the Rheidol (after Wootton, 1973b).

the female does not shrink in length (Wootton, unpublished). For the group of leiurus fish described above, the relationship between the number of eggs spawned and the weight of the female after spawning was given by:

$$EP = -11.9 + 89.3W$$

where W was measured in grams.

The eggs are about 1.5 mm in diameter and weigh when fresh 0.0014–0.0025 g, and after drying to constant weight 0.00025–0.00044 g, the water content of the egg representing about twenty per cent of the total weight. For leiurus females, the relationship between egg production measured as fresh weight in grams and the weight of the fish, also measured in grams, was:

$$EP = -0.043 + 0.188W.$$

Food supply determines the maximum number of times that a female of a given size will spawn during the breeding season. On an *ad libitum* ration a female weighing a gram or more can spawn as many as twenty times in a breeding season of about sixty days, whereas a female of similar size receiving only about two per cent of her body weight of food per day will spawn only two or three times. Until there are quantitative estimates of food consumption under natural conditions, the total egg production in a natural population of sticklebacks cannot be estimated. If the food supply enables the females to consume the equivalent of eight per cent or more of their body weight per day, then the egg production is likely to form a significant proportion of the total annual production of the stickleback population. Consider a female weighing a gram and consuming the equivalent of eight per cent or more of her body weight of food per day during the breeding season. At each spawning she will produce around eighty eggs weighing about 0.150 g, and there will be perhaps ten spawnings during the breeding season. Thus the female will produce 800 eggs which weigh 1.5 g. The calorific value of the eggs is 5400 calories per g dry weight, so the female will have produced:

$$1.5 \times \frac{20}{100} \times 5400 \text{ calories of eggs,}$$

i.e.   1620 calories of eggs.

As described above, the efficiency of egg production is such that 30 calories of eggs will be produced by 100 calories of food consumed, so to produce 1620 calories of eggs, 5400 calories of food will have been consumed. If, as in Chapter 3, it is assumed that the food of the stickleback has a calorific value of 5000 calories per g dry weight and the dry matter represents twenty per cent of the total fresh weight of the food, then to produce the 800 eggs the stickleback will have consumed 5.4 g of food. Since in Chapter 3, it was estimated that it takes between 9 and 19 g of food to produce a stickleback weighing a gram, the total cost of producing the female and the eggs will be between about 14 and 24 g of food. The provisional nature of these calculations must be remembered, but they do indicate the amount of food that must be available for each fish in a population of sticklebacks.

Nikolskii (1969) suggested that food supply might affect not only the number of eggs produced by a fish, but also the quality of the eggs. A fish population, according to this theory, responds to a good food supply with both an increase in the number of eggs produced and an improvement in the quality of the eggs. In the case of the stickleback, the evidence for this dual mechanism is conflicting. In one study no relationship was found between either the level of the food supply and the size of the eggs or the size of the females and the size of the eggs produced (Wootton, 1973a, b). In contrast to this, Russian workers found that if they divided fish into "fast" growing and "slow" growing groups, the faster growing fish weighed more at maturity, produced relatively more eggs, but that these eggs weighed less and had a lower lipid and protein content than the eggs produced by the "slow" growing group. The individuals that grew most rapidly had a higher fat content in the body. The ecological significance of the differences in quality between the eggs of the "fast" and "slow" growing groups was not discussed (Potapova et al., 1968). Experiments in which females are kept on known food rations and their eggs analysed for lipid, protein and carbohydrate content would clarify the effect of food supply on egg quality.

The reproductive biology of the stickleback presents the intriguing picture of females producing, in spite of their small size, relatively large numbers of eggs, and the males expending considerable amounts of time, and perhaps energy, in caring for these eggs. It tends to be conventional biological wisdom that those animals which show parental care produce far fewer eggs or young than species that do not exhibit such care. The ability of the female stickleback to spawn several times during the breeding season means that far more eggs are produced than would seem likely from the number of eggs produced at a single spawning, this ability allied to the parental care shown by the male ensures that in spite of their small size, the parental sticklebacks produce sufficient eggs to provide adequate replacement for losses from the parental generation. The abundance and wide geographical distribution of the stickleback indicate just how successful this reproductive strategy has been.

10. Reproduction: The Male I
(Spermatogenesis and the Secondary Sexual Characters)

More has probably been written on the reproductive biology of the male three-spined stickleback than for any other single species of fish. Most of this attention has been directed at the behaviour of the male, and the importance of such studies for the development of ethological theory has already been mentioned. The physiological aspects have received less attention but a thorough, if in some places a tentative, account of most aspects of the reproductive biology of the male can now be given.

The paired testes of the male lie in a ventro-lateral position in the body cavity supported by mesenteries from the dorsal wall of the cavity. In mature males in spring, each testis is about 1.5 mm long and 0.9 mm in diameter and accounts for about one per cent of the total body weight. The thin visceral peritoneum which covers the testes contains many melanophores so that in contrast to a female's ovaries a male's testes are pigmented black. Why the testes should be heavily pigmented while the ovaries are virtually unpigmented remains unknown. Blood for each testis is supplied by a genital artery which enters the testis dorsally. Also found dorsally in each testis is the vas deferens, the tube which carries the sperm away from the testis to be released into the water at spawning. The vasa deferentia from each testis fuse and the common duct opens into the cloaca between the anus and the opening of the urinary bladder (Craig-Bennett, 1931). Sperm production is the primary function of the testes, but they are also endocrine organs producing steroid hormone(s), androgen(s), which are essential for the development of the secondary sexual characteristics of the mature male stickleback.

In each testis, the sperm-producing zone consists of between 150 and 200 tubules which radiate outwards from a dorsal hilus, where the primary tubules unite to form the vas deferens. The walls of the tubules consist of a layer of epithelial cells and a layer of connective tissue. Throughout the year a few spermatogonia or germ cells lie pressed against the wall of the tubule, while the cells which are thought to synthesise and secrete the androgens, the interstitial cells, are found in the tissue between the tubules. These interstitial cells reach their maximal development just prior to spawning (Courrier, 1921, 1922; Stanworth, 1953) (Fig. 36).

In young male sticklebacks the differentiation of the genital ridges into testes does not take place until the fish is about 14 mm long. As the fish grows in length, the germ cells continue to divide and the melanophores appear in the peritoneal covering of the testes. By the time the male is 25 mm long, the testes have become fully differentiated and contain most of the stages in the maturation of the sperm (Swarup, 1958c). However, the male does not become functionally mature, that is capable of completing a breeding cycle, until he is about 40 mm long.

Maturation of the spermatozoa in the male stickleback follows a pattern similar to other teleost fishes so far studied. Spermatogonia, the germ cells, which initially are about 6 μ in diameter, divide and grow giving rise to the primary spermatocytes which are 12 μ in diameter. These primary spermatocytes are contained in a sac or cyst. The origin of this sac is in some doubt. Early studies suggested that it was formed by the walls of the tubule, but a recent study of spermatogenesis in the brook stickleback (*Culaea inconstans*) has suggested that the sac is formed when a so-called companion cell enfolds the spermatogonium in folds of its plasma membranes (Ruby and McMillan, 1975). Within the sac, the primary spermatocytes derived from the original spermatogonium develop into secondary spermatocytes which can be distinguished from the primary spermatocytes because the chromatin material in the nucleus of the cells has condensed. The secondary spermatocytes give rise to the spermatids and these in turn develop into mature spermatozoa. Formation of the spermatids and spermatozoa is associated with the breakdown of the sac so that the sphermatozoa are released into the lumen of the tubule to be transported to the vas deferens (Stanworth, 1953). Mature spermatozoa have a flattened disc-shaped head which contains the paternal genetic material, a distinct middle piece containing mitochondria, and a tail which is a typical flagellum and is used for propelling the spermatozoa along (Swarup, 1958c).

Gametogenesis in the male seems to be less nicely controlled by the interaction of external environmental factors than it is in the female. In those males that survive for more than a year, division of the spermatogonia that will produce the following year's sperma-

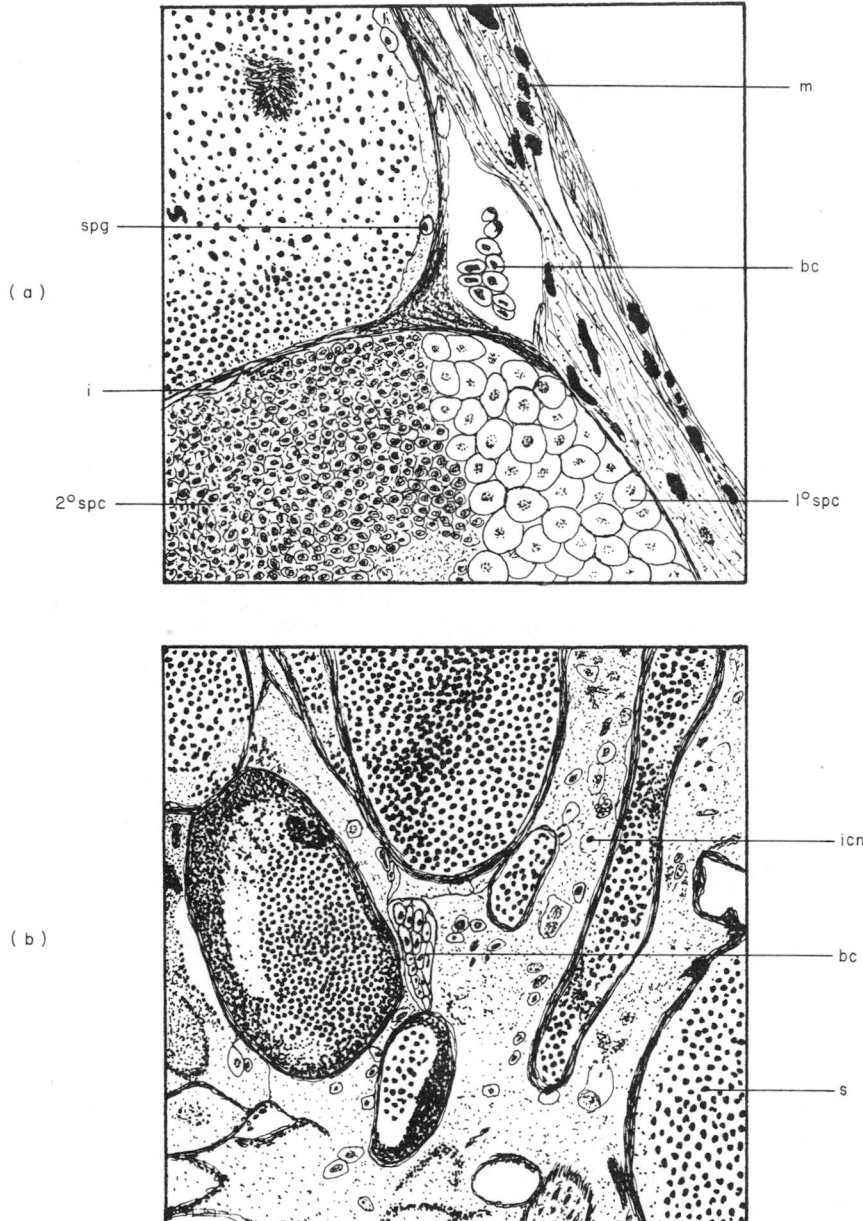

Fig. 36. Drawing of histological sections of testis of male *Gasterosteus aculeatus* (after Craig-Bennett, 1931). (a) Winter condition, reduced interstitium; (b) condition during breeding, wide interstitium and tubules full of spermatozoa. Key to lettering: bc, blood cell; i, interstitial cell; icn, nucleus of interstitial cell; m, melanophore; s, sphermatozoa; 1°spc, primary spermatocytes; 2°spc, secondary spermatocyte; spg, spermatogonium.

tozoa starts after the spermatozoa have been discharged during the current breeding season. If temperatures remain relatively high during the autumn the testes can, by mid-winter, contain mature sperm capable of fertilizing eggs (Craig-Bennett, 1931). But at this time the male is not behaviourally mature. Low temperatures and short daylengths inhibit sperm formation. The effects of high temperatures combined with short daylengths probably depends on the stage of spermatogenesis that has been reached. Stanworth (1953) reported that at high temperatures sperm formation from secondary spermatocytes went to completion in complete darkness, but Ahsan and Hoar (1963) and Schneider (1969) both showed that high temperatures combined with short daylengths inhibited spermatogenesis. It seems probable that long daylengths are the most important external factor controlling spermatogenesis.

Long daylengths are critical for the functional development of the interstitial cells. Only under conditions of long daylengths do the interstitial cells secrete sufficient androgen for the male to become sexually mature (Baggerman, 1957). When males were kept on a short photoperiod (8L 16D), the injection of mammal gonadotropic hormone, luteinizing hormone (LH), stimulated spermatogenesis and even the development of secondary sexual characters in some fish (Ahsan and Hoar, 1963). This suggests that both the maturation of the sperm and the development of the interstitial cells depends on a gonadotropic hormone released from the pituitary, and that the pathway by which light stimulates the onset of sexual maturation involves the hypothalamic region of the brain which in turn regulates the activity of the gonadotrope cells in the pituitary.

If a male stickleback is castrated, then maintained at long daylengths such as 16 hours of light and 8 hours of dark, he fails to develop the characteristic red throat and blue irises of the sexually mature male, the kidney tubules do not become modified to produce the glue used in nest-building and he fails to build a nest or show any sexual behaviour (Ikeda, 1933; Hoar, 1962a, b; Baggerman, 1966). All these characters can be evoked in a castrated male by hormone therapy with testosterone, a typical androgen.

Of the androgen-dependent secondary sexual characters of the male stickleback, the breeding colours are the most immediately striking, although the extent to which the breeding colours develop can vary considerably (Semler, 1971). Typically, the first sign of the appearance of the nuptial colours is the development of a patch of blue in the upper part of the iris and eventually the entire iris becomes blue. A blueish tinge also develops on the back. As the iris becomes blue, a red coloration develops in the throat region as the erythrophores expand. At the maximum expression of the nuptial colours, the underside of the mouth, the throat and fore-belly and the opercular region are all red. Because of a contraction of the melanophores, which contain a black pigment, the ground colour of the body lightens considerably. The blue colour of the iris is due to a reduction in the amount of guanin crystals in the guanophores (Titschack, 1922). An analysis of pigments from the throat region of mature males indicated that three pigments were present which together produced the characteristic red colour. The major pigment could not be defined chemically but behaved like a mono-hydroxy xanthophyll; two minor components were a carotene ester and astaxanthin. Even in immature males, the first two of these pigments were present though in reduced concentrations, which suggests that the appearance of the red colour is primarily a result of an increase in pigment concentration rather than a qualitative change in the pigments present (Brush and Reisman, 1965).

As the nuptial coloration develops, the tubules in the kidneys become modified for the production of the mucus required for glueing the nest together (Fig. 37). This glue is stored in the urinary bladder, which is larger in the male than in the female. In the bladder, the mucus is a clear, glutinous material which consists of closely-packed, fine fibrils in a matrix (Wourms, 1973). The cells of the kidney tubules increase in height from about 12 μ to 31 μ and an accumulation of secretory granules takes place; clear mucus-secreting cells also appear (Wai and Hoar, 1963). At this time, the kidney tubule can be divided into three sections. The section closest to the glomerulus remains unmodified and retains the appearance of proximal tubule cells found in males outside the breeding season and in females and immature fish throughout the year (see Chapter 8). In the next section, the cells are much taller and have a glandular appearance, though they retain the microvilli characteristic of unmodified kidney tubule cells. In this second section the cells produce two types of granules. The first type is produced only for a short period; they have a diameter of 200–250 nm and their production ceases as the second type of granule starts to appear. This second type of granule is assumed to be the precursor of the mucus. The third section of the tubule consists of cells that are so modified as to be unrecognisable as kidney tubule cells. Instead they are glandular, mucus-secreting cells. The apical region of a cell in this section is occupied by a large number of vesicles derived from the precursor granules and contains clear material. During the transformation of the granules, the contents undergo a chemical change which alters their staining properties (PAS positive to PAS negative).

In the zones of transition between the three sections of the tubule, the cells have an intermediate appearance which suggests that the cells show a progressive differentiation as they move further from the glomerulus. The cells of the collecting ducts also become modified to produce a mucus, but the formation of this mucus does not pass

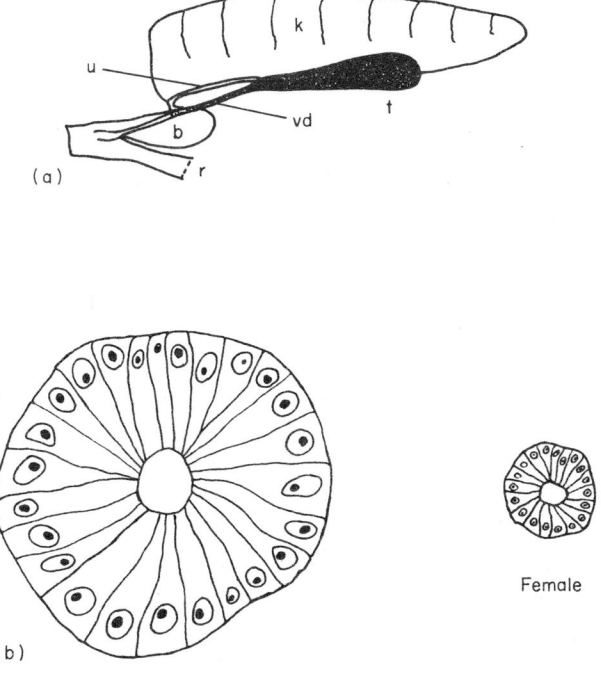

Fig. 37. Kidney of male *Gasterosteus aculeatus* in the breeding season. (a) Lateral view of uninogenital system (after Ikeda, 1933, and Rinkel and Hirsch, 1940); (b) comparison of the diameter of the kidney tubules of male and female (after Titschack, 1922). Key to lettering: b, urinary bladder, k, kidney; r, rectum (cut); t, testis; u, ureter; vd, vas deferens.

through a precursor granular stage. This product of the collecting ducts is chemically distinct from the mucus produced by the tubule cells for it is an acid mucopolysaccharide, whereas the tubule product is a neutral mucosubstance (Mourier, 1970; Hentschel, 1973). Other changes within the kidney of the male at this time include a slight increase in the thickness of the basement membrane in the Bowman's capsule and an increase in the size of the feet of the podocytes of the epithelium of the capsule. A layer of smooth muscle cells develops under the tubule cells (Opperman, 1973).

Although these changes are not normally shown by females or immature sticklebacks, they can be evoked by treatment with testosterone. Three days of treatment were required to reach the stage at which the tubule cells were ready to discharge mucus, but only two days of treatment induced mucus production by the cells of the collecting ducts. The first structural change which indicated that testosterone was influencing the differentiation of a proximal tubule cell was an increase in the size of the nucleolus in the cell nucleus, followed by the appearance of numerous ribosomes (the site of protein synthesis) free in the cytoplasm and the rapid development of the endoplasmic reticulum. These changes were accompanied by the growth of the cell (Mourier, 1972). The precise causal sequence by which testosterone brings about these changes is not known.

A further change that occurs as the male matures is the enlargement of the musculature of the pectoral fins; presumably this is an adaptation in preparation for the fanning behaviour by which the male ventilates his nest (Titschack, 1922).

Since androgen therapy of castrated males will evoke all these secondary sexual characters, it is presumed that in intact males the interstitial cells of the testes produce androgens. Evidence that the testes do synthesise androgens was obtained by Gottfried and Mullem (1967) who used the analytical technique of chromatography. They identified and measured androgen levels in the testes of mature, territorial males and also in males that were not sexually mature. A number of steroids were found in the testes of the mature males; testosterone, androstenedione, hydroepiandrosterone and progesterone. Testosterone was not found in the testes of immature males and the total level of steroids in the testes of mature males was five to seven times the level in immature males.

The interstitial cells, which are assumed to be the main site of androgen synthesis in the testes, are derived from undifferentiated pericapillary cells, which multiply and start to differentiate in early spring. As they differentiate into steroid-producing cells they enlarge and show changes in their ultrastructure, the most obvious of which are an increase in the size and number of vesicles of endoplasmic reticulum and an increase in the number of free ribosomes in the cytoplasm of the cells (Follenius, 1968b).

Although androgen therapy restores the secondary sexual characters of castrated males, there is some evidence which suggests that the development of full sexual maturity of the male requires the joint action of both androgens and gonadrotropic hormone produced by the pituitary. Males that had been castrated and then kept at short daylengths (8L 16D) were much less responsive to androgen therapy than castrated males kept at long daylengths (16L 8D). It is assumed that at long daylengths, the pituitary is more active in producing gonadotropin than at short daylengths (see also Chapter 9) (Wai and Hoar, 1963; Baggerman, 1968).

As in the female stickleback, there are marked changes in the relative size and dry matter content of the liver during the reproductive cycle of the male (Immers, 1953). In the autumn, the liver of the male forms about five per cent dry matter. But as the breeding season approaches, both the size and the dry matter content of the liver declines, with the size reaching a minimum of about three percent of total body weight during the breeding season, and the dry matter content reaching a minimum of twenty-five or twenty-six per cent in the period immediately after spawning. For the male, the liver forms the main storage organ of the carbohydrate, glycogen, and the changes in the glycogen content of the liver parallel the changes in its size. Although the glycogen content of the gonads forms only a small proportion of the total glycogen content of the fish, it reaches a peak early during the spawning period. The liver of the male is smaller than that of the female, but males injected with estrogen, a female gonadal hormone, showed an increase in the size of their livers up to the female level (Oguro, 1957).

These then are the major physiological and morphological correlates of the male's reproductive cycle, accompanying them are major changes in the male's behaviour.

11. Reproduction: The Male II
(Nest Building and Territorial Behaviour)

The reproductive behaviour of the male stickleback can be divided into several phases which follow on from the migration into the breeding area which was described in Chapter 8. The first phase, the nest building phase, is marked by the onset of territorial behaviour, the selection of a nest site and the subsequent building of a nest. This phase is succeeded by a sexual phase during which the male will court females. If the male is successful in inducing females to lay their eggs in his nest, then he enters the parental phase during which he guards and ventilates the eggs and then cares for the newly hatched young.

Territorial behaviour involves two aspects, site attachment and aggression. Site attachment means that the male stickleback confines the bulk of his activities to a restricted area, the area around the nest. This restricted area is defended by the male who behaves aggressively towards all conspecifics except for gravid females during his sexual phase. Other species are also attacked, though to a lesser extent.

Experiments in which males were placed on their own in a large ditch have indicated how the behaviour of the male changes as he starts to show site attachment and settles down in one particular area of the ditch (van den Assem, 1967). Initially when placed in the ditch, a male tended to swim almost from end to end, turning relatively infrequently. But this pattern of movement gradually changed with the male making many shorter moves, turning frequently so that he began to spend most of his time in one half of the ditch. This was the half in which the male eventually built his nest.

Several factors seem to influence the site which the male selects as the point at which he will build his nest. These factors include the nature of the substance, the topography, the presence of vegetation, the presence of conspecifics and light intensity.

In an experimental situation in which the male had the choice between a sandy substrate and a muddy substrate, trachurus males preferred to build their nests on the sand while the leiurus males preferred the muddy substrate. These preferences correlated with the substrate on which the two forms nested in their natural habitats in the Little Campbell River (Hagen, 1967). When the favoured substrates are absent, the males will build nests on gravel, amongst stones or fragments of sea-shells, and if kept in an aquarium with a bare glass floor will still try to build a nest even on such a completely unsuitable substrate. Usually the nests are built in shallow water, only a few centimetres deep.

Several experiments have sought to analyse the effect of the presence of vegetation and conspecifics on the site selected for the nest. These experiments have also indicated that factors which have a particular effect in some situations may have a quite different effect in other situations.

In a glass aquarium 60 or 120 cm long with a row of plants planted along one side wall, males tended to build their nests away from the row, although not at the maximum distance away that was physically possible. If only one plant was present in an otherwise bare aquarium, the males tended to nest away from the plant, but when both a row and a single, isolated plant were present, some males built their nests close to the single plant (van Iersel, 1958). In tanks that were 300 to 600 cm long, a row of plants at one end no longer had a repellant effect on the nest site. Indeed several males built their nests within the row. If the row of plants was away from an end wall, then a high proportion of males built their nests close to the row (Jenni, 1972).

In the experiments described so far, only one male was present in the aquarium at any one time, so that the choice of nest site was made without interference from or interaction with other males. The presence of a conspecific male has a repellant effect on the nest site. This effect has been shown in several ways. When, in a long aquarium, a male was confined behind a transparent glass plate at one end of the tank, a male placed in the large section of the tank generally built his nest in the half away from the confined male. If males were placed behind glass plates at both ends of the tank, a third male usually built his nest in the middle region of the tank, although not precisely equidistant from the two confined males. Thus the presence of conspecific males has an effect on the site of the nest even though there is only visual contact between the males, direct physical contact being prevented by the glass plates (Jenni, 1972). When two males were simultaneously introduced into a 600 cm long tank so that they could interact both visually and physically, the two nests were built on average seventy-one per cent of the greatest possible distance apart. If the two males were introduced successively so that the first male had built his nest before the second male was introduced, then the two nests were on average eighty-five per cent of the maximum distance apart. An established male seems to have a greater repellant effect on another male's nest site than if the males are establishing themselves at the same time (van den Assem, 1967).

When the presence of a conspecific male and a row of vegetation were combined, the vegetation seemed to reduce the repellant effect of the conspecific male, so that the nest was built closer to the conspecific than would have been the case if the vegetation was absent (Jenni, 1972).

A study of the combined effect of a number of factors presented simultaneously on the site selected by the male for his nest showed that males preferred the combination of plants in the corner, subdued lighting and a striped exterior pattern, to the combination of stones in the corner, bright lighting and an external pattern of circles (Tschanz and Schärf, 1971).

The experience of the male before being placed in an aquarium and allowed to build a nest also affects the position of the nest. Males kept under conditions that made them very sensitive to disturbances, in particular males which had been kept in total isolation, tended to nest in the corner of an aquarium. Males which were accustomed to disturbances still showed some preference for the corners, but built nests throughout the aquarium (Jenni et al., 1969).

There are relatively few descriptions of the sites chosen for nests in natural populations of sticklebacks. In splash pools on the west coast of Vancouver Island, the nests of trachurus males were built in low tufts of algae, rock crevices, close to vertical walls and sometimes on bare patches of silt (Black and Wootton, 1970). In the River Wear in Durham City, male leiurus sticklebacks built their nests on a shallow, muddy shelf. Most of the nests were out in the open, but two conspicuous exceptions were that one nest was built inside a tin can and one inside a milk bottle (Wootton, 1972a). In the Little Campbell River (British Columbia), the leiurus males built their nests on a mud substrate near the bank of the stream at an average depth of 24 cm. Although the nests were in the open, they were close to stands of water plants in areas where the water was still. Trachurus males built their nests on a sandy substrate, within or on the downstream edge of a bed of *Elodea* (Canadian pond weed). The nests tended to be in the centre of the stream where there was a detectable current and at an average depth of 50 cm (Hagen, 1967). The basic pattern of nest sites seems to be determined by the aggressive interactions between the males, but males will take advantage of available cover when selecting a nest site. Of the five genera of sticklebacks, the three-spined stickleback is exceptional in its preference for nesting in open areas of the substrate rather than amongst thick vegetation. It is argued that the emancipation of the three-spined stickleback from areas of vegetation is a consequence of its effective, morphological adaptations that deter predators (see Chapters 5 and 16).

As well as influencing the position of the nest, the presence of conspecifics and vegetation also influences the rate at which the nest is completed. Males kept in tanks that lacked material suitable for nest building or in which such material was inaccessible were less likely to build nests than males who had access to such material. The deprived males spent far more time fluttering, that is swimming up and down the side of the tank, before starting to construct a nest (Schütz and Tschanz, 1971). Wunder (1930) had suggested that the presence of females stimulated nest-building while Reisman (1968a) used models of gravid females as well as male and neutral models to investigate the effect of conspecifics on nest-building and other secondary sexual characters. The most stimulatory situation was the presence of a female model together with material suitable for nest-building, but models on their own and nest material on its own also had some stimulatory effect. The character most affected by the presence of models and nest material was the development of the red coloration in the throat region of the male. If males are induced to mature prematurely by keeping them on long day-lengths at high water temperatures, they will often start to build nests before they develop the full nuptial coloration, which indicates, as does Reisman's study, that the development of the various secondary sexual characters is only loosely synchronised. The effect of the presence of other males on the rate at which a male builds his nest depends on the physiological state of the male under observation. To investigate this problem, van den Assem (1967) used an aquarium 60 cm long divided in half by a transparent glass partition. The experimental male was placed in one half and the other half was left empty or contained another male; sometimes vegetation was also present in the aquarium. If the experimental male was just at the start of the breeding season, then both the other male and the vegetation had a stimulatory effect on the rate at which the male completed his nest. But if the experimental male had, for at least a week before the start of the experiment, experienced a photoperiod of 16L 8D, that is a regime which accelerates the rate at which the male becomes sexually mature, then the presence of the other male had an inhibitory effect on the rate at which the nest was completed. This inhibitory effect was only temporary. When there are several males present in a tank that is only large enough for a single territory, only one male becomes fully mature while the remainder remain immature. Once the mature male is removed, another male will become mature. Crowding sticklebacks together is frequently used as a means of slowing the rate at which they become mature.

In a natural situation, the stimulatory effects of the presence of both conspecifics and vegetation will normally be present. There is some evidence that males take up territories and complete their first nests within a few days of each other. This has been seen in a lake in southern Finland (Sevenster, cited in van den Assem, 1967) and in the River Wear in Durham (personal observation).

Nest-building consists of a group of distinct behaviour patterns, the sequential organisation and integration of these patterns over a period of time results in the completion of a functional nest. This process is dependent on the androgen(s) produced by the testes, and can be induced in castrated males that have been kept on long day-lengths by treatment with testosterone. Castration of males that have already built nests causes them to abandon all care of the nest, nor do they attempt to build another unless treated with testosterone. When gonadectomised females were treated with testosterone, a small proportion built nests, but these nests were very inadequate when compared with the nests built by males (Wai and Hoar, 1963).

The first behavioural component of the nest-building sequence to appear is sand-digging. The male swims into an almost vertical position with his head down and then takes a mouthful of sand from the bottom. He swims for some distance away from the site where he digs and spits the sand out. Although at first, the male digs at several sites, eventually he concentrates his activity in one area with the result that a shallow pit is dug, usually 4 or 5 cm wide and 8 or 9 cm long. While he digs this pit, the male also starts to pick up small pieces of vegetation. At first, he spits these bits out immediately, but then he starts to drop the bits into the nest pit. In some cases the male seems to test material, repeatedly spitting out and then sucking it back into his mouth until finally, the material is either rejected or carried back to the nest pit. Van Iersel (1953) suggested that the male rejected pieces that sank or rose rapidly but took pieces that floated back to the nest. The material brought to the nest pit is placed in the rear of the pit. Where a male has built a nest previously he will make repeated trips to the old nest site in order to collect material for use in the new nest (Wootton, 1972a). Curiously, material near the nest does not seem to be preferred to material at some distance from the nest. Even more curiously, where males have adjoining territories, material that is at or just beyond the territorial boundary seems to be preferred (van den Assem, 1967).

There have been few studies on the properties that the material must possess in order to be selected by the male. Slender pieces are taken in preference to broad pieces, and some experiments have indicated that the colour of the material may influence the male's choice. Morris (1958) supplied males with pieces of different coloured cottons for use in nest-building. Initially one male used green threads, but as the building progressed, the proportion of green threads used declined while the proportion of red threads used increased. Neither blue nor yellow threads were used much. Other males showed an initial preference for the yellow threads, but again the preference switched to red threads as the building progressed. In some cases, the use of this red thread resulted in a bright ring of colour around the nest entrance. It might tentatively be suggested that a male gains some advantage by having a conspicuously coloured nest entrance perhaps because a female can find the nest entrance more easily (Wunder, 1930). In a natural situation in which there will often be a restricted range of material for use in nest-building such preferences may not be relevant.

Material that the male brings to the nest pit is glued with the mucus secretion of the kidneys. The glueing behaviour of the male is very conspicuous. He swims smoothly over the nest using what van Iersel (1953) describes as "peculiar" movements of the pectoral and anal fins. Both his head and tail are raised and the cloacal region is pressed against the nest material. Each bout of glueing lasts only a few seconds during which the male may circle around the nest or swim straight across it.

The nest is consolidated by pushing, in which the male moves into a head-down position and pushes his snout into the nest material, usually in a bout of several quick thrusts. Another technique that the male uses to anchor the nest is sucking, in which he sucks sand into his mouth then forces it out through the opercular slits. This sucking is performed especially at the rim of the nest and eventually results in the formation of a series of holes round the nest, then the edges of the nest get pushed down into these holes and are partially covered with sand (van Iersel, 1953).

With the accumulation of a mass of material in the nest pit, the male starts to show boring which resembles pushing except that the body of the fish is almost horizontal rather than vertical. Boring tends to be concentrated in one place so that it results in the male forcing a tunnel into the middle of the heap of material. At about this time, he tends to bring material to the mouth of the tunnel and to glue around this area so that a distinct nest entrance is formed.

As the nest reaches completion, the male starts to show fanning. This behaviour, which is usually associated with the parental phase and is described in detail in Chapter 13, ventilates the nest by driving a current of water through it. Although the amount of time spent fanning does not reach a peak until the parental phase of the male, the behaviour is seen both in the nest-building and sexual phases.

A climax of the nest-building phase is reached when the male pushes his way right through the nest and emerges at the back of the nest. This creeping through of the male produces a continuous tunnel, with a distinct entrance and exit. The first appearance of creeping through is generally regarded as marking the end of the nest-building phase and the onset of the sexual phase during which the male attempts to seduce the female into laying her eggs in his nest.

A male usually takes about five or six hours to complete his first nest, although the time taken can vary from four hours to several days (van Iersel, 1953). The temporal sequence of events during nest-building is shown in Fig. 38. This orderly sequence of events provokes the question of what factors control the organisation of nest-building behaviour.

Experiments with gonadectomised females showed that although treatment with testosterone could induce some females to build nests, these nests were not comparable to the nests made by males. The females showed most of the relevant behaviour patterns but the organisation of these patterns was not adequate for the production of a proper nest. The nest pit was shallow, there was little pushing and, although glueing occurred, the vegetation was not neatly glued together so that the end product was merely a flat mass of vegetation lying in a shallow pit (Wai and Hoar, 1963). Males that had had their entire fore-brain removed could still dig, collect material and glue, but they failed to orientate these activities to one particular site so that a coherent nest was never built, although males that had had only the olfactory bulbs removed did build nests (Schönherr, 1955; Segaar, 1956, 1961).

Guiton (1960) studied some aspects of the temporal organisation of nest-building. He was interested in the problem of whether the changes in behaviour during the nest-building phase were solely a result of the changing external stimuli as the nest took shape or whether there were intrinsic changes in the male such that the

responsiveness of the male to the external situation was also
changing. A point to note in this context is that the phases during
the nest-building sequence are not discontinuous, the digging phase
does not abruptly stop and the phase of collecting material abruptly
start, rather there is a sort of orchestration of behaviour patterns

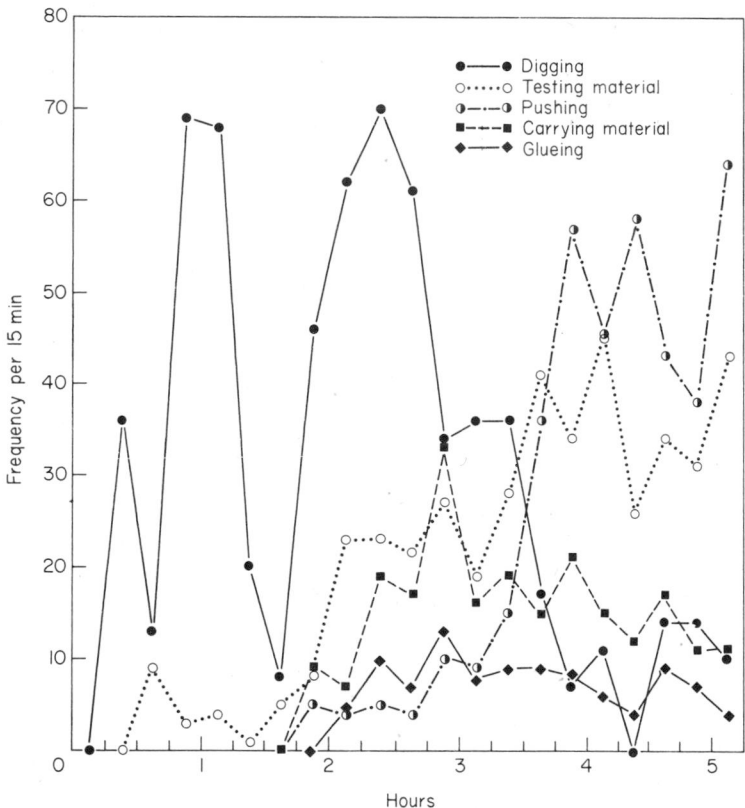

Fig. 38. Behavioural changes during a five hour period of nest building by a male
Gasterosteus aculeatus (after van Iersel, 1953).

such that at one time one behaviour pattern is dominant and others
are less prominent, while at another time another behaviour pattern
predominates. These changes in relative dominance may be fairly
rapid or relatively gradual. The transition from digging to collecting
and pushing is rapid in that collecting, pushing and glueing appear
somewhat abruptly, but the frequency of digging declines slowly.

　　Guiton found that if he obliterated the nest pit soon after the transition from the digging phase to the collecting phase, the male would continue to collect material for five or ten minutes, but then this activity declined rapidly and the male increased the frequency of his digging so that a new pit was started. This was not a total reversal to the digging phase for some collecting still continued while the frequency of digging did not reach a high, stable level. When the nest pit was obliterated later in the nest-building sequence, the male did not resume digging for about thirty minutes, nor did he immediately stop glueing but instead he continued to glue at the nest site although this was no longer an appropriate behaviour pattern in the changed external circumstances. A very similar situation can be seen if a mature male is kept in an aquarium that has a bare glass floor. Such a male sometimes attempts to build a nest from fragments of algae and faeces. but these bits usually disperse as the male tries to push and bore them, nevertheless, the male will glue across the glass floor in the region of the appropriate site. These experimental results and observations suggest that the successful completion of the nest is a consequence of the combination of the male's response to the changing external situation as the pit is dug and material accumulated, together with changes in the male's state that are intrinsic to the male and which mean that components of the nest-building sequence can appear even in the absence of suitable external conditions.

That changes intrinsic to the male do take place during his breeding cycle is indicated by other experiments of Guiton (1960), who examined the effect of obliterating the nest pit when the male was in the sexual phase. Normally during the sexual phase, the male is ready to show intensive courtship behaviour to a suitable female and displays a low level of nest-building activities with digging and collecting material being particularly low. When the nest was obliterated in this phase, the frequency of all activities associated with nest-building decreased except for digging which showed a slight increase but never reached the levels characteristic of the early phases of nest-building. Even an hour after the removal of the nest, the male still showed relatively high levels of courtship behaviour towards a gravid female although the male now lacked a nest in which the female could lay her eggs. If the nest was replaced within a few hours, and before the male had started to build a new nest, then the male rapidly re-adopted his old nest and showed the behaviour characteristic of a male in the sexual phase of the breeding cycle.

The male's response to the change in the external situation brought about by the disappearance of his nest lags behind that change. The cause for this lag is not clear, perhaps both neural and hormonal factors are implicated. It is not known whether the presence of a nest has any affect on the hormonal status of the male, and the details of the physiological control of the nest-building sequence remain to be analysed.

The end product of these behavioural events, the nest, is a mass of vegetation anchored in a small pit, the vegetation bound together with the glue from the kidneys. Nests vary in size and shape, and at least one author has tried to classify nests into distinct forms. Leiner (1929) described three types of nest, the tube nest, the round nest and the sand nest. The tube nest was about 5 or 6 cm long and 2 or 3 cm across; the round nest lay in a pit some 5 cm deep and was 12 to 15 cm in diameter. A sand nest consisted of a round nest which the male had covered with sand. A male often brings sand to his nest towards the end of the nest-building phase, dropping it on the nest especially around the entrance (van Iersel, 1953), so the formation of a sand nest implies that this bringing of sand occurred at a relatively high frequency. Vrat (1949) describes nests built by sticklebacks in a Californian population which consisted entirely of sand. However a strict classification of nests is probably arbitrary for forms occur which are intermediate to the ones described by Leiner. There are no accounts of the effect that the nature of the substrate or the availability of building material has on the form of the nest. It seems that males are versatile in using the materials available when building their nests. For example, in an aquarium in which only fine gravel was provided, a male built a nest which consisted of a circular pile of gravel together with scraps of algae 3 or 4 cm high. This nest was used successfully, the male fertilised eggs in it and the eggs hatched.

A male stickleback uses several cues in order to locate his nest after he has swum away from the site. In an environment in which there are few landmarks, a male often builds his nest close to any distinct objects and locates his nest using the objects as a guide (van den Assem, 1967). Other experiments have suggested that in addition to objects in the immediate area of the nest, more distant objects and the pattern of light intensity may also be used for orientation (Tschanz and Shärf, 1971). When a plate of glass is placed over the nest so that the male can see it but cannot touch or smell it, the male still orientates his nest-directed activities at the correct site. A male who has recently abandoned a nest site, even if he has already started to build a nest at a new site, will sometimes attempt to lead a gravid female down to the old nest although only useless fragments of the old nest remain. Males seem to retain, at least for a short period, the memory of the site of a former nest. All the evidence suggests that a male is very familiar with the topography of his territory and the position of his nest so that he can find his nest quickly and accurately.

When a male's nest is moved by an experimenter, he becomes unsure and in some cases will fail to adopt the nest even if it is in clear view. In a very bare and homogeneous environment a male may adopt a nest that is moved up to 30 cm away from its original site. But in a natural situation such displacements of the nest are not likely to happen.

Male sticklebacks react to changes in the immediate environment of their nests. A male removed stones from the nest entrance and small sticks placed around the nest and attempted to remove material restricting access to his nest (Muckensturm, 1965). It is of course important for the male to maintain the nest in a suitable condition for use by the female.

The area around the nest is defended as a territory. This defence by the male is primarily directed against other males, but females, other species of fish and some invertebrates are also attacked. Attacks on females and other species usually consist of a direct and rapid charge by the male towards the intruder, and if the intruder fails to flee the male bites and in extreme cases carries it bodily out of the territory.

In encounters between males, especially between territorial males, the fighting becomes more elaborate. The following account is based largely on the descriptions of van Iersel (1953) and Hall (1956), who distinguish several distinct behaviour patterns that can occur during a fight between two males. An encounter often begins with one of the males charging rapidly towards his opponent and such a charge frequently ends with the male biting his rival. The bite can be directed at any part of the opponent's body, but the area around the eyes and the caudal peduncle are frequent targets. Sometimes the male brakes suddenly before getting close enough to deliver a bite, a response that has sometimes been called a low intensity attack. If the opponent flees, the male will give chase, attempting to bite the fleeing fish. In a confined space, in which a beaten fish cannot flee, the dominant male can quickly kill the subordinant fish, male or female. A beaten fish that cannot escape usually remains still at the surface of the water in a tail down position. If the dominant fish approaches, the subordinate raises the pelvic spine on the side from which the attacker is approaching. Sometimes when attacked a fish will roll its dorsal surface towards the attacker, a move that usually inhibits the attacker from delivering a bite. When there is a conflict between two males close to the border between their territories, the males may start to circle each other rapidly. Each has his dorsal spines and the pelvic spine nearest the opponent errect. This rapid circling with spines erect was labelled spine-fighting by van Iersel, but in some ways this is a misleading description for the spines are not used as weapons. Roundabout fighting or carouselling are preferable labels. Another component of fights between territorial males is the head-down threat. In this head-down threat, a male adopts a vertical

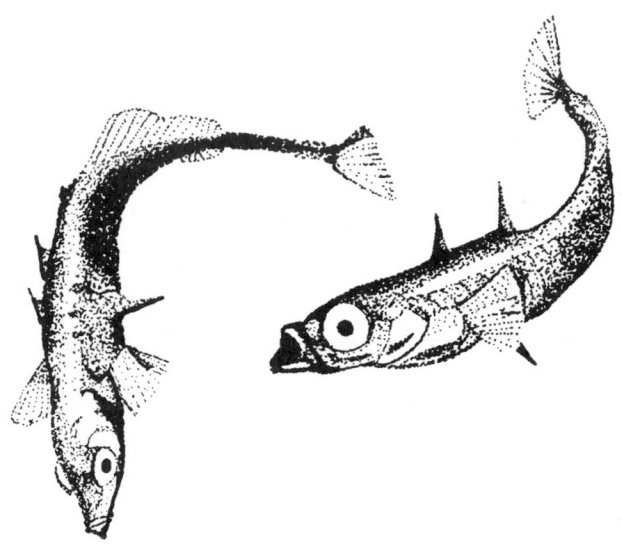

Fig. 39. Male *Gasterosteus aculeatus* fighting. Male on the left is adopting the head-down threat (after Pelkwijk and Tinbergen, 1937).

orientation with his head pointing to the substrate and his flank directed towards the opponent (Fig. 39). He erects his dorsal spines and usually the pelvic spine nearest the opponent. This head-down threat may be performed by just one of the males in mid-water, but frequently both males will adopt the head-down threat, approaching each other closely and diving down to the bottom where they jerk up and down rapidly. Often such a mutual threat will end with one of the males swimming away towards the middle of his territory.

The effect of this head-down threat on the male that is threatened depends on the position of the threatening male in relation to the territorial boundaries. When a male was confined in a narrow glass tube which prevented him displaying the threat, a neighbouring male encroached into the imprisoned male's territory although the glass tube was in that territory. But when the male was kept in a tube in which he could display the threat, the neighbouring male respected the boundary, although the male in the tube could not physically attack an intruder. In contrast, a threat delivered within the threatened male's territory elicits attacks by the threatened male (ter Pelkwijk and Tinbergen, 1937; Tinbergen, 1951).

Ethological theory suggests that such threat postures are adopted when an animal engaged in an aggressive encounter is unable to make a direct attack on its opponent. This may be because the animal is in an ambivalent motivational state with the tendency to attack and the tendency to flee both strong or because a direct attack is being thwarted. In such situations the animal may show apparently irrelevant behaviour such as feeding, preening or sleeping and these "irrelevant" behaviours are called displacement activities (Tinbergen, 1951). The head-down threat of the male stickleback has been interpreted as having evolved from displacement sand digging (Tinbergen and van Iersel, 1947). Their evidence for this interpretation comes from observations on the fighting that occurred when several males were put in a small aquarium. The males spent most of their time fighting, and in this situation digging also became very frequent so that the males dug several deep holes. In contrast, when the males were isolated, they showed no threat behaviour and no holes were dug with the exception of the nest pit. This correlation between the frequency of threatening and the frequency of digging suggested that head down threatening was derived from sand digging. Alternative explanations for this correlation can be given, so that it is not certain that the threat is derived from sand digging. In most cases the threat does not include the male taking sand into his mouth, so that it can be suggested that the correlation between digging and threatening is a consequence of the similarity in the orientation that the male takes up to perform them. Both involve the male adopting a head-down position so that transitions between the two behaviours may be facilitated although motivationally they are quite distinct. A detailed analysis of the temporal relationships between threatening and digging during aggressive encounters might shed some light on the problem. Other species of sticklebacks also show head-down threats during fights between males, but do not show sand digging which indicates that the one behaviour pattern can occur without the other (Tinbergen, 1952).

When a fish is swimming through the territory of a male another type of behaviour is occasionally seen. The male takes up a position alongside and a few centimetres from the intruder. The two fish then swim parallel to each other to the border of the territory where the male moves away from the intruder as the latter passes out of his territory.

By far the most spectacular fights are those that take place between males that have adjacent territories. Each male is dominant in his own territory but subordinant in his rival's territory, so a male that at one moment is vigorously chasing will in the next moment be fleeing as his chase takes him over the territorial boundary. The fight pendulums back and forth in a rapid sequence of chases and fleeings interspersed with bouts of roundabout fighting or threatening. It is as though each male was attached by a piece of elastic to the centre of his territory, with the elastic stretching just far enough for the male to invade his neighbours' territory, but becoming very taut in the process.

During fights, the spines may be raised or lowered, yet they are not used as weapons. Perhaps a fish may become impaled on a spine, but this would seem to be a rare accident and not because the spines are offensive weapons. The role of spines as defensive weapons giving protection against predators is described in Chapter 5. Some attempts have been made to link the erection of spines during a fight with the motivational state of the male. Early analyses along these lines suggested that the erection of the dorsal spines was a sign that the male was highly aggressive, whereas the erection of the pelvic spines indicated that the tendency to flee was relatively strong (van Iersel, 1953; Morris, 1958). A detailed analysis of the correlations between spine-raising, biting, fleeing and zig-zagging did not support this simple interpretation (Symons, 1965). Symons' study showed that the erection of the dorsal spines was correlated with zig-zagging, that is a behaviour usually interpreted as courtship, whereas erection of the pelvic spines was correlated with biting and also zig-zagging. In a comparison of the behaviour of a male at his territorial boundary with his behaviour within his territory, Symons showed that the erection of the pelvic spines was also correlated with the tendency to flee. These results refer to experiments in which the male was usually reacting to another fish confined within a transparent tube. That different conclusions might be drawn in a situation in which both fish were unconstrained is suggested by the observation that in such a situation males that approached fish with their pelvic spines erect tended to make their approach in a slow and hesitant fashion. When a fish has been badly beaten it stays still with its tail down, and if the dominant male approaches, the beaten fish erects the pelvic spine on the side from which the tyrant approaches.

A major problem in assessing the motivational significance of spine erection is that the spines are modified fins, so that in some cases the erection of spines may be correlated with changes in the aspect of the fins as the fish swims, rather than directly with changes in the factors that control biting, fleeing or zig-zagging. There seems to be no published evidence that the spines are used to give intraspecific signals which indicate the motivational state of the signalling animal to conspecifics. Experiments in which the effect of the removal or the exaggeration of the spines on the interactions with conspecifics have not yet been reported. In this context it may well be that the orange pigmentation of the pelvic spines in some sexually mature males is significant.

Although aggressive behaviour is typically shown by sexually mature males during defence of their territories, it is not completely confined to this situation. Juvenile sticklebacks occasionally chase and bite each other and females also show aggressive behaviour in some situations. Sexually mature females were confined in small tanks with juvenile fish, which they chased and harried often killing the juveniles. When pairs of females were kept in small tanks, one of the pair often, but not invariably, became dominant, chasing and biting the subordinant who was sometimes killed. In none of these situations does threatening or roundabout fighting occur with any frequency, these patterns are confined to the interactions of territorial males. But when considering the causation of aggressive behaviour in the stickleback, it has to be remembered that aggressive behaviour is not solely restricted to mature males during the breeding season though this is its most characteristic expression.

Aggression cannot be manifested unless there is some stimulus against which the aggression can be directed. Much research on the male stickleback has been concerned with the nature of the stimulus that releases aggressive behaviour. A mature male has a red throat and fore-belly (exceptions to this are described in Chapters 5 and 14). This coloration is an attraction for the females (Chapter 9), but does it also have an effect on the behaviour of other males? In a classic series of experiments, Tinbergen and his colleagues showed that red acted as a releasing stimulus for male agression. In the early experiments dead sticklebacks were stuck on pieces of wire and dangled within the territory of a male. The male attacked dead, red males much more vigorously than dead females or pale, immature males. A dead female coloured red was attacked more vigorously than she had been before being coloured. This difference in response persisted even when the dead fish were within a glass container to prevent the male obtaining any olfactory or gustatory information about the fish (ter Pelkwijk and Tinbergen, 1937). A male presented with a series of models some of which were painted silver-grey all over and some of which had red ventral surfaces attacked the red models more than the silver-grey models. If the red model was made even more male-like by painting in blue eyes and a blueish back, then this had a slight additional effect on the stimulation of the male's aggression, but the red ventral surface seemed to be the most important signal. In these

Tinbergen's series   Peeke *et al*'s series

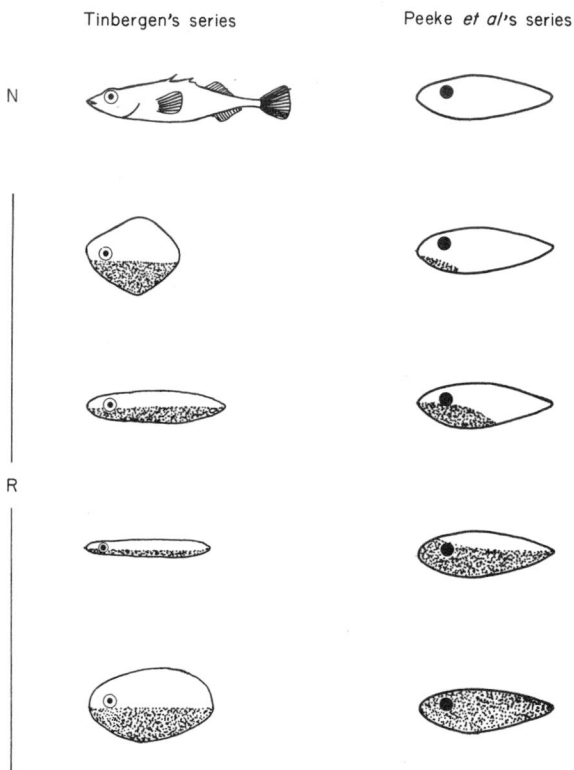

Fig. 40. Models used to test the effectiveness of red as a releaser for the aggression of male *Gasterosteus aculeatus* (after Tinbergen, 1951, and Peeke *et al.*, 1969). Red areas on models are stippled; R, red series; N, non-red series.

experiments, the presence of the red underside seemed to be more important for the release of the male's aggression than the size or shape of the model. An almost perfect model of a stickleback not coloured red was attacked less than crude, oddly-shaped models with red undersides (Fig. 40) (Tinbergen, 1939, 1942, 1948, 1951). There is even a description of males attempting to attack a distant, red, post-office van. When such a van passed by the window of the laboratory, the male sticklebacks would dash to the side of their tanks nearest the window (Tinbergen, 1953).

Red is not a necessary condition for the male to show aggressive behaviour to a stimulus. Even neutral models may be attacked, though usually at a lower intensity than red models. Fighting, often intensive, can take place between a pair of males even when one or both of them lack the full development of the red underside (Muckensturm, 1967). When a series of models with undersides of various colours was presented to males, it was not necessarily the model with the red underside that was attacked most. Individual males differed with respect to which colour evoked the most attacks from them, and it was suggested that the colour served to orientate the male towards the model but did not act as a releaser specifically for aggressive behaviour (Muckensturm, 1968). In the context of this experiment it must be remembered that in natural populations, the males' interactions are either with females that have silver undersides or with males with red undersides and that fish with blue or yellow undersides are not encountered.

Not all experiments have confirmed the importance of red as a releasing stimulus. In an experiment on the effect of repeated presentations of models on the aggressive behaviour of male stickle-backs, models with different amounts of red on their undersides were presented to the males (Fig. 40). There were no significant differ-ences in the amount of biting directed at models that had some red on their undersides and a model that had no red on it (Peeke et al., 1969). Another curious finding regarding the response of males to models was described by Peeke (1969). He presented males with a model for fiteeen minutes a day for ten successive days. The model was painted grey with a red "throat" and blue "eyes". Over the ten day period, the number of bites and charges aimed at the model declined significantly. On the eleventh day, the males were presented with a live male confined within a glass tube. The aggression shown towards the live male was similar to the level shown by males that had not been presented with a model for ten previous days. The decline in the aggression shown to the model had not influenced the aggression shown to a live male, which could be interpreted as an indication that the males were not confusing the model with a live conspecific male. Although males will vigorously bite at models as they will bite at rival males, they make most of their approaches towards the models with both dorsal and pelvic spines erect, whereas they will usually approach a live male with either no spines or just the dorsal spines erect (Wootton, 1971a). This again raises the question of whether the males are really treating the model as a conspecific and a potential rival. But there is some evidence that supports the belief that males do treat correctly coloured males as rival males. As will be described in Chapter 13, males show distinct changes in the level of aggression during their parental phase. When males were presented with models that were all the same shape and size, three of which had a patch of red and a fourth that was all silver, the aggression shown towards the red models varied in approximately the same manner as the aggression shown to con-specific males during the parental phase. The aggression shown towards the silver model varied in the same way as aggression towards female conspecifics (Wootton, 1971a).

On balance, the evidence suggests that red does tend to release the aggressive behaviour of the male, when the stimulus carrying the red is within the male's territory. If the stimulus is presented outside the male's territory, then the male is intimidated and is less likely to cross his territorial boundary. So, as with the head-down threat, the effect of colour on aggressive behaviour is a function of the geography of the situation. However, the use of models to demon-strate the effect of red as a releasing stimulus is not always successful. Males vary considerably in their response to models. In some populations a majority of males will respond vigorously to models, whereas the males from another population may show little or no aggressive response to models, even those coloured red.

During the early phase of the reproductive cycle of the male, before a nest had been built, females were attacked as vigorously as males, but after the nest had been built, males with red underparts were attacked more vigorously than females or immature fish (Wootton, 1970). This change was partly because the male started to show courtship behaviour towards the females, but there was also some evidence that there was a real enhancement of the aggression shown towards sexually mature males. Such an enhancement might result if the sensitivity of the male to the colour red increased at about the time of nest-building. Females showed a decrease in their threshold for detecting red during the breeding season (Chapter 9), but males showed no change in threshold at either the red or the blue end of their visual sensitivity throughout the year (Cronly-Dillon and Sharma, 1968). Unfortunately in the description of this study, it was not made clear whether the males tested during the breeding period were dominant males with nests, for there are distinct hormonal differences between dominant and other males, with the dominant males having far higher levels of androgen in their testes (Gottfried and Mullem, 1967). There remains the possibility that the red sensitivity of the male stickleback might vary with his hormonal status. The neural properties of the visual system of frogs can be altered by treating the frogs with hormones (Oshima and Gorbman, 1969).

Since most of the mature males in a population are similar in size, it is unlikely that size is an important factor in determining levels of aggression. An experiment, in which the effect of the size of the opponent on a male's aggression was studied, did not yield any consistent results (Wootton, 1970). Very large models inhibit the attacks of the male, even when the model has a red underside (Tinbergen, 1953) but sticklebacks will attack minnows 3 or 4 cm larger than themselves.

Once the male has built his nest, the level of his aggression is a function of the distance of the male from his nest. An early but elegant demonstration of this is due to Tinbergen, who set up a tank that was large enough to hold two territorial males. Each of the males was allowed to build a nest, then they were placed in transparent tubes wide enough for them to swim around in. The two tubes were placed close together so that the males could see each other. One of the males attempted to attack the other who tried to flee. The attacker was the male whose territory the tubes were in. But when the tubes were moved a sufficient distance to bring them within the territory of the second male, the male that had been attacking now started to flee, while the second male became the attacker (Tinbergen, 1953).

This relationship between the aggression of the male and the distance from the male's nest has since been investigated in more detail. A male was allowed to build a nest, then a second, mature, fully coloured male was placed in a transparent glass tube, which could be put at various distances from the nest. The number of bites the nest owner aimed at the male in the tube was taken as a measure of the owner's aggression. This technique of using a fish confined in a glass tube as the test stimulus has been commonly used to measure the aggression of male sticklebacks under reasonably standard conditions (van Iersel, 1958; Sevenster, 1961; Symons, 1965; Wootton, 1971a), and recent evidence indicates that it does indeed provide a reasonable measure of the male's level of aggression (Huntingford, 1974). The results of the experiment showed that the aggression of the male declined with increasing distance from the nest. At about 30–40 cm from the nest there was often an abrupt decrease in aggression. The introduction of a row of vegetation in a previously barren tank resulted in a change in the distribution of aggression, with it being relatively high on the nest side of the row and relatively low on the other side. This direct influence of a topographical feature on the aggression of a male indicates how the size and shape of a territory can be influenced by such features (van Iersel, 1958). Other studies have confirmed that the aggression of a territorial male declines with increasing distance from the nest (Symons, 1965; Black, 1971).

The results have suggested the concept of a "landscape" of aggression in which the peak levels of aggression are around the nest with gradients of decreasing aggression sloping away from this peak (Fig. 41) (van den Assem, 1967). Such a concept provides the basis for an explanation of the pattern of nest sites observed when more than one male builds a nest in a particular area. Both in natural environments and in laboratory tanks, the distribution of nests is rather regular (van den Assem, 1967; Black and Wootton, 1970; Wootton, 1972a). When a male builds a nest in a large tank there will be an area some 30–40 cm in radius around the nest in which the male is very aggressive. In areas very distant from the nest, aggression will be low. Another male will be able to set up a territory in that area where the aggression of the first male is low. Around the nest of this second male there will be an area in which he is highly aggressive, so that when a third male is added, this third fish is most likely to succeed in carving out a territory in that area of the tank where the resultant aggressive levels of the first two males are at a minimum. This is the area where the total number of attacks that the third male has to experience is a minimum. In this way successive males can set up territories until each territory has reached the minimum size tolerated by the resident male. From then on, no further males could be accommodated unless a territorial male was ousted from his territory or there was a decrease in the minimum size of the territory. (During the parental phase, males tolerate a reduction in the size of the territories they are defending.)

It is not clear why there is a relationship between distance from the nest and the level of aggression. Even when a male is on his own in tank and never comes into direct physical contact with a rival such a relationship is present (van Iersel, 1958). Perhaps the fearfulness or timidity of a male increases with increasing distance from his nest, and this inhibits aggressive behaviour. Another possibility is that males are only willing to spend so much time away from the nest, and that time spent swimming to and from an opponent is subtracted from the time spent fighting rather than from time spent at the nest.

Territory size is related to a number of factors, of which three seem to be of primary importance: topography, the aggressiveness of the male and the synchrony with which males take up their territories. Topography is important in determining the site of the

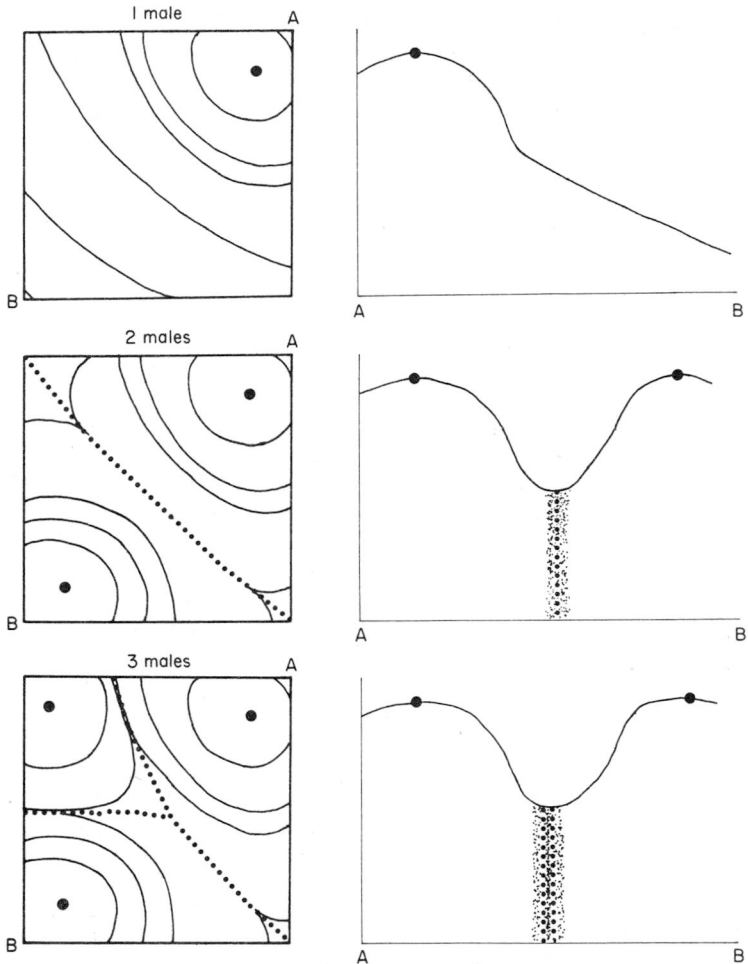

Fig. 41. The "aggression landscape" model of territorial settlement by male *Gasterosteus aculeatus*. On left, a contour map representation; on right, a sectional map representation. Contour lines join points where the frequency of biting at a confined, male conspecific is equal; border between adjacent territories marked by row of dots; border area, stippled; single dots mark position of nests.

nest and may also provide physical barriers which prevent males seeing each other so that they build their nests closer than would be tolerated if they could easily see their neighbours. In a tank of a given size, more territorial males were accommodated when opaque partitions were used to divide the tank up into compartments, even though the compartments inter-communicated (Wunder, 1930). More aggressive males would be expected to hold larger territories than less aggressive males. This expectation was supported by the observation that there was a positive correlation between the size of territory that a male held and the number of aggressive interactions with other males initiated by that male (van den Assem, 1967). Huntingford (1974) found that the most aggressive males in one phase of the sexual cycle also tended to be the most aggressive males in other phases, which suggests that males that take up large territories can maintain those territories. A more surprising factor found to influence territory size was the synchrony with which a group of males took up their territories. When males simultaneously took up territories a greater number of males was accommodated in a given area than when the males were introduced successively with a twenty-four hour delay between the successive introductions (van den Assem, 1967).

Since not all males succeed in taking up territories when there are many males present, there must be a minimum size for a territory. In an investigation of the minimum territory size, thirty males were placed in a ditch 600 cm long and 100 cm wide. When the males were added simultaneously, about thirty per cent of them succeeded in building nests within ˉseventy-two hours. The territories were about 45 cm by 45 cm. This value agrees with the sizes of territories observed in natural situations. Bertin (1925) reported that the maximum density of nests observed in nature was four to five per square metre. More precise measurements have indicated that the minimum distance between nests is some 30 to 50 cm (Sevenster, cited in van den Assem, 1967; Black and Wootton, 1970; Wootton, 1972a). Some measurements of territory size from a natural population of sticklebacks are shown in Table VIII.

In a situation where more than one male is present, the males fight in order to obtain territories, but once a male has established himself on a territory it would seem, at least intuitively, advantageous if the territorial male reduced the level of his aggression towards established territorial neighbours, but remained aggressive towards any intruders into his territory. If the incidence of fighting between neighbours is reduced then there is less chance of a fish being damaged in a fight; the males will spend less time fighting and therefore there will be more time available for maintaining the nest, courting females and feeding; and the males will conserve energy that would otherwise be dissipated in the often hectic activity that characterises territorial disputes.

Evidence has accumulated that a reduction in fighting does take place between adjacent, territorial males. Two males were placed one on either side of a transparent glass partition that divided a tank into two halves. Initially the males attempted to bite each other through the partition, but with time the frequency of biting waned and threatening became the predominant activity (van den Assem, 1967). When males settle in adjacent territories, observers have gained the impression that the frequency of high intensity aggressive behaviour between the males declines over a period of days (van den Assem and van der Molen, 1969).

Systematic studies of this phenomenon of the waning of levels of aggression have made use of both live males and models as test

TABLE VIII

Distances between adjacent nests of male *Gasterosteus aculeatus* in the River Wear, Durham City, in June and July, 1969.

(a) Frequency distribution of inter-nest distances

Class interval (cm)	0–49	50–99	100–149	150–199
Number of inter-nest distances	0	10	8	9
Class interval (cm)	200–249	250–299	300–349	350
Number of inter-nest distances	10	5	2	7

(b) Average inter-nest distances

Period of observation	Number of distances measured	Average inter-nest distance (cm)
8 June–13 June	19	237 ± 21.8
30 June–8 July	12	143 ± 25.4
10 July–16 July	10	149 ± 34.2
17 July–23 July	10	199 ± 34.2

stimuli. In almost all cases a decline in the level of aggression occurred with repeated presentation of the stimulus. When such repeated presentation of a stimulus leads to a waning in a specific behavioural response to that stimulus, the process is usually referred to as habituation. Some authors have argued that habituation is the process by which the level of fighting between adjacent males is reduced (van den Assem and van der Molen, 1969; Peeke and Peeke, 1973).

In a demonstration of habituation, males with nests were presented with a series of five models. The models had increasing amounts of red on them. Once a day each male was presented with the five models in turn, a model being presented for a two minute period. Over a twelve day period, the frequency of biting at all five models declined (Peeke *et al.*, 1969). For another demonstration, the experimental males, all of whom had nests, were presented either with a live male confined in a glass tube or with a male-like model. Initially the frequency of biting at the live male was far higher than at the model when each was presented for fifteen minutes per day. But after ten days, the amount of biting at both stimuli had declined, that to the live male so dramatically that there was no difference between the frequency of biting at the male and at the model. Even within the fifteen minute presentation period, there was clear evidence of a decline in the frequency of biting, charging and orientating towards the stimulus (Peeke, 1969), In these experiments, the experimental males saw the test stimulus for only a few minutes each day, and for the rest of the time they received little or no stimulation from an object to which an aggressive response would appropriate.

A different experimental situation also provided evidence for the habituation of the aggressive response (van den Assem and van der Molen, 1969). Tanks were divided in half with transparent glass partitions. In the control situation, a single male was placed in one half of the tank while the other half was left empty, whereas in the experimental situation a male was placed in each half of a tank. The aggression of the control and experimental males was measured by placing a male confined in a glass tube in the appropriate section of the tank and recording the number of bites directed at the male in the tube. Where there was a male in both halves of a tank, one of the males was removed while the aggression of the other was being measured, so that the latter male was not distracted by the activity of the male in the other half of the tank. The experimental males showed significantly less biting than the control males, which probably indicated that the presence of a neighbouring male had significantly reduced the aggressiveness of the experimental males. An alternative hypothesis would be that the isolated males, the control males, had become hyper-aggressive. Other experiments showed that the effect of the presence of the neighbouring male was obtained in the absence of the partition, that is in a situation in which the pair of males could interact freely, and also when the neighbours could see each other only intermittently. There was one situation in which the presence of a rival male did not seem to modify the aggression shown to a male in the tube. The results described above were obtained for males that had built nests. When males which had not built nests were tested in the same way, many of them failed to show the modified aggressive response to the male in the tube. This result suggests that the presence of the nest has a significant effect on the aggression of a male, though it is not clear how the nest has an effect.

These experimental studies clearly support the hypothesis that aggression between adjacent, territorial males can habituate. But for a male to maintain his territory, he must continue to respond aggressively to intruders or potential usurpers. This implies that the habituation should be specific to the neighbouring males and not to other males. This specificity could be achieved either because the male habituates to rivals that are in a specific geographical or topographical relationship to him, or because the male learns to recognise neighbouring males as individuals (Peeke and Peeke, 1973).

Some evidence for the specificity of the modification of the aggressive response was obtained when a male stickleback was placed in one half of a tank which contained a goldfish in the other half, visible through the glass partition. Such a male was found to be as aggressive to a male confined in a glass tube as the control males who could see neither a stickleback nor a goldfish in the other half of the tank, and far more aggressive than males that had a conspecific male in the other half of the tank (van den Assem and van der Molen, 1969). But attempts to analyse this specificity further have given contradictory results. Evidence that both positional cues and the individual recognition of fish can contribute to the specificity has been obtained (Peeke and Veno, 1973), but no evidence of individual recognition of rivals was obtained in the experimental situation where the rivals were separated by a glass partition (van den Assem and van der Molen, 1969). Since experience of a rival visible through a glass partition leads to a reduction in the aggression shown to a different male in a glass tube placed within the living space of the male, this also suggests that the waning of aggression is not very stimulus specific.

Another difficulty with the hypothesis that habituation plays an important role in determining the aggressive levels of territorial males comes from the observation that it is often the neighbouring males that are most assiduous in trying to encroach into a territory and interfere with the nest of the resident male (Wootton, 1971b). In this situation, a specific habituation to neighbours would seem to be a grave disadvantage, unless the habituation is specific to the sight of the neighbour in his own territory. Several questions remain to be answered before the role of habituation in the interactions between territorial males can be assessed. Is the waning of aggression an artefact of the experimental situations or can a similar waning be observed between free-living males? If such a waning is observed, is the rate of waning related to the intensity of the interactions during fighting? What are the specific advantages gained from the waning?

So far the discussion has been centred on the factors that

determine the level of aggression observed in particular situations in terms of external factors such as the nature and frequency of presentation of the stimulus, but the increase in the males' aggression that takes place at the beginning of the breeding season takes place even if these extrinsic factors are kept constant. The aggression of the males is an essential component of their reproductive behaviour, for males which are not aggressive and cannot defend territories will not breed. It might therefore be expected that the hormonal factors which are important for other aspects of the reproductive behaviour of the male will also be important in the causation of aggression. Hormones produced by the testes are essential for nest-building and courtship behaviour, but what effect does the removal of the testes have on the aggressive behaviour of the male? Somewhat surprisingly, the aggression of the male is to a large extent not dependent on the presence of the testes, and so cannot be dependent on the presence of androgens produced by the testes. When males were kept on a light regime of 16L 8D and castrated before they had built nests, they showed no decline in the levels of their aggression, but over a period of a month became more aggressive (Hoar, 1962b), a result confirmed by Baggerman (1966). If the castrated males were kept on a light regime of 8L 16D, there was little or no increase in the level of the aggression which was low at the start of the experiment (Hoar, 1962b). The castrated males kept at 16L 8D did not develop nuptial colours or build nests, so that the castration had dissociated the aggressive components of the males' reproductive behaviour from the nest-building and courtship components and from the morphological, secondary sexual characters. Note that the aggression of the castrated males on the long day-lengths was high although none of the fish had developed the red underside characteristic of the sexually mature male.

Males castrated during their parental phase still showed the changes in aggression that are characteristic of intact males in the parental phase including the marked increase in aggression after the young hatch (Baggerman, 1968).

The situation during the sexual phase of the male, that is the period between the completion of the nest and the start of the parental phase, is less clear. Males castrated nine to twelve days after they had completed their nests showed a significant decline in the level of aggression that they displayed to a male opponent. The decline was similar to that seen in normal males after the end of their breeding cycle and the level of aggression reached was far lower than that seen in intact males before they built nests or in males that had been gonadectomised before they had built nests. This result led to the hypothesis that in the course of the breeding cycle, the hormonal control of the aggressive behaviour passed to the gonadal hormones from the gonadotropic hormone which, as discussed below, is thought to control aggression throughout most of the breeding cycle (Baggerman, 1966). An attempt was made to replicate the results of the effect of castration on males that had built nests. A different and, it was hoped, a standardised method of measuring aggression was used. Males were castrated either just before or in the week after they built nests, then tested four weeks later. The males that had been castrated after they had built nests showed a decline in the level of their aggression back to a level characteristic of males shortly before they had built nests. The castrated fish did not maintain their nests so that after four weeks they did not have nests (Wootton, 1970). This suggests the possibility that the high level of aggression of males with nests is to some extent dependent of the presence of the nest. If the male loses the nest because he is no longer in the hormonal state required for its maintenance, then there is also a decline in his aggression. Some support for this hypothesis comes from the observation that even intact males whose nests had been removed showed a reduction in the level of aggression that they displayed to other males (Symons, 1965).

Attempts to induce an increase in the aggressiveness of males by treating them with exogeneous testosterone have not been successful, although treatment will evoke the development of secondary sexual characters (Wai and Hear, 1963; Baggerman, 1968).

If the aggression of the males is not dependent on gonadal hormones, what is likely to be the causal basis for the increase in aggression that characterises the onset of the breeding cycle of the male? Three obvious possibilities are that there is a change intrinsic to the central nervous system induced by the increasing day-lengths, or that another peripheral endocrine organ produces a hormone or hormones in response to the output of hormones from the pituitary, or thirdly that a product of the pituitary itself induces the increase in aggressiveness.

This third possibility has received most experimental support. Hoar (1962a) has argued that as the day-lengths increase, the pituitary produces more gonadotropin which in addition to stimulating the production of androgens by the testes also has a direct effect on the level of aggressive behaviour. High levels of aggression are associated with high levels of gonadotropin. At short day-lengths the pituitary produces little or no gonadotropin, the testes are not stimulated to produce androgens and as a direct result of the low gonadotropin levels, the levels of aggression are very low. When males were kept on short day-lengths and injected with a mammalian gonadotropin, luteinising hormone (LH), they showed an increase in the level of their aggressive behaviour (Hoar, 1962a, b). Other mammalian pituitary hormones tested were the thyroid stimulating hormone (TSH) and the gonadotropin, follicle stimulating hormone (FSH), but neither of these induced an increase in aggressive behaviour. Methallibure (dithiocarbamoylhydrazine) is a drug that is believed to block the formation of gonadotropin. Males kept on long day-lengths and treated with methallibure showed a decrease in their aggressive behaviour (Carew, 1968), a further piece of evidence which supports the hypothesis that pituitary gonadotropic hormone is casually involved in controlling the level of aggression in the male stickleback.

Although this indirect evidence supports the hypothesis that changes in the level of aggression of the male depend on changes in the level of gonadotropin, there is also some evidence that gonadal hormone must be present for the increase in aggression to take place at the beginning of the breeding season. Males were kept for two or three months on a photoperiod of 8L 16D, then castrated and placed on a photoperiod of 16L 8D. This treatment would be expected to increase the secretion of gonadotropin from the pituitary gland and so lead to an increase in the level of aggression. But the males showed no appreciable increase in their aggressive behaviour (Baggerman, 1968). A problem with this and the other experiments on the relationship between gonadotropins and aggression is that there have been no direct measurements on the levels of gonadotropin during the various phases of the breeding cycle, so that any evidence that high levels of gonadotropin and high levels of aggression coincide is indirect.

Although some of the differences in the level of aggression between individual males may be environmentally induced, there may also be an underlying genetic difference. Sevenster (cited in Huntingford, 1974) has shown that selection for high and low levels of aggression can be successful, which could only occur if some of the variance in the levels of aggression had a genetic basis.

Two other types of behaviour seem to be correlated with levels of aggression shown by males. Dominant males were found to be more active than subordinant males when the males were placed individually in a strange environment. A comparison of mature males with immature males showed that, although over a period of eighteen or more hours the two groups did not differ in the amount of activity they showed in the strange environment, the mature males started to explore sooner than the immatures (Anthouard, 1967). A second correlation found was between the degree of boldness shown by male sticklebacks towards predators or in a strange environment during the non-reproductive period and the level of aggression during the breeding period. The boldest males tended to be the most aggressives males (Huntingford, 1974). The functional significance of these correlations has still to be determined.

In spite of all the research efforts that have been devoted to the aggression of the male stickleback, there are still many gaps and uncertainties in our understanding of this aspect of the reproductive behaviour, and even more problems as to the nature and role of the male's aggression will be raised in the next chapter.

12. Reproduction: The Male III
(The Sexual Phase)

At the beginning of the nest-building phase of the male's reproductive cycle, the sight of a female induces only an aggressive
response from the male. Towards the end of the nest-building phase
the male may approach a gravid female with a few zig zags rather
than a direct charge, but he does not lead the female back to the, as
yet, incomplete nest. The beginning of the sexual phase of the cycle
is signalled when the male creeps through the nest forming a distinct
tunnel for the first time. Now the male is ready to lead a gravid
female back to his nest and to induce her to spawn in the nest
(Sevenster, 1961).

The courtship of the male serves several functions, some more
obvious than others (Tinbergen, 1953). Each courtship follows a
fairly predictable temporal sequence which serves to synchronise the
activities of the male and female. The initial approach of the male to
the gravid female is made in a series of zig zags quite unlike the
normal swimming pattern of the stickleback. This unique mode of
approach advertises the presence of a male in the sexual phase to the
female. In the courtship the male leads the female back to the nest
and indicates the position of the nest entrance. In this way the male
ensures that the eggs are laid at the correct site; the courtship has an
orientating function. The distinctive courtship of the three-spined
stickleback also ensures that the male only mates with females of his
own species, thus enhancing the reproductive isolation between
closely related species such as the three-spined and nine-spined
stickleback (see Chapter 16). Recently it has also been suggested that
the courtship of the male functions to maintain the male in the
correct motivational state to achieve a successful mating. Both an
excessive tendency to behave aggressively towards the gravid female,
and more surprisingly, an excessive tendency to show sexual behav-

(a)

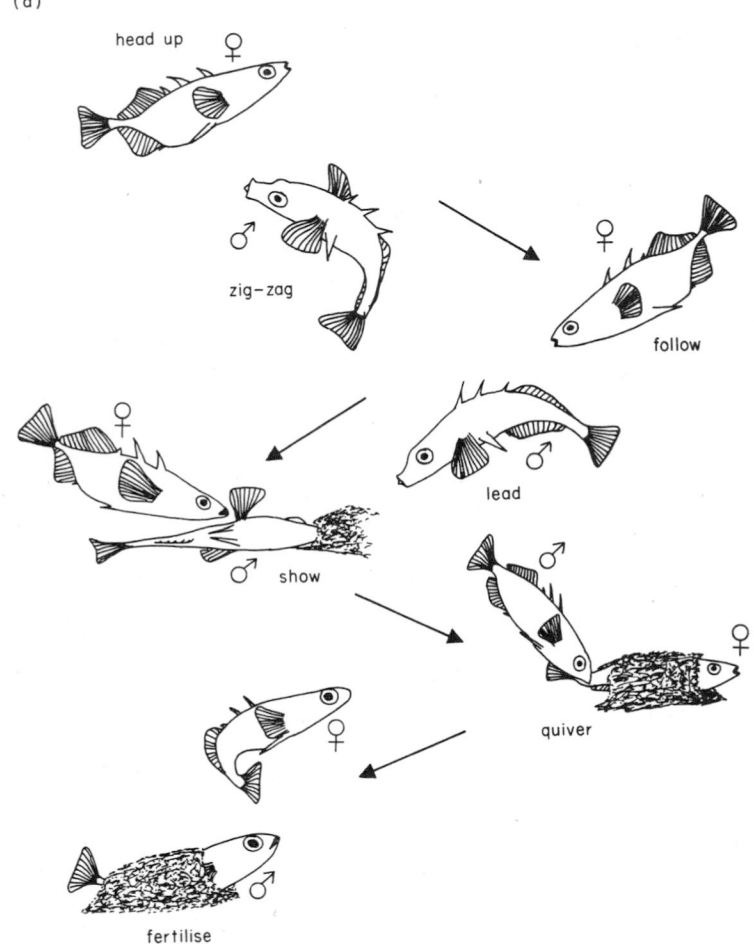

Fig. 42. Courtship of *Gasterosteus aculeatus*. (a) Zig-zag, lead, show sequence.

iour interfere with the chances of mating (Sevenster, 1961; Wilz, 1972). In this context courtship behaviour has a homeostatic function.

Each behavioural element in the male's courtship repertoire is distinctive and easily recognised (Fig. 42).

The zig-zag dance of the male consists of a series of jumps in which the male jumps first away from and then towards the female with his mouth open and usually with spines erect (Tinbergen, 1953). A male may approach the female or dance around her, and

(b)

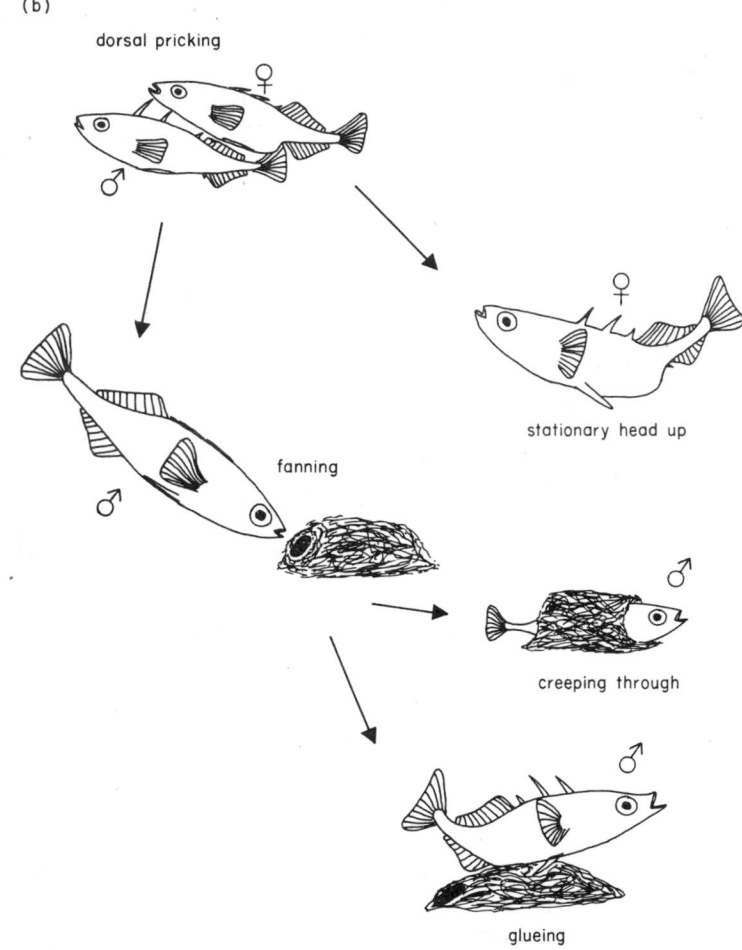

Fig. 42 (continued). (b) Dorsal pricking, next visit sequence.

sometimes a series of zig zags ends with the male biting or butting the female although more often the dance ends a short distance from her. This zig-zagging of the male is usually interpreted as being composed of two elements. Each leap away from the female represents the intention of leading the female back to the nest, while each leap forward represents an intention of attacking the female. Thus zig-zagging is seen as an alternation of aggressive and sexual tendencies (van Iersel, quoted in Sevenster, 1961).

A gravid female responds to the zig-zagging of the male by

adopting the head-up posture (Chapter 9). The male then swims directly and rapidly back to the nest, leading the female to the nest. If the female follows the male down to the nest, the male pokes his snout slightly into the nest tunnel and turns on his side so that his back is towards the female. In this position the male jerks to and fro slightly as if indicating the position of the nest entrance. This is the showing component of the male's courtship. A gravid female slips past the male into the nest. If the female is not quite ready to spawn she may merely nose part of the way into the nest and then retreat. In some cases the female may even fail to find the nest entrance and thrust in inappropriate directions as though unable to interpret the showing of the male correctly.

If a female is repeatedly nosing into and then backing out of the nest, the male sometimes positions himself above the female and erects his ventral spines. This behaviour has been described as "helping" the female into the nest (Leiner, 1930), but it rarely seems to result in an unwilling female entering the nest.

Once the female is in the nest the male quivers giving a series of quick pushes on the flanks and caudal peduncle of the female. Only when she receives this stimulus (or its equivalent) does she spawn. When the female has spawned the male pushes his way through the nest depositing his sperm over the eggs and so fertilising them.

The sequential or temporal organisation of this courtship has been described as a reaction chain (Tinbergen, 1951). Each behaviour of one of the actors serves as a stimulus evoking the response of the coactor. Thus the zig-zagging of the male is evoked by the appearance of the gravid female with her silvery, distended stomach. Then the head up response of the female is evoked by the zig-zag approach of the male and so on (Fig. 43a). But the reaction chain illustrated in Fig. 43a represents an idealised courtship sequence, although occasionally a courtship is seen which almost exactly follows this idealised sequence. Two types of deviation from the sequence occur. Some steps may be omitted or repeated (Morris, 1958) or, more interestingly, additional elements appear in the male's response to the appearance of a gravid female (Fig. 43b).

Instead of leading the gravid female directly back to the nest, a male often adopts the posture called dorsal pricking (ter Pelkwijk and Tinbergen, 1937; Wilz, 1967, 1970b). The male positions himself below and across the female and with his dorsal spines erect moves backwards as though to prick the belly of the female. While in this position the pair tend to swim round in circles. Next, the male breaks off the dorsal pricking and circling and swims back to his nest. But in this case, if the female attempts to follow the male, he changes

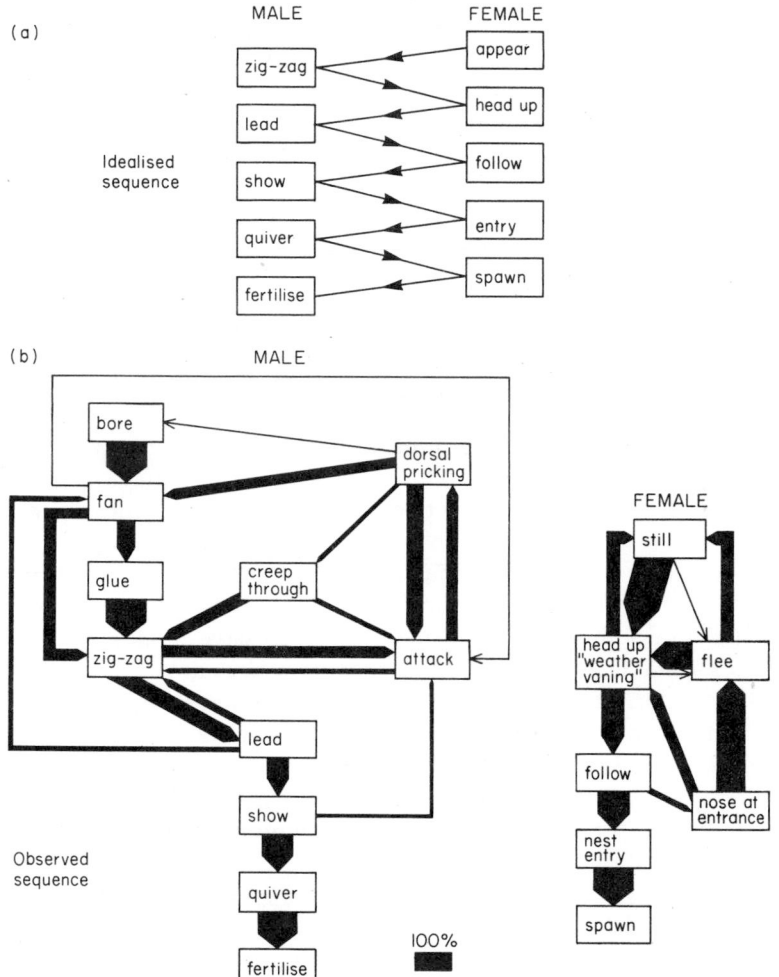

Fig. 43. Courtship sequence of *Gasterosteus aculeatus*. (a) Idealised sequence (after Tinbergen, 1951); (b) observed sequences, data from 15 consummated courtships have been pooled; width of arrow is proportional to the percentage of times with which a behaviour is followed by another.

direction abruptly and usually resumes dorsal pricking, or starts biting the female. Either of these activities results in the male manoeuvering the female away from his nest. When the male does get back to the nest he performs activities which, from a functional point of view, would be regarded as characteristic of the nest building or parental phases of the reproductive cycle. Typically, the male bores slightly at the entrance of the nest and then either creeps through or starts fanning. This fanning is identical in form to the fanning seen in the parental phase when the nest contains eggs. The fanning is usually followed by glueing, again the form of which is identical to that seen during nest building although the time spent glueing is usually shorter. Only if the male successfully completes the fanning—glueing sequence does he then show high intensity courtship behaviour with zig-zagging and leading. Fanning not followed by glueing, or creeping through, tends to be followed by less intense courtship with bouts of dorsal pricking and even attacks on the female.

The puzzling aspect of this variation on the male's courtship behaviour is that it incorporates elements such as fanning, glueing and creeping through which do not seem relevant in the context of courtship behaviour. The dorsal pricking behaviour even seems to dissuade the female from coming to the male's nest rather than serving to entice her there. The evolution of a behaviour pattern which seems to disrupt a sequence of behaviour that ends in mating seems very paradoxical.

In order to resolve, at least partially, this paradox, the relationship between the aggressive tendency and the courtship tendency of a territorial male must be considered. Aggressive males hold large territories and males with large territories are more successful in courtships than males with small territories. When several males were present in a large container there was a direct relationship between the success a male had in getting females into his nest and the size of the territory he held (van den Assem, 1967). From this it might be concluded that high levels of aggression favour success in matings. But the gravid female still presents sufficient stimulus properties to be able to release attacks by the male, and such attacks are likely to drive the female out of the male's territory into a rival male's territory. A male must resolve the problem of maintaining a high level of aggression in order to maintain a large territory in the face of pressure from his neighbours, but also be able to switch from attacking intruders to courting an intruder if the latter is a gravid female.

There is now evidence which indicates that the dorsal pricking and circling behaviour of the male, and the activities the male performs at the nest are concerned with the balance between the sexual and aggressive tendencies of the male.

Early studies on this facet of the male's courtship had suggested that the activities at the nest, the fanning, glueing and creeping through were what ethologists called displacement activities. Displacement activities are behaviours that appear in a context in which they seem, at least from the observer's point of view, to be irrelevant.

Thus in the male's courtship, the performance of the nest building and fanning activities would seem to be irrelevant to the task of inducing the female to lay her eggs in the nest, especially as the performance of these activities requires that the male leaves the female to return to the nest alone. It was suggested that these activities occurred when the female was reluctant to follow the male down to the nest, and so the male's sexual tendency was thwarted (Tinbergen and van Iersel, 1947).

As closer attention was paid to the context in which these so-called displacement activities appeared in the male's sexual behaviour, the view that they were a product of the thwarting of the male's sexual drive was found to be inadequate. Although such activities were most prominent during the courtship they also occurred in the absence of a female. Fanning is first seen towards the end of the nest building phase, but when the male enters the sexual phase a clear cycle of fanning can be seen (Sevenster, 1961; Nelson, 1965). For a period after a male has crept through his nest little fanning occurs, and on visits to the nest the male tends to spend his time nosing at the nest. At this time the male is also prone to perform the zig-zag dance towards inappropriate stimuli such as air bubbles or moving snails. Such zig zags are called "vacuum" zig zags. As the period since the creeping through lengthens, the male shows more and more fanning at the nest, while the time spent nosing at the nest declines. Eventually the male creeps through the nest again and the cycle is repeated (Figs 44 and 45). Although this cycle, the creeping through cycle, was first analysed in isolated males, it certainly occurs in natural situations (Wootton, 1972a).

Normally once a male has crept through there is an interval of at least seven minutes before he does so again, but in some populations there are males that on occasions creep through two or more times in rapid succession. These males are called creeping through "maniacs". Once a male showing the "maniac" behaviour has crept through two or more times in rapid succession, he then shows the refractory period of at least seven minutes before creeping through again. It is as though the succession of passages through the nest by a "maniac" is equivalent to the single passage of a normal male. The "maniac" trait has a genetic basis; breeding experiments suggested that the genetic factor involved in the trait showed simple Mendelian inheritance with the normal condition dominant over the "maniac" condition. The trait was not linked to sex or the number of lateral plates. However, the expression of the trait depends to a marked degree on the conditions under which males known to be genetically "maniacs" are raised. Males that had been brought to sexual maturity

prematurely by maintaining them under long day-lengths and at high
water temperatures usually expressed the "maniac" trait. Males from
the same stock but maintained for some months under winter
conditions and then brought to sexual maturity failed to express the
trait (Sevenster and Hart, 1974).

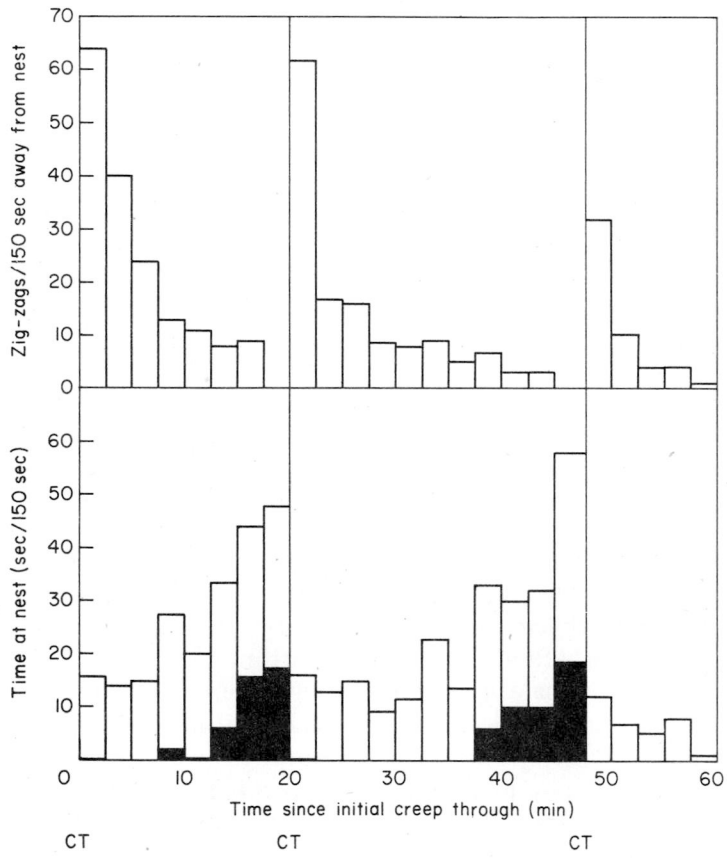

Fig. 44. The creeping through cycle of male *Gasterosteus aculeatus* showing changes in
zig-zagging and time at nest (after Metz, 1974). Black bars represent time at nest spent
fanning; CT, creeping through.

In the sexual phase of the male the creeping through, glueing,
fanning and other nest-orientated activities occur even in the absence
of a gravid female but the presence of the female usually results in
these activities appearing at a higher frequency. The observation that
the male shows "vacuum" zig-zagging most prominently in the
period immediately after creeping through suggests that at this point

the male has a high tendency to show courtship behaviour (a high sexual drive) (Sevenster, 1961). Creeping through has already been noted as a behaviour which demarcates the nest building phase from the sexual phase, so that creeping through seems to mark a transition

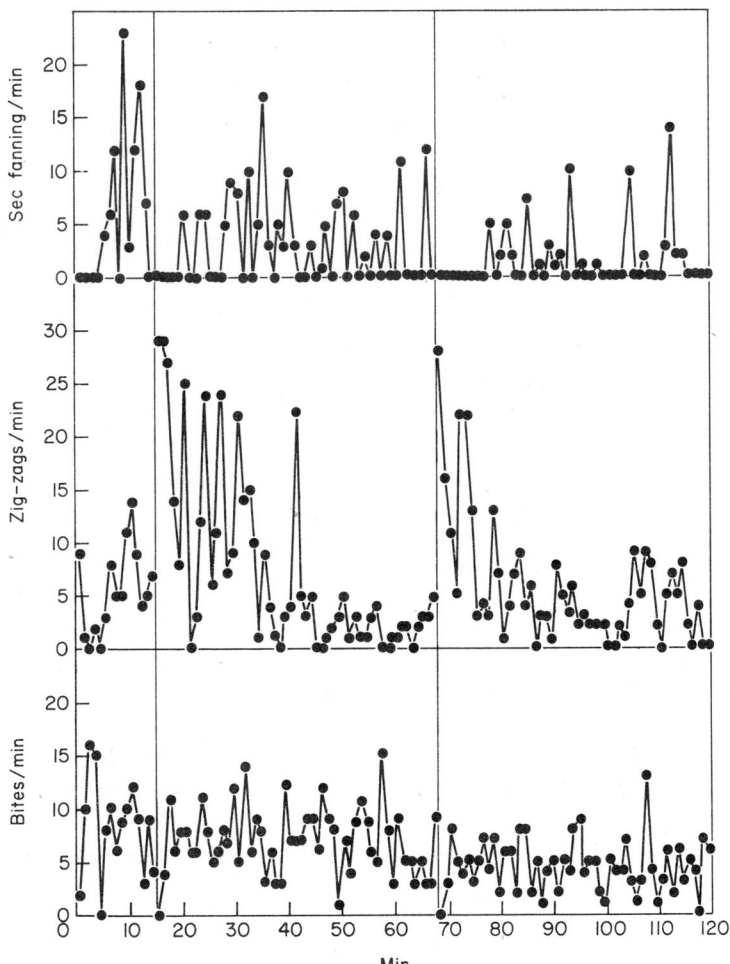

Fig. 45. Creeping through cycle of a male *Gasterosteus aculeatus* showing changes in fanning, zig-zagging and biting in the presence of a confined male conspecific. Vertical line indicates occurrence of creeping through.

to a period of enhanced sexual behaviour. But this raises the question of the behavioural state of the male prior to creeping through. The first occurrence of creeping through marks the transition from the nest building to the sexual phase. In the nest building phase the male is highly aggressive even towards females, so that it seems logical that even in the sexual phase creeping through should mark a transition for the male from a relatively aggressive state to a relatively sexual state (Sevenster, 1961).

There would, of course, be no problem if the male stickleback could switch immediately from aggressive behaviour to courtship behaviour and back again as the appropriate stimuli appeared. But the relevant stimuli for these two types of behaviour have overlapping stimulus properties and so are likely to release both types of behaviour. There is also strong evidence that the aggressive and sexual behaviour of the male are mutually inhibitory. This means that high levels of aggression will prevent high levels of courtship behaviour and vice versa. Evidence for this inhibitory relationship will be presented later, but here the concern is with the consequences of this relationship in the sexual phase of the male.

It is now possible to interpret the creeping through cycles of the male during the sexual phase as indicating a cyclical fluctuation in the relative strengths of the aggressive and sexual tendencies of the male, with creeping through marking the point at which the sexual tendency becomes predominant (Sevenster, 1961). But this interpretation does not explain the cyclical changes in the amount of fanning that the male shows. Fanning in the sexual phase can be shown to be influenced by the same factors that influence it in the parental phase of the male (Sevenster, 1961). For example, passing water containing high levels of carbon dioxide through the nest causes an initial increase in the amount of fanning. Normally those factors which stimulate fanning such as eggs in the nest or changes in carbon dioxide in the water, inhibit sexual behaviour. This suggests that factors that enhance parental behaviour inhibit sexual behaviour, and there is evidence of mutally inhibitory relationships between parental, sexual and aggressive behaviour (Fig. 46) (Sevenster, 1961). Given this situation it is possible to interpret fanning behaviour in the sexual phase, both during courtship and in the absence of a female as occurring when the balance between the aggressive and sexual tendencies of the male is such that neither of them can retain their usual inhibition on the parental activity of fanning. Fanning therefore occurs as a disinhibited behaviour (Sevenster, 1961).

This attractive hypothesis interprets the appearance of fanning, creeping through and the other activities as symptoms of underlying changes in the relative strengths of the tendencies of the male to show courtship or aggressive behaviour.

That this is not the whole story is indicated by more recent work. One of the striking features of the creeping through cycle is its

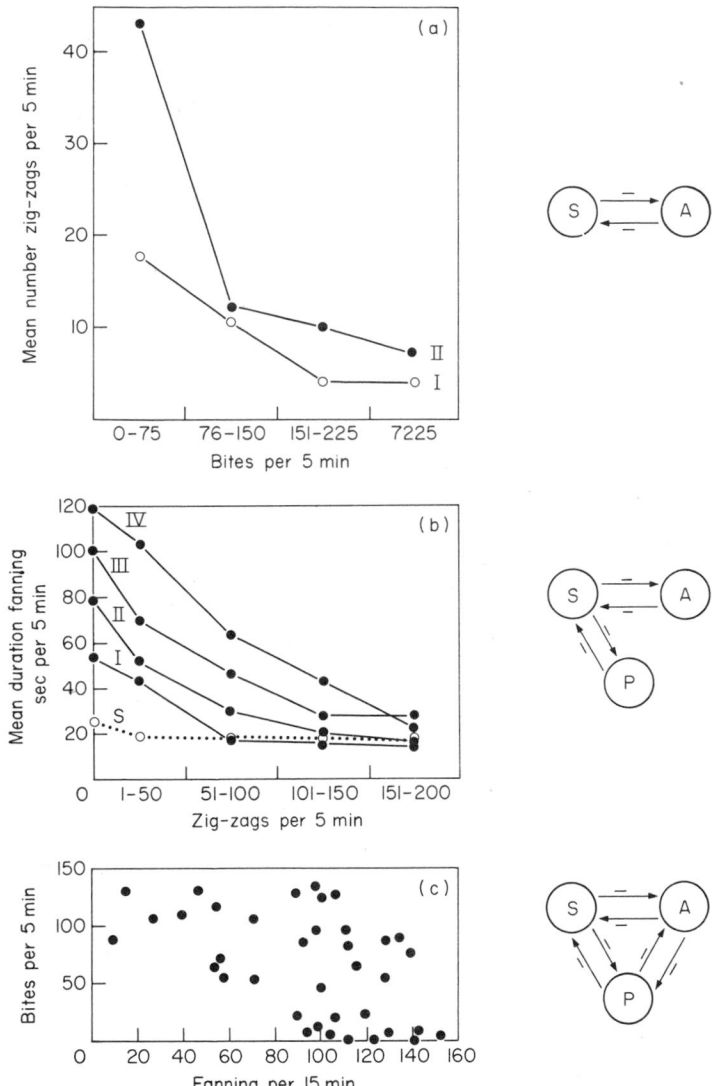

Fig. 46. Some evidence for Sevenster's (1961) scheme of the mutually inhibitory relationships between the sexual (S), aggressive (A) and Parental (P) tendencies of the male *Gasterosteus aculeatus*. (a) Relationship between frequency of zig-zagging and biting directed at a confined male conspecific. I, males, that showed more than 125 zig zags/5 min. towards a confined gravid female; II, males that showed fewer than 125 zig zags/5 min; (b) relationship between amount of fanning and frequency of zig-zagging when males presented with a confined gravid female during the parental phase (I–IV) and the sexual phase (S). Males classified by amount of fanning in sec./30 min. shown when female not present: I, 0–500; II, 500–1000; III, 800–1200; 1000–1500. (c) correlation between frequency of biting at confined male conspecific and duration of fanning during 15 min. before male presented.

remarkable regularity. In some situations the interval between successive creeping throughs, in the absence of the appearance of a female,
increases geometrically with almost mathematical precision. This
feature enabled a sophisticated mathematical analysis of the creeping
through cycle to be made (Nelson, 1965; Metz, 1974). The models of
the system that resulted from this analysis indicated that it was not
essential to postulate the involvement of the aggressive tendency in
the inhibition or disinhibition of fanning. Further evidence comes
from a single experiment in which the behaviour of a male towards a
test male confined in a glass tube was observed for more than an
hour. There were no clear-cut changes in the amount of biting shown
towards the test male, although the male crept through the nest three
times and zig-zagging showed the changes typical of the interval
between successive creeping throughs (Fig. 45).

The very predictability of the interval between successive creeping
throughs indicates that creeping through has a causal role in the
cycle. The timing of the creeping through cycle depends, to some
extent, on the performance of creeping through. The length of the
interval could be altered by altering the length of the nest, so altering
the time it took for the male to push his way through (Nelson,
1965).

Although these studies have thrown light on the causation of the
creeping through cycle, they shed no light on its functional significance. It is in the context of courtship that clues emerge as to the
function of the events seen in the creeping through cycle. The
appearance of fanning, glueing and creeping through during courtship
can be interpreted as displacement activities which lack any functional significance but rather appear as symptoms of underlying
motivational conflicts (Sevenster, 1961). But a more satisfactory
concept of the role of these prominent activities is one which assigns
them a role in enabling the male to switch from an aggressive
response towards the more appropriate courtship response (Wilz,
1967, 1970a, b, c).

Evidence for this function was found when the performance of
these nest directed activities was prevented after the male had been
presented with the model of a gravid female. A male that was unable
to gain access to his nest, then failed to show the full courtship
response to the model. Instead he showed considerable amounts of
dorsal pricking and circling rather than attempting to lead the model
back to the nest. When the male was allowed to perform fanning,
glueing or creeping through at his nest, he showed little dorsal
pricking on his return to the model, but instead attempted to lead
the model directly to the nest and show it the nest entrance. This

finding that the performance of the nest directed activities makes it less likely that the male will subsequently show dorsal pricking to the female, refocuses attention on the cause and function of dorsal pricking.

In what circumstances does dorsal pricking form an important component in the courtship of the male? Experimental and observational evidence suggests that it occurs when the male is relatively aggressive. A male that was made more aggressive by presenting him with another male confined in a glass tube for a few minutes, then showed considerable amounts of dorsal pricking when presented with a model of a gravid female (Wilz, 1970b). But a male that had been sexually stimulated by a presentation of the model female showed relatively low levels of dorsal pricking on the next presentation of the model. The amount of time spent dorsal pricking increased the longer the period between the initial presentation of the female model and the subsequent presentation (Wilz, 1970b). Dorsal pricking may also be seen when a male courts a female that is initially outside his territory. The male leads the female into his territory, but may begin dorsal pricking as soon as he crosses the boundary into his own territory, that is when the female becomes an intruder (van den Assem, 1967).

Dorsal pricking is a response to the approach of a female maintaining a head up posture. It is not seen if the female does not approach and attempt to follow the male. The effect of dorsal pricking and circling is to cause the female to stop following the male and to hold her position, usually retaining the head up posture. While the female holds her position the male has an opportunity to return to his nest without being followed by the female. At the nest he can perform those nest directed activities which seem to enable him to switch from a predominantly aggressive motivation to a predominantly sexual motivation. Successful leading of the female to the nest entrance can then take place (Wilz, 1970b). The entire behavioural complex of dorsal pricking, circling, return to the nest and the performance of nest directed activities seems to be a necessary component of the male's courtship pattern which enables the male to switch from a relatively aggressive behavioural state which is necessary for the maintenance of a territory, to a relatively sexual behavioural state necessary for successful mating.

This suggests that one function of courtship, at least in this fish, is to achieve a behavioural homeostasis such that neither a very strong aggressive nor a very strong sexual motivation develops, for both can interfere with the success of the courtship (Wilz, 1972). A very aggressive male will drive a female from his territory, while a male with a high sexual motivation turns to lead the female back to the nest after making only one or two zig-zags, and so never gets very far from his nest with the result that the advertising function of his courtship is neglected and a female often fails to follow his leading (Sevenster, 1961). When a male was given eggs stripped from a female which he had not had the chance of courting, he was most likely to fertilise the eggs when he was in a state that suggested a "balance" between the aggressive and courtship tendencies (Sevenster-Bol, 1962).

If the male was fearful this might also interfere with courtship. Wilz (1970c) found that mildly frightening the male led to an increase in the nest directed activities.

Interestingly enough, the nine-spined stickleback (*Pungitius pungitius*), which seems to be less aggressive during courtship than the three-spined stickleback, has no equivalent to dorsal pricking and does not leave the female during the courtship sequence (Chapter 17) (Wilz, 1971).

A somewhat different way of looking at the relationship between courtship and nest directed activities has been discussed by McFarland (1974). He suggests that a function underlying the organisation of courtship is maintenance of the nest so that it is kept in a suitable condition to receive the female. During courtship, the male must pay attention both to the female and to the nest, and this is achieved by time-sharing. Although attention to the female is the dominant activity and has priority, at times the sub-dominant activity of nest care is permitted; that is the two activities share the available time. A difficulty with this interpretation is that it does not explain why the frequency of nest visits by the male should increase during the period of courtship. This occurs in the three-spined stickleback, but does not occur in other stickleback species in which nest care must still be relevant. However, the interpretations of Wilz and McFarland are not mutually exclusive, so that it is possible that in the three-spined stickleback the opportunity has been taken, during the evolution of the courtship behaviour, to make use of nest visits to influence the relative balance of the sexual and aggressive tendencies.

Both the displacement activity and the functional interpretations of the nest directed activities during the courtship of the male stickleback imply that there is a mutually inhibitory relationship between the tendency to show sexual behaviour and the tendency to show aggressive behaviour. High levels of aggression are incompatible with high levels of courtship behaviour and high levels of courtship behaviour are incompatible with high levels of aggressive behaviour. Four major lines of evidence support this assumption.

In an interaction between a male and a gravid female, a male may approach the female in a direct straight line or may approach in a series of zig zags. While the direct approach frequently ends with the male biting the female sometimes causing her to flee, a zig-zag approach much less frequently ends in the male biting the female and the male usually returns to his nest, leading the female down, or returning to bore and fan. In some situations the male may dance around the female in a series of slight zig zags, but with his mouth open as though about to bite her, but the bite is rarely made. It is as though the male, while zig-zagging, is inhibited from biting (Sevenster, 1968).

The second piece of evidence for the inhibitory relationship comes from studies in which either a male or a gravid female was placed in a tube and presented some centimetres away from the nest of a male. The male with the nest can attempt to bite the fish in the tube or can zig-zag towards it. In such tests, it was found that the frequency of biting was inversely related to the frequency of zig-zagging (Fig. 46). It is not simply that there was not sufficient time for high frequencies of both to occur, for the effect is greater than can be accounted for simply by a lack of sufficient time (Symons, 1965). For a time after a tube containing a male was removed, there was a reduction in the amount of zig-zagging, leading and showing if the male with the nest was then presented with a real or model female. So a period during which the aggressive behaviour of the male predominated is followed by a period of reduced sexual behaviour even when the stimulus evoking the aggressive behaviour has disappeared and has been replaced by a stimulus which normally evokes considerable courtship behaviour (Wilz, 1972).

A third piece of evidence comes from the studies discussed in the previous chapter in which a waning in the aggressive response of a male was induced by the repeated presentation or continual presence of a male conspecific. In this case the waning in the aggressive responses of charging and biting at a male conspecific was accompanied by an increase in the frequency of zig-zagging to a female conspecific (Peeke, 1969; van den Assem and van der Molen, 1969). Although there were some differences in the results of these two studies, probably caused by the different methods used, the clear conclusion emerged that a waning in the aggressive response of a male in the sexual phase tended to favour an increase in the tendency to show sexual behaviour. In the next chapter a situation will be described in which a waning in aggression is not associated with an increase in courtship behaviour.

Fourthly, the most intriguing piece of evidence comes from studies in which the male had to learn a particular task in order to gain a chance of displaying courtship behaviour to a gravid female. Male sticklebacks were trained either to swim through a ring or to bite at a rod. If they performed the task correctly, they were allowed to view for twenty or thirty seconds a gravid female confined in a transparent container. The rate at which the task was performed, the response rate, was higher when the task was swimming through a ring than when it was biting a rod. Yet this was not because the act of biting itself caused the delay, for if the reward was no longer given, the trained animal would start to bite the rod more rapidly than when the reward, the gravid female, was given. Detailed observations of the behaviour of the male after he had bitten the rod clarified why the male took such a relatively long time to bite the rod again. When the male could see the female, he performed his courtship to her until the end of the presentation period. For a short time after the disappearance of the female the male sometimes performed activities at the nest or showed "vacuum" zig-zagging. This behaviour occurred whether the male's task was to swim through a ring or bite a rod. But when the male did swim to the rod, and this was usually relatively soon after the disappearance of the female, he did not bite the rod but tended to dance around it in a series of small zig zags and often with his mouth open. Only after the zig-zagging declined did the male again bite the rod. These observations can be interpreted as showing that the courtship behaviour such as zig-zagging stimulated by the sight of the female was incompatible with the biting the male must perform in order to obtain another exposure to the female (Sevenster, 1968, 1973).

Although these pieces of evidence indicate a mutually inhibitory relationship between the tendencies to show courtship and aggressive behaviour this is not the whole story.

A most obvious point is that both courtship and aggressive behaviour of the male tend to be at their peak in the same period of his life, during the breeding period and more specifically the sexual phase of the period. So taken over the whole life cycle of the stickleback, there is a positive correlation between aggressive and sexual behaviour. Even during the courtship sequence itself a male may show abrupt changes from courtship to aggressive behaviour. This is especially true if the female starts to flee from the male. Finally it was found that although the short-term effect of exposing a male to another male for ten minutes was to reduce the frequency of glueing at the nest, both when the male was present and for up to five minutes after the tube was removed, this depression was followed by levels of glueing higher than observed before exposure to the male (Wilz, 1972). Glueing is also seen at high frequencies during courtship behaviour, so it may be that over a longer period of time the stimulation of aggressive behaviour also stimulates sexual behaviour. This possibility remains conjectural at the moment, but it implies that when discussing inhibitory relationships between aggressive and sexual behaviour it has to be remembered that the relationship may be a function of time and that, when a relatively long period of time is considered, what was an inhibitory relationship in the short term, may have become a neutral or even a stimulatory relationship. In a natural situation a male has to be prepared to show aggression towards his neighbour and yet be able to respond with courtship to any gravid female that enters or passes near his territory.

Clearly, the courtship of the male stickleback has been, and still is, the subject of elegant behavioural analysis and has provided much of the data on which ethological theory has been built. It is, therefore, disappointing that the physiological correlates of this behaviour have received so little study.

Males kept under long day-lengths (16L 8D) but gonadectomised did not build nests and did not show courtship behaviour (Hoar, 1962b; Wai and Hoar, 1963). When males were gonadectomised shortly before they had built nests, but after they had started to show some nest building and courtship behaviour, they showed a decline in courtship behaviour to very low levels over about twenty-four days. These males also stopped nest building. Similar results were obtained when the males were gonadectomised several days after they had completed nests. In this case the decline in courtship occurred mainly in the first three days after the gonadectomy with a gradual decline thereafter (Baggerman, 1966).

When males which had been gonadectomised were treated with testosterone and kept under a long day-length, most of them built nests and showed the full male courtship repertoire when presented with gravid females. These males even went through the motions of fertilising the eggs although of course they could emit no sperm (Wai and Hoar, 1963). When this experiment was repeated with the difference that the males were kept on short day-lengths (8L 16D), very few males built nests or showed any courtship behaviour.

Females treated with testosterone after they had been gonadectomised occasionally built rather token nests which lacked the tunnel. These females also showed glueing and fanning but did not show zig-zagging or leading when presented with normal gravid females (Wai and Hoar, 1963). This indicates that the glueing and fanning behaviour seen during the courtship of the male probably has a different causal basis from the zig-zag and lead components of courtship, although the behavioural analysis described previously had suggested that these behaviours can share, at least partially, common causal factors (Wilz, 1972).

A provisional hypothesis regarding the endocrine basis of the male's courtship behaviour assumes that level of the pituitary gonadrotropic hormone is high when the fish is experiencing long day-lengths and low when the fish is experiencing short day-lengths. Male courtship behaviour requires high levels of gonadotropin and male gonadal hormone and probably that the fish is a genetic male. This scheme remains tentative and requires further studies to modify it (Baggerman, 1966, 1968).

Whatever the physiological basis of courtship, its function is to ensure the successful fertilisation of eggs in the nest of the male. With fertilised eggs in the nest, the male moves into the parental phase of the reproductive cycle.

13. Reproduction: The Male IV
(The Parental Phase)

After the male fertilises eggs his behaviour changes. Some of the changes are short lived and are reversed within an hour or so. Other changes are much longer lasting and form the main behavioural events that characterise the parental phase of the male, a phase that lasts several days.

The male pushes through the nest depositing sperm over the eggs soon after the female has laid them. Both visual and chemical stimuli probably play a role in releasing the act of fertilisation. Males will attempt to fertilise the mucus taken from freshly laid eggs, which suggests significant chemical stimuli, but males which had had their nasal cavities cauterised would still fertilise fresh eggs placed in the nest by an experimenter (van Iersel, 1953). Males will not fertilise eggs that have become hard and stiff, a process that takes about fifteen to thirty minutes. Usually the fertilisation is performed as soon as or even as the female leaves the nest, but in some cases the male attacks the female as she leaves the nest and chases the female away. Then the eggs are not fertilised until the male returns to his nest which may not be for several seconds.

After the eggs have been fertilised and the female driven out of the male's territory, the male begins to attend to the eggs. At this stage the eggs are usually lying in the nest entrance forming a rather rounded mass. The male pushes the eggs inwards and downwards onto the floor of the nest. Once the eggs are well in the nest the male takes a vertical position directly over them and presses them into the bottom in a series of short bouts of pushing. This is succeeded by a boring-fanning movement. The male appears to fan very rapidly, but in this case the pectorals beat in an opposite direction to that seen in normal fanning so that the male swims rapidly downwards pushing and flattening the egg mass against the bottom of the nest with his mouth. These activities result in the egg mass being flattened into a sheet, and further egg clutches can be laid partially on top of the preceding, flattened layer. Half an hour after the fertilisation, egg pushing and bore-fanning no longer occur, and the male starts a short phase of nest building which lasts about twenty minutes. This results in the nest being lengthened and the nest entrance narrowed to the size it was before the female had pushed her way into the nest. The extra length of the nest ensures that the next clutch of eggs is not laid directly on top of the preceding clutch, instead the successive clutches lie like roof tiles on top of each other. This arrangement probably ensures a more efficient ventilation of all the eggs than would be achieved if all the eggs were just lying in one large rounded mass (van Iersel, 1953).

In the time spent pushing and boring the eggs well down into the nest and while he is lengthening the nest, the male does not show courtship behaviour towards other gravid females. Indeed from the time that the female is in the nest until about an hour after a successful fertilisation the male is relatively aggressive and unwilling to respond sexually even to suitable females (Fig. 47). The events that surround the successful fertilisation of eggs seem to result in changes in aggressive and sexual behaviour that last for up to an hour.

The relevant factors which lead to the changes in the aggressive and sexual behaviour of the male were analysed in an ingenious series of experiments, which systematically compared the effect of the presence and absence of possible factors (Sevenster-Bol, 1962). These experiments showed that the most important factor was the presence of fresh eggs in the nest. With fresh eggs in the nest, a male showed a marked reduction in his tendency to show courtship behaviour and a marked increase in his aggressive behaviour. The presence of eggs also slowed down the rate at which the male returned to his original behavioural state. A second factor which had some effect, though not as great an effect as the presence of eggs, was the performance of quivering. This is the behaviour by which the male stimulates the female to spawn (see previous chapter). Surprisingly there was no evidence that the act of fertilisation with the emission of sperm brought about these relatively short-term changes in sexual and aggressive behaviour.

The inhibition of sexual behaviour and the enhancement of aggressive behaviour seems to be most marked in the vicinity of the nest. When a gravid female was presented in a tube 160 or 260 cm from a nest where the male had just fertilised eggs, the male initially approached the female in a direct line as though about to attack her, but about 1 m from the nest the male started to zig zag. If the female was presented 20 or 90 cm from the nest, the male showed only aggressive behaviour towards her. Before the eggs had been fertilised, the male showed maximum levels of zig-zagging when the female was 90 cm from the nest (Sierksma and Sevenster, quoted in Sevenster-Bol, 1962).

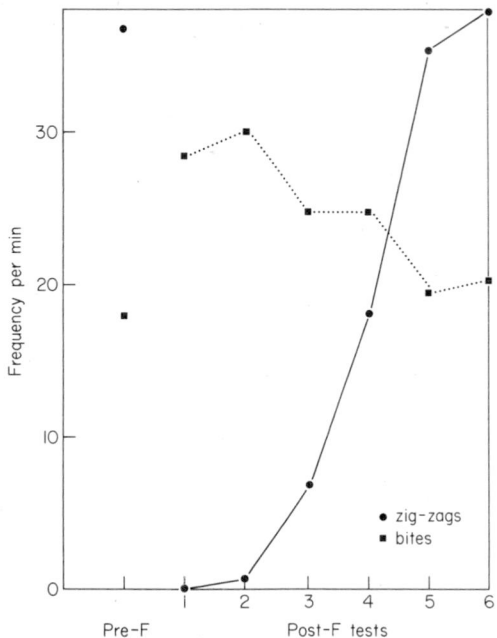

Fig. 47. Changes in the frequency of biting and zig-zagging by male *Gasterosteus aculeatus* after fertilising one clutch of eggs (after Sevenster-Bol, 1962). Biting measured as frequency directed at a confined conspecific male and zig-zagging as frequency directed at confined gravid female, test animals at 50 cm from nest. Pre-F, pre-fertilisation; Post-F, post fertilisation.

The increase in aggressive behaviour shown by a male after he has fertilised eggs seems to be primarily a change in the rate at which the male attacks an opponent rather than a change in the amount of time the male spends attending to the opponent. The intensity of the male's aggressive behaviour changes rather than the time devoted to aggressive behaviour. These high rates of attack shown by the male are also notable for the high proportion of attacks which are made with dorsal spines erect. In this situation there is a correlation between high levels of aggression and high levels of spine raising (Wootton, 1972b).

About an hour after the fertilisation, the male is again ready to attempt to court gravid females and will, in a day or two, fertilise up to seven clutches. Although this number is based on laboratory studies, field studies have also indicated that a male may collect as many as seven clutches although the average number normally collected is lower than this (Moodie, 1972b).

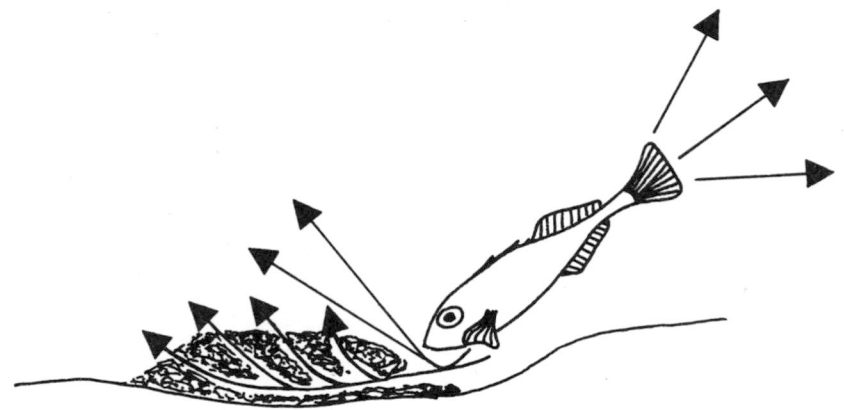

Fig. 48. Currents of water through nest created by fanning of male *Gasterosteus aculeatus* (after Tinbergen, 1951).

As days pass the male spends more and more time at or close to the nest, and becomes less and less likely to court passing females. The male spends the bulk of his time at the nest fanning, although other behaviours are also characteristic of this parental phase.

When fanning, the male moves so that his snout is within a centimetre or two of the nest entrance and angles his body at about 30 to 40 degrees with the horizontal plane, in a vertical plane through the longitudinal axis of the nest (Fig. 48). The tail and hind part of the body move as though the fish was going to swim rapidly forward, but this forward thrust is countered by the action of the pectoral fins so that the fish stays still but drives a current of water over the nest. The pectoral fins beat in alternation and in synchrony with the tail, so that as the right pectoral moves forwards the tail moves to the left—thus the fish does not pivot about the vertical axis. When each pectoral fin moves forward, all the fin rays move simultaneously but in the backward movement the dorsal rays move backwards first, the others following, so that the fin travels back obliquely. The tail fin is kept spread and the rays move synchronously, the amplitude of each tail beat is about 4 mm. Fanning is such a characteristic behaviour that it can be recognised even when it occurs, as it occasionally does, away from the nest. In these cases, the male remains horizontal in the water, but obviously fans (van Iersel, 1953; Sevenster, 1961).

A judicious use of potassium permanganate crystals showed that fanning produces a current of water through and across the top of the nest ensuring that any de-oxygenated water around the developing eggs is rapidly removed (Fig. 48) (Kristensen, cited in Tinbergen, 1951). A male can use several cues to maintain the correct orientation during fanning. The tilt of the body is maintained relative to the long axis of the nest, so that if the nest is tilted the male alters his angle relative to the horizontal plane to maintain a constant angle to the nest. To maintain his position relative to the nest as a whole, the male uses cues such as the entrance of the nest and even more important, other objects in view (Baerands, 1971). When there is a current of water, the male usually fans into the current. This was graphically demonstrated by a group of males which had built nests in a relatively fast running stream. A male would fan, facing into the current, and when he stopped fanning the current swept the male several centimetres downstream and he had then to swim upstream to his nest. Unfortunately a period of flooding made it impossible to tell whether these males successfully hatched any fry. From a functional point of view it seemed absurd for the males to try to push water against the water current (Wootton, 1972a).

Under normal circumstances the fanning of the nest is essential for the successful development of the eggs. In the absence of adequate ventilation the eggs become mouldy and die (Wunder, 1930; van Iersel, 1953). Although fanning is the predominant behaviour of the parental phase, other behaviours also serve a parental function. Eggs that die and become mouldy are picked out and eaten by the male. Any eggs that lie outside the nest are picked up and pushed back into the nest. As the parental phase progresses, the male makes holes in the roof and around the rim of the nest; the most likely function of these holes is that they ease the ventilation of the nest at a time when the eggs are metabolically very active (Leiner, 1930). Eventually the male starts to tear the nest apart leaving a heap of nest material lying in the nest pit with the recently hatched fry lying in the tangled mass of vegetation. As the young become active most of the nest material is carried away from the nest pit. The parental phase is characterised by the progressive destruction of the nest (Fig. 49).

Days after
fertilisation

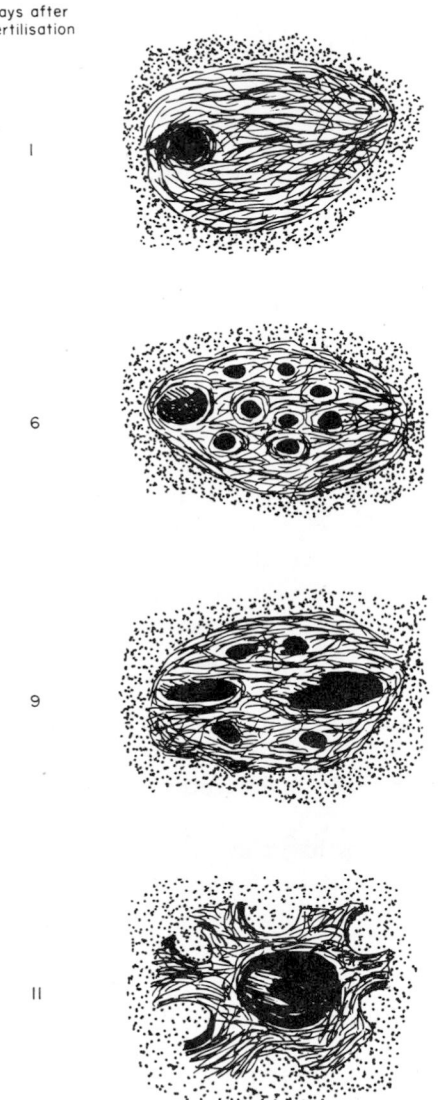

I

6

9

II

Fig. 49. Changes in the structure of the nest of male *Gasterosteus aculeatus* during the parental phase (after Wunder, 1930).

During the parental phase the male loses his bright courtship coloration. Over a period of days, the dorsal surface of the male becomes dark, sometimes almost black, the red colour of the underside becomes restricted to the most forward part of the belly, and the blue of the iris fades. As a result of these changes the male becomes more cryptic, and this presumably provides further protection for the nest, because the male no longer acts as a coloured beacon advertising the nest site (van Iersel, 1953).

The length of the parental phase depends on the rate of development of the eggs, which in turn depends on the water temperature (Chapter 3). At 18 to 20°C, the young hatch in seven or eight days, and there then follows a period in which the male attempts to keep the young together. Any fry that move away from the nest are sucked into the male's mouth and spat out into the nest pit. The length of this phase during which the male guards and retrieves the young, but no longer fans the nest, is a matter of some debate. In one study, males were observed to round up their fry at night for up to fourteen days after the young had hatched (Benzie, 1965). But in other studies the males have lost all parental behaviour by a week after hatching (van Iersel, 1953). A single field observation is that the male abandoned the nest site and the young only a few days after the fry had hatched (Wootton, 1972a).

The parental phase is characterised by distinct changes in the amount of fanning shown by the male, and by changes in his aggressive and sexual behaviour. These changes raise questions about the factors which control these temporal changes in behaviour. In a study, which must be one of the most cited studies in ethology, van Iersel (1953) analysed the factors which control the changes in fanning and sexual behaviour during the parental phase. This study was so comprehensive that it may have inhibited further research on the problem, and this is a great pity because like all the best research van Iersel's study poses as many problems as it solved. In particular, modern techniques of systems analysis and the statistical analysis of time series data could probably be profitably applied both to van Iersel's data and to further studies.

After eggs have been fertilised, the amount of fanning shown by the male rises and reaches a peak a day or two before the young hatch. After the eggs hatch, there is a relatively rapid decline in the amount of fanning behaviour (Fig. 50). The initial increase in fanning consists both of an increase in the number of times the male initiates a bout of fanning and in the average length of a bout of fanning. In the early days of the parental phase, a spell of parental behaviour, in particular fanning, is followed by a period of sexual behaviour, which in turn is followed by a period of nest building behaviour. As the male moves further into the parental phase, the parental behaviour becomes more and more dominant, sexual behaviour drops out entirely and nest building is shown at very low frequencies.

The amount of fanning shown influences the rate of development

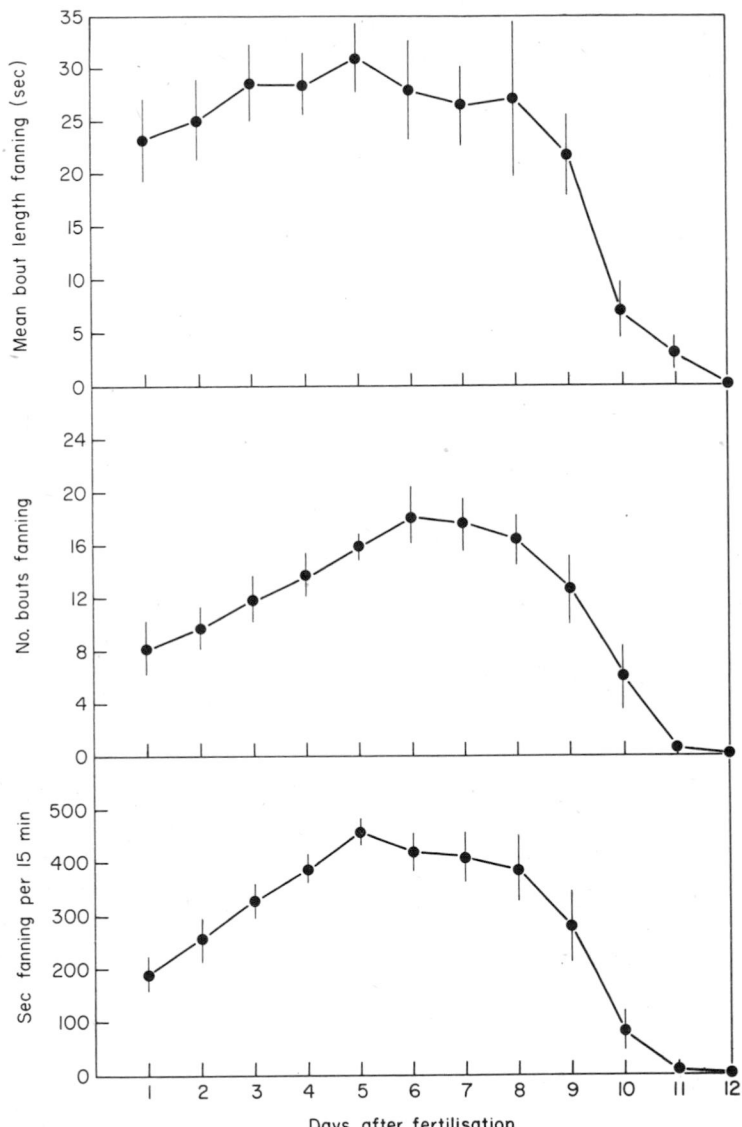

Fig. 50. Fanning cycle of male *Gasterosteus aculeatus* after fertilising one clutch. Mean values ± 1 standard error ($N = 13$).

of the eggs within the limits set by the water temperature. The rate of development was better correlated with the average length of bouts of fanning rather than with the total amount of fanning. Development of the eggs is favoured by relatively fewer long bouts rather than by relatively more short bouts (van Iersel, 1953; Cane, 1961).

A male does not enter the parental phase unless fertilised eggs are present in his nest. A male allowed to court a female and fertilise her eggs stays in the sexual phase of his reproductive cycle if the eggs are removed from the nest. A male can be kept in the sexual phase for many days, although he may be fertilising eggs every day, simply by removing the eggs soon after the male has fertilised them. Conversely, a male can be induced to enter a parental phase by placing eggs fertilised by another male into the empty nest. It is not essential for the male to experience the fertilisation for him to pass from the sexual phase to the parental phase.

The importance of the presence of eggs for parental behaviour suggests that the changes in the amount of fanning may be related to the changes in the rate of metabolism of the eggs. To test this hypothesis, van Iersel ran water that was rich in carbon dioxide but poor in oxygen through the nests of males that were in the parental phase. He found that this "bad" water stimulated an increase in the amount of fanning. There was also an increase in the amount of boring, pulling and noseing at the nest, while other nest building activities such as pushing and bringing material declined in frequency. The changes in the condition of the water are detected by receptors in the pharynx which are innervated by the sensory, pharyngeal branches of the ninth and tenth cranial nerves (Segaar, 1966).

This experiment also provided data which suggested that the pattern of the parental cycle was not solely determined by a response to changes in the metabolic state of the eggs. The response to the "bad" water decreased as the parental cycle advanced, so that an increase in fanning was not stimulated by the "bad" water when the male was five or six days into the cycle. Either the male was fanning at the maximum rate possible by this time, or there had been a decrease in the responsiveness of the male to the "bad" water.

Further evidence that there were changes intrinsic to the male occurring during the parental phase came from an experiment in which a male was allowed to keep his first eggs until the day they hatched. They were then exchanged for two freshly fertilised clutches. The male entered a second cycle of fanning until this second batch of eggs hatched. Then the exchange was repeated with the male receiving a third batch of freshly fertilised eggs. Again the male started a fanning cycle. Three exchanges were made successfully and young were hatched, but a fourth exchange was unsuccessful for the eggs were eaten by the male about five days after the exchange. Although the fanning cycles induced by the exchanged eggs were similar in form to the first, natural cycle, the fanning peak reached before hatching was lower after each exchange. The male became less and less "parental" until he finally started eating the eggs. After the eggs had been eaten, the male built a new nest and five days later a full parental cycle was again induced by giving him two fresh clutches.

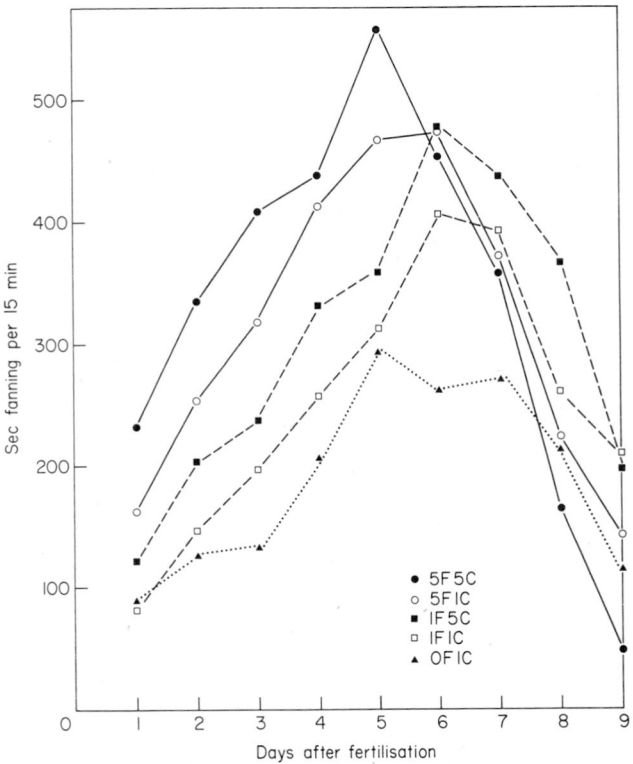

Fig. 51. Effect of the number of fertilisations (F) and number of clutches present in nest (C) on the fanning cycle of male *Gasterosteus aculeatus* (after van Iersel, 1953).

The next step in van Iersel's study was the investigation of the effect of the number of clutches and the number of fertilisations performed by the male on the male's fanning cycle. More fertilisations (up to five), and the presence of the additional clutches from those fertilisations led to a faster development of the fanning cycle and to a higher peak of fanning. But the decline from the peak was also faster than if fewer fertilisations had been performed (Fig. 51). On the other hand, where males were induced to become parental by supplying them with eggs freshly fertilised by other males, the amount of fanning performed still increased with an increasing number of clutches but the decline in fanning after the eggs hatched was slower when more clutches were present. A comparison was made between males that had the same number of clutches; some males having fertilised the clutches themselves whilst others had been given fertilised eggs. The comparison showed that the males that had experienced fertilisation showed higher levels of fanning than males that had their fanning cycle induced. The fertilisation of eggs influences both the subsequent amount of fanning and the timing of events during the parental phase. These effects are manifested some days after the fertilisations have taken place, which means that the experience of fertilisation alters the internal state of the male. In general the amount of fanning was better correlated with the number of fertilisations the male had experienced than with the number of clutches present in the nest, an observation which serves to underline the importance of the act of fertilisation as a factor influencing the fanning cycle.

The question that can be asked now is what are the contributions to a particular fanning cycle of the direct stimuli from the eggs and the internal state of the male. To answer this question, van Iersel carried out three types of investigation. In one group of experiments the eggs of a male were removed at various stages in the fanning cycle and the nest left empty so that there was no stimulation from eggs. In a second set of experiments the male's eggs were again removed at various points in the fanning cycle, but in this case were replaced by freshly fertilised eggs. In this experiment the stimulation from eggs is assumed to be lowered because they have only just started their development. In the third type of experiment, males were given developing eggs of various ages, so that it was assumed that there was an increase in the stimulation from the eggs.

In the experiments in which eggs were removed and not replaced there was usually a sudden drop in fanning and the decline continued until there was no parental fanning. If the eggs were removed on the first two or three days of the fanning cycle, the male then reverted to the sexual phase of his reproductive cycle, and showed the type of behaviour described in the previous chapter. If the change was made on the third, fourth or in some cases the fifth day of the fanning cycle, the male destroyed the nest and entered the nest building phase of the reproductive cycle. In this case no fanning was seen on the following day. When the change was made even later into the fanning cycle, the male showed relatively large amounts of parental fanning even though there were no eggs in the nest. The amount of this "residual" fanning was increased by delaying the time of the removal of the eggs until the peak levels of fanning were almost due, and was greater the more clutches there had been in the nest. Occasionally males showed a peak of fanning just before the eggs were due to hatch, although there were no longer any eggs in the nest. These results indicate that in the presence of eggs there is a progressive change in the internal state of the male which makes it more and more difficult for the male to revert to his sexual phase and more and more likely that the male will continue to show parental behaviour even in the absence of the appropriate stimuli. The nature of this progressive change is not known, but it seems to make the male less responsive to external stimuli. The "bad" water experiments described earlier indicated this change in responsiveness, and the egg-removal experiments also indicate such a change.

This picture of a progressive change in the internal state of the male as the fanning cycle progresses is further reinforced by the experiments in which a male's own eggs were replaced by eggs freshly fertilised by another male. The exchange results in a lowering of the external stimulus, and so it might be predicted that there would be a drop in the male's fanning to a level more appropriate to fresh eggs. Such a drop was observed after some exchanges but was more marked the earlier in the fanning cycle the exchange was made. In other words, the amount of fanning shown to the fresh eggs was higher the later in the fanning cycle the exchange was made. A second feature of these experiments was that in many cases the males showed a peak of fanning just before the hatching of their original clutch was due, so that the temporal pattern of the original fanning cycle was maintained although there had been a marked change in the stimulus value of the eggs in the nest. There was also a second peak induced by the second batch of eggs. The development of a peak in fanning at a time appropriate to the hatching of the original eggs was favoured by two factors; the number of fertilisations the male had experienced and the length of time the male had been exposed to the original eggs before the exchange took place. So again, the picture emerges of a male undergoing a change in internal state as the parental cycle progresses, a change induced by the act of fertilisation and by exposure to the developing eggs. The change results in a tendency for the male to continue a normal fanning cycle in spite of marked changes in the stimulation coming from the contents of the nest. It is not only the temporal patterning of fanning that is influenced by this internal change, the timing of the opening up of the nest is even more rigidly determined by the internal state of the male. But the male's behaviour is not totally dependent on this internal state, for there are changes from a normal fanning cycle induced by a change in the stimulus from the eggs. For example, in the experiments described above, a second peak of fanning occurred just before the subsititue eggs hatched.

In the third type of experiment, males were given older eggs. These were either exchanged for the male's own fresh eggs, or placed directly in an empty nest. The result is to suddenly increase the stimulation coming from the nest. If a male is responding to the stimulus from the eggs, a rise in the amount of fanning would be expected. In practice the effect of the exchange was always that the level of fanning was lower than would be expected from the age of the eggs placed in the nest. Those experiments in which the eggs were placed in the empty nest of a male which had experienced neither fertilisations nor the presence of newly fertilised eggs gave a curious result. When only one clutch was given, the level of fanning showed little change with an increase in the age of the donated eggs, but when two or three clutches were given there was an increase in the level of fanning with an increase in the age of the donated eggs. Yet the levels of fanning shown to clutches two or three days old were below those shown to a single clutch of a similar age. Another odd result was that the height of the peak of fanning induced by the donated eggs was not simply related to the number of clutches, but depended on both the number of clutches and the age of the eggs when they were placed in the nest. When the eggs were freshly fertilised, the peak induced was higher when there were more clutches, but when the eggs were three or four days old, and so represented a stronger stimulus, the peak induced was highest when only one clutch was given.

Other experiments showed that if the male had experienced fertilisation and exposure to fresh eggs for a few hours before the exchange of eggs was made, the male was better able to respond to the change in stimulus strength and showed a level of fanning more appropriate to the new situation, although still not comparable to undisturbed fanning cycles. A short exposure to fresh eggs, but without the experience of fertilisation, made the male more responsive to the substitute eggs if those eggs were two to four days old. But if the substituted eggs were older than this, a previous exposure to fresh eggs had no effect. The experience of fertilisation led to higher peak values of fanning whatever the age of the donated eggs, further evidence that the act of fertilisation has relatively long-term effects on the internal state of the male. A second factor which led to the heightening of the peak levels of fanning was the length of exposure to the donated eggs.

Van Iersel's interpretation of these complex results is that when a strong stimulus in the form of well developed eggs is suddenly given, the full development of fanning is hampered, unless the stimulus given is strong enough to overcome the "resistance" to fanning. The experience of fresh eggs can to some extent oppose this "resistance" and the experience of fertilisation does so to an even greater extent.

Among the other results from this type of experiment was the discovery that even a short exposure to fresh eggs could sometimes lead to a peak of fanning related to the hatching time of these eggs, even though the older eggs which had been exchanged had already hatched.

In some experiments, the male ate the donated eggs. This was more likely to happen the older the eggs were at the time of donation, and was less likely to happen if the male had been briefly exposed to fresh eggs and had experienced fertilisations.

With this picture of changes intrinsic to the male making the male more likely to complete a fanning cycle and less responsive to changes in external stimulation, the next stage of the investigation was to relate these changes to changes in the sexual behaviour of the male. Van Iersel measured the sexual behaviour of the male by recording the number of zig zags the male displayed towards a gravid female confined in a glass tube for five minutes.

Sexual behaviour disappears entirely in the course of the parental phase and does not reappear until the male initiates a new reproductive cycle. The decline in sexual behaviour occurs abruptly, but the level of sexual behaviour was lower and the decline occurred earlier in the parental cycle the more fertilisations the male had experienced and the more clutches the male retained (Fig. 52). If the male had been induced to become parental by being given eggs fertilised by other males, his sexual behaviour persisted well into the parental cycle, sometimes even beyond the time when the eggs hatched. Then there was a very rapid decline and sexual behaviour was no longer shown. This rapid decline occurred earlier the more clutches the male had been given. The experience of fertilisation has a profound effect on the subsequent decline in sexual behaviour.

What is the effect of several fertilisations on the level of sexual behaviour on subsequent days if the fertilised eggs are removed so that a parental cycle does not develop? Fertilisation did cause a drop in the level of sexual behaviour, and this drop was greater and the subsequent recovery slower the more fertilisations the male experienced. Unnaturally long periods of courtship that were not allowed to lead to a successful fertilisation also caused a drop in the level of sexual behaviour, 120 minutes of unsuccessful courtship caused about the same drop as five fertilisations, but the subsequent recovery was much more rapid. Since the total duration of courtship associated with five fertilisations was only about twenty minutes, it is the fertilisations rather than the associated courtship behaviour

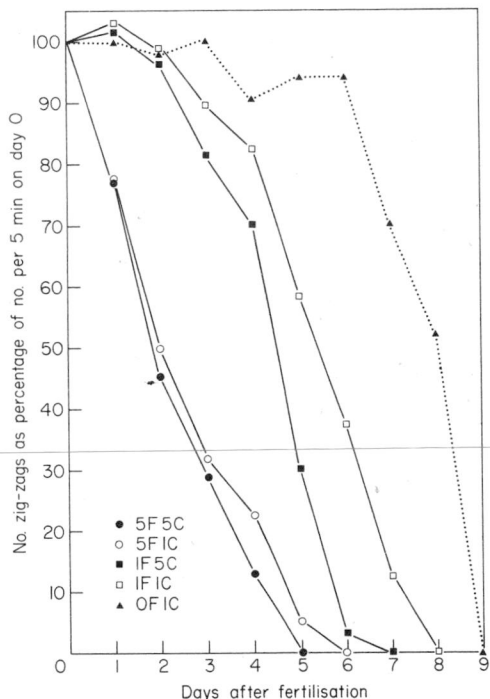

Fig. 52. Effect of number of fertilisations (F) and number of clutches in nest (C) on relative frequency of zig-zagging by male *Gasterosteus aculeatus* at confined gravid female (after van Iersel, 1953).

that has the profound effect on the subsequent level of sexual behaviour.

There is one odd finding from these experiments. The decrease in the level of sexual behaviour on the day after the fertilisation was greater if the eggs were removed than if the male was allowed to retain them. For the first few hours, the presence of eggs in the nest seems to augment sexual behaviour, although over the parental cycle there is an overall inhibition of sexual behaviour.

A comparison of the course of sexual behaviour during the parental cycles of males which have fertilised eggs and males which have had parental cycles induced by the donation of eggs indicates that the relatively early decline noted in the former group is an effect of the fertilisations. But even in the absence of the experience of the act of fertilisation, there is an incompatability between parental behaviour and sexual behaviour which shows itself as the time of hatching approaches.

There is evidence that the relationship between sexual behaviour and parental behaviour is one of reciprocal inhibition. When a male was allowed to court a gravid female who was restrained in a tube and that male showed a reasonable level of sexual behaviour (more than twenty zig zags in a five minute period) there was a decrease in the level of parental fanning shown by the male after the test. It took about thirty minutes for parental fanning to recover to its pre-test level (Sevenster, 1961). On the basis of this sort of evidence, van Iersel suggested that the tendency to show sexual behaviour acts as an inhibitory factor on the build up of parental behaviour during the first few days of the parental phase, that is, it acts to "resist" the development of the fanning cycle, but that this inhibitory effect is reduced by the influence of fertilisations and exposure to eggs.

The events that surround the act of fertilisation have both short- and long-term effects on the level of sexual behaviour. A short-term reduction in the level of sexual behaviour which occurs in the first hour after fertilisation is reversible and is accompanied by changes in the level of aggression, such that the highest levels of aggression coincide with the lowest levels of sexual behaviour. A long-term reduction which depends both on the number of fertilisations and on the presence of eggs in the nest is irreversible in the context of a single reproductive cycle.

This long-term, irreversible reduction in the level of sexual behaviour during the parental cycle is not accompanied by an increase in aggressive behaviour. Although the interrelationship between parental behaviour and aggressive behaviour has not been analysed in the same detail as that between parental and sexual behaviour, a clear picture of the changes in aggressive behaviour has emerged.

Van Iersel had noted that during the first half of the parental cycle the aggressiveness of the male declined and the male no longer showed strong defence of his territorial boundary. A more complete description of the changes in levels of aggression was obtained by placing a tube containing a mature male 23 cm from the experimental male's nest and recording the number of bites the experimental male aimed at the male in the tube during a three

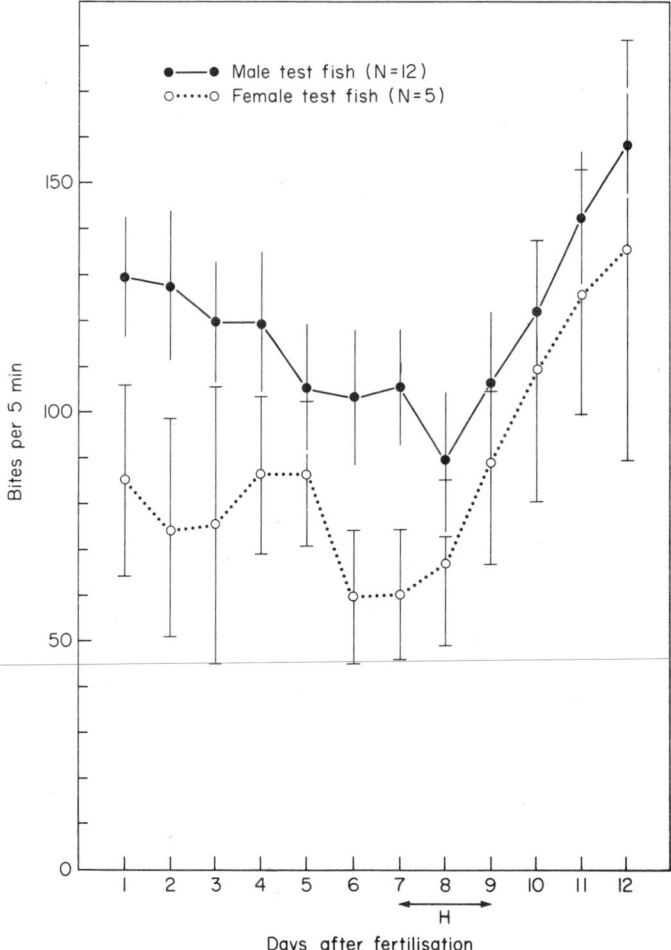

Fig. 53. Changes in frequency of biting at a confined male and confined female conspecific during the parental phase of male *Gasterosteus aculeatus* that had fertilised one clutch. Mean value ± 1 standard error; H, eggs hatching.

minute period. A test was made each day from the day of fertilisation to two days after the eggs hatched. The number of bites stayed steady for the first three or four days but then declined, reaching a minimum about the day of hatching. Once the young hatched there was an abrupt recovery in the level of biting (Fig. 53) (Segaar, 1961).

A similar technique was used to investigate the effect of the distance that the stimulus was from the nest site on the decline in aggression. The tube containing the test male was placed at either 10, 100 or 280 cm from the nest. Only at the two greater distances was the decline noted. In the immediate vicinity of his nest, the male maintains his aggressiveness through the parental cycle (Symons, 1965; Black, 1971).

The most obvious explanation for these changes would be that, as the male devotes more and more time to the care of the eggs, there is less and less time available for aggressive behaviour. Once the young had hatched, this situation would be reversed. But this is not the complete story. In experiments in which the test stimulus is provided by a male confined in a tube, only a very short period of the day is taken up by such a test. The male can spend the rest of the time caring for the eggs undisturbed. In practice, during such tests, the male spends a considerable proportion of the test period orientated towards the male in the tube, and during the parental period the time spent orientated towards the test male does not first decline and then increase (Wootton, 1971a; Black, 1971). The change in aggression is primarily a change in the rate at which the male attacks rather than the time devoted to aggressive behaviour (Wootton, 1971a). There have been no studies published on the effect that the number of fertilisations or the number of clutches has on the pattern and size of the changes in aggressive behaviour.

All the studies on the parental phase described up to now have concerned males that were kept isolated and only encountered other fish during aggression and sex tests. Such tests take up only a small part of the day. But in a natural situation, the male will be holding a territory in the presence of other territorial males, females and fish of other species. How does this complexity affect the changes in parental, sexual and aggressive behaviour discussed above?

Although the temporal patterning of the fanning cycle remains the same when other fish are present, the total amount of fanning is reduced. This reduction occurs because the presence of other fish leads to a reduction in the average length of bouts of fanning, and there is not a sufficient change in the number of bouts of fanning which are initiated to compensate for the reduction in the average length of the bouts. Other fish, through their movements and territorial intrusions cause a male to break off fanning sooner than they would do if no other fish are present (van den Assem, 1967; Wootton, 1971a). This effect of the shortening of bout lengths of fanning may have some influence on the success of rearing the eggs. The time of hatching of the eggs has been found to be better correlated with the average bout length of fanning than with the total time spent fanning (van Iersel, 1953). A reduction in average bout length will also tend to lengthen each parental cycle because of this retardation in the rate of development of the eggs.

Field observations showed that the fanning cycles of fish in a natural situation were similar to those of fish kept in the laboratory (Wootton, 1972a).

A change in a male's aggression in the presence of other males would be expected to have consequences for the size of territory that the male could hold (Wootton, 1971a). The changes in aggression measured during the parental cycle would indicate that before the eggs hatch, the size of the territory would decline, but after hatching there would be an increase in territory size. Laboratory studies have shown that both of these changes do take place. In an experiment in which four or six males were kept in large containers, the territory held by a parental male decreased in size up to the time the young hatched. All the other males had nests, but they were not all parental at the same time (Black, 1971). An increase in territory size after the young hatch has also been recorded (Morris, 1958).

A weakness of these laboratory studies is that the number of fish in a particular area was kept constant. In a natural situation the number of males in an area will fluctuate. Some will be territorial, while others will be attempting to claim territories. A decline in territory size during the parental cycle has been observed in a natural population of sticklebacks. For example one male was watched on most days of his parental cycle, and initially the nearest nest to his own was 170 cm away and he actively defended the boundary. But he spent more and more time at his nest and another male successfully built a nest only 75 cm from the parental male's nest. This second male successfully maintained his territory even after the eggs of the original male had hatched and the young had started to swim. When there is strong pressure for territories, it seems unlikely that a male, having abandoned the outer regions of his territory, will be able to reclaim them. The increase in aggression associated with the hatching of the eggs is not necessarily followed by an increase in the size of territory held by the male (Wootton, 1972a).

Perhaps the most spectacular effect of the presence of other fish, in particular other males, is the phenomenon of nest raiding. This peculiar behaviour was first described for the nine-spined stickleback by Morris (1952), but the same phenomenon is also prominent in the three-spined stickleback. There is close agreement between the various descriptions of nest raiding that have been published, but little agreement on the function of nest raiding, although it is a prominent component of interactions between breeding males.

A male attempting to raid another male's nest shows a distinct sequence of actions. On reaching the border of the territory containing the nest to be raided, the raider sinks to the bottom, his dorsal spines are kept erect, but he becomes cryptically coloured as the bright breeding colours fade. He approaches close to the nest in a series of slow glides, resting on or close to the bottom between glides. The last few centimeters to the nest are covered in a final rapid dash. If the raider is detected by the resident before the nest is reached, the raider will retreat rapidly when the resident male charges. But if the raider succeeds in reaching the nest, the resident often has considerable difficulty in ejecting the intruder.

There seem to be three distinct situations in which nest raiding takes place. The first of these is where the raider steals nest material and sometimes uses this material in his own nest. Such raids occur even when the owner of the raided nest is not in the vicinity of the nest. In other words, the raider does not have to be guided to the nest. The second situation occurs when the owner of the nest is courting a female. In this case, the raid is only made when the owner is at the nest. What happens next seems to depend partly on the behaviour of the owner and partly on the raider himself. If the owner is creeping through the nest, the raider may quiver on the tail of the owner then bore at the nest, or the raider may also creep through the nest. If the owner is boring or fanning at the nest, the raider will also bore, usually on the roof of the nest. In those cases where the owner is showing a female the nest or the female had just entered the nest, the raider disrupts the courtship by boring at the nest or lying motionless in the nest pit. When the female is already in the nest, she usually spawns, but the presence of the raider can considerably lengthen the time the female spends in the nest before laying the eggs. Once the eggs are laid, the raider attempts to fertilise them and, in some cases, succeeds in depositing his sperm over them before the owner of the nest does. The third situation occurs when the nest being raided contains eggs. The raider steals the eggs and tries to take them back to his own nest. When a raider has succeeded in fertilising the eggs during a raid, he makes further raids in an attempt to steal the eggs. If a raider steals eggs before he has a nest to take them to, the eggs are eventually eaten (Morris, 1952; van den Assem, 1967; Wootton, 1971b).

A feature of nest raiding is that the disturbance created frequently serves to attract other fish who also begin tearing and pulling at the nest. A graphic example of this occurred during a field experiment in which a resident territorial male was removed from his territory. A male from an adjacent territory raided the absent male's nest and tried to remove the eggs. His activities rapidly attracted other sticklebacks, so that eventually nearly thirty fish were around the nest at one time. These fish ate the eggs and destroyed the nest within minutes, but remained aggregated around it for many minutes (Black and Wootton, 1970).

Although parental males do not make nest raids, this activity can have an important effect of their parental cycle, because they may suffer from egg robbing. This disturbing effect is in addition to the effect that other fish have on fanning which has been described earlier. When males were kept on their own, parental success was high, with usually over ninety per cent of the original eggs developing successfully. And when two or more males were present and all had eggs, then parental success was still high. In this case some nests contained more eggs than expected, while others had fewer, which suggested that egg robbing redistributed eggs between the males. A significant lowering of parental success occurred when two or more males were present but only one male had obtained eggs by a successful courtship. In this situation egg robbing had a very detrimental effect, because the robber was frequently unsuccessful at rearing the eggs, often eating them. This failure may be caused by several interacting factors such as the raider stealing too few eggs for a parental cycle to be induced, experiencing too few fertilisations to have moved towards a parental mood, and the generally high level of aggressive interactions in such a situation (van den Assem, 1967).

Eggs are robbed not just after they have been spawned, but almost up to the time of hatching. Such well developed eggs are rarely adopted by the raider and are usually eaten (Black, 1971).

Males, which at the start of the parental cycle have larger territories, suffer fewer egg losses and have a better chance of hatching their clutches (van den Assem, 1967; Black, 1971). But this observation has been made only on groups of fish held in the laboratory. There seems to be no data published on the hatching success of clutches in natural populations.

As something of a digression, it is worth-while asking what is the function of nest raiding and egg robbing. That this behaviour has a function is indicated both by the unique behavioural sequence involved in making a raid and by the frequency with which it can occur both in laboratory and natural situations. During observations on a wild population, a male was seen to make four attempts to raid his neighbour's nest in twenty minutes (Wootton, 1972a).

The earliest interpretation of nest raiding was that the raider was showing pseudo-female behaviour. This interpretation could be applied only to raids made during courtship when, it was argued, the raider was sexually frustrated (Morris, 1952). The observation that nest raiding occurred at times other than in association with courtship led to another hypothesis. This was that raiding was a response to a shortage of some resource. A nest containing eggs is a concentration both of material suitable for nest building and food. If either of these resources are in short supply, nest raiding might have a distinct survival value (Wootton, 1971b). Nest raiding which ends with the fertilisation of eggs in a rival's nest, is clearly likely to increase the number of offspring left by the raider, especially if the gravid females are the resource in short supply. But from the evidence presented above, egg robbing seems to lead to a reduction in parental success since the robber may frequently fail to rear the eggs. If a raider succeeds in fertilising eggs in a rival's nest, it would seem to make more sense to allow the rival to expend time and energy rearing those eggs, while the raider is left free to make more raids or court other females. What advantage will the raider gain by stealing the eggs? A suggestion is that each male has more success in hatching eggs if all males in the area are also involved in parental activities. Aggression tends to be low and each male restricts most of this activities to the area of his own nest (Black, 1971; Wootton, 1971b). Egg robbing is seen as a mechanism for distributing eggs between males to ensure a degree of synchrony in their reproductive cycles (van den Assem, 1967).

Whether this interpretation is valid remains to be seen, but there is some evidence of the synchronisation of breeding cycles from studies on the growth and length frequency distributions of young fish (van Mullem, 1967). Other observations on natural populations have indicated that males with adjacent territories can be completely out of synchrony (Wootton, 1972a). Nor is there any direct evidence linking synchrony with egg robbing.

Returning now to the main theme, the behavioural analysis of the parental phase has provided a clear picture of the major changes during the phase and had also indicated some of the factors important in the control of parental behaviour. As with other aspects of the stickleback's reproductive cycle, the analysis of the physiological correlates of parental behaviour has lagged behind the purely behavioural analysis. Even worse than this, some of the studies which have been published seem mutually contradictory, so that as yet no clear picture of the physiological control of parental behaviour has emerged; certainly not one that could satisfactorily be merged with the behavioural data.

Both nest building and courtship are dependent on gonadal hormones, so the obvious question is what is the effect of gonadectomising males during the parental phase? An early report suggested that a male castrated during the fanning cycle continued the cycle normally, though with lower levels of fanning than normal (van Iersel quoted in Baggerman, 1957). This finding was put in doubt with the report that males castrated on the second or third day of the fanning cycle removed the eggs on the fourth or fifth day and stopped fanning (Smith and Hoar, 1967). But almost immediately, a further study indicated that males gonadectomised on the third and fourth days showed virtually normal fanning cycles. Indeed the parental cycles of such males were so normal that they even showed the distinct increase in aggressive behaviour after the young hatched (Baggerman, 1968). To reconcile these contradictory results is not possible at the moment. One possibility is that gonadal hormones are important in the initiation of the parental cycle so that gonadectomy soon after the start of the cycle causes it to come to an end, but once the parental cycle is well-established it becomes independent of gonadal hormones. Clearly, the aggression seen after the young hatch is independent of gonadal hormone.

In many vertebrates, especially mammals, the pituitary hormone prolactin is important in the control of parental behaviour. Fish prolactin has been implicated in the control of osmo-regulation (Chapter 8), but it is natural to ask whether it also has a role in the control of the parental behaviour of the male. Two studies have been made of this possibility. When 0.45 IU of prolactin were injected into males, there was a reduction in the amount of courtship fanning they showed. Injection of a higher dose (6 IU) of prolactin on the third or fourth day of the fanning cycle caused no significant change in the amount of fanning (Smith and Hoar, 1967). The inhibition of courtship fanning by doses of 0.45 IU of prolactin has been confirmed, but it has also been shown that courtship fanning can be increased above normal values by smaller does of prolactin. As little as 0.006 IU had an effect, but 0.12 to 0.14 IU were most effective. Higher doses inhibited fanning. Sand digging, boring and glueing were also increased by doses of 0.06 to 0.14 IU. A critical factor determining the degree to which fanning was increased was the state of maturity of the male fish. Immature males showed hardly any response, but the response was strongest in males with full nuptial coloration (Molenda and Fiedler, 1971). There is no evidence that variations in the level of prolactin are responsible for the changes in fanning during parental cycle.

Another approach to the analysis of the physiological correlates of the reproductive behaviour has been to lesion small parts of the fore-brain or telencephalon of the male and observe the subsequent parental, sexual and aggressive behaviour. These experiments have shown that the mutual relationships between fanning, courtship and aggression can be changed by such small lesions.

When either the frontal or bilateral regions of the fore-brain were removed, the level of aggressive behaviour was significantly reduced, courtship behaviour disappeared relatively early in the parental phase but the level of fanning was significantly higher. Large lesions in the mediocaudal region of the fore-brain resulted in the reverse situation, aggression was high, sexual behaviour persisted throughout the parental cycle and parental fanning was significantly lowered. One breeding cycle passed into the next without a new nest being built. Other patterns were obtained when smaller lesions were made in this mediocaudal region. Small lesions in the lateral part of this region led to almost normal levels and changes in courtship and aggression, but parental fanning tended to occur in two waves, and when fanning increased both courtship and aggression tended to decrease. This decomposition of the fanning cycle into two waves was even more marked when small lesions were made near to the midline of the mediocaudal region, although courtship and aggression were normal. The first wave of fanning peaked about four days after fertilisation at a level reached on the same day by normal fish. But the second peak, reached about the time of hatching, was higher than a normal peak. Lesions in the medial border of the mediocaudal region caused a complete disruption of normal fanning, males treated in this way showed very high levels of fanning on the day after fertilisation (1570 sec. in 1800 sec.) but then the level of fanning declined, although the level remained abnormally high. In spite of these marked changes in fanning behaviour, the levels of aggression and courtship were suprisingly normal (Segaar, 1956, 1961; Segaar and Nieuwenhuys, 1963).

Animals can show typical aggressive, sexual or parental behaviour after these lesions, but the mutual relationship between these behaviours and their integration over time into functional sequences of behaviour seems to depend on the integrity of the fore-brain. As yet, it is not possible to weave the behavioural, endocrinological and neurophysiological information into a coherent and integrated pattern describing the parental phase of the male's reproductive cycle.

An aspect of the parental cycle and indeed the entire reproductive cycle of the male stickleback that has received little attention is the cost of the process. These costs take several forms. By becoming conspicuous and showing conspicuous behaviour, the male is increasing the chance that he will be detected by a predator, so one of the costs is the extra risk of being eaten. A male spending considerable time within his own territory has to rely on that area to provide the necessary food, he cannot move from one area of food concentration to another in the way that the schools of females can be seen doing. Time devoted to aggression, courtship and parental behaviour is not available to be spent searching for food. Another cost in terms of time occurs because the male stops courting females during the parental phase. The male sacrifices the possibility of fertilising more eggs in favour of tending for the eggs he has already fertilised, so for a significant portion of the breeding season the male is not willing to court gravid females. There is also the energetic cost of territorial defence, courtship, nest building and parental behaviour, a cost that would not have to be met in the absence of these complex behavioural patterns.

In the face of these costs, what advantages does the male stickleback gain from this breeding strategy? In the nest, the eggs the male has fertilised are concentrated together and so can be defended by the male. This defence and the subsequent guarding of the young until they are free-swimming means that the male's offspring are protected in the period when they are most susceptible to predation. Clearly, the increased survival of eggs and young more than compensates for the fertilisations the male sacrifices in the parental phase.

Throughout the reproductive cycle the nest forms the focus of all the activities of the male. It, and its immediate neighbourhood, form an area where the male's aggressiveness is always high. Even when the outer-lying areas of the territory are abandoned during the parental phase, the nest is still vigorously defended. Once the nest contains eggs, the male spends more and more time at it, fanning and altering the state of the nest. Only after the young have become free-living does the male abandon this focal point. Even for rival males the nest is an object of specific interest, as the phenomenon of nest raiding testifies.

Given the importance of the nest and its contents, defence of the area around it becomes inevitable. Both conspecifics and other predators must be excluded, otherwise the time and energy devoted to obtaining and rearing the eggs will be wasted. Males with larger territories are more successful in raising eggs, because they suffer less from egg robbing. So it is not surprising that these males are also more successful in obtaining eggs, for the females will be most likely to contribute to the gene pool of the next generation if they deposit their eggs in the nests of males most likely to raise these eggs. An aggressive male, a male who is likely to obtain a large territory, should advertise the fact of his aggression so that females can recognise him, and so the male has the bright nuptial coloration which both attracts females and intimidates rivals. In the parental phase, the male is no longer concerned with attracting females but with guarding the nest, and so the advertising colours fade and the male becomes cryptic until the parental phase is completed and the male is once again back in the business of attraction and intimidation.

14. Genetics and Evolution

The morphological, physiological and behavioural variation of the three-spined stickleback has attracted the attention of biologists who seek to understand the process of evolution. They wish to know the origin of such variation, the factors that maintain it and the selective advantages that accrue from it. Because the leiurus and trachurus forms described in Chapter 1 are so distinct, though obviously related, some authors have argued that the two forms are separate species, *Gasterosteus aculeatus* and *Gasterosteus trachurus* (Hagen, 1967). On the other hand, the occurrence, sometimes in large numbers, of the morphologically intermediate semiarmatus form indicates that at least in some areas the trachurus and leiurus forms interbreed readily. In order to examine both the systematic status of the stickleback and the significance of the variation, the first question that must be answered is the extent to which the observed variation is a product of variations in the environment or a reflection of an underlying genetic variation.

The earliest detailed analysis of the problem of the morphological variation seen in the stickleback suggested that the variation was primarily a product of environmental factors. According to this theory fish that experienced high salinities and relatively low temperatures completed their development right through to the trachurus stage characterised by the complete row of lateral plates and a fully developed caudal keel. Fish that experienced only low salinities and relatively high temperatures reached sexual maturity at the leiurus stage and lacked the full complement of lateral plates and the caudal keel. On this interpretation the leiurus, semiarmatus and trachurus forms represent ontogenetic stages. The stage reached before any further development is halted by the onset of sexual maturity depends on the environmental conditions experienced by the fish, in particular the temperature and salinity regimes (Bertin, 1925).

That this was not the true situation was shown by a detailed study of the distribution, physiology, morphology and breeding of the stickleback in Belgium (Heuts, 1947a, b). In the streams in Belgium, Heuts found that two distinctive populations occurred. Populations of type A had a low mean length, a relatively high mean number of vertebrae and a low number of lateral plates. These populations were found in the east of the country, away from the coast and they remained in fresh water during the winter. In the west of the country, near the coast of the North Sea, populations of type B occurred. Type B populations were characterised by a relatively high mean length, a low mean number of vertebrae and a high number of lateral plates. They spawned in the lower reaches of the river and overwintered in the sea. Type A represents what is now called the leiurus form (in older literature, the gymnura form), and type B the trachurus form. There was little mixing or interbreeding between the two types of populations, and individuals that were morphologically intermediate (semiarmatus) formed only a small proportion of the total sample, and were found principally in the western populations. The differences between the two forms seemed to depend on genetic differences.

Since the studies by Heuts, other evidence has confirmed that there is an underlying genetic difference between the leiurus and trachurus forms. Crosses of leiurus x leiurus, trachurus x trachurus, and trachurus x leiurus showed that differences in the number of lateral plates, number of gill rakers and in body shape were all primarily under genetic control. In contrast to these characters, the differences in the number of rays in the dorsal and anal fins did not have a genetic basis but were a consequence of differences in environmental factors during the life history of the fishes (Hagen, 1967). Evidence from trachurus x leiurus crosses suggested that a simple genetic mechanism underlies the difference in number of lateral plates between the two forms. Münzing (1959, 1963a) proposed that at a single genetic locus there were two possible alleles, T and t. Fish homozygous for T, i.e. TT, fall into the trachurus range of plate numbers, fish homozygous for t, i.e. tt, fall in the leiurus range, while the heterozygotes, Tt fall into the hybrid or semiarmatus range. The trachurus allele, T, was considered to be dominant over the leiurus gene t. The expression of these major genes may be modified by many other genes (Heuts, 1947a, b; Münzing, 1963a). More recent studies have indicated that this model for the genetic control of plate number may be too simple, but this point will be discussed below.

Hay (1974) showed that the possession of a particular lateral plate, plate I (see Chapter 1), was under genetic control. This led him to consider that the criterion for distinguishing between semiarmatus and leiurus fish should be the presence of plate I in the former and its absence in the latter. Crosses between fish possessing plate I gave offspring some of whom had the plate (semiarmatus) and some of whom did not (leiurus). Crosses between leiurus fish never gave offspring that had plate I.

No visible differences were found between the chromosomes of leiurus and trachurus fish. Both forms had a diploid number of forty-two chromosomes (Muramoto, *et al.*, 1969).

Along the Pacific coast of northwest America, populations of sticklebacks that live permanently in fresh water exhibit a considerable range of variation, particularly in number of lateral plates and number of gill rakers. Three forms or plate morphs have been recognised, the low plated morph, the partially plated morph and the completely plated morph. The low plated morph is morphologically similar to the leiurus form and perhaps should be regarded as the leiurus form. The completely plated morph is similar to the trachurus form, but was originally distinguished from the latter because it does not over-winter in the sea but remains as a permanent resident in fresh water. The partially plated morph is morphologically intermediate between the low and completely plated morphs, and it has a caudal keel, but the row of lateral plates is not complete, so it is similar to the semiarmatus form (Hagen and Gilbertson, 1972). The interpretation of the status of these three morphs must be considered later on, but first it must be established how much of the variation has a genetic basis and how much is environmentally determined.

Breeding experiments using fish drawn from monomorphic populations, that is populations in which only one of the three morphs was represented, showed that the difference in plate numbers of the three morphs had a genetic basis. Low plated morphs crossed with low plated morphs produced offspring that were low plated. Under the same rearing conditions, completely plated parents produced completely plated offspring, and partially plated parents produced partially plated offspring. Most crosses between low and completely plated parents produced partially plated offspring. Some of the results of this breeding experiment suggested that the morphs were controlled by one gene locus with two alleles, that is T and t, and that the partially plated morphs were heterozygotes, Tt. This is the same model that was used to explain the inheritance of leiurus and trachurus plate numbers. But other evidence showed that this model of inheritance of plate number was inadequate, for example crosses between low plated and completely plated forms sometimes gave progeny all of which were completely plated. Nor if this model was correct could there be populations composed entirely of partially plated individuals, yet such monomorphic populations do occur (Hagen and Gilbertson, 1973b). Whether such considerations also invalidate the model when used to account for the inheritance of leiurus and trachurus plate numbers is not known. Any model that does explain the inheritance of plate morphs has also to account for the observation that crosses between low plated parents taken from a population which contained all three morphs produced both low and partially plated morphs. However, whatever genetic model ultimately accounts for the inheritance of plate morphs, there is no doubt that the differences between the three morphs reflect a genetic and not an environmental effect.

Even within a particular morph there is variation both in the number of lateral plates and in the number of gill rakers. Breeding experiments have shown that this intra-morph variation has a strong genetic component, so that variation in plate number or gill raker number within a particular morph reflects an underlying genetic variation (Hagen, 1973).

The importance of the demonstrations that both inter- and intra-morph variation has a genetic basis cannot be overstressed, because natural selection can operate only on variation that has this underlying genetic component. If the variation merely reflected the effects of various environments acting on an identical genotype, then selection pressures resulting from predation, salinity, temperature or any other environmental factor could not produce evolutionary change within a population.

Although much of the variation seen in the three-spined stickleback has a genetic basis, environmental effects are not absent altogether.

Since the trachurus form over-winters in the sea, and generally has a more northerly distribution than the leiurus form, the two environmental factors that would be expected to influence the differences in morphology between the two forms are salinity and temperature. The effect of these two factors has been analysed by raising offspring from the same parents, or from parents belonging to the same population, under various regimes of temperature and salinity. Such experiments have shown that a number of morphological characters are indeed affected by the environment in which the fish were reared. Some characters are more strongly influenced by these environmental factors than others.

Leiurus fish were found to have a slightly lower average number of lateral plates, the lower the temperature at which they were raised. This effect was relatively weak and would in no way account for the very marked difference in plate number between leiurus and trachurus forms or between the low and completely plated morphs of the Pacific northwest. Nor were variations in the salinity of the water sufficient to cause a marked variation in the number of lateral plates (Lindsey, 1962a).

The number of vertebrae in leiurus fish was influenced by the temperature at which they were raised. With an increase in temperature the mean number of vertebrae first decreased but then increased, so that the relationship between vertebral count and temperature was V-shaped. The minimum average number of vertebrae was obtained when the rearing temperature approximated the temperature at which there was optimal survival of the eggs and young. The increase in vertebral count that occurred at the higher temperatures resulted principally from an increase in the anterior half of the vertebral column. Higher rearing temperatures also led to a higher average number of the basal plates associated with the dorsal spines (Lindsey, 1962a).

In contrast to this, higher rearing temperatures caused a lowering in the number of rays in both the dorsal and anal fins. But in this case there was evidence of an underlying genetic difference between the leiurus and trachurus forms. In leiurus fish, this effect of high temperature was most marked when they were reared in water of low salinity, but for trachurus fish the effect was most marked at high salinities (Heuts, 1949). This effect of environmental factors on the number of fin rays means that when populations are found that differ in the average number of fin rays, this difference cannot be used to indicate a genetic difference between the populations (Hagen, 1967).

These experiments taken together with the breeding experiments indicate that the major differences between the various forms of the three-spined stickleback are a consequence of genetic differences rather than direct effects of the different environments in which sticklebacks live.

This conclusion raises the question as to the origins of these differences. Such a question might partially be answered if it were known when in geological time and under what environmental conditions the various forms evolved. Unfortunately the fossil record of the stickleback is too sparse to answer these questions.

The earliest fossil of a *Gasterosteus* comes from Pliocene deposits in North America, deposits which are probably at least 10 million years old (Bell, 1974). A species named *Gasterosteus doryssus* was found in western Nevada, this *Gasterosteus* was a low plated form (Hay, 1907). Some of these Pliocene sticklebacks have a reduced pelvic girdle, only one or, more rarely, two or three dorsal spines and few or no lateral plates and Mural (1973) named these *Gasterosteus apodes*. Bell (1974) pointed out that amongst living three-spined sticklebacks there are a few populations which contain a high proportion of individuals with a reduced or missing pelvic girdle, reduced dorsal spines and no lateral plates, yet these forms are retained within *G. aculeatus* so *G. apodes* should be regarded as a junior synonym of *G. doryssus*. A fossil referable to *G. aculeatus* has been found in middle Pliocene deposits of southern California. This fossil was originally described as *Pungitius* (David, 1945), but reexamination showed that it was *G. aculeatus* (Bell, 1973b).

Further remains of *G. aculeatus* occur in early Pleistocene deposits in California (Bell, 1973a). A major feature of the Pleistocene period was the series of ice-ages separated by inter-glacials during which the ice retreated. The early Pleistocene deposits in which the sticklebacks were found were laid down in the period of the Kansan glaciation (in Europe the equivalent gaciation was the Mindel). Of particular interest is the finding that these fish had a low number of lateral plates and in this respect were similar to the modern leiurus or low plated forms, a similarity which is enhanced by the evidence that the deposits were accumulated in a fresh water lake which lay some 300 metres above sea level.

No fossils of the trachurus form have yet been described, perhaps because its habit of over-wintering along the coast in the sea has meant that it is less likely to be fossilised in a recognisable condition. Yet it seems unlikely that there were no completely plated sticklebacks in existence during the Pliocene, so that the fossil record can be interpreted as showing that a separation of a low plated form and a completely plated form had occurred as early as the Pliocene and perhaps even before that. The alternative hypothesis is that one form has repeatedly given rise to the other in the appropriate environments; most commonly it is suggested that the marine trachurus form has given rise to the leiurus form on several occasions (Bell, 1974). This latter hypothesis implies that the modern leiurus form has had a polyphyletic origin, with populations that are morphologically similar arising independently from trachurus stock. Unfortunately there is still doubt whether the low plated stickleback from the west coast of North America is genetically similar to and shares a common origin with the European leiurus form or even whether the European leiurus is monophyletic and genetically homogeneous. This problem will be taken up again later.

As was described in Chapter 2, evidence from the modern distribution of the three-spined stickleback in Europe suggested that the trachurus and leiurus forms existed in the last inter-glacial period, the Riss/Würm interglacial (the American equivalent was the Sangamon Interglacial). Indeed it has been suggested that the European leiurus form, which has the more southerly distribution in Europe, evolved when a population of sticklebacks was isolated in the Great Siberian Ice Lake (Svärdson, 1961). So this evidence suggests that the leiurus and trachurus forms have been distinct since at least the last inter-glacial, that is about 100,000 years, and possibly even longer.

In view of this relatively long period in which the two forms have probably been distinct, and also in view of the distinct morphological, physiological and behavioural differences between the two forms, it is now worth asking how much gene flow there is between the two forms in the various geographical areas where they coexist. Two types of study have provided evidence on this point. There have been at least two detailed studies on the distribution of and degree of overlap between leiurus and trachurus populations within a restricted geographical area (Heuts, 1947a; Hagen, 1967). Other studies have been made on the distribution of these two forms and their presumed hybrid, the semiarmatus form, over wide geographical areas (Münzing, 1959, 1963a; Penzak, 1962, 1965).

In Belgium, Heuts found that the leiurus and trachurus forms (Heuts' types A and B) lived in discrete populations; the trachurus form moved into the estuaries and lower reaches of the rivers in spring, bred, and moved to the sea to overwinter, while the leirus form lived further upstream and remained in fresh water all the year round. Although intermediates did occur, they were uncommon, which suggested that gene flow between the populations was restricted. In an attempt to establish the mechanism which restricted the gene exchanges between the two forms, the eggs of crosses between leiurus and trachurus fish were raised in various salinities. Similar experiments with eggs from trachurus x trachurus and leiurus x leiurus crosses had shown that the two forms had different optimum salinities for egg development. The survival of leiurus x leiurus eggs was maximum in fresh water and in low salinities, whilst the survival of trachurus x trachurus eggs was a maximum at moderately high salinities (about half-strength sea water). Eggs from trachurus x leiurus crosses had an optimum salinity for development that corresponded to the optimum for the maternal form. When the female was a trachurus fish, the eggs had an optimum similar to that of trachurus x trachurus eggs, whereas when the female was a leiurus fish the eggs had an optimum similar to leiurus x leiurus eggs. This type of maternal inheritance means that the hybrids were not truly intermediate in character. Heuts argued that these physiological properties of the hybrid eggs was one of the factors that limited gene flow between the trachurus and leiurus populations (Heuts, 1946, 1947b). Yet the type of controlled, stable environmental factors used in these experiments is not typical of the natural environment, where rapid fluctuations in both temperature and salinity can occur within twenty-four hours. So it is not clear how relevant the physiological experiments carried out under laboratory conditions are to events in the natural environment.

Hagen (1967) examined a number of the possible mechanisms that could restrict gene flow between leiurus and trachurus populations in a geographically restricted area. The Little Campbell River which drains into the Pacific near the Canada/U.S.A. border is only about 20 km long. In the head waters there is a leiurus population (in later publications, Hagen refers to it as a population of the low plated morph) and a trachurus population breeds in the lower stretches of the river. The trachurus population is a typical anadromous population with the complete row of lateral plates and the caudal keel. A short stretch of the river about 1.5 km long is the only region of the river in which hybrids between the trachurus and leiurus forms are found.

There are several possible mechanisms by which gene flow between closely related species can be restricted and so maintain the genetic isolation of these forms. These isolating mechanisms can operate either by preventing mating between the two forms, that is, pre-mating isolation, or by reducing the success of any such matings, post-mating isolation (Mayr, 1963).

If the two forms breed at different times of the year, then this temporal isolation ensures that no inter-breeding takes place. In the Little Campbell River, there was a partial separation of the breeding seasons of the leiurus and trachurus forms. Leiurus fish bred from March through to June, while trachurus fish bred between the middle of May and the middle of September. Only the early spawning trachurus fish could make any major contribution to hybridisation between the two forms. There was some evidence that these early breeding trachurus were genetically distinct from the bulk of the trachurus population. They moved into the river from the sea about a month before the bulk of the trachurus population, they moved further upstream settling in the hybrid zone, and they had significantly more lateral plates. Curiously, there was a form of seasonal isolation within the hybrid forms. Mature hybrid males were found in April and May and so could breed only with leiurus females, while female hybrids were gravid in June and July and so were more likely to breed with trachurus males.

Hagen found no evidence which suggested that the fish used behavioural cues during courtship to ensure that they mated with a partner of the same form. When males of either form were presented with a trachurus and a leiurus female of equal size and gravidity and allowed to court them until one of the females laid her eggs in the males nest, the males showed no preference either for females of the same form or females of the other form. In a second series of test, gravid females were given the opportunity of responding to either a trachurus male or a leiurus male. A positive response was recorded when the female orientated towards one of the males and showed the head up posture (see Chapter 9). Again the females showed no preference for males of the same form as themselves. However, in a series of tests in which a positive response was only recorded when the female entered or was about to enter the nest, leiurus females chose leiurus males significantly more often than they chose trachurus males, while trachurus females chose trachurus males significantly more often than they chose leiurus males (Hay and McPhail, 1975). These preferences were by no means absolute and may not provide a very strong barrier to inter-breeding. Behavioural isolation is probably more important in preventing inter-breeding between species of sticklebacks, such as between *Gasterosteus aculeatus* and *G. wheatlandi* (Reisman, 1968b) or between *G. aculeatus* and *Pungitius pungitius* (Wilz, 1970d, 1971).

When crosses were made between the leiurus and trachurus forms from the Little Campbell River, they provided no evidence of hybrid inviability or infertility, so that the normal post-mating mechanisms do not prevent genetic exchange between the two forms. Yet in the Little Campbell River, hybrids are restricted to a narrow stretch of the river, and there is no evidence of a diffusion of trachurus genes into the leiurus population or leiurus genes into the trachurus population. In other words, introgression does not seem to be occurring, which means that there must be an effective mechanism restricting gene flow between the leiurus and trachurus populations.

The efficiency of this mechanism can be gauged from the analysis of plate counts of the leiurus population in the Little Campbell. If there was gene flow between the trachurus and leiurus population, it would be expected that the leiurus population closest to the sea would have the highest numbers of lateral plates, because this would be the population closest to the breeding areas of the hybrids and trachurus populations and so be most influenced by a flow of genes from these populations. But the situation was found to be the reverse of this expectation. The leiurus fish closest to the hybrid and trachurus zones had the lowest average number of lateral plates of any leiurus fish from the entire stream (Fig. 54). This reversed cline in plate counts indicates that there is very strong selection against any exchange of genes between the leiurus and trachurus populations.

By detailed field observations and careful laboratory experiments,

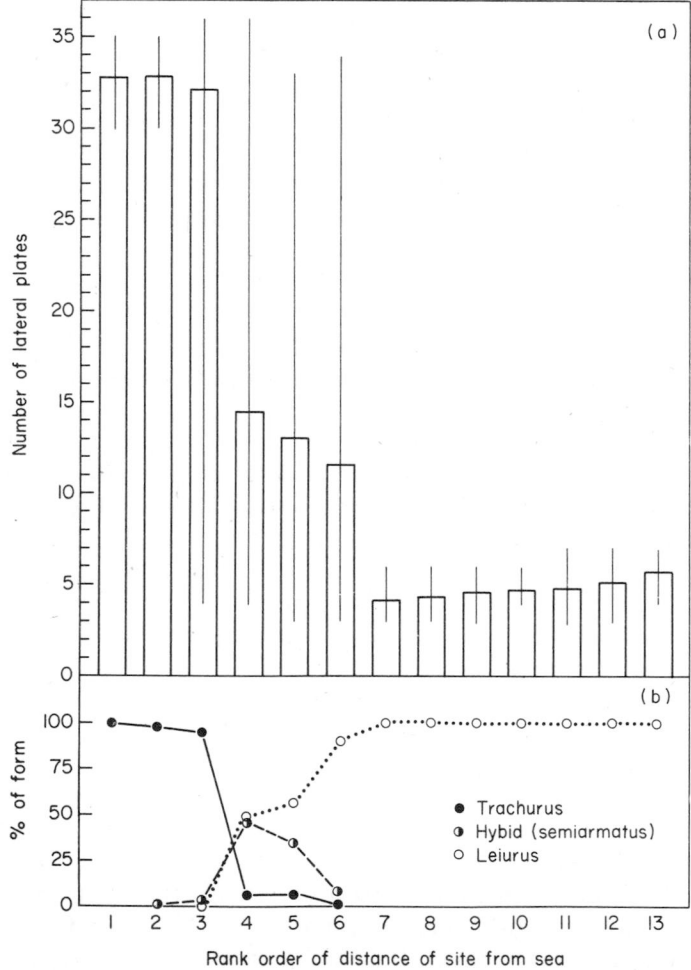

Fig. 54. Variation in number of lateral plates and population composition of *Gasterosteus aculeatus* from Little Campbell River (after Hagen, 1967). (a) Mean and range of number of lateral plates at each sampling station; (b) population composition at each station. Sampling stations ranked by distance from sea, station 1 closest to sea. Note reversed cline in number of lateral plates for the leiurus component of the population.

Hagen showed that even during the breeding season, when the trachurus and leiurus populations were sharing the same river, the populations were occupying different habitats within the river, and showed different habitat preferences. The two populations were ecologically separated and adapted to somewhat different environments. Trachurus fish bred in a stretch of the stream that had a sandy bottom, a slow current and beds of *Elodea* and *Myriophyllum*. The leiurus fish lived and bred in quiet or still backwaters or ponds where the bottom was muddy, the vegetation dense and the water discoloured. When trachurus fish were transferred to the head waters of the river normally occupied only by leiurus fish, the trachurus transfers disappeared within a month. Many dead individuals were found, which indicates that the trachurus fish were poorly adapted to living in the leiurus zone of the river.

The rather more slender shape of the trachurus form suggests that it is better adapted to living in water currents than the deeper-bodied leiurus form. Behavioural tests showed that while leiurus fish avoided a water current, trachurus fish would spend periods of time riding the current.

The gill rakers of the trachurus form were more numerous and longer than those of the leiurus form, whose rakers were short and thick. This difference suggests that the two forms had somewhat different food preferences. Analysis of the stomach contents confirmed this difference for trachurus fish were feeding largely on planktonic organisms while the leiurus fish were feeding primarily on benthic organisms.

These differences between the two forms indicate that each is well adapted to a particular habitat in the river, but hybrids between the two are unlikely to be well adapted to either the typical trachurus habitat or the typical leiurus habitat. In the trachurus habitat, the hybrids will be excluded by trachurus fish, and in the leiurus habitat they will be excluded by the leiurus fish. Thus the gene flow between the trachurus and leiurus populations is restricted because the hybrids between them are at a disadvantage in both the typical leiurus and typical trachurus habitats and so cannot act as a "bridge" for the gene flow.

In some circumstances such gene flow does take place, so that apparent leiurus x trachurus intergrades, the semiarmatus form, constitute an important component of the stickleback populations. This is the situation in anadromous populations of the North Sea and Western Baltic (Fig. 11, p. 26). The proportion of semiarmatus in this area tends to increase from north to south, from about forty-three per cent in coastal northern Germany to just over fifty per cent in the populations off the Belgium coast. The proportion of trachurus in these anadromous populations declines from fifty-three per cent in the north German populations to forty per cent off the Belgium coast. South of the English Channel only leiurus populations confined to fresh or brackish water occur, while north of the Baltic the coastal waters of Norway contain pure trachurus populations. These northern populations are characterised by their large size and more strongly developed body armature (Münzing, 1959, 1963a).

The presence of the semiarmatus form in the coastal areas of western Europe was interpreted as marking the zone where the trachurus and leiurus populations isolated during the last glaciation (Würm) came into contact when the ice retreated. The relatively high proportions of semiarmatus in these populations indicates that the intergrades are not at a selective disadvantage when compared with the trachurus and leiurus forms in this particular area. Indeed the increased proportion of the semiarmatus form in the more southerly coastal populations indicates that under some environmental conditions the semiarmatus form has a selective advantage over the trachurus form (Münzing, 1959, 1963a, 1972). The mechanisms which maintain the particular proportions of the three forms in these polymorphic coastal populations are not known, but deserve study.

The situation in central and eastern Europe is interesting for in this region both semiarmatus and trachurus populations occur as permanent residents of freshwater. They must therefore be regarded as the European equivalents of the partially plated and completely plated morphs which are permanent residents of fresh water in northwest America. Whether this phenotypic similarity reflects a genetic similarity is not known. In the region between the Elbe and Oder rivers in central Europe, trachurus, semiarmatus and leiurus forms coexist as permanent residents in fresh water. Semiarmatus fish form a smaller proportion of these polymorphic populations than of the North Sea populations, but the trachurus form does not seem to be at any selective disadvantage compared with the leiurus form. This distribution pattern in central Europe has been interpreted as a product of contact between the leiurus form isolated in south-western Europe in the last ice age and a trachurus form isolated in the Black Sea area that has spread north-westwards as the ice receded (Paepke, 1970; Münzing, 1972).

In eastern Europe, the trachurus form occurs both in rivers that flow into the Baltic and in rivers that flow into the Black Sea. Some of the localities are so remote from the sea that it is probable that the trachurus populations are permanent residents in fresh water. Leiurus and semiarmatus fish occur only in the watersheds of rivers flowing into the Baltic and occur in relatively small numbers both in monomorphic populations and in polymorphic populations in association with the trachurus form. The leiurus form may not be adapted to survive the very cold winters of eastern Europe, but this hypothesis needs experimental confirmation (Penczak, 1962, 1965, 1966).

On the eastern side of North America there are landlocked trachurus populations in Lake Ontario and other isolated lakes in the Ottawa Valley (Miller and Hubbs, 1969; Garside and Hamor, 1973; McPhail, personal communication). There are also landlocked populations which contain a very high proportion of the semiarmatus form (Coad and Power, 1974), but a full account of the variation in this geographical area has still to be given. This area is particularly interesting because five species of sticklebacks are found on or close to the Atlantic coast of North America, *G. aculeatus*, *G. wheatlandi*, *Pungitius pungitius*, *Apeltes quadracus* and *Culaea inconstans*, and it would be interesting to know whether this geographical overlap has led to particular evolutionary trends in any of the species.

Along the Pacific coast of North America, the anadromous trachurus form extends from Alaska to the area of the San Lorenzo River south of San Francisco. Freshwater populations of leiurus extend into Baja California just south of the U.S.A./Mexico border (Miller and Hubbs, 1969). From Alaska to California there are many landlocked populations which are polymorphic for the three plate morphs, that is the populations consist of various proportions of the low plated morph (probably leiurus), the partially plated morph (semiarmatus?) and the completely plated morph (trachurus?) (Hagen and Gilbertson, 1972). The existence of these polymorphic, landlocked populations provokes the question: what factors determine the relative frequencies of the morphs within a given population? Two suggestions have been made.

The first of these explanations is that much of the variation between these landlocked populations reflects variation in the amount of gene flow between the low plated and completely plated morphs, or in more coastal districts between anadromous trachurus fish and low plated (leiurus) fish. On this interpretation, hybridization has allowed an exchange of genes between the two forms resulting in populations which show the results of this exchange of genes. This process of intergradation and introgression is seen almost as an accidental process with little adaptive significance as no morph is at a distinct selective advantage or disadvantage compared to another (Miller and Hubbs, 1969).

But as was described earlier, two studies have shown that gene

flow between trachurus and leiurus populations can be very restricted with a limited zone of hybridisation and no introgression (Heuts,
1947a; Hagen, 1967) which, if also true for crosses between the low
plated morph (leiurus) and the completely plated morph (trachurus),
implies that the variation between the polymorphic populations must
have an adaptive significance and be the result of natural selection.
Other evidence also suggests that selective forces rather than introgression may determine the relative proportions of the three morphs
in polymorphic populations. Several lakes which have been isolated
from the sea for at least 10,000 years contain all three morphs. Yet
the isolation from the sea ensured isolation from an anadromous
trachurus population so the fully plated morph could not have been
maintained by gene flow from a trachurus population, but must
represent an adaptive genotype in the environment of the lake. A few
lakes have a very high proportion of the partially plated morph
although the fully plated morph is absent or present only as a very
low proportion. In this situation the partially plated morph cannot
be regarded as a simple hybrid whose presence in the population is
maintained by inter-breeding between the low and completely plated
morphs, but must be regarded as a fully adaptive genotype, in the
same way as the semiarmatus form in the North Sea seems to
represent an adaptive genotype. Another piece of evidence is that in
the Chehalis River in Washington State, the resident fresh water
populations that live in the lower reaches of the river consist
predominantly of a single morph, although anadromous trachurus
populations also enter the lower reaches of the river and so there is
ample opportunity for introgression and intergradation to occur. In
contrast, in the headwaters of the Chehalis, which are over 100 km
from the sea and hence far from trachurus influence, the populations
are polymorphic and the frequency of the three morphs changes
markedly over short distances (Hagen and Gilbertson, 1972).

This sort of evidence has led to attempts to identify the selective
factors that operate to produce particular proportions of the three
morphs in polymorphic populations from different localities. No
correlation was found between the proportions of the three morphs
and several environmental factors which might have been relevant.
These factors were temperature, distance of the site from the sea and
the pH of the water. One significant correlation showed that the
higher the total dissolved solids (TDS) in the water, the lower the
proportion of the partially plated morph (Hagen and Gilbertson,
1972). But the range was largely restricted to low levels of TDS and
it is perhaps unlikely that the negative correlation reflects an
important effect of TDS on population composition (Garside and

Hamor, 1973). As yet the search for the environmental factors which may determine the relative proportions of the three morphs at a particular site has been unsuccessful. Until progress is made in this direction, the relative importance of selection and introgression in determining morph frequencies in the stickleback populations of the Pacific northwest remains an unsolved problem.

Nevertheless, studies on these landlocked populations have demonstrated some effects of selection. When populations from streams and lakes were compared, the lake fish were found to have a higher average number of gill rakers, a higher average number of vertebrae and more slender bodies than stream fish. In these characters, the lake sticklebacks tended to resemble the anadromous trachurus form more than the stream fish. This may be the result of evolutionary convergence, since dwelling in a large lake is in some respects more similar to living in the sea than to living in streams. The high number of gill rakers is probably a trophic adaptation which enables the fish to feed more efficiently on planktonic organisms (see also Chapter 4). The significance of the body shape and high vertebral count is less obvious but again it may be related to a pelagic rather than a fluvial mode of life (Hagen and Gilbertson, 1972), although this interpretation has been questioned (Garside and Harmor, 1973).

The most potent environmental factor yet detected that influences these fresh water stickleback populations in the Pacific northwest is the presence of predatory fish. These predators include the squawfish (*Ptychocheilus oregonensis*), the cutthroat and rainbow trout (*Salmo clarki* and *S. gairdneri*), the chars (*Salvelinus malma* and *S. alpinus*) and the pike (*Esox lucius*). In areas where predators were common, the sticklebacks' dorsal and ventral spines were significantly longer than those of sticklebacks from areas where predators were absent or sparse. Since spines are an effective defence mechanism against predators (Chapter 5), this is not a surprising correlation (Hagen and Gilbertson, 1972).

A more curious observation was that at sites where predatory fish were common, the number of anterior lateral plates of the low and partially plated morphs tended to show a strong mode at seven (Fig. 55). Where predators were scarce or absent, there tended to be no strong modal class for plate numbers, and few or no fish with seven lateral plates. This suggests that fish with seven plates are at a distinct selective advantage over other sticklebacks when predatory fish are present, but this advantage disappears when predators are not an important factor in the environment (Hagen and Gilbertson, 1972). Direct evidence of this advantage comes both from field observations and laboratory studies.

Lake Wapato is a lake in central Washington State, lying to the east of the coastal mountains so that the stickleback population in the lake is isolated by a mountain range from the populations in the coastal strip. The lake also contains rainbow trout which prey upon the sticklebacks, the heaviest predation occurring in the winter. Hagen and Gilbertson (1973a) found that the stickleback population

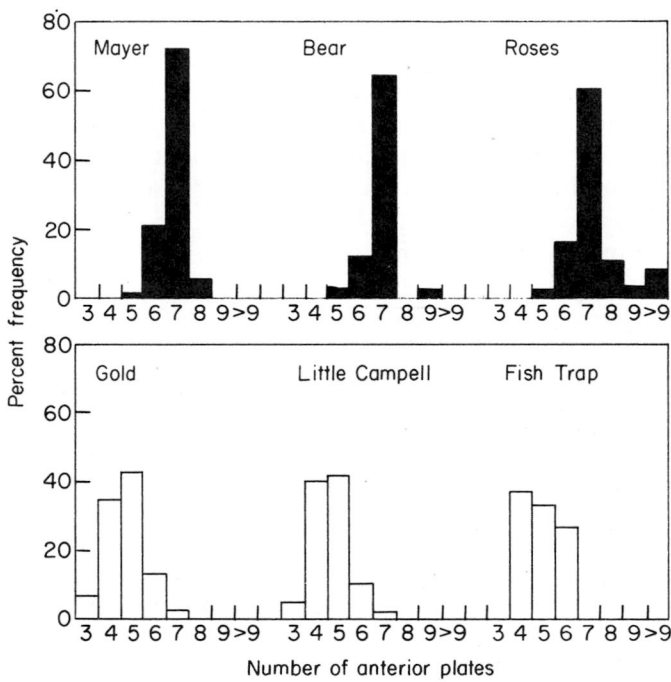

Fig. 55. Frequency distribution of number of anterior lateral plates for six populations of *Gasterosteus aculeatus* from Pacific northwest (after Hagen and Gilbertson, 1972). Black bars for sites where predatory fish common; open bars for sites where predatory fish absent or rare.

showed a strong mode for seven lateral plates. A comparison of samples of sticklebacks caught in a seine net with those found in the stomachs of trout indicated that sticklebacks with seven lateral plates occurred less frequently in the stomachs than would have been expected on the basis of their frequency in the population as a whole. Sticklebacks with less than seven lateral plates and those with nine were at a strong disadvantage during predation. A similar situation was observed by Moodie (1972a, b) during a study of the sticklebacks of Mayer Lake on the Queen Charlotte Islands. These sticklebacks were eaten by cutthroat trout, and a comparison of samples taken by seine netting with those from trout stomachs showed that sticklebacks with eight lateral plates were eaten more than would have been expected from their frequency in the whole population. The population showed a strong mode of seven plates, though the mode for female fish was less prominent than that for male fish.

In laboratory experiments in which predatory fish were allowed to feed on groups of sticklebacks with a predetermined composition with regard to plate number, the predators took relatively fewer sticklebacks with seven plates than with more or fewer than seven plates. This result was obtained when the fish were kept under "winter" conditions of low temperature and short photoperiod. Under "summer" conditions, the seven plated sticklebacks were found to be no longer at an advantage during predation, a laboratory result that conflicts with data from natural populations (Moodie *et al.*, 1973).

It is not clear why sticklebacks with seven lateral plates have an advantage in environments in which predators are common. One possibility is that it is not the plates themselves that are important, but a behavioural trait that is correlated with the morphological trait. Moodie (1972b) found that males with seven lateral plates tended to nest in deeper water and closer to cover than males with six plates. Perhaps relevant in this context is the finding that male sticklebacks that are relatively bold in the presence of a predator outside the breeding season tend to be more aggressive towards conspecifics during the breeding season (Huntingford, 1974). The former trait may make them more likely to be eaten by a predator but the latter trait will enable them to reproduce more successfully (see Chapter 13). A question that remains concerns the geographical distribution of this relationship between seven platedness and predation. Is the phenomenon confined to the Pacific northwest, or is a similar phenomenon shown by stickleback populations in Europe and Asia?

Predation is also implicated as an important factor in the evolution of several unusual populations in the Pacific northwest.

The first of these populations was discovered in the Chehalis River system in Washington State and subsequently analysed by McPhail (1969). Over almost the whole range of the three-spined stickleback, the reproductively active male assumes a red throat and blue eyes (Chapter 10), but in the Chehalis system are found males which become jet black during the breeding season (outside the breeding season these males are a dull mottled colour). Normal sticklebacks also live in the Chehalis system. Breeding experiments showed that a genetic difference underlies the difference in nuptial colours between the "black" sticklebacks and the typical sticklebacks. There are also differences in the number of gill rakers and the positioning of the dorsal spines which have a genetic basis. The "black" sticklebacks, both as eggs and adults, were far less tolerant of high salinities than the normal fish.

The mere presence and continuing survival of the "black" stickleback in several parts of the Chehalis system indicates that in these areas the "black" stickleback has a selective advantage over the typical stickleback. The question thus arises of what is the selective advantage of the "black" stickleback, and how does it maintain its unique genotype although sharing the same river system with populations of typical sticklebacks?

A unique feature of the Chehalis system is the presence of the small carnivorous fish *Novumbra hubbsi*, the western mudminnow. This fish is endemic to this area of Washington. Although too small to be a predator of adult stickleback, the two species being of similar size, *Novumbra* takes sticklebacks' eggs and larvae. Laboratory experiments showed that *Novumbra* was less successful at catching larvae of the "black" stickleback than those of typical sticklebacks. This was because the "black" larvae were more successful in evading attacks by *Novumbra* (Chapter 5). Experiments also showed that *Novumbra* tended to orientate towards normal males when in their breeding colours more than towards "black" males in breeding condition. Typical males are more conspicuous and so may signal the site of their nest to *Novumbra* more than "black" males. In addition, the "black" males fade rapidly to a drab colour when disturbed, whereas typical males lose their red coloration only slowly.

The evolution of the "black" stickleback of the Chehalis can be seen as a response to the presence of a specific predator, *Novumbra*. There are at least two ways in which the black of the breeding males may be adaptive. Firstly it may make the male less conspicuous and so less likely to advertise the site of the nest. Secondly it may represent an evolutionary convergence which makes the male stickleback resemble the predator. During its breeding season, the male *Novumbra* is dark chocolate or black, and the blackness becomes more intense during courtship and fighting. Like the male stickleback, the male *Novumbra* is strongly territorial during the breeding season, defending an area both from conspecifics and from sticklebacks (Hagen, *et al.*, 1972). By resembling the male *Novumbra*, the male "black" stickleback may be able to intimidate this predator of eggs and larvae in a comparable manner to the way in which the red throat of the typical stickleback may intimidate conspecifics from nest-raiding (see Chapters 11 and 13).

For this adaptation of the "black" stickleback to be effective, it must not be swamped by gene flow from other populations of typical sticklebacks. Breeding experiments suggested that there was a slight reduction in the viability of hybrids between "black" and typical sticklebacks, compared with offspring of crosses between parents of the same type. The hybrids were intermediate in both morphology and in breeding coloration, and were slightly less fertile than the parental types. Male hybrids had a curious behavioural handicap, for when they were parental they did not show normal fanning cycles (Chapter 13), but fanned at very low levels so that they were relatively unsuccessful at rearing eggs. Backcrosses between hybrids and either of the parental types showed on average a fifty per cent reduction in viability. All these handicaps of the hybrids and backcrosses will restrict gene flow between "black" and typical stickleback populations. Hybrids do occur naturally, and experiments showed that there were no behavioural barriers to gene flow between "black" and typical populations. Indeed, when given a choice between a "black" male and a typical male, females from the "black" population tended to prefer to mate with typical, brightly coloured males (see also Chapter 9). The genetic integrity of the "black" stickleback populations seems to be maintained by the selective advantage in the presence of *Novumbra* and by the disadvantage suffered by hybrids (McPhail, 1969).

A relationship between the nuptial coloration of the male stickleback and predation is also implied by the unusual situation in Lake Wapato, where the stickleback population is polymorphic for male breeding colours (Semler, 1971). Only about fourteen per cent of the males develop the typical red throat during the breeding season, the other males have ventral surfaces that are silver, drab mottled black, or completely black. Semler found that during the breeding season, the proportion of red males declined. In choice tests, females from the Wapato population preferred to mate with males with the red nuptial coloration rather than non-red males. Even when the choice was betweeen a non-red male that had been artificially coloured red and an untreated non-red male, the females preferred the male with the red colouring. So red males have a distinct advantage over non-red males in terms of attracting females. But it is likely that the red that signals to the females is also conspicuous to the rainbow trout that feed on the sticklebacks so that the red sticklebacks suffer heavier rates of predation than the non-red fish during the breeding season. The precise mechanisms that maintain the colour polymorphisms at the levels observed are not known, though O'Donald (1973) developed mathematical models which suggested that the polymorphism could be maintained by a balance of sexual and natural selection. The sexual selection would operate through the females' preference for red males, while the natural selection would operate through the disadvantage that red males suffer during predation by the trout.

Yet another example of predation apparently acting as the major selective force leading to the evolution of an unusual stickleback has come from studies on the sticklebacks of the Queen Charlotte Islands

TABLE IX

A comparison of the morphological characters of sticklebacks from Mayer Lake and adjoining streams. Sample sizes are shown in brackets (from Moodie, 1972b).

Character	Mayer Lake sticklebacks Mean and SE	Leiurus sticklebacks from adjoining streams Mean and SE
Number of lateral plates	6.8 ± 0.054 (295)	4.7 ± 0.126 (152)
Number of gill rakers	21.2 ± 0.092 (250)	16.6 ± 0.151 (205)
Number of vertebrae	34.0 ± 0.041 (157)	32.5 ± 0.072 (71)
Number of dorsal fin rays	11.6 ± 0.085 (92)	10.9 ± 0.064 (140)
Number of anal fin rays	9.4 ± 0.060 (92)	8.3 ± 0.053 (139)
Ratio of body length to body depth	4.6 ± 0.011 (455)	4.4 ± 0.017 (219)
Ratio of body length to pelvic spine length	5.3 ± 0.005 (457)	6.4 ± 0.034 (221)

(Moodie, 1972a, b; Moodie and Reimchen, 1973). These islands lie off the coast of British Columbia (53° 40' N, 132° 02' W). A population of sticklebacks characterised by their unusually large size occurs in Mayer Lake on one of the Queen Charlotte Islands. The largest fish taken during Moodie's study was a female with a standard length of 116 mm. This unusual population is confined to the lake; the streams draining into the lake contain populations of typical leiurus sticklebacks (equivalent to the low plated morph). The morphological differences between the lake fish and fish from the adjoining streams are shown in Table IX. The lake fish are longer, have longer pelvic spines, a more streamlined body, and a higher number of gill rakers, vertebrae and dorsal and anal fin rays. The phenotype of the lake fish has remained stable for at least forty years. Apart from size, the most distinctive feature of the lake sticklebacks, is their colour. Outside the breeding season, the fish are black except for the opercular and the anteroventral surfaces which are bright silver. Sexually mature males lose this silver coloration, and although a small proportion of the males develop red throats, most of them develop grey or sooty black throats. They usually lack the blue eyes and iridescent back of the typical sexually mature male.

Although the elongated shape and high number of gill rakers of the Lake Mayer sticklebacks probably represent adaptations to the lacustrine mode of life, most of the unusual characteristics of this population can probably be best interpreted as adaptations that reduce the intensity of predation by the piscivorous fish living in the lake. The most important of these predators is the cutthroat trout, though the prickly sculpin (*Cottus asper*) takes stickleback eggs, young and small adults. Large size, long spines and inconspicuous nuptial coloration are all likely to reduce the intesity of predation, the first two by making it less likely that the stickleback can be captured successfully, the third by reducing the risk of detection by a predator at a time in the male's life history when his behaviour is likely to make him most conspicuous. Both field observations and some experimental data support this interpretation. Sticklebacks taken from the stomachs of trout in Mayer Lake tended to have shorter spines than the average for the population. Only the largest trout were found to take the largest of the lake sticklebacks. In laboratory experiments, when presented with a choice, cutthroat trout attacked sticklebacks with red throats significantly more often than they attacked sticklebacks with dull throats (Moodie, 1972a).

These populations are not the only atypical sticklebacks found along the Pacific coast, although they have received the most attention. On the Queen Charlotte Islands, there are populations of sticklebacks with one or more of the dorsal spines absent, a population in which the majority of the fish lack pelvic spines and have much reduced pelvic skeletons, and populations in which most individuals lack lateral plates (Moodie and Reimchen, 1973). Texada Island also lies off the mainland coast of British Columbia; on it a population was found in which the fish lacked lateral plates, had no pelvic spines or pelvic skeleton and had only rudimentary dorsal spines (Hagen and McPhail, 1970). Such plateless forms with reduced or absent spines seem to occur most frequently in isolated lakes where there are no predatory fish (McPhail, personal communication). As described earlier, fossil *Gasterosteus* with a reduced pelvic skeleton, few or no lateral plates and reduced dorsal spines are known from Pliocene deposits (Bell, 1974). Bell argues that this condition has evolved several times in *Gasterosteus* populations and does not imply that all such forms are descended from the same ancestors. A similar condition has been observed in populations of the nine-spined stickleback (*Pungitius pungitius*) and the brook stickleback (*Culaea inconstans*) (see Chapters 16, 17).

Although most studies on variation in the stickleback have relied on morphological characteristics, physiological and biochemical differences also occur. In Chapter 8, the differences in the osmo-regulatory abilities of the anadromous trachurus form and the leiurus form were described. At a biochemical level, there are differences in the electrophoretic patterns of muscle proteins from leiurus and anadromous trachurus fish (Hagen, 1967), and there are also differences in the electrophoretic patterns of some enzymes (Muramoto *et al.*, 1969), though the functional significance, if any, of these differences is not known. Even within a single morphological form, there may be differences at a biochemical level. In Italy, all sticklebacks belong, morphologically, to the leiurus form. Some populations migrate into saline lagoons and canals and these migratory populations differ from populations that are resident in fresh water. All fish from permanent fresh water populations have the same type of haemoglobin, Hb^A (identified from its electrophoretic pattern). Fish from migratory populations have Hb^A or another haemoglobin which has a different electrophoretic pattern, Hb^B, or an intermediate haemoglobin, Hb^{AB}. This biochemical polymorphism seems to be linked to the migratory habit but again the functional significance of the differences between the haemoglobins is not known (Raunich *et al.*, 1972).

The modern distribution and variation of the three-spined stickleback suggest that three factors have had a most important influence on its evolution. These factors are the ice-ages of the Pleistocene, the temperature and salinity of the environment and predation by piscivorous fishes. The variation that has evolved in response to these and other factors imposes tremendous difficulties on attempts to classify neatly the three-spined stickleback. Early authors tended to describe almost every morphological variation as a distinct species so that over forty species of *Gasterosteus* have been described (Table X), but this trend was reversed when all the morphological variations were brought into one species *Gasterosteus aculeatus* by Bertin (1925). His solution has persisted until now, but the recent studies reviewed above have again emphasised the amount of variation found in the stickleback and have shown that much of this variation has a genetic component.

Species are often erected on the basis of morphological features; in

TABLE X

Synonyms of *Gasterosteus aculeatus* (from Münzing, 1959).

	Specific name	Authority		Equivalent form
Europe	G. trachurus	Cuv. and Val.	1829	trachurus
	G. leiurus	Cuv. and Val.	1829	leiurus
	(= gymnura)			
	G. semiarmatus	Cuv. and Val.	1829	semiarmatus
	G. semiloricatus	Cuv. and Val.	1829	semiarmatus
	G. argyropomus	Cuv. and Val.	1829	leiurus
	G. brachycentrus	Cuv. and Val.	1829	leiurus
	G. tetracanthus	Cuv. and Val.	1829	leiurus
	S. spinulosus	Jenyns	1835	leiurus
	G. quadrispinosa	Crespon	1844	leiurus
	G. nemausensis	Crespon	1844	leiurus
	G. ponticus	Nordmann	1840	trachurus
	G. biarmatus	Nordmann	1840	trachurus
	G. neustrianus	Blanchard	1866	semiarmatus
	G. bailloni	Blanchard	1866	leiurus
	G. argentatissimus	Blanchard	1866	leiurus
	G. elegans	Blanchard	1866	leiurus
	G. algeriensis	Sauvage	1874	leiurus
	G. hologymnus	Regan	1909	leiurus
Atlantic Coast	G. bispinosus	Walbaum	1792	trachurus
of North America,	G. noveboracensis	Cuv. and Val.	1829	trachurus
Greenland and	G. niger	Cuv. and Val.	1829	trachurus
Iceland	G. biaculeatus	Cuv. and Val.	1829	leiurus
	G. loricatus	Reinhardt	1838	trachurus
	G. dimidiatus	Reinhardt	1838	?
	G. biaculeatus	Dekay	1842	trachurus
	G. cuvieri	Girard	1849	semiarmatus
	G. atkinsi	Bean	1879	semiarmatus
	G. suppositus	Sauvage	1874	?
	G. islandicus	Sauvage	1874	leiurus
	G. gladiunculus	Kendall	1895	leiurus-semiarmatus
	G. cataphractus	Pallas	1811	trachurus
	G. insculptus	Richardson	1855	trachurus
	G. williamsoni	Girard	1854	leiurus
	G. microcephalus	Girard	1854	trachurus-semi-armatus
Pacific Coast of	G. plebeius	Girard	1854	leiurus
North America	G. inopinatus	Girard	1854	leiurus
and Japan	G. serratus	Ayres	1855	trachurus
	G. intermedius	Girard	1856	trachurus
	G. pugetti	Girard	1856	leiurus
	G. santae-annae	Regan	1909	leiurus
	G. japonicus	Franz	1910	leiurus

the case of the stickleback, for instance, the degree of development of the row of lateral plates has often been used as a character of taxonomic importance. But the studies of Hagen and his co-workers on the stickleback populations of the Pacific northwest have shown that features such as number of lateral plates, number of gill rakers and body shape are subject to strong selection pressures. This means that the morphology of the stickleback in a particular area may represent an adaptation to the environmental conditions prevailing in that area rather than providing clues as to the evolutionary origin or systematic status of the stickleback (Hagen and McPhail, 1970; Moodie, 1972a). Biologically, the most satisfactory definition of the species is one which emphasises that distinct species are reproductively isolated from each other, so that there is no significant gene flow between different species. Such reproductive isolation maintains the genetic integrity of a species by preventing introgression. Yet even this concept of the species does not help to clarify the systematics of *Gasterosteus*. At certain times and in certain places leiurus and trachurus populations show reproductive isolation and so are acting as good species (Hagen, 1967), but at other times and in other places, the hybridisation between the two forms is extensive and integrades form an important proportion of the stickleback populations as is the case in the North Sea. In these populations, the hybrids do not seem to be at a selective disadvantage compared with the parental types (Münzing, 1963a, 1972). In the Chehalis system, the "black" stickleback described by McPhail (1969) is reproductively isolated from the typical stickleback; should this "black" stickleback be regarded as a good, distinct species?

If, conservatively and provisionally, all the morphological variations including such forms as the Chehalis River and Lake Mayer sticklebacks are retained within the single species *Gasterosteus aculeatus*, there remains the problem of the status of the forms or morphs within the species.

The completely plated form exists as both the anadromous trachurus form and the landlocked form which is usually also referred to as trachurus, but which Hagen in his publications refers to as the completely plated morph. There is significant morphological variation within the trachurus form, for example the trachurus populations from Norwegian coastal waters have a more strongly developed body armature than more southerly trachurus populations. Narver (1969) found that he could distinguish two phenotypes in the completely plated sticklebacks of the Chignik River system in Alaska. The estuarine phenotype had larger lateral plates and a better developed caudal keel than the lacustrine phenotype. A major problem concerning the fully plated morph is the relationship between the anadromous trachurus form and the landlocked fully plated forms which occur on both sides of the North American continent and in eastern Europe. The most plausible relationship is that the landlocked forms have been derived from originally anadromous populations. Because it spends a proportion of its life in the sea, the trachurus form is presumably pre-adapted to life in large lakes and in such an environment will not be at a selective disadvantage to the leiurus form. A second feature of the trachurus form is that it adapted to colder waters than the leiurus form and this may enable it to penetrate into areas such as eastern Europe which have a continental climate with very cold winters. The other hypothesis for the origin of landlocked populations of the completely plated form is that they have evolved from partially or low plated morphs in response to particular environmental factors.

The partially plated, keeled form, usually described as semiarmatus, sometimes exists as a very small proportion of the total stickleback population of a river system maintained through interbreeding between leiurus and trachurus populations but at a selective disadvantage compared with either of the parental types (Hagen, 1967). In other situations the semiarmatus form constitutes a significant proportion of the stickleback population in an area, and does not seem to be at a selective disadvantage compared with either of the other two forms and occurs at too high a frequency to be maintained only by hybridisation (Münzing, 1959, 1963a, 1972). Finally, in some situations the semiarmatus form constitutes all or the vast majority of the stickleback population in an area. In this situation, there is no question of this form being maintained only by hybridisation but it must represent an adaptive phenotype in its own right (Hagen and Gilbertson, 1972).

Nor does the status of the low plated, unkeeled leiurus form pose any fewer problems of interpretation. The main morphological variation in the leiurus form is the presence, especially towards the southern limits of its range, of populations in which all or a high proportion of the individuals lack any lateral plates. This situation occurs in Europe (Bertin, 1925) and in North America (Miller and Hubbs, 1969). It is not known what selective advantage these unplated forms possess, though the absence of predatory fish may have been an important factor in their evolution (McPhail, personal communication; Ross, 1973). An important question is whether all leiurus populations are derived from the same ancestral stock that can be traced back in the fossil record to the early Pleistocene (Bell, 1973a), or whether the leiurus form has repeatedly been derived from the anadromous, trachurus form. Because of the relatively high salinity tolerance of the leiurus form, especially outside the breeding season (Chapter 8), it can probably spread between adjacent fresh water systems via the sea, so it is not necessary to postulate that within every river system in which the trachurus and leiurus forms coexist, that the latter has evolved from the former within that system. There is some tendency for populations almost certainly derived from the anadromous trachurus form but which are now landlocked to show a reduction in the number of lateral plates. Examples of this are provided by the populations in Lake Techirghiol and Lake Iznik, near the Black Sea. In Lake Techirghiol, this reduction in number of lateral plates has taken place although the lake is saline (Münzing, 1962a, 1963a).

For those populations that are polymorphic with respect to plate morphs, there is the problem of accounting for the maintenance of the polymorphism. The problem of polymorphism in animal populations has received considerable attention recently (Ford, 1964; Levins, 1968), but specific models that explain the situations found in many populations of the stickleback are still required.

Some authors have used sub-species when classifying *Gasterosteus aculeatus*. In particular the populations in southern California which consist predominantly of fish lacking lateral plates and, associated with this platelessness, a reduction in the size of the spines and a tendency for the margins of the fins to be more rounded than in the typical leiurus form, have been described as *G. aculeatus williamsoni* (Jordan and Hubbs, 1925; Miller, 1960). Leiurus fish from the Pacific coast of North America are designated *G. aculeatus microcephalus*, and complete plated forms as *G. aculeatus aculeatus* (Miller and Hubbs, 1969). Hybridisation between *williamsoni* and *microcephalus* occurs where their distributions overlap, but there is no overlap between *williamsoni* and *aculeatus*. There is some evidence that crosses between *williamsoni* and *microcephalus* are slightly less fertile than crosses within the sub-species but there is little evidence that gene flow between the two forms is restricted by isolating mechanisms (Ross, 1973). This designation of distinct sub-species for the sticklebacks of the Pacific has two disadvantages. Firstly, it ignores the existence of populations of plateless forms as far north as Texada Island and the Queen Charlotte Islands off the coast of British Columbia which have apparently evolved from the typical leiurus form in isolated lakes in the absence of predatory fish (Hagen and McPhail, 1970; Moodie and Reimchen, 1973). Secondly, it distinguishes between the leiurus form in the Pacific coastlands and the leiurus form of eastern America and Europe, which in view of the close morphological, behavioural and physiological similarities between leiurus forms from all these areas seems an unnecessary sub-division.

Penczak (1964) designated leiurus sticklebacks from Iceland as a distinct sub-species *G. aculeatus islandicus*. The most distinctive feature of these Icelandic sticklebacks was a relative reduction in the pelvic skeleton, yet this is a condition which seems to recur repeatedly in isolated populations of the three-spined stickleback. Whether this feature and the other distinguishing characters of the Icelandic stickleback are sufficient to justify sub-specific recognition is questionable.

While studies are still being pursued on the evolutionary signifi- cance of the various morphological forms of the three-spined stickle- back, it is probably best to retain them all within the species *Gasterosteus aculeatus* and not to recognise distinct sub-species, but to ensure that careful morphological descriptions and details of the site of origin are provided for specimens used in studies of any kind on the stickleback. Only extensive breeding experiments, and morphological, anatomical, biochemical, physiological and behav- ioural studies will provide a firm basis for the classification of the three-spined stickleback. Perhaps the various morphological forms are in the process of speciating, or perhaps they are in the process of reintegrating into a single, morphologically less variable species. The very dynamism of the situation prevents taxonomists from applying strict rules, yet it is this dynamism that makes the studies of the evolution of the stickleback so exciting, providing the opportunity for research on the action and consequences of natural selection on a vertebrate species.

Part 2

THE OTHER GASTEROSTEIDS

15. *Gasterosteus wheatlandi:*
The Black-Spotted Stickleback

Although at the moment the most convenient way of classifying the three-spined stickleback, *Gasterosteus aculeatus*, is to retain all the morphological forms within the single species, there is a fish, obviously closely related to the three-spined stickleback, which must be regarded as a distinct species. This is *Gasterosteus wheatlandi* Putnam, 1867, the black-spotted stickleback (Hubbs, 1929; McAllister, 1960; Leim and Scott, 1966). Because it is very similar to the three-spined stickleback it has probably often been confused with that species, but recent studies have served to underline its distinctiveness (Fig. 56).

Gasterosteus wheatlandi has a very restricted distribution, for it is confined to coastal waters and a few freshwater localities from Newfoundland to New York (Fig. 57). Within its range, it is sympatric with *G. aculeatus* and also with the four-spined stickleback *Apeltes quadracus* and the nine-spined stickleback, *Pungitius pungitius*. Indeed it would seem possible that all four species may be breeding in the same waters along parts of the North Atlantic seaboard. If such a situation does occur it would provide an ideal opportunity for a study on reproductive isolating mechanisms between closely related species. In the waters of Long Island, N.Y., *G. wheatlandi* and *G. aculeatus* could be seen co-existing in water less than a metre deep over a coarse, gravelly substrate (Perlmutter, 1963).

Although it is primarily a marine fish, morphologically *G. wheatlandi* resembles the leiurus form of *G. aculeatus*; the number of lateral plates varies from five to eleven, and these are confined to the anterior region of the body, a caudal keel being absent (Nelson, 1971a). *G. wheatlandi* differs morphologically from *G. aculeatus* in a number of respects. The posttemporal and supracliethra bones of the pectoral girdle are missing (cf. Fig. 7 p. 16). Each pelvic fin consists

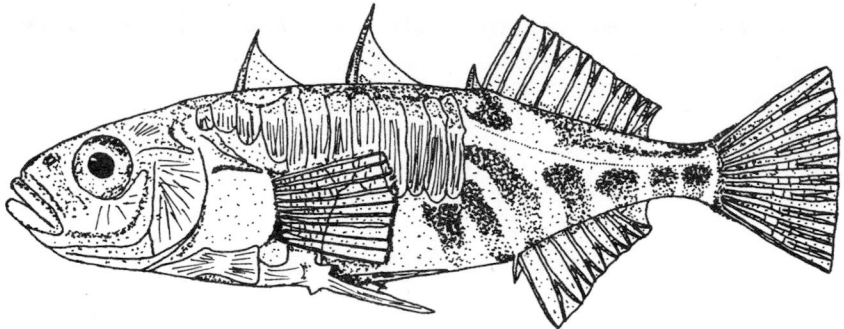

Fig. 56. *Gasterosteus wheatlandi* Putnam.

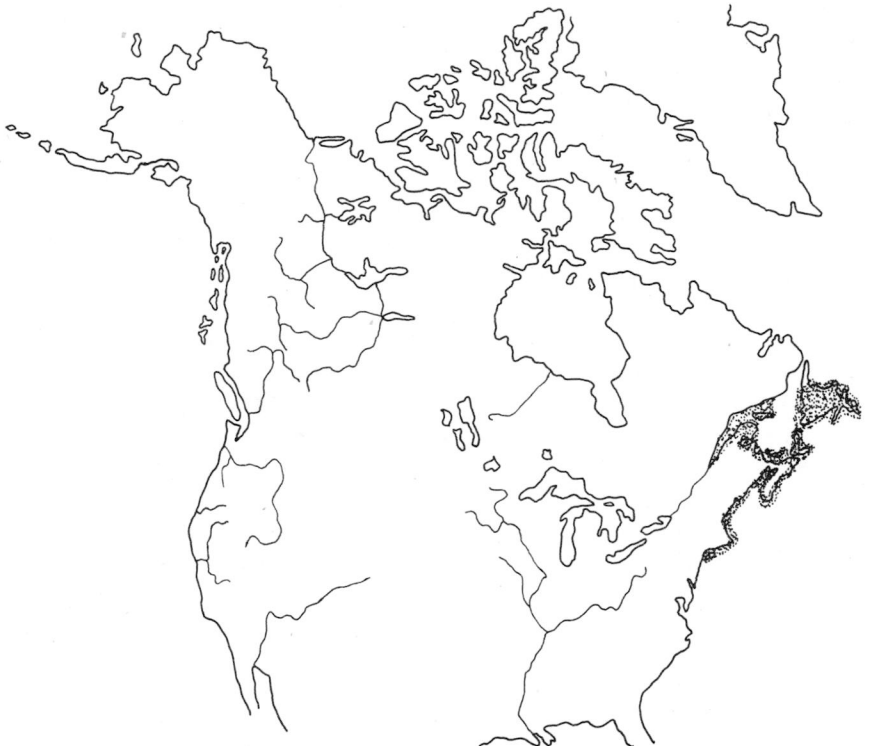

Fig. 57. Distribution of *Gasterosteus wheatlandi*.

of a spine and two fin rays, and the pelvic spine has a base with a well-developed cusp (Fig. 56). Normally there are twenty-eight vertebrae, a lower number than is usually found in *G. aculeatus*. Most of these differences can be detected only by careful examination, but a notable difference beween the two species is found in the colours of the breeding male. *G. wheatlandi* males do not develop a red throat or blue eyes, but they have a greenish gold body colour with a series of black markings behind the pelvic spines. The pelvic spines are orange (McInerney, 1969; Leim and Scott, 1966; Scott and Crossman, 1973).

G. wheatlandi is largely confined to the sea, penetrating brackish water to spawn and occurring only occasionally in freshwater. Studies in New Brunswick and Quebec have found that breeding

TABLE XI

Parasites recorded from the black-spotted stickleback (*Gasterosteus wheatlandi*).

Platyhelminthes

1. CESTODA
Schistocephalus solidus (Müller, 1776) (b).

Arthropoda

1. CRUSTACEA

(i) COPEDODA
Thersitina gasterostei (Pagenstechner, 1861) (a).

(ii) BRANCHIURA
Argulus canadensis Wilson, 1916 (b).

Sources. (a) Hanek and Threlfall, 1969a. (b) Hoffman, 1967.

takes place in brackish water, often in water whose salinity changes with the tidal cycle. Only one size class was found which suggests that breeding takes place in one season and the fish die after breeding. Otoliths have been used to age fish and this method also indicates that the fish breed the year after their birth and die relatively soon after breeding (McInerney, 1969; Coad and Power, 1973c). In Newfoundland the maximum length recorded was 64 mm, while from the Altantic coast a maximum length of 76 mm has been noted (Scott and Crossman, 1973).

Only a few species parasitic on *G. wheatlandi* have yet been recorded (Table XI).

Although the breeding behaviour of *G. wheatlandi* is basically the same as that of the three-spined stickleback, there are a number of interesting differences. The zig-zag approach of the male to the gravid female is performed with the head down so that the male makes an angle of about 30 degrees with the horizontal. If the female is receptive, showing a head-up posture and orientating towards the male, the leading sequence begins. This sequence is markedly different from that of *G. aculeatus* described in Chapter 12. The male moves close to the substrate and maintains a head-down position, with his pelvic spines erect. His body is held so that the ventral surface is concave and he quivers. One author has compared this behaviour to fanning except that it is not performed at the nest (Reisman, 1968b). The female swims beneath the male but retains her head-up posture. She nudges the male between the pelvic spines and the male swims slowly forward quivering continuously. Leading does not consist of a direct and rapid movement to the nest, instead a devious route may be followed so that the leading phase can take a minute or more. Once at the nest, the male "shows" the female the nest entrance. The courtship sequence of the male includes few nest building activities and dorsal pricking has not yet been described in this *Gasterosteus*. Fertilisation of the eggs and the parental cycle are similar to those of the three-spined stickleback although fanning levels are somewhat less (McInerney, 1969).

A collection of females whose mean standard length was 33 mm produced between 75 and 168 eggs with a mean of 126. The eggs ranged in diameter from 0.86 to 1.12 mm, somewhat smaller than the eggs of *G. aculeatus* (Coad and Power, 1973c). But Scott and Crossman (1964) examined twenty ripe females and found that the number of eggs ranged from 171 to 272 and that the diameter of the eggs varied from 1.2 to 1.5 mm, which is within the *G aculeatus* range.

In preference tests, males of both *G. wheatlandi* and *G. aculeatus* courted females of either species with equal vigour, but the females responded preferentially to males of their own species. Even where a courtship between a male and a female from the two species was started, it broke down at the leading stage. *G. wheatlandi* females would not follow *G. aculeatus* males when the latter led rapidly to the nest, while *G. aculeatus* females did not respond appropriately to the *G. wheatlandi* males when they adopted the head-down position at the start of the leading sequence. Thus there seem to be behavioural mechanisms that restrict gene flow between these two closely related species (Reisman, 1968b; McInerney, 1969).

In *G. wheatlandi* the apparently unusual combination of a marine distribution and low number of lateral plates occurs. Clearly then, a high number of lateral plates is not an essential adaptation for a stickleback living in the sea (see also Chapter 18). It is not known whether *G. wheatlandi* is an offshoot of the trachurus form of *G. aculeatus* which has subsequently shown a reduction in the number of lateral plates, or an offshoot of a low plate form which has become adapted to saline conditions. On morphological evidence this seems the more likely, but the time and the circumstances in which this eastern American *Gasterosteus* evolved remain as yet unstudied.

The close relationship between the two has recently been emphasised by a study of the chromosomes. In both species the diploid number of chromosomes is 42, and only a single paracentric inversion would be required to derive the *G. wheatlandi* arm number of 52 from the *G. aculeatus* arm number of 54. But the circumstances and consequences of such a change in chromosome morphology are yet another feature of *Gasterosteus wheatlandi* that awaits study (Chen and Reisman, 1970).

16. *Pungitius pungitius:*
The Nine-Spined Stickleback

(Synonyms: *Gasterosteus pungitius* L.;
Pygosteus pungitius (L.))*

Of the other four genera of sticklebacks, *Apeltes, Culaea, Pungitius* and *Spinachia*, only *Pungitius* and specifically *P. pungitius*, the nine-spined stickleback, rivals *Gasterosteus aculeatus* in its widespread distribution and morphological variability. *Pungitius* has received less attention from biologists than *G. aculeatus* but a reasonably detailed description of its morphology, distribution and life history can be given.

Pungitius is a small fish; it probably never exceeds 10 cm in total length and is usually only about half this size. It has a slender body with a very slender caudal peduncle so that it looks a more delicate fish than *Gasterosteus* (Fig. 58). The most obvious feature that distinguishes *Pungitius* from *Gasterosteus* is the high number of dorsal spines of the former. Although, as the common name suggests, the usual number of spines is nine, there is a range from seven to twelve. Even the common name of the fish reflects this variation for it is often called the ten-spined stickleback! Unlike the spines of *Gasterosteus*, which lie directly in line with each other along the dorsal mid-line, the dorsal spines of *Pungitius* incline alternately to the left and right of the mid-line. They are relatively short compared to the two anterior spines of *Gasterosteus*. Behind the row of dorsal spines lies the dorsal fin with between nine and twelve fin rays. The anal fin is inserted directly below the dorsal fin and contains seven to eleven soft rays preceded by a small spine. As in *G. aculeatus* each pelvic fin consists of a spine with usually one soft ray, though the

* Lindsey (1962b) showed that the generic name *Pungitius* (Coste) has priority over *Pygosteus* (Gill) which has commonly been used by European workers.

266

soft ray may be absent or there may be two. The body lacks scales but lateral plates may be present, the number of plates varying from 0 to 34, and a caudal keel may also be present (Nelson, 1971a).

On the basis of morphological variations and geographical distribution, two species of *Pungitius* have been recognised: *P. pungitius* (the nine-spined stickleback), and *P. platygaster* (the Ukrainian stickleback). The latter species is restricted to the region of the Black, Caspian and Aral Seas. Several sub-species of *P. pungitius* have also been recognised, though whether these should be regarded as species, sub-species or as morphological variants of *P. pungitius* that

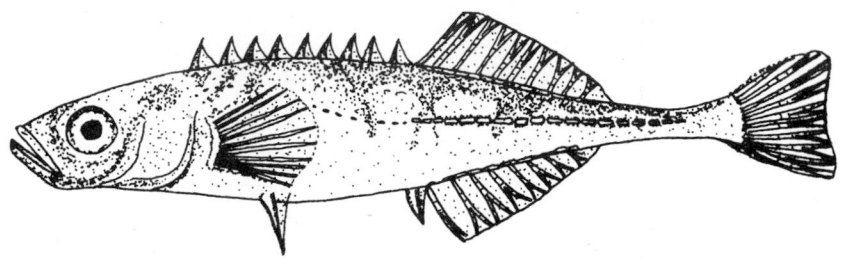

Fig. 58. *Pungitius pungitius* (L.).

are not of sub-specific status remains an open question. The most widely distributed form, *P. pungitius pungitius* (L.), usually has a distinct caudal keel together with a row of small lateral plates along the lateral line in the anterior region of the body. It has well developed ascending processes in the pelvic skeleton rather like those in the pelvic skeleton of *Gasterosteus* and has long pelvic spines. *P. pungitius laevis* (Cuvier) is similar to *P. pungitius pungitius* but lacks all lateral plates and its caudal peduncle is unkeeled. Two further forms are restricted to east Asia, *P. pungitius tymensis* (Nikolsky) and *P. pungitius sinensis* (Guichenot). The former is distinguished by a reduction in the size of the pelvic skeleton, for the ascending processes are hardly developed, the pelvic spines are short and there are no soft rays. In this form the dorsal spines are also very short. *P. pungitius sinensis* has a complete row of lateral plates that stretch from the keeled caudal peduncle to the anterior region of the body; it is the most heavily armoured *Pungitius*. In all forms of *P. pungitius* the diploid number of chromosomes is 42, but while the karyotypes of *P. pungitius pungitius* and *P. pungitius tymensis* are indistinguishable, that of *P. pungitius sinensis* is slightly different. There are also some differences in the electrophoretic patterns of some enzymes from the skeletal muscles (Muramoto *et al.*, 1969). *P. platygaster* also has a more or less complete row of lateral plates, but those on the caudal peduncle are small, rounded and loosely arranged. Two sub-species have been described: *P. platygaster platygaster* (Kessler) which has serrated pelvic spines and *P. platygaster aralensis* (Kessler) in which the pelvic spines are usually smooth (Münzing, 1969). Considerable work is required to elucidate the relationships between these forms before the taxonomy of *Pungitius* can be regarded as satisfactory but, in general, the forms are geographically more

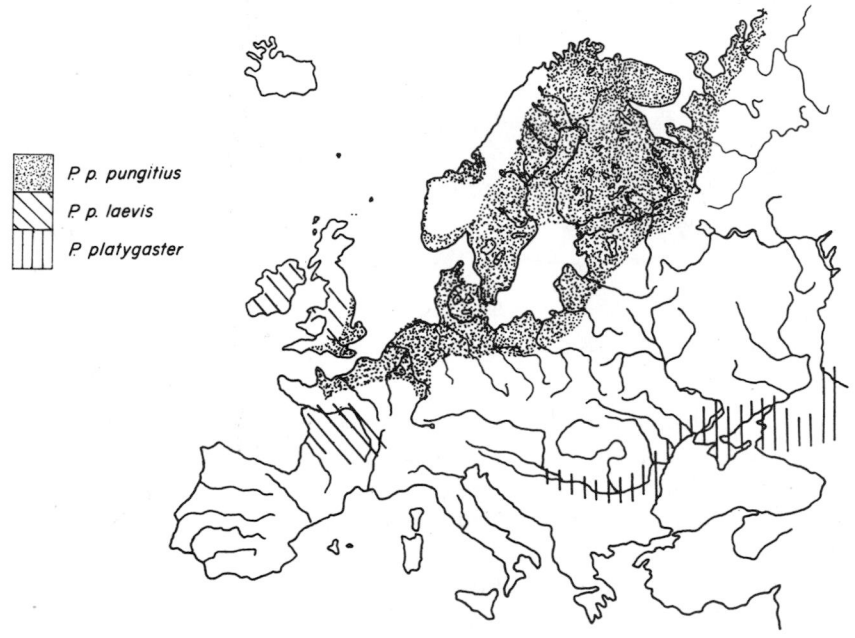

P. p. pungitius

P. p. laevis

P. platygaster

Fig. 59. European distribution of *Pungitius*.

distinct than is the case with the leiurus, semiarmatus and trachurus forms of *G. aculeatus*.

P. pungitius has a more northerly distribution than *G. aculeatus* and is less restricted than the latter species to coastal areas. In Europe, *P. pungitius* reaches only as far south as southern France (the River Loire), but northwards it reaches the Arctic Ocean. The populations in the coastlands of the English Channel, North Sea, Baltic Sea, North Atlantic and Arctic Ocean consist of *P. pungitius pungitius*, but those of Ireland, northwest England and southern France consist of the unplated *P. pungitius laevis* (Fig. 59). In marked contrast to *G. aculeatus*, *P. pungitius* is found along the Arctic Ocean coastline of the U.S.S.R., so that the species has an almost continuous circumpolar distribution, for it is also found on the northern coast of North America (Münzing, 1969).

Three sub-species occur in the coastlands of the eastern Pacific (Fig. 60). *P. pungitius pungitius* reaches as far south as Korea and is

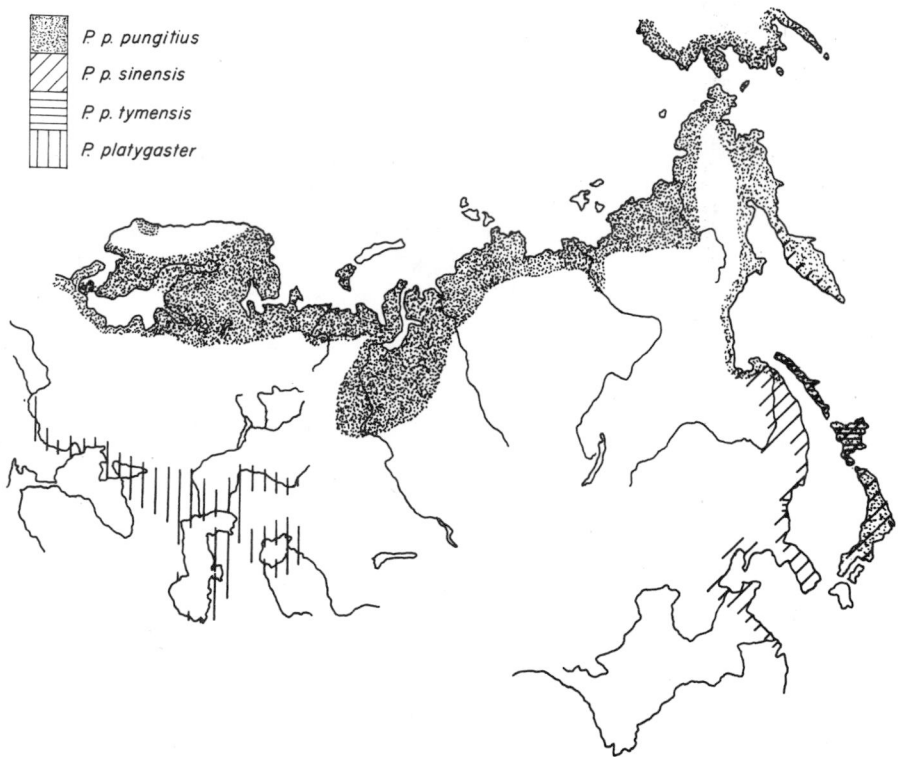

Fig. 60. East European and Asian distribution of *Pungitius*.

found on the islands of Hokkaido and Honshu in Japan. *P. pungitius sinensis* ranges from the southern coastline of Kamchatka to the Yangtse River and also Japan. *P. pungitius tymensis* has a much more resistricted distribution which includes the islands of Hokkaido (Japan) and Sakhalin (U.S.S.R.) and the western coastline of the Sea of Japan (Berg, 1949; Okada, 1959/60; Münzing, 1969)

The North American distribution of *P. pungitius* is significantly different from that of *G. aculeatus* for *Pungitius* is absent from most of the Pacific coastline (Fig. 61). In the north Pacific, it occurs on the Aleutian Islands and in Alaska as far south as Kodiak Island and

Cook Inlet. To the east of Alaska, it is found in the Mackenzie River system, Bear Lake and Great Slave Lake. Still further east, it is found around Hudson's Bay, on Baffin Island and along the Atlantic Coast of North America as far south as New Jersey. It is also found in the heart of the continent in the Great Lakes system (although it is

Fig. 61. North American distribution of *Pungitius pungitius* showing range of the Bering and Mississippian forms (after McPhail, 1963).

apparently absent from Lake Erie), and in Manitoba and Saskatchewan, two of the prairie provinces of Canada. *P. pungitius* has also been collected in the Mississippi drainage in Indiana. Thus its North American distribution is primarily east of the Rockies, and therefore more similar to the distribution of the brook stickleback (*Culaea inconstans*) than to *G. aculeatus* (McPhail, 1963; Nelson, 1968b; McPhail and Lindsey, 1970; Scott and Crossman, 1973).

McPhail and Lindsey (1970) also recorded *P. pungitius* as present on Greenland, though it is apparently absent from Iceland.

The second species of *Pungitius, P. platygaster* lives in the river systems of the Black Sea, the Caspian Sea and the Aral Sea, and so is geographically isolated from *P. pungitius*. This geographical isolation and some morphological differences are the reasons why *P. platygaster* is recognised as a distinct species. Whether the two species will hybridise when allowed to come into contact must be determined by breeding experiments (Münzing, 1969). Little is known about the biology of *P. platygaster* and so for the rest of the chapter *Pungitius* will refer to *P. pungitius* unless otherwise stated.

As with *G. aculeatus*, the glaciations of the Pleistocene seem to have been the primary factor which has led to the contemporary distribution of *Pungitius*. Fossils of the genus *Pungitius* are known from pre-Pleistocene deposits, for example in upper tertiary (Pliocene) deposits in Russia and China (Berg, 1940; Liu Hsien-T'Ing and Wang Nien-Chung, 1974), although a fossil in middle Pliocene deposits of California and originally described as *P. haynesi* (David, 1945) has since been shown to be a *Gasterosteus* with the characteristic split hypural plate of that genus (Bell, 1973b). During the ice-ages of the Pleistocene, various populations of *Pungitius* retreated to ice-free refugia and the results of such movements and the subsequent reinvasions of areas left free of ice as the glaciers retreated is shown by the North American populations of *Pungitius* (McPhail, 1963). On the basis of counts of dorsal spines and gill rakers, two forms of *Pungitius* were distinguished. One form, characterised by a relatively high number of dorsal spines and a relatively low number of gill rakers had basically a coastal distribution stretching from Alaska to the Atlantic coast. The second form had a more inland distribution including the Great Lakes, Lake Winnipeg and the Mackenzie Basin. The coastal form seems to have spread eastwards from an ice-free refugium in the area of the Bering Straits, whilst the inland form spread north-west and north-east from a fresh water refugium in the head waters of the Mississippi as the last ice sheet (the Wisconsin glaciation) retreated (Fig. 61). A population found in Crooked Lake, Indiana, which is in the Mississippi drainage basin, may represent a relict of this refugial population (Nelson, 1968b). Although the period of isolation of the Bering Straits and Mississipian forms was not sufficient for separate species to evolve and now the two forms readily hybridise, the morphological differences do seem to have a genetic basis (McPhail, 1963).

P. platygaster probably evolved from a fully plated form of *P. pungitius* which became isolated in the Caspian Sea area at least as long ago as the last but one ice age, the Riss glaciation (Münzing, 1969).

TABLE XII

Parasites recorded from *Pungitius pungitius*.

Protozoa

1. FLAGELLATA
Cryptobia branchialis (Chen, 1956). U.S.S.R. (a).

2. SPOROZOA
Sphaerospora elegans Thelohan, 1892. U.S.S.R. (a).
Myxobilatus gasterostei (Parisi, 1912). U.S.S.R. (a).
M. medius (Thelohan, 1892). U.S.S.R. (a).
Henneguya pungitii Akhmerov, 1953. U.S.S.R. (a).
Glugea anomala (Moniez, 1887). U.S.S.R. (a).
Plisthophora typicalis (Gurley, 1893). U.S.S.R. (a).

3. CILIATA
Hemiophrys branchiarum (Weinrich, 1925). U.S.S.R. (a).
Tripartiella pungitii Bogdanova and Shtein. U.S.S.R. (a).
Trichodina domerguei (Wallengren). U.S.S.R. (a), U.K. (c).
T. domerguei f. latispina Dogel', 1940. (a).
T. gracilis Polyanskii, 1955. U.S.S.R. (a).
T. tenuidens Faure-Fremiet, 1943. U.K. (c).
Glossatella conica Timofeev, 1962. U.S.S.R. (a).
G. amoebae (Grenfell, 1887). U.S.S.R. (a).

Platyhelminthes

1. MONOGENEA
Gyrodactylus bychowskyi Sproston, 1946. U.S.S.R. (a).
G. rarus Wegener, 1909. U.S.S.R. (a).
G. elegans Nordmann, 1832. U.K. (c).
G. avalonia Hanek and Threlfall, 1969. North America (b).
G. canadensis Hanek and Threlfall, 1969. North America (b).

2. DIGENEA
Azygia lucii (Müller, 1776). U.S.S.R. (a).
Sphaerostoma bramae (Müller, 1776). U.S.S.R. (a).
Bunodera luciopercae (Müller, 1776). U.S.S.R. (a), North America (b).
Bucephalus polymorphus Baer, 1827. U.S.S.R. (a).
Cotylurus pileatus (Rudolphi, 1802). U.S.S.R. (a).
Diplostomum spathaceum (Rudolphi, 1819). U.S.S.R. (a), North America (b), U.K. (c).
Posthodiplostomum cuticola (Nordmann, 1832). U.S.S.R. (a).
Hemiurus appendiculatus (Rudolphi, 1802). North America (b).
Derogenes varicus Müller, 1784. North America (b).
Brachyphallus crenatus (Rudolphi, 1802). North America (b).

3. CESTODA
Triaenophorus nodulus (Pallas, 1781). U.S.S.R. (a).
Bothriocephalus scorpii (Müller, 1776). U.S.S.R. (a).
Diphyllobothrium dendriticum (Nitzsch, 1824). U.S.S.R. (a).
D. norvegicum Vik, 1957. U.S.S.R. (a).
Schistocephalus pungitii Dubinia, 1959. U.S.S.R. (a).

TABLE XII—*continued*

S. solidus (Müller, 1776). North America (d), U.K. (c).
Proteocephalus filicollis (Rudolphi, 1802). U.S.S.R. (a), U.K. (c).

Aschelminthes

1. NEMATODA
Raphidascaris acus (Bloch, 1779). U.S.S.R. (a).
Camallanus lacustris (Zoega, 1776). U.S.S.R. (a).

2. ACANTHOCEPHALA
Neoechinorhynchus cristatus Lynch, 1936. U.S.S.R. (a), North America (b).
N. rutili (Müller, 1780). U.S.S.R. (a), North America (d).
Paracanthocephalus curtus Akhmerov and Domrovskaya-Akhmerov, 1941.
    U.S.S.R. (a).
Echinorhynchus clavula (Dujardin, 1845). U.S.S.R. (a).
Acanthocephalus lucii (Müller, 1776). U.S.S.R. (a).
A. lateralis (Leidy, 1851). North America (b).
Corynosoma semerme (Forssell, 1904). U.S.S.R. (a).
C. strumosum (1802). U.S.S.R. (a).

Annelida

1. HIRUDINEA (Leeches)
Piscicola geometra (L. 1761). U.S.S.R. (a).

Arthropoda

1. CRUSTACEA
(i) COPEPODA
Thersitina gasterostei (Pagenstechner, 1861). U.S.S.R. (a), North America (b),
    U.K. (c).
(ii) BRANCHIURA
Argulus foliaceus (L. 1758). U.S.S.R. (a).

Sources. (a) Bykhovskaya-Pavlovskaya *et al.*, 1964. (b) Hanek and Threlfall, 1970c.
(c) Kennedy, 1974. (d) Scott and Crossman, 1973.

Although the classification of *Pungitius* depends primarily on morphological evidence, environmental factors such as temperature and salinity can influence the morphological characters, though the effect is relatively slight compared with the differences between the various species and sub-species of *Pungitius* (Lindsey, 1962b). One morphological peculiarity is that some populations of *P. pungitius* contain a high proportion of individuals that lack the pelvic fin and associated skeletal elements. So far, such populations have been reported only from Ireland and northern Canada (Nelson, 1971b; Coad, 1973), although the pelvic skeleton of the Asian form *P. pungitius tymensis* is relatively weakly developed. Populations of *G. aculeatus* and *C. inconstans* in which all or a high proportion of the individuals lack pelvic spines are also known (Bell, 1974; Nelson,

1969a). The adaptive significance of this loss is not known, most commonly it is suggested that it only occurs in isolated lakes and rivers in which predators are scarce or absent, but a population of *Pungitius* in which twenty per cent of the individuals lacked pelvic spines was found co-existing with a population of pike (*Esox lucius*).

There is experimental evidence that the spines of *Pungitius* are less effective in deterring piscine predators than the more robust spines of *G. aculeatus* (Hoogland *et al.*, 1957), (see Chapter 5), but this does not necessarily mean that *Pungitius* is more likely to be taken by a predator than *G. aculeatus*. The behaviour of *Pungitius* when confronted with a predator or a potentially frightening situation is significantly different from that of *G. aculeatus* (Benzie, 1965). *Pungitius* is less likely to approach a predator and more likely to retreat or stay in the weed. Even with no previous experience of predatory fish, *Pungitius* reacts to a predator at a greater distance than similarly inexperienced three-spined sticklebacks. So while *Gasterosteus* seems to rely relatively more on its morphology to protect it from predation, *Pungitius* relies more on its behavioural adaptations. This difference between the two species in their adaptations to predation is thought to have had consequences for their reproductive behaviour, a point that will be taken up later on. As yet, there are no data from field studies to indicate the rates of predation on *Gasterosteus* and *Pungitius* when they are living in the same area. The relevant data would have to include both the intensity of predation on the two species and their population densities. Among predatory fish known to feed on *Pungitius* are pike, lake trout, char, grayling, pike perch and walleyes (McPhail and Lindsey, 1970; Scott and Crossman, 1973).

Pungitius is host to a similar collection of parasites as *Gasterosteus* (Table XII), but the records of *Schistocephalus solidus* are suspect for *P. pungitius* was shown to reject *S. solidus* infestations (Orr *et al.*, 1969).

A study of the feeding habits of *Pungitius* in the River Birket in north-west England where it co-exists with *G. aculeatus* showed that the diets of the two species were very similar except that *Pungitius* was less likely to eat algae (Hynes, 1950). *Pungitius* had a higher proportion of individuals with empty stomachs which suggests that it feeds more sporadically than *G. aculeatus*. Feeding was also more disrupted by the onset of the breeding season. Nevertheless, the overall impression is that of two species occupying very similar feeding niches.

Matamek Lake, in Quebec, also contains both *G. aculeatus* and *P. pungitius*, but their feeding habits in this situation were different, for *Pungitius* took cladocerans and chironomid from the littoral zones while *G. aculeatus* took pelagic zooplankton (Coad and Power, 1973d). Chironomid larvae, cladocerans and other zooplankters such as cyclopoid copepods also formed the summer diet of *Pungitius* living in Ikroavik Lake in northern Alaska (Cameron *et al.*, 1973). In contrast, *Pungitius* living in Lake Superior, one of the Great Lakes, fed principally on the amphipod *Pontoporeia affinis* and the mysid

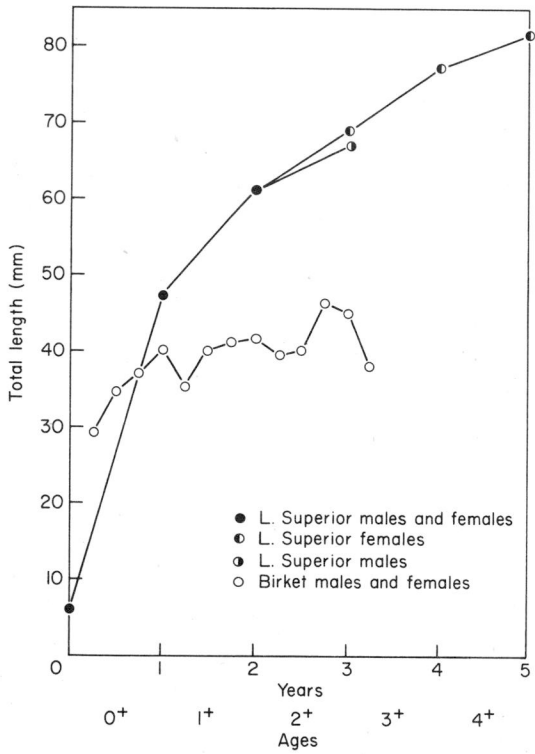

Fig. 62. Growth in length of *Pungitius pungitius* from Lake Superior (Griswold and Smith, 1973), and the Birket (Jones and Hynes, 1950). Values for L. Superior population are mean values for a six year period; values for Birket population based on samples taken over one year.

Mysis relicta, with cladocerans and chironomid larvae forming an insignificant portion of the diet (Griswold and Smith, 1973).

An examination of their otoliths indicated that the *Pungitius* living in the River Birket had a maximum life span of three and a half years. Their initial growth rate was greater than that of the three-spined sticklebacks living in the same river, but after the first year growth almost ceased so that mature *Pungitius* tended to be smaller than mature *G. aculeatus* (Fig. 62) (Jones and Hynes, 1950). In the

Pungitius populations of Ikroavik Lake, three age-classes were detected: young-of-the-year (0^+), fish born the previous year (1^+), and
fish born two years previously (2^+) (Cameron *et al.*, 1973). A similar
age structure was present in the population of *Pungitius* in Matamek
Lake, but the *Pungitius* from the Matamek River system rarely
reached two years old (Coad and Power, 1973d). In Lake Superior,
females as old as five years were found, but the males had maximum
life span of three years (Griswold and Smith, 1973). In comparison
with the Birket population, all the North American populations
showed a more rapid growth rate with the fish reaching a larger size,
but the Lake Superior fish had by far the fastest growth rate reaching
a total length in excess of 45 mm in the first year (Fig. 62). Other
unusual characteristics of the Great Lake nine-spined sticklebacks
will be noted later on.

The relationship between the length (L) and weight (W) of
Pungitius can be described by the equation:

$$W = aL^b$$

where a and b are constants. For the Lake Superior fish, the value of
the exponent b was 3.219, whereas for the Lake Ikroavik fish the
exponent was only 2.745.

In comparison with *Gasterosteus*, *Pungitius* tends to prefer habitats that have relatively thick vegetation, but it is by no means
confined to such areas. Some evidence suggests that *Pungitius*
tolerates partially de-oxygenated water, such as might develop when
vegetation decayed, better than *G. aculeatus*. When fish of similar
weight were compared *Pungitius* had a slower rate of oxygen
consumption than *G. aculeatus* and survived longer in a closed
container (Lewis *et al.*, 1972). The composition of the blood of
Pungitius under conditions of low oxygen tensions has been analysed
by Zhiteneva (1971). Although the salinity tolerance of *Pungitius* is
less than that of *Gasterosteus*, it is still considerable (Heuts, 1943;
Nelson, 1968a). As with *G. aculeatus*, the tolerance of saline water is
lowest during the breeding season, but outside the breeding season
some populations over-winter in the sea. McPhail's (1963) analysis of
some North American populations showed that in tidal areas the fish
had well-developed lateral plates. The modal number of anterior
lateral plates for these tidal populations ranged from three to five but
was commonly four. In some populations from the Atlantic coast of
North America, the fish have a complete row of lateral plates
(McPhail and Lindsey, 1970). In contrast, McPhail found that populations from inland fresh water systems consisted of fish with either a
few weakly developed plates or none. So, as with *G. aculeatus*,

there tends to be a positive correlation between the number of lateral plates and salinity tolerance. During the breeding season *Pungitius* is found only in fresh or slightly brackish water.

The reproductive biology of *Pungitius* is similar in broad outline to that of *Gasterosteus*, but the differences between the two illustrate the niceties of the adaptations to what may seem minor differences in the biology of these closely related genera. This point is brought out even more clearly by the discovery that the reproductive behaviour of *Pungitius* shows a wider range of variation between populations than has been found in *Gasterosteus* and that these differences can be related to the environments of the populations.

Pungitius probably breeds for the first time in the summer following the year of birth, and certainly nearly all fish of both sexes are mature by the age of two. In the River Birket, the breeding season was from April to June, whereas in Ikroavik Lake, which has an ice-free period of only about two months, breeding occurred in June and July. This is when the lake margin is flooded by water released as the ice melts and it was in this flooded marginal area that *Pungitius* was found in the summer months. June and July were also months of spawning in the Matamek system and Lake Superior (Coad and Power, 1973d; Griswold and Smith, 1973).

As with the other sticklebacks, the female *Pungitius* plays no role other than the production of the eggs and spawning these eggs in the appropriate place, the nest of a male. It is the male who is responsible for building the nest, guarding a territory around the nest and for tending the eggs in the nest. *Pungitius* females tend to lose their normal cryptic olive or brown colour and develop black dorsal surfaces and silver ventral surfaces as they become mature. As they become gravid the belly becomes visibly distended with eggs (Morris, 1958). Females from a population in Lake Huron, another of the Great Lakes, did not develop the dark dorsal surface but had brown backs with darker brown blotches (McKenzie and Keenlyside, 1970). The females may become relatively aggressive during the reproductive season, and when held in an aquarium will hold territories adjacent to territories held by males. When ready to spawn a female will leave her territory but take it up again after spawning (Morris, 1958). Whether females hold territories in natural situations is not known, because *Pungitius* normaliy breeds in vegetated areas so that it is difficult to make observations on their reproductive behaviour in the wild. The Lake Huron females were not observed defending territories either in aquaria or in their natural environment.

The ovaries of the female are similar to those of *Gasterosteus* and the development of the oocytes follows the same pattern (see

Chapter 9). When spawned, the eggs of *Pungitius* are surrounded by a jelly-like mucus, as indeed are the eggs of *Gasterosteus*. Yamamoto (1963) showed, in a study of the ovary of *P. pungitius tymensis*, that when the eggs have ovulated into the lumen of the ovary they are surrounded by this mucus which is probably secreted by the cubical, epithelial cells that line the ovarian lumen. This substance coagulates in water and may help to attach the eggs to the nest. Females spawn more than once in a breeding season and the interval between successive spawnings has been reported as being as low as six hours and up to forty-eight hours (Griswold and Smith, 1972). This represents a much shorter interval than has been found for *Gasterosteus*, but the egg production per spawning seems to be smaller than is found in *Gasterosteus*. *Pungitius* females from a population in Lake Superior and ranging in length from 58 to 81 mm produced between 61 and 112 eggs per spawning (Griswold and Smith, 1973).

The reproductive period of the male can be divided into the same phases as that of *G. aculeatus* (Chapter 11). In the initial phase the male takes up a territory within which he builds a nest. Upon completion of the nest-building phase, he enters the sexual phase during which he courts gravid females. Once he has accumulated eggs in his nest he enters the parental phase in which the bulk of his activities are directed towards the care of the eggs.

Reproductively mature males usually become black all over, with very prominent white pelvic spines which stand out clearly against the dark ventral surface of the fish (Morris, 1958). But the males from the populations in Lake Huron and Lake Superior do not become dark all over; instead they develop a grey patch mid-ventrally, against which the bluish white spines are conspicuous. This patch becomes jet black when a male courts a female or is guarding eggs. These Great Lake populations belong to the Mississippian form of *P. pungitius* in North America; the coastal Bering form has populations in which the males do become black during the breeding season (McKenzie and Keenlyside, 1970). The breeding coloration and other secondary sexual characteristics of the male such as the modification of the kidney tubules to produce the glue used to stick the nest together fail to develop if the male is castrated (van Oordt, 1923, 1924). That the testes must be present for the secondary sexual characteristics of the stickleback to appear was thus first demonstrated on the nine-spined stickleback, although, subsequently, studies on the hormonal control of these characteristics used the three-spined stickleback as the experimental animal (see Chapter 10).

The male *Pungitius* defend territories, and in most respects the behaviour shown during this defence is similar to that shown by *G. aculeatus*. Much of the fighting takes the form of direct chases and attempts to bite the opponent. The main threat posture is a head-down threat, with the male turning his body broadside to his opponent with his pelvic spines erect. While in this position, the male tends to alternate between positions that are oblique to the direct line of attack, first turning slightly towards and then slightly away from his opponent. When two males are simultaneously showing this head-down posture to each other, they may beat their tails, moving steadily down through the water. If a fish is badly beaten and cannot escape, it assumes a tail-down posture and loses its dark coloration. In *Pungitius*, the erection of the pelvic spines is correlated with a tendency to attack (Barraud, 1955; Hall, 1956; Morris, 1958).

Within the defended area the male builds a nest. Three distinctly different types of nest have been observed, but the type most commonly associated with *Pungitius* consists of a bundle of fine pieces of vegetation forming a mass about 4 cm in diameter and positioned among the branches and leaves of aquatic vegetation. The nest is usually between 2 and 20 cm off the substrate, with between 10 and 15 cm the preferred height. A tunnel is pushed through the bundle of material and this tunnel is inclined so that the entrance is lower than the exit. Some authors have distinguished tube nests from ball nests on the basis of their shape, but these shapes merely represent the ends of a continuum of nest shapes so perhaps little significance should be assigned to this variation. Since the male builds this nest off the substrate, his repertoire of nest-building activities differs from that of the ground-nesting *Gasterosteus*. The male *Pungitius* selects a suitable site, pushing through the branches and leaves of a plant. He then brings material to the site, the favoured material being threads of *Spirogyra* or *Fontinalis* (willowmoss). Material is sometimes stolen from the nests of neighbouring males, a thievery also observed in *Gasterosteus*. Once the male reaches the nest site, he bores in amongst the vegetation, pushing forwards and obliquely upwards. He drops the material then backs out. Any long strands are looped up and pushed back into the nest. The male repeats this collecting and boring so that he accumulates a bundle of vegetation lodged amongst the leaves of a plant and with a distinct indentation where he pushes into the bundle. As this bundle increases in size, the male bores further and further into it until eventually only his tail may be visible before he backs out. Once he has collected a substantial amount of material he starts glueing it together. Two forms of glueing behaviour occur. In superficial glueing, the male swims over the surface of the nest with a slow jerky motion, secreting the glue produced in the kidneys. The underside of the body is held concave so that his body curls round the nest as he swims around. Each bout of superficial glueing lasts less than thirty seconds. Superficial glueing occurs only during the nest-building phase and not subsequently, which is in contrast to *Gasterosteus*, but it is superseded by insertion glueing which is not seen at all in *Gasterosteus*. Insertion glueing begins with the male circling and bending his head and tail towards each other. A drop of glue is extruded from the cloaca and forms a thread which the male catches in his mouth. He then swims to the nest with this thread. At the nest, the male bores in and deposits the glue in the interior of the nest, he then backs out giving a series of conspicuous gulps. Insertion glueing appears towards the end of the nest building phase and persists until a day or two after the fertilisation of eggs. Its function seems to be to cement and consolidate the inside of the nest, and perhaps to stick the eggs in place and so prevent the female dragging them out with her as she leaves the nest after spawning. About halfway through the nest-building phase, the male starts to perform a bout of fanning at the nest after he has bored into it. This fanning is like that seen in *Gasterosteus* except that the male *Pungitius* retains a horizontal position in the water.

As the nest reaches completion, the male creeps through it making a tunnel with a distinct entrance and exit. This creeping through is repeated at intervals throughout the sexual phase and, as with *Gasterosteus*, the appearance of creeping through can be regarded as a sign that the male has entered the sexual phase during which he will court gravid females.

Once completed, the nest is kept intact by the addition of more material and glue. The male will also push at the nest from the outside increasing its compactness. He clears an area in front of the nest, tearing off offending bits of weed and carrying them away from the nest before discarding them.

This description, based on the accounts of Leiner (1931b), Hall (1956) and Morris (1958), applies to what might be called the typical *Pungitius* nest. Occasionally a male will build a nest such that it lies amongst vegetation but rests on the bottom. When this happens the male may excavate a pit in front of the nest entrance by vigorous lateral beats of the tail which sweep away the sand. Digging comparable to that shown by *Gasterosteus* is used only when the male is removing sand that has lodged inside the tunnel of the nest (Morris, 1958).

Males of the *Pungitius* populations of Lake Huron build unusual nests. These fish were observed breeding in areas that lack rooted plants. Their nests were built under or between rocks in water ranging in depth from 25 cm to 2m. They were made from algal and detrital fragments glued together with insertion glueing; superficial glueing was not seen. Sand was removed from the nest by digging in a manner comparable to that of *Gasterosteus* and not swept away by tail-beating. Some of the nests lacked a complete tunnel so that when a female spawned in such a nest both she and the male entered and backed out of the nest by the same hole. When given a choice between nesting in rooted vegetation or rock crevices, the Lake Huron males chose the rock crevices. One male given only rooted vegetation did build a nest off the ground, but it was loosely constructed, not glued on the outside and soon disintegrated (McKenzie and Keenlyside, 1970).

In Lake Superior, sexually mature males and females were collected both in dense beds of *Nitella* sp. and over highly organic muds several metres down. In aquaria, the males built nests in the mud. The nest consisted of a burrow about a centimetre in diameter and 3 or 4 cm long, but lacked a complete tunnel so that the male and a spawning female entered and left the nest through the same hole (Griswold and Smith, 1972, 1973).

Clearly, the nest building behaviour of *Pungitius* is a relatively plastic characteristic, and the type of nest built depends very much on the environment in which a population evolves. No comparable range of nest types has been reported for the other species of sticklebacks.

Once he has completed the nest, and this is usually signalled by the formation of a complete tunnel, the male is ready to go through the full courtship sequence with a gravid female. In *Gasterosteus*, nest building inevitably precedes the sexual phase, but in *Pungitius* the two phases may occasionally get reversed, so that the male passes from the preliminary territorial phase into the sexual phase without building a nest. Such a male may persuade a very ripe female to lay her eggs in a clump of weeds and then the male builds a nest around the eggs (Morris, 1958). Normally, however, the male has a completed nest. When a gravid female enters a male's territory, he dances towards her. This dance is somewhat similar to the zig-zag dance of *G. aculeatus* but while the three-spined stickleback usually maintains an approximately horizontal orientation, the *Pungitius* male dances in a head-down position. *G. wheatlandi* adopts a partially head-down position while zig-zagging (Chapter 15). The dance of the *Pungitius* male consists of a series of jumps, each of which has a forward, and upwards and a sideways component. During the courtship the ventral surface of the male becomes or remains very dark; the prominent white pelvic spines are held erect but the dorsal surface of the male becomes lighter. When she sees the male, the gravid female assumes a head-up position, which makes her distended belly even more prominent, and moves towards the dancing male. When she reaches him, she places her snout close to the erected pelvic spines of the male who then dances towards the nest with the female following slightly below the male with her tail held down. The male does not always dance directly back to the nest, but may follow a circuitous route. In reaching the nest, the male assumes a head-down position with the tip of his snout placed just above the nest entrance, makes a few gulps and starts fanning. This fanning in a head-down position seems to be the equivalent of showing at the comparable stage in the courtship of *Gasterosteus*. The female noses into the nest, often making several attempts before entering the nest. She lies with her head protruding from the nest exit and her tail from the entrance. The male quivers on her flanks in a manner similar to that shown by a *Gasterosteus* male at the equivalent stage in the courtship. Once she has spawned, the female leaves the nest, then the male pushes straight through, fertilising the eggs. He then chases the female out of his territory (Fig. 63) (Morris, 1958).

The Lake Huron males showed an interesting variation on this courtship sequence. The male danced to the female but he did not dance back to the nest, instead he swam directly back to the nest, so that in this respect the behaviour of the Lake Huron males is similar to that of *G. aculeatus* males. The female followed the male back to the nest with her snout close to or touching the dark patch on the ventral surface of the male in a slightly head-up position. At the nest the male assumed the head-down position with his snout on the upper rim of the nest entrance but he did not fan. Other aspects of the courtship followed the conventional *Pungitius* pattern (McKenzie and Keenlyside, 1970).

Although the male will bite the female during the courtship sequence, especially after a bout of dancing to a female who responds by fleeing or remaining still, the *Pungitius* male is significantly less aggressive towards the female during courtship than is the *G. aculeatus* male. Perhaps correlated with this is the absence of an equivalent to the dorsal pricking and circling behaviour of the male *G. aculeatus* discussed in Chapter 12, and the absence or very low frequency of nest visits, fanning and glueing during courtship (Morris, 1958; Wilz, 1971).

Once the male has fertilised the eggs and chased the female from his territory, he returns to the nest and pushes the eggs deeper into the nest. He then shows a phase that lasts one or two hours in which boring and fanning increase to a peak of around thirty seconds of fanning per five minutes. After this peak is reached, fanning declines and there follows a phase of nest building which presumably prepares the nest to receive another clutch of eggs (Hall, 1956).

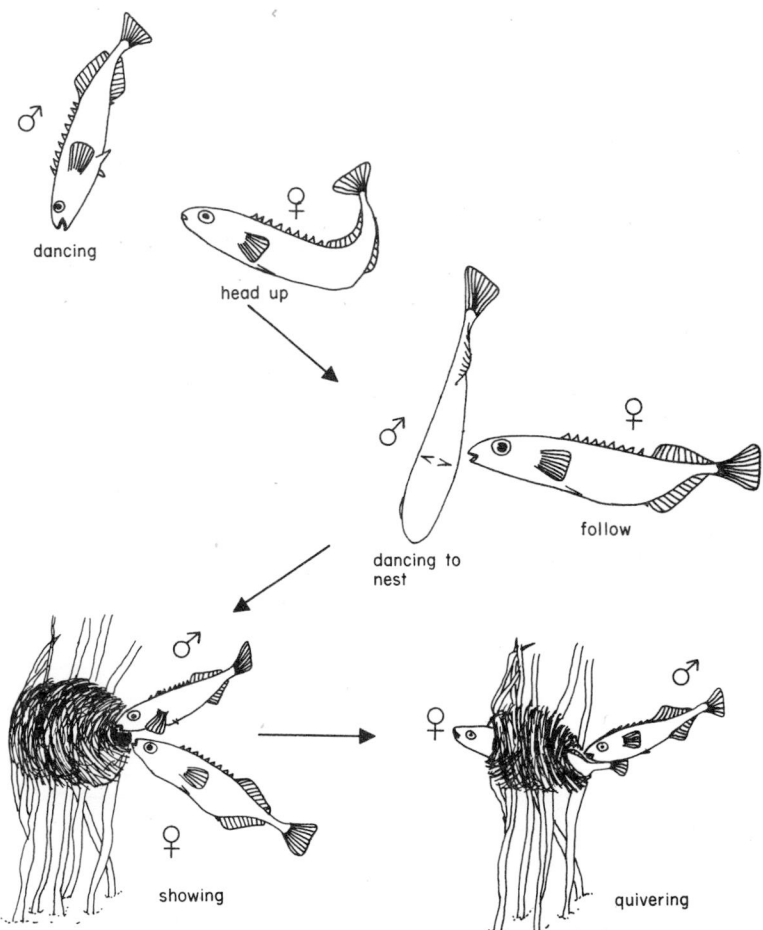

Fig. 63. Courtship of *Pungitius pungitius* (after Leiner, 1931b and Morris, 1958).

The ensuing parental cycle resembles that of *Gasterosteus* (Chapter 13). Fanning becomes the major parental activity, reaching a peak just before the eggs hatch and then showing a rapid decline (Fig. 64). *Pungitius* males spend less time fanning than *G. aculeatus* males and it has been suggested that a plausible explanation for this difference is that since the nest is off the substrate and is enmeshed in living, photosynthesising plant tissue, it is better ventilated and oxygenated than the ground nest of the three-spined stickleback. Two observations militate against this hypothesis. Although the fanning behaviour of the ground-nesting *Pungitius* of Lake Superior and Lake Huron has to be analysed in detail, some data suggest that the amount of time spent fanning is somewhat higher than that

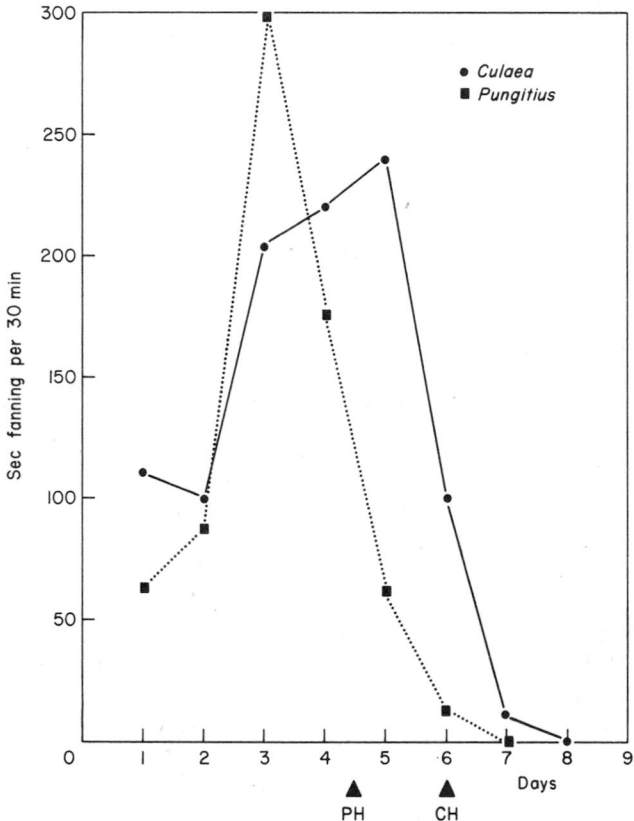

Fig. 64. Fanning cycles of male *Pungitius pungutius* and *Culaea inconstans* that have fertilised a single clutch (after Morris, 1958, and McKenzie, 1974). PH, *P. pungitius* hatching; CH, *C. inconstans* hatching.

shown by typical *Pungitius* males but is not as high as that of *G. aculeatus*. Secondly, the amounts of fanning shown by *G. wheatlandi*, which is a ground-nester, are comparable to the levels shown by *Pungitius*. Explanations for the differences between fanning levels may have to be sought in factors such as the metabolic rate of the eggs, the average clutch size, the average number of eggs that a male has in his nest and the efficiency with which the fanning ventilates the eggs.

The young hatch some six to seven days after fertilisation at 15-16°C, and after four or five days at 18-19°C. These times to hatching are somewhat shorter than for *Gasterosteus* at similar temperatures, so the lower level fanning does not result in longer parental cycles (Morris, 1958).

Other activities related to the care of the eggs also occur during the parental phase. The male will remove dead eggs, but will often retrieve groups of eggs that have become dislodged from the nest. With the nest situated off the substrate there is a real danger of the eggs dropping out of the nest so the male will attempt to secure any eggs that become dislodged. Perhaps it is because of the danger that the eggs will be dragged out of the nest that the male stops creeping through once the nest contains eggs (Morris, 1958).

Occasionally a male removes the eggs from the nest and transfers them to another site either having previously built a new nest at this site or building a new nest around the eggs. This egg removal and rehousing seems to occur when the original nest has deteriorated badly, but such a transfer may be unsuccessful and the eggs are then eaten by the male or by other fish (Morris, 1958).

After hatching, the young tend to remain motionless, hanging with the tail vertically down and resting against a strand of alga. Any young that jump out of the nest are retrieved by the male. At this time, the male frequently collects together a loose network of strands of vegetation just above the nest. This shapeless mass of material forms a nursery. As the nest disintegrates, the male transfers his young to the nursery, although while the nest is still in relatively good condition the young may be returned either to the nest or to the nursery (Morris, 1958). The ground-nesting males of Lake Huron do not build a nursery, straying young are returned to the nest (McKenzie and Keenlyside, 1970). Three or four days after hatching, the young start to visit the surface to fill their swim bladders with air. They then hide in the vegetation near the surface so that the male cannot easily retrieve them, and so, shortly, the male ceases to show any parental behaviour (Benzie, 1965).

During the parental phase, the male *Pungitius* shows changes in sexual and aggressive behaviour comparable to those that occur in *Gasterosteus* (see Chapter 13). Sexual behaviour declines as the fanning cycle proceeds so that by the time the young hatch the male has stopped showing sexual behaviour altogether. Aggressive behaviour also declines over the first part of the parental cycle so that the male defends a smaller area around the nest. But after the young hatch, there is a marked increase in the aggressiveness of the male. After the young disperse, the aggression of the male declines. The parental male retains an overall dark coloration, and experiments with model fish suggest that males which are very aggressive will attack a black model more frequently than models of other colours. The black of the male *Pungitius* seems to function as a releaser for aggressive behaviour in a way that is comparable to the red colour of *G. aculeatus* (Sevenster, 1949; Morris, 1958).

Although in many ways *Pungitius* and *G. aculeatus* are similar, the differences between them pose questions about the adaptive significance of these differences. Ecologically, the two differ in that *G. aculeatus* tends to nest in the open, whereas *Pungitius* nests amongst vegetation, though in the Great Lakes, where *Gasterosteus* is absent, ground-nesting *Pungitius* are found. If this exceptional situation is ignored for the present, then it can be argued that the difference between nesting in the open and amongst vegetation can be correlated with a difference in the anti-predator adaptations of the two genera. *Gasterosteus* usually has long, stout spines which make it difficult for a predator to swallow, whilst the spines of *Pungitius* are shorter and less robust, and are less effective in deterring a predator (see also Chapter 5). In a frightening situation such as the presence of a predator, *G. aculeatus* is bolder than *Pungitius* and less likely to remain hidden in vegetation (Benzie, 1965). These differences suggest that when *G. aculeatus* and *Pungitius* are sympatric, *G. aculeatus* is able to exploit open areas successfully, relying for protection on its morphological adaptations, whereas *Pungitius* is relatively restricted to areas of vegetation, where its main protection is its behaviour. The situation in the Great Lakes suggests that at least in some areas where *Pungitius* is present but *Gasterosteus* is absent, then *Pungitius* can exploit open areas for breeding.

Living out in the open, in full view not only of predators but also of rival males, a male *G. aculeatus* must be aggressive to be successful. As described in Chapter 12, male *G. aculeatus* with large territories are more successful in inducing females to lay eggs in their nest and subsequently are more successful at guarding those eggs from nest raiders. But this high level of aggression tends to interfere with the courtship and so the courtship of the male *G. aculeatus* has evolved to include sequences which serve to change the male's motivation from the predominantly aggressive mode to a predominantly sexual mode. The courtship sequence includes the dorsal pricking and circling component followed by the male returning to his nest unaccompanied by the female. A period of courtship by the male *G. aculeatus* is also marked by an increase in the frequency with which he performs nest-directed activities such as fanning and glueing (see Chapter 12). In the less open habitat favoured by *Pungitius*, the male is less likely to be in full view of rival males and so probably needs to be less aggressive with the result that aggression does not seriously interfere with courtship. Wilz (1971) showed that at various stages in the courtship sequence, the probability that the male *Pungitius* will bite the female is lower than for the *G. aculeatus* male at comparable stages in the sequence. Nor did an increase in the frequency of biting by male *Pungitius* lead to a marked decline in the frequency of zig-zagging, although in *G. aculeatus* there is a marked inhibitory relationship between biting and zig-zagging (Chapter 12). But in a heavily vegetated area, the courtship must be performed without the male and female losing contact with each other, so that whereas in the courtship of *G. aculeatus* the male frequently leaves the female, in the courtship of *Pungitius* the male and female stay close together. A male *G. aculeatus* leads a female back to the nest by swimming there rapidly and directly, with the female following some distance behind. In contrast, a male *Pungitius* leads slowly back to the nest with the female staying close to him. An exception to this is the Lake Huron *Pungitius*, for in this population of ground-nesting nine-spined sticklebacks, the male leads the female directly back to the nest. There are also some intriguing parallels between the "typical" *Pungitius* courtship and that of *G. wheatlandi*. Although *G. wheatlandi* is a ground-nester the male leads back to the nest slowly with the female following below the male visually fixing the male's pelvic spines. Another similarity is that *G. wheatlandi* performs the zig-zag dance in the head-down position and shows relatively few nest-directed activities during the courtship. The functional significance of these similarities has still to be analysed.

Also correlated with the differences between *G. aculeatus* and *Pungitius* in their habitats is their breeding coloration. *G. aculeatus* living in the open, adopts a bright red and blue nuptial dress, while *Pungitius*, living amongst vegetation, adopts a dark dress. The brook stickleback *Culaea inconstans*, which also nests in dense vegetation, also adopts a dark nuptial coloration.

Thus many of the differences between *G. aculeatus* and *Pungitius* can be interpreted as a consequence of the emancipation of *G. aculeatus* from areas of vegetation by virtue of its morphological adaptations against predation (Morris, 1958; Benzie, 1965; Wilz, 1971), while some of the similarities between *Pungitius* and *Culaea*, which will be described in Chapter 17, may be a result of the preference of both species for weedy habitats. It would be of interest to know whether the similarities between *Pungitius* and *G. wheatlandi* are fortuitous or indicate that in some aspects of its biology *G. wheatlandi* resembles *Pungitius* more than *G. aculeatus*.

Although the evidence suggests that *Pungitius* is less aggressive than *G. aculeatus*, male *Pungitius* do engage in raiding the nests of other males, indeed this phenomenon was first described in detail for *Pungitius* rather than for *G. aculeatus* (Morris, 1952). Morris interpreted nest raiding as an expression of sexual frustration or thwarting on the part of the raider, and presented some evidence that in certain situations the raider behaved like a gravid female. A raiding male would follow a model of a mature male when the latter was made to zig-zag in the same way as a gravid female would follow a dancing male. However, the analysis of nest raiding in *G. aculeatus* has cast considerable doubt on Morris' interpretation, though it has to be admitted that no satisfactory explanation of the causation or significance of nest raiding has emerged (van den Assem, 1967; Wootton, 1971b). This phenomenon is discussed in more detail in Chapter 13.

In spite of their preferences for slightly different habitats, *G. aculeatus* and *Pungitius* frequently occur living side by side in the same stream or pond. In the laboratory, hybrids between the two species have been obtained (Leiner, 1934, 1940, 1957), but they have not been recorded from natural waters. Wilz (1970d) analysed the importance of the differences in the courtship behaviour in keeping the two species reproductively isolated. *Pungitius* and *G. aculeatus* males were relatively undiscriminating, courting gravid females of either species with equal vigour, but the response of the females was far more discriminating. A majority of the females of both species failed to respond to the attentions of the heterospecific males. Even when a female did show a response, and this occurred more frequently for *Pungitius* females than for *G. aculeatus* females, the courtship usually failed because the female responded less and less during the course of the courtship. A final behavioural barrier to inter-specific mating was that *Pungitius* females followed the male from underneath, a positioning that was inappropriate when it was a *G. aculeatus* male attempting to lead the female down to his nest. *G. aculeatus* females followed the male from above. So, in addition to the differences in the sites chosen for breeding, there are behavioural differences during courtship which will prevent inter-specific crosses. Even if such crosses do occur occasionally, Leiner (1940) found that hybrids between *Pungitius* and *G. aculeatus* were sterile. Usually the gonads of the hybrids failed to develop, but a few males did show signs of becoming sexually mature with their undersides becoming dark and a few red spots developing. These males never built nests.

G. aculeatus and *Pungitius* are, in terms of their geographical distribution, the most successful of the sticklebacks and they are also the most thoroughly studied. The three other genera have received comparatively little attention, but they show interesting differences from *Pungitius* and *Gasterosteus*.

17. *Culaea inconstans:*
The Brook Stickleback
(Synonym: *Eucalia inconstans* (Kirtland))*

Culaea inconstans, the brook stickleback, is restricted to inland waters of North America. Only in Hudson's Bay and south-eastern New Brunswick is it found in coastal areas. Although it has a lower salinity tolerance than the other sticklebacks, its tolerance is still higher than many other freshwater fishes of North America and it is found in saline lakes and brackish water (Winn, 1960; Nelson, 1968a).

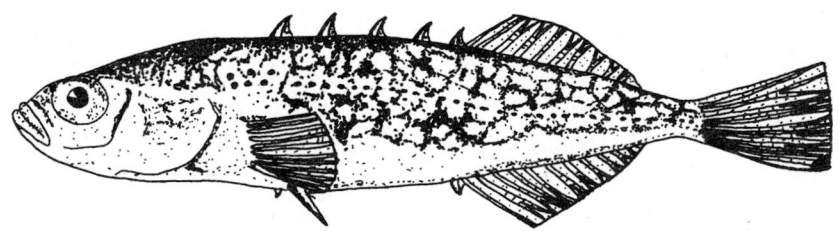

Fig. 65. *Culaea inconstans* (Kirtland).

Morphologically, *Culaea* is similar to *Gasterosteus* and *Pungitius*, for it is a small fish rarely exceeding 65 mm in length and has a body outline typical of the short-snouted sticklebacks (Fig. 65). For most populations of *Culaea*, the modal number of dorsal spines is five, with the vast majority of fish having four, five or six spines, although a few individuals with as few as two or as many as seven have been found (Lawler, 1958; Nelson, 1969a). In this character, *Culaea* is intermediate between *Pungitius* and *Gasterosteus*. Like *Gasterosteus*,

* Whitley (1950) indicated that the generic name *Eucalia* was preoccupied by a butterfly and proposed the name *Culaea* which has since been accepted.

the dorsal spines lie directly in line one behind the other and not inclined to one side or the other as they are in *Pungitius*. Unlike the other two genera, the membranes of the dorsal spines of *Culaea* are pigmented with melanophores which makes the spines conspicuous. The pelvic fins consist of one spine and one soft ray. The dorsal fin usually has ten soft rays, but the normal range is from eight to thirteen, and the anal fin, which is inserted slightly anterior to the dorsal fin, contains a small anterior spine and 10 soft rays (with a range of seven to twelve). The truncate caudal fin has eleven or twelve rays. On superficial examination, *Culaea* appears to be naked, lacking both scales and bony plates, but careful study has shown that there is a row of thirty to thirty-six small, non-overlapping lateral plates. The first few anterior plates are paired with up to five additional plates which are out of line with the main row. These lateral plates are too small to offer any significant protection to the flanks of the body (Nelson, 1969a, 1971a).

In North America, the distribution of *Culaea* is predominantly within the heartland of the continent, which is in marked contrast to the distribution of *Gasterosteus* (Fig. 66). There is no stickleback in Eurasia with a distribution that is so continental. The northern limit of *Culaea* occurs in Canada, on the border between Alberta and the North-West Territories (60° N), in the Hay River region of the Great Slave Lake. The southern limit is approximately 40° S except for a population that is found in north-west New Mexico. To the west, the limit is set by the Rocky Mountains; *Culaea* is not found to the west of this range (Nelson, 1969a; Scott and Crossman, 1973). The present distribution of *Culaea* indicates that it spent the last glaciation of the Pleistocene (the Wisconsin) in the ice-free area of the upper Mississippi Valley (McPhail and Lindsey, 1970).

Within this geographical distribution there is significant variation in spine length for both the dorsal and pelvic spines. The longest spines occur in populations from Wisconsin to Ohio, the mid-western region of U.S.A., while the shortest spines are found in populations from the north-western part of the range in eastern British Columbia and Alberta. The cause or causes of this clinal variation in spine length are not known, but it is possible that there is a relationship between spine length and the density of predators. There is also some geographical variation in the shape of the body. In the south-western part of its range, *Culaea* is relatively deep-bodied, so that sympatric populations of *Culaea* and *Pungitius* in Indiana differ significantly in the relative depth of the body. But in the north-western part of its range, *Culaea* resembles *Pungitius* in being relatively slender. The size of the pelvic skeleton is another character that shows geographical

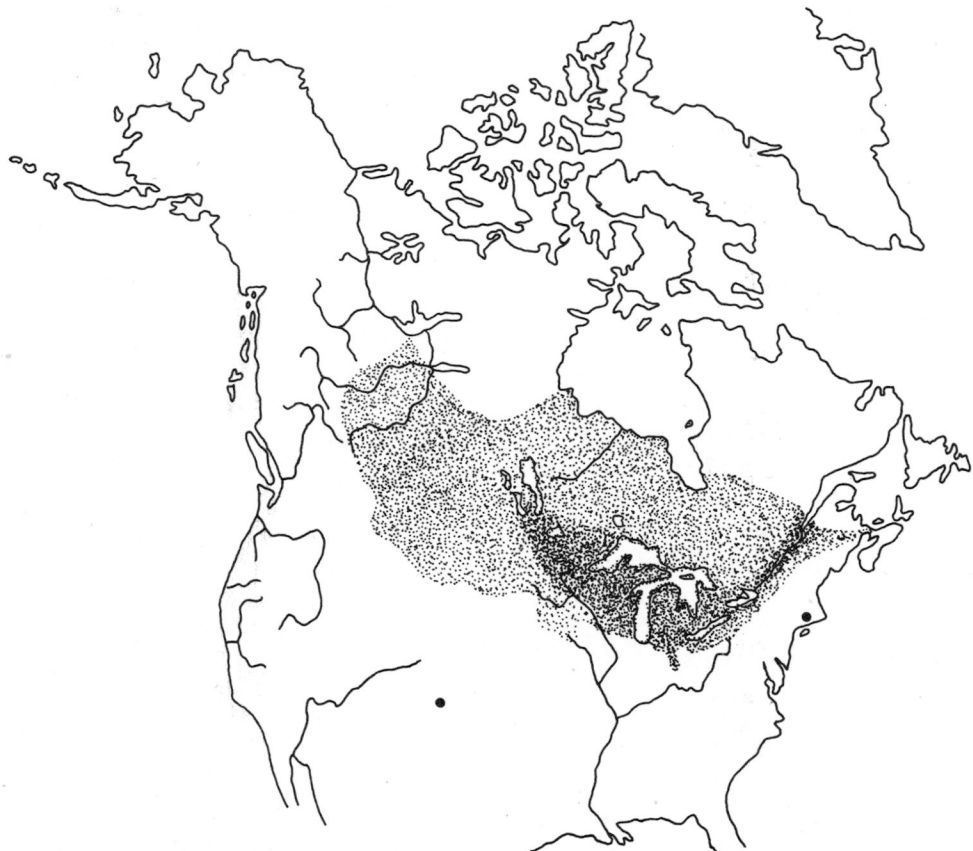

Fig. 66. Distribution of *Culaea inconstans*.

variation. In relation to body size, the pelvic skeleton is largest in populations in the Great Lakes area of U.S.A. from Wisconsin to New York State, and smallest in the north-western part of *Culaea*'s range. So the picture emerges of north-western populations in which the fish are more slender, have lighter skeletons and shorter spines than *Culaea* populations from the Great Lakes area (Nelson, 1969a).

Some of the populations of Alberta and Saskatchewan contain a high proportion of individuals which entirely lack or have only a partially developed pelvic skeleton and so lack pelvic spines. These populations are interspersed with populations in which the pelvic skeleton is small but normally developed. Among the locations in which individuals lacking the pelvic skeleton occur is Pine Lake in northern Alberta. This lake also contains a population of *Pungitius* in which a significant proportion of the individuals also lack pelvic spines. But, as with the overall geographical variation in the size of the pelvic skeleton, the causative factors in the origin of these aberrant populations of *Culaea* (and *Pungitius*) remain unknown (Nelson, 1969a; Nelson and Atton, 1971).

The preferred habitat of *Culaea* is cool, clear, heavily weeded water such as spring-fed streams and ponds. But populations also occur in the sheltered bays, the swampy margins and the bogs of lakes (Winn, 1960; Reisman and Cade, 1967). This requirement for a heavily vegetated habitat suggests that the ecological requirements of *Culaea* are more similar to those of *Pungitius* than of *Gasterosteus*. Since the distribution of *Culaea* overlaps far more with *Pungitius* than with *Gasterosteus*, this apparent similarity is surprising for it might be expected that *Culaea* would have diverged from *Pungitius* to avoid inter-specific competition. Until a detailed comparison of the ecological relationships of sympatric populations of *Culaea* and *Pungitius* becomes available, this paradox will remain unresolved.

Although *Culaea* does occur in brackish water and in lakes that are relatively saline, it is unable to tolerate salinities greater than about 21 ‰ . In water with a salinity of 7 ‰ *Culaea* showed an increase in oxygen consumption, but in higher salinities the oxygen consumption decreased. In salinities higher than 10.5 ‰ *Culaea* became sluggish and feeding was reduced. Fish that died in high salinities turned black before dying (Armitage and Olund, 1962; Nelson, 1968a).

Culaea is carnivorous, eating aquatic insect larvae and crustacea as well as snails, oligochaetes, water mites and fish eggs. Algae have also been found in the stomachs of some individuals (Winn, 1960). In turn, *Culaea* forms the prey of predatory fish such as pike (Hunt and Carbine, 1951; Lawler, 1965), fish-eating birds such as kingfishers, gulls and terns, and piscivorous mammals such as otters (Lagler and Ostenson, 1942; Winn, 1960).

Laboratory studies indicate that the brook stickleback is a skittish, shy fish compared with *Gasterosteus* or even *Pungitius*. *Culaea* will burrow into soft silt to conceal itself, though it cannot penetrate into sand. Degraeve (1970) observed burrowing in three contexts while watching brook sticklebacks living in a small creek. Some fish fled from a source of disturbance then dived into the silt head first, propelling themselves with rapid lashes of the tail. Other fish, when disturbed, tunnelled through the silt, covering distances of up to 60 cm in the silt before emerging and swimming off. Burrowing was also seen in association with feeding; fish would thrust their heads into the silt then grub around for food. These observations suggest that *Culaea* relies more on behavioural than on morphological adaptations to minimise predation.

Culaea is host for several species of parasites (Table XIII).

Although the data are scanty, *Culaea* probably breeds in the spring and summer of the year after that of its birth, when about a year old. The bulk of a population is probably made up of fish in their first year, but two and three year old fish may be present (Winn, 1960). Comparative data for the growth rate and age structure from several populations would clarify the situation and enable comparisons to be made with *Gasterosteus* and *Pungitius*.

As might be guessed from its geographical distribution and preferred habitats, *Culaea* is a cold water fish. Its tolerance of high water temperatures is low even when compared with other species with which it is sympatric (Brett, 1944). This restriction to cold water is reflected in its breeding biology for breeding is inhibited at temperatures higher than 19°C, although breeding is stimulated by lengthening days (Winn, 1960; Reisman and Cade, 1967; Braekevelt and McMillan, 1967).

In spring, brook sticklebacks migrate into the shallower water in which they breed from the deeper water in which they over-winter. Such a migration has been described in the Roseau River in Manitoba (MacLean and Gee, 1971). As the river ice broke up, the fish moved upstream from the main river into meltwater ponds and ditches. They chose water that was warmer than that of the river, but avoided water that was above 19°C. When the water temperature did go above 19°C, the fish showed a downstream movement. Laboratory experiments showed that mature fish had a preference for water that was between 15 and 19°C. Upstream movement tended to occur in daylight, but any downstream movement was usually at night. The spawning migration took the fish into shallow water that was clear, slow-moving and heavily vegetated and away from the river which was deep, turbid, swift and sparsely vegetated.

The life history and reproductive biology of *Culaea* are similar in outline to those of *Pungitius* and *Gasterosteus*. Breeding takes place in spring and early summer. In Ontario, the breeding season is from April to the end of June or mid July (Braekevelt and McMillan, 1967), and a comparable breeding season has been reported in Michigan (Winn, 1960), while in New York a population of the brook stickleback was observed to start breeding in the middle of May and end in mid July (Reisman and Cade, 1967). The end of the breeding season usually coincides with a time when water tempera-

TABLE XIII

Parasites recorded from the brook stickleback (*Culaea inconstans*).

Protozoa

1. SPOROZOA
Myxosoma eucalii Guilford, 1965.

2. CILIATA
Trichodina sp.

Platyhelminthes

1. MONOGENEA
Dactylogyrus eucalius Mizelle and Regensberger, 1945.

2. DIGENEA
Bunoderina eucaliae Miller, 1936.
Crepotrema funduli Miller, 1934.
Diplostomulum baeri eucaliae Hoffman and Hundley, 1957.
Echinochasmus donaldsoni Beaver, 1941.
Neascus sp.
Posthodiplostomum minimum
Tetracotyle sp.

3. CESTODA
Proteocephalus filicollis (Rudolphi, 1802).
Schistocephalus solidus (Müller, 1776).
Triaenophorus nodulosus (Pallas, 1781).

Aschelminthes

1. NEMATODA
Contracaecum sp.
Rhabdochona cascadilla Wigdor, 1918.
Spinitectus gracilis Ward and Magath, 1916.
Spiroxys sp.

2. ACANTHOCEPHALA
Leptorhynchoides thecatus (Linton, 1891).
Neoechinorhynchus rutili (Müller, 1780).
Pomphorhynchus bulbocolli (Linkins, 1919).

Annelida

1. HIRUDINEA (Leeches)
Illinobdella sp.

Arthropoda

1. CRUSTACEA
(i) BRANCHIURA
Argulus stizostethi Kellicot, 1880.

Source. Hoffman, 1967.

tures go above 20°C for prolonged periods of time. The spawning ceases, the females resorb any mature eggs that are unspawned and the males cease to build nests or defend territories. At the end of the spawning period the fish migrate downstream (Lamsa, 1963).

Female *Culaea* have a reproductive cycle like that of *Gasterosteus*. After spawning the ovary contains predominantly small oocytes derived from the oogonia. These oocytes grow and from September onwards vesicles of primary yolk form in the oocytes. This stage is reached even when the water is just about freezing and food is not abundant, but there is no further maturation of the oocytes until the following spring. Then, as the day-length increases and the temperature of the water starts to rise, the oocytes start to fill with secondary yolk and by April or May eggs are ready to be spawned. Immediately after the end of the breeding season the ovary forms only one to two per cent of the total body weight, then this percentage increases during the autumn to four per cent but shows little further change over the winter months when days are short and water temperature low. In spring, the ovaries of mature females constitute ten to twenty per cent of total body weight (Braekevelt and McMillan, 1967). Reports on the number of eggs laid at a spawning give a range from 40 to 250 or more (Hall, 1956; Winn, 1960), which represents a comparable range to that reported for *Gasterosteus* (Wootton, 1973b), and probably reflects differences in the size of the females (see Chapter 9). It has been claimed that in *Culaea* a year's crop of oocytes mature together so that there is only one spawning (Braekevelt and McMillan, 1967), but both *Pungitius* and *Gasterosteus* will spawn several times in a breeding season and it would seem likely that the same is true for *Culaea*. Indeed it is possible that for such small fish a strategy of multiple spawning is the only way in which a sufficient number of eggs can be produced to ensure that recruitment is adequate to replace losses in the parental generation.

The testes of the male also undergo cyclical changes and light and electron microscope studies of the testes during these changes have clarified some aspects of the formation of sperm in teleosts (Ruby and McMillan, 1970, 1975). In July, at the end of the breeding season, the spermatogonia in the testes start to develop into primary spermatocytes which will develop into secondary spermatocytes. Each spermatogonium gives rise to all the spermatocytes lying in a sac or cyst and these sacs come to fill the tubules of the testes. There is no germinal epithelium lining the walls of the tubules; instead the spermatogonia lie in the interstitial tissue between the tubules. The spermatogonia are most numerous in the interstitium just prior to the spawning of the mature sperm that is in the tubules. As the sacs develop, the number of spermatogonia in the interstitium declines. The formation of a sac depends on the presence of a companion cell which lies in the tubule. A companion cell extends broad cytoplasmic processes through gaps in the wall of the tubule into the interstitium and enfolds a spermatogonium in its plasma membrane. Within the folds of the companion cell's membrane, the spermatogonium divides and the sac begins to expand into the tubule. The companion cell withdraws the cytoplasmic processes from the interstitium and the gaps in the wall of the tubule close. Development of the spermatocytes into spermatids take place within the sac lying in the tubule and in about October they start to metamorphose into sperm. When the sperm are mature they are released from the sac into the lumen of the tubule while the companion cell is reduced to a nucleus with a thin layer of cytoplasm. During the period of sperm release in spring, some companion cells may be enfolding a spermatogonium from the interstitium, while still enfolding some residual sperm in the tubule. Once spawning has begun, the tubules are invaded by phagocytes which engulf sperm that are not released during spawning, but after spawning the number of phagocytes declines so that when sacs of spermatocytes start to fill the tubules no phagocytes are visible. (There is some ambiguity in the description which suggests that in some aspects the behaviour of companion cells and phagocytes may be confounded.) Although mature sperm are present in the testes by the onset of winter, the male *Culaea* does not become reproductively mature until spring, presumably because reproductive maturity depends on the presence of gonadal hormones secreted by interstitial cells of the testes. Compared with the ovaries, the testes show a much more restricted cycle of weight change over the reproductive cycle. At a minimum they form 0.3 to 0.5 per cent of the total body weight in late July. By the autumn this has increased to about one per cent, but then declines somewhat during the winter period. At the start of the breeding season, the testes again account for about one per cent of body weight, but as the breeding season progresses and sperm is used, there is a decline to the July minimum.

On the breeding grounds the males become aggressive and defend territories. Outside the breeding season, *Culaea* are cryptically coloured, usually olive green or brownish with a dark, variegated pattern on the back and flanks. But reproductively mature males are darker, although the exact colour depends on the behavioural context. Their eyes, which have yellow irises, develop a black bar of malanophores which runs vertically through the eye. Their dorsal and anal fins and the dorsal spines also become dark (Hall, 1956;

Reisman and Cade, 1967). Females also change colour when they become sexually mature, the variegations become more prominent (Scott and Crossman, 1973).

At the start of an aggressive encounter between two males, the attacker approaches his opponent directly, and as he nears his opponent he erects his dorsal spines and spreads his dorsal and anal fins while finally the pelvic spines are sometimes erected. The attacker may then adopt a head-down posture while still maintaining a frontal orientation towards the opponent. This head-down posture is also often combined with a broadside posture similar to the broadside head-down threat shown by *Pungitius*, but in *Culaea* the broadside may also be elaborated into a sigmoid posture in which the male draws his tail towards the head, contorting the body sideways, Usually, the male erects his pelvic spines during the broadside and sigmoid postures. When a male is broadside to his opponent, he frequently beats his tail, swinging the tail laterally with an amplitude of about a centimetre four to ten times a second. When two males are displaying a broadside posture towards each other so that they are head to tail, they will frequently make the transition to circular (roundabout) fighting, circling around each other rapidly. A broadside posture combined with tail beating is frequently followed by a direct charge at the opponent, culminating in an attempt to bite or bump the rival male. A beaten fish will respond to the approach of an attacker by turning broadside to the latter, and rolling the dorsal surface towards the attacker. This dorsal roll, which is also seen in *Pungitius* and *Gasterosteus* in similar circumstances, seems to inhibit the attacker from pressing home his charge. When badly beaten and unable to flee, a fish holds a tail-down posture with its head just below the surface (Hall, 1956; McKenzie, 1969a). Very aggressive males become completely black or blue-black and the dark bar in the eye becomes accentuated so that the whole eye may look black (Hall, 1956).

In a large, though not densely planted, aquarium, territory size of male brook sticklebacks varied from as large as 1600 sq cms down to 250 to 300 sq cm. The larger territories were often established first, and males that held the larger territories had more success in obtaining clutches of eggs (Reisman and Cade, 1967), a finding like the results discussed in Chapter 12 for *G. aculeatus* (van den Assem, 1967).

Female *Culaea* have been described as aggressive and territorial (Hall, 1956), but most reports suggest that mature females form small groups in areas that do not form part of a male's territory (Reisman and Cade, 1967; McKenzie, 1969a).

Like *Pungitius*, the *Culaea* male builds his nest off the substrate in vegetation, though the nests are commonly close to the bottom. Unlike *Pungitius*, the nest is attached to a stem or placed in the fork between two branches, not positioned amongst the leaves of plants. In the absence of suitable nest sites, males will attach nests to the vertical surfaces of rocks, and even on thermometers and siphon tubes in aquaria (Reisman and Cade, 1967). The nest is a small spherical mass of vegetation such as filamentous algae, plant remains and small twigs. It has a diameter that may vary from about $1\frac{1}{2}$ to 3 cm, which is smaller than the nests of *Pungitius* and *Gasterosteus* (Hall, 1956; Winn, 1960; Reisman and Cade, 1967).

Nest building begins with the selection of a suitable site by the male. He then glues at the site, depositing a tangle of glue; each bout of glueing lasts about thirty seconds. Then plant material is brought to the site and spat into the tangle of glue. As material accumulates, the male starts to push his snout into the bundle of vegetation before spitting out the fragment that he has collected. The pushing and boring forms an indentation in the nest mass which marks the entrance of the nest. Later, as the nest grows, material is spat onto the exterior of the nest, often on the outside of the top rim of the entrance. The male forms a cavity in the nest by pushing his snout well into the nest and twisting his head from side to side. He strengthens the nest by glueing over the external surface, a behaviour comparable to the superficial glueing shown by *Pungitius*. The appearance of insertion glueing signals the completion of the nest and the collecting of material wanes. When performing insertion glueing, the male catches globules of glue in his mouth and deposits them in the interior of the nest. Fanning appears quite early in the nest building phase, but at first the bouts of fanning are very short; then the length of the fanning bouts increases to between one and five seconds with about fifteen bouts per half hour. Fanning is usually preceded by a bout of glueing. The completed nest is neater and more compact in appearance than that of *Pungitius*, but unlike the nests of *Pungitius* and *Gasterosteus* that of *Culaea* does not have a complete tunnel with an exit (Hall, 1956).

A somewhat aberrant aspect of nest-building in *Culaea* is that some males collect stones which they drop in the entrance of the nest. The functional significance of this behaviour is not known, and as the observations were made on fish kept in an aquarium it is possible that the behaviour is a consequence of the artificial environment rather than a normal part of the nest building behaviour (Hall, 1956). Both aggressive behaviour and nest-building were inhibited when food was scarce (Smith, 1970).

The transition from the nest building phase to the sexual phase is not marked by the male creeping through the nest as it is in *Gasterosteus* and *Pungitius*, rather there is a relatively gradual transition. In the sexual phase, the male assumes a more or less jet black coloration, while ripe females assume a variegated pattern of brown speckling on a pale background.

When a male in the sexual phase sees a gravid female he turns slowly towards her, erects the dorsal and ventral spines and rapidly vibrates his pectoral and caudal fins. He approaches the female slowly until within 10 to 15 cm of her, then he suddenly lunges at her striking her on the head or flanks with his snout. The male pummells the female who sinks to the bottom; this pummelling is repeated if the female starts to swim away. Once the female is still, he turns and swims towards the nest, adopting a distinctive mode of swimming. All his spines are erect and his body is arched so that the back is convex, and he often holds his mouth open. He moves slowly forward, with his tail lowered but the caudal fin well spread; he beats his tail in a stiff, exaggerated manner at about five strokes a second with the body pivoting slightly from side to side. In some populations the tail is a conspicuous whitish colour. At the nest, he presses his open mouth against the upper rim of the nest and fans. If the female has not followed him to the nest, he returns to her and may show the aggressive broadside display before resuming the pummelling of the female. If the female does follow the male when he leads to the nest she stays a few centimetres below and just behind him. At the nest, she rides the current caused by the male's fanning for a few moments, then thrusts her way into the nest. Once she is in the nest, the male starts to quiver on her flanks in a manner similar to that seen in *Gasterosteus* and *Pungitius* at the equivalent point in the courtship sequence. For most of the time the female lies passively in the nest, but at intervals she shakes her body violently, then after a period of time that can vary from just over a minute to as long as ninety minutes, but which averages seven to ten minutes, she leaves the nest slowly forcing her way out of the nest through the back wall. The male pushes through the nest, fertilising the eggs without pausing in the nest. Female *Culaea* seem to spend far longer in the nest while spawning than either *Gasterosteus* or *Pungitius* females. After spawning, the male chases the female out of his territory (Fig. 67) (Hall, 1956; Reisman and Cade, 1967; McKenzie, 1969b). Some observations suggest that the courtship sequence may be abbreviated because a very ripe female will creep right up to the nest without being led by the male (Hall, 1956; Reisman and Cade, 1967).

Courtship may be interspersed with bouts of aggressive behaviour

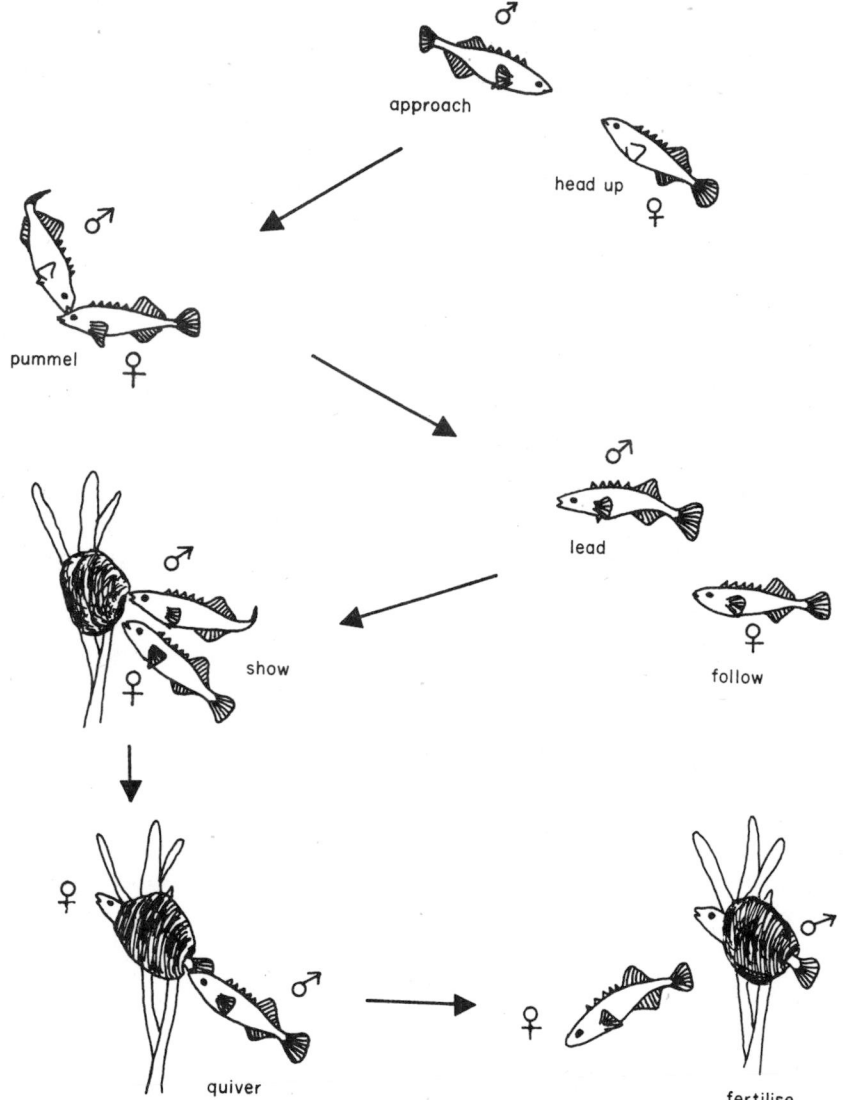

Fig. 67. Courtship of *Culaea inconstans* (after McKenzie, 1969b).

or bouts of boring and fanning at the nest, but there is no equivalent
to the dorsal pricking–nest visit sequence so characteristic of *G.
aculeatus* courtship described in Chapter 12. The pummelling component of the *Culaea* courtship makes the sequence look more
aggressive than the courtship of *Pungitius* or *Gasterosteus*. It is as
though, far from interfering with the successful courtship, aggressive
behaviour is an important component of *Culaea*'s sexual behaviour.

After the male has fertilised the eggs and chased the female away, he pushes the eggs well into the nest so that they lie on the floor of the nest cavity. Then for about an hour the male shows a high level of fanning. As this initial phase of fanning subsides, it is succeeded by a phase of nest building, during which the male repairs the exit caused by the passage of the female and male through the nest, and enlarges and strengthens the nest ready to receive another clutch of eggs (Hall, 1956; McKenzie, 1974).

For two or three days after this initial fertilisation, the male still courts gravid females and the level of fanning remains low. But then fanning takes up more and more time and the male stops courting females. The fanning cycle is similar to those of *Gasterosteus* and *Pungitius*, although far less time is spent fanning than is shown by *Gasterosteus*, so a male with only one clutch of eggs had a maximum level of fanning of 250 seconds per thirty minutes (Fig. 64, p. 284). The young hatch in five to nine days depending on the temperature. They attach themselves to the walls and roof of the nest, hanging by the mouth, and remain still. Any young that jump out of the nest are retrieved by the male. Once all the young have hatched the male shows little fanning and starts to pull at the nest loosening its structure. He builds a nursery area above the nest; this nursery consists of a loose tangle of threads into which he transfers the young as the nest disintegrates. He shows slight fanning at the nursery, especially immediately after he has retrieved one of the young and spat it back in. But within two or three days the young become more active and start to disperse from the nursery. Once the young are sufficiently active to escape from the male's attempts to retrieve them, the parental phase comes to an end. In some cases the male will interrupt the fanning cycle to transfer the eggs to a new nest constructed at a different site. Material from the old nest is incoporated in the new nest and the eggs are moved to the new nest shortly before the old one is demolished. As in *Gasterosteus* and *Pungitius* nest raiding and egg stealing take place (Hall, 1956; McKenzie, 1974).

In most respects the reproductive cycle of *Culaea* resembles that of *Pungitius*. In both species the male assumes a dark colour on reaching maturity, both build their nests off the ground, and both build nurseries just above the old nest to accommodate the young after they hatch. The major difference between the two occurs during courtship, and the courtship sequences of the two are sufficiently unlike to make it doubtful that successful inter-specific mating ever occurs under natural conditions, though in both species the male is dark coloured so a simple visual discrimination is less likely to be a barrier to cross mating than it would be between either of these two species and *Gasterosteus*.

An outstanding problem that remains is how much of the likeness between *Culaea* and *Pungitius* is because they are closely related species and how much because they occupy rather similar ecological niches and so have responded to similar selection pressures in comparable ways.

18. *Apeltes quadracus:*
The Four-Spined Stickleback

Apeltes quadracus, like *Culaea*, is restricted to the North American continent but, in complete contrast to *Culaea*, which is restricted to freshwater localities, *Apeltes* is found principally in salt or brackish water though it does occur in a few freshwater sites. Its tolerance of saline conditions is greater than that of *Culaea, Pungitius* and even *Gasterosteus* (Nelson, 1968a). Although slightly deeper bodied than

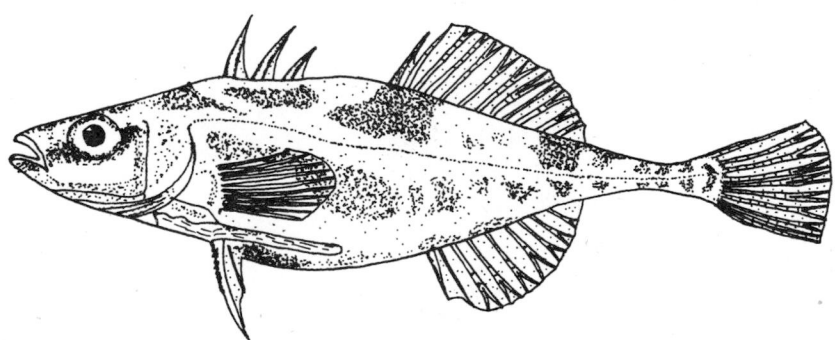

Fig. 68. *Apeltes quadracus* (Mitchill).

Culaea or *Pungitius, Apeltes* morphologically resembles them and *Gasterosteus* (Fig. 68). The most obvious differences are in the complete absence of lateral plates and in the number of dorsal spines.

Apeltes is naked, lacking both scales, as do the other Gasterosteids, and lateral plates. It also lacks a caudal keel. This lack of lateral plates is surprising in view of the general correlation in *Pungitius* and particularly *G. aculeatus* between plate number and salinity tolerance (see Chapter 8). *Spinachia*, which is entirely confined to salt waters, also has a complete row of lateral plates, though *G. wheatlandi* has relatively few lateral plates in spite of being predominantly a fish of brackish and marine waters. A further point of similarity between *Alpeltes* and *G. wheatlandi* is that they are both restricted to the eastern seaboard of North America.

In most populations of *Apeltes* the modal number of dorsal spines is four, though some populations have a mode of five spines. The vast majority of individuals have three, four or five dorsal spines, but occasionally two-spined or six-spined individuals are found. There is some correlation between salinity and the number of dorsal spines, for populations with a relatively high proportion of five-spined individuals often occur in water that is fresh or has a low salinity (Cox, 1923; Kreuger, 1961). The first two spines are longer than the posterior spines and the last one in the row is attached to the anterior edge of the dorsal fin. As in *Pungitius*, the spines incline to the left and right of the midline. The pelvic spines are long and serrated and each is associated with two soft rays to make up a pelvic fin (Leim and Scott, 1966; Scott and Crossman, 1973).

Apeltes has a maximum length of about 6 cm but is frequently smaller than this. The small mouth is set at the end of the snout, with the lower jaw projecting slightly beyond the upper jaw. In the dorsal fin there are between nine and fourteen soft rays, but twelve is the most common complement. The anal fin is inserted slightly behind the dorsal fin, and has one spine at the anterior margin with between seven and eleven soft rays, nine being the usual number. The tail fin is rather rounded, and the caudal peduncle is slender (Kreuger, 1961; Nelson, 1971a; Coad and Power, 1973a).

The geographical range extends from the Gaspé Basin of Quebec in the north to Virginia in the south, including Newfoundland (Fig. 69). This means that *Apeltes* has the most southerly based distribution of the five genera of sticklebacks, but *Gasterosteus aculeatus, G. wheatlandi* and *Pungitius* all overlap with *Apeltes*. Although primarily restricted to coastal areas, in Nova Scotia, Newfoundland, and further south in Pennsylvania, it is found up to 20 km from brackish water (Kreuger, 1961; Leim and Scott, 1966; Dadswell, 1972a).

Little has been published on the general ecology of *Apeltes* although there is no reason to suppose that it differs in broad outline from that of *Culaea, Pungitius* or *Gasterosteus*. A population living in freshwater in the Matemek River in Quebec included females in their third year and males in their second year, and similar age structures have been reported for populations in the Miramichi River, New Brunswick, and from Maryland (Coad and Power, 1973a; McInerney,

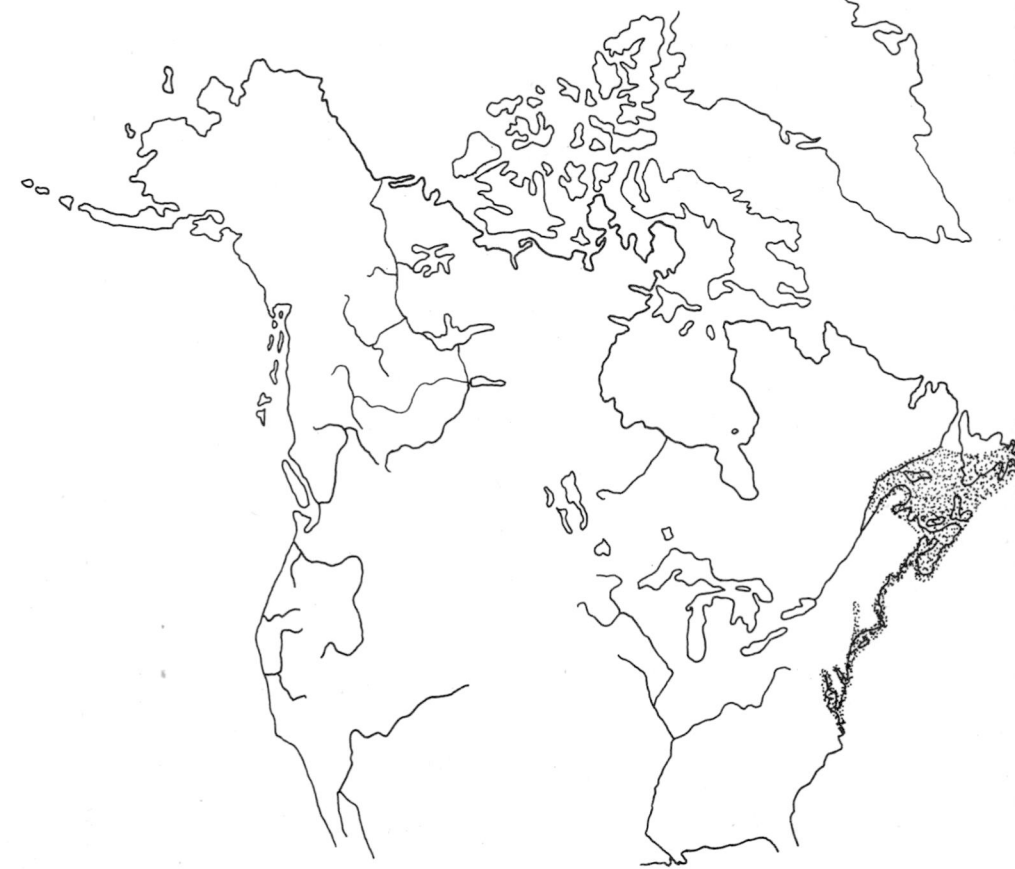

Fig. 69. Distribution of *Apeltes quadracus*.

1969; Schwartz, 1965). The freshwater population of the Matamek feeds on cladocerans, chironomid larvae, ephemeropteran larvae and other arthropods, while marine populations feed on gammarids, isopods and chironomids.

Throughout the year, *Apeltes* retains a cryptic coloration of a brownish olive back mottled with black patches and a silvery underside. Hall (1956) reports that in an aquarium, the fish backed away from a source of disturbance, at the same time moving upwards so that it came to rest in a head-down position. When a fish backed into a vertical surface such as the side of the aquarium, it crept backwards up the side, with its head pointing vertically downwards. *Apeltes* takes cover in vegetation, usually lying at right angles to the main branches but it can also conceal itself by half burying in sand or gravel, or by creeping into small crevices. These observations suggest that *Apeltes* relies on its behaviour rather than its morphology to protect it from predation, although its spines are well developed.

TABLE XIV

Parasites recorded from *Apeltes quadracus*.

Platyhelminthes

1. MONOGENEA
Gyrodactylus avalonia Hanek and Threlfall, 1969.
G. cameroni Hanek and Threlfall, 1970.
G. canadensis Hanek and Threlfall, 1969.
2. DIGENEA
Podocotyle atomon Rudolphi, 1802.
3. CESTODA
Proteocephalus sp.

Aschelminthes

1. NEMATODA
Cystidicola farionis Fischer, 1798.

Source. Hanek and Threlfall, 1970b.

An interesting aspect of the ecology of *Apeltes* is its behaviour as a cleaner species. *Apeltes* has been seen removing and eating an ectoparasite from the skin of the rainwater fish *Lucania parva*. The parasite was a monogenean trematode *Gyrodactylus*. The rainwater fish solicited *Apeltes*, the cleaner fish, by assuming a rigid vertical posture, with its snout pointed up and its pectoral fins vibrating rapidly. The flank was always presented to the stickleback and the client fish would solicit several times in succession. Although the observations of this cleaning behaviour were made on fish held in an aquarium, *Apeltes* and *Lucania* co-exist in shallow weed beds and this cleaning behaviour may well be a naturally occurring interaction between the two species and not simply an artefact of the aquarium environment (Tyler, 1963). *Lucania* is a small fish about the same size as *Apeltes*, so that the cleaning symbiosis between the two is biologically less bizarre than that reported between *Gasterosteus* and the fish-eating pike described by Bartmann (1973).

In spring, when the reproductive period of *Apeltes* starts, the males become territorial. Mature males may be recognised by their red pelvic spines. As in the other sticklebacks, the testes of males contain mature spermatozoa by the winter prior to breeding, but the males do not become reproductively mature until the following spring. High water temperatures accelerate the rate at which the spermatozoa become mature. In contrast, the females do not develop mature oocytes until the spring and early summer prior to breeding. High water temperatures in autumn slow down the rate of maturation of the oocytes. Long day-lengths are essential for the complete maturation of the oocytes of the female and for the development of behavioural maturity in the male. This latter effect is presumably mediated by the secretion of gonadotropin from the pituitary and the stimulatory effect of this hormone on the interstitial cells of the testes which secrete androgens (Merriman and Schedl, 1941).

Once the female is reproductively mature she will spawn at intervals of three to four days, producing fifteen to twenty eggs at each spawning (Hall, 1956).

The reproductive behaviour of *Apeltes* has received comparatively little study, but descriptions of aggressive encounters suggest that it is a relatively unaggressive species with a simple repertoire of agonistic behaviour patterns. When a fight between males occurs, the attacker approaches his opponent, erecting the dorsal and pelvic spines as he does so. If the opponent is an intruder in the attacker's territory, the intruder will usually flee, but if the latter stands his ground, the attacker stops a few centimetres in front of his opponent. Both erect their dorsal and pelvic spines, but then the spines of one of the pair start to flicker and are eventually lowered. The fish that lowers his spines starts to turn away, backing away slowly and turning broadside with the head slightly down. He hesitates slightly and then swims away. In encounters close to a territorial border, one of the males may adopt a head-on threat in which he faces his opponent in a head-down position. In this position the erect, red pelvic spines are very conspicuous. A lateral head-down threat may also occur. Direct attacks with biting may be relatively rare (Hall, 1956; Rowland, 1974a).

Although *Apeltes* builds a nest among the branches of a water plant or attached to its stem, the nest is far smaller than those of *Culaea* and *Pungitius* and may be hardly more than 5 mm in diameter. The nest is cup shaped with only a few strands of material forming the roof. After a male has selected a suitable site, he may either lay down a matrix of glue, pivoting around the nest site in a bout of glueing that may last over a minute, or he may bring a few pieces of material to the site then glue. A bout of glueing lasts for about forty seconds on average, far longer than the comparable behaviour in *Pungitius* or *Culaea*. Once the matrix of glue is laid down, the male brings small fragments of plant material to the site and spits them into the matrix. The alternation of collecting and glueing results in the accumulation of a small clump of material. The outer surface of this nest is smooth and rounded, for, in each bout of glueing over the surface, the male erects the pelvic spine nearest the centre of the nest and uses this spine as a pivot to stabilise his movements as he curves around the nest. By pushing into the nest before spitting out the material he has brought to the site, the male forms a depression which is both the entrance and central cavity of the nest. Some nests have a layer of sand sprinkled over the outer surface. The nest may be almost at substrate level or 20 cm or more off the substrate; the location of the nest is probably determined by the type of vegetation available and the preferences of the males (Hall, 1956; Rowland, 1974a). When sexually mature males were kept in aquaria that lacked water plants, they built nests on the ground, but it is not known whether females will lay eggs in such nests (Rowland, 1974b).

Apeltes does not fan the nest, either during the nest building phase or the sexual phase or the parental phase. Ventilation of the nest is achieved by a behaviour called sucking. This behaviour first appears towards the end of the phase of nest building. The male puts his snout in the nest entrance, and with a series of gulping movements draws water into his open mouth and expels it through the opercular slits. While sucking, the male holds his pectoral fins pointing backwards at an angle of about 45 degrees to the body and they vibrate rapidly. The tail fin may also vibrate, but there is no muscular tail beating. So although sucking seems to appear in the same contexts and serves the same function as the fanning of *Culaea, Pungitius* and *Gasterosteus* it is a distinctly different behaviour pattern (Hall, 1956).

As in *Culaea*, the transition from nest building to sexual phase is relatively gradual and is not signalled by creeping through the nest as in *Pungitius* and *Gasterosteus*. In some populations, the males during the sexual phase, in addition to their bright red pelvic spines, develop two dark bands of pigment which stretch from the eye to the posterior margin of the skull. The lower of these bands may lead into a dark band which stretches the length of the body and is formed by the vertebral column showing through the semitransparent musculature of the body (Hall, 1956).

A gravid female swims slowly, often close to the bottom, in a slightly head-up posture. When he sees her, the male approaches, erecting his dorsal and pelvic spines. The initial approach is slow, but then the male leaps forward and starts to strike the female rapidly on the side of the head or the flanks. When pummelled like this, the female stops swimming and sinks towards the bottom. After a bout of pummelling, the male swims rapidly away from the female, following a spiral or circular path; he stops somewhere between the female and the nest and displays his red pelvic spines. He then performs a further bout of pummelling and spiralling, and with a series of pummels forces the female right to the bottom. Eventually, a gravid female will swim to the male as he pauses after the completion of his spiral dance. She takes up a position closely behind and underneath the male with her snout almost touching his body between the pelvic spines. With both his dorsal and pelvic spines erect, the male swims slowly towards the nest moving in short jerks. The male may interrupt the leading with more bouts of pummelling. If the female does not follow the male, he may return to the nest alone and perform glueing, or other nest building activity, or sucking, before resuming the courtship. But if the female successfully follows the male, he presses his snout into the nest entrance and gives a few strong beats of the tail. During this brief showing display, the male is usually in a head-down position. The female then pushes her way into the nest, thrusting; diagonally upwards so that she comes to rest with her head higher than her tail, and the nest forming a flimsy ring around her belly. Once she is in the nest, the male takes up a horizontal position at right angles to her, and gently bites her tail fin repeatedly. This display is distinctly different from the quivering shown by *Culaea, Pungitius* and *Gasterosteus* males at a similar point in the courtship sequence. After the female has spawned the eggs, she wriggles forwards out of the nest, and the male pushes through fertilising the eggs. The male may pause for a few seconds in the nest while fertilising the eggs, but once he has left the nest he chases the female out of his territory (Hall, 1956; Reisman, 1963; Rowland, 1974a). Although the spiral dance is unique to the courtship of *Apeltes*, film analysis has shown that during the spiral dance the male performs very rapid zig zags (Rowland, 1974a), which may be comparable to the zig zags which figure so prominently in the courtship of *Gasterosteus* and *Pungitius*.

After a brief pause which follows the fertilisation of the eggs, the male starts a period of nest building which results in repairs to the nest which contains the eggs, and the construction of a second nest sitting on top of the first. This second nest will hold the eggs from the next successful spawning. This process is repeated after each spawning so that the male builds tiers of small nests arranged one above the other (Ryder, 1882; Breder, 1936; Hall, 1956; Reisman, 1963; Rowland, 1974a).

For a day or two after the first fertilisation, the male shows low levels of sucking, the mode of nest ventilation in *Apeltes*. But then the amount of time spent sucking increases steadily as both the number of bouts of sucking and the average length of the bouts increase. A male remains responsive to gravid females and will continue to acquire more clutches of eggs, which is in contrast to the other species described up to now in which there is a decline and finally the disappearance of sexual behaviour of the male as the parental cycle proceeds. By about the sixth day after the first fertilisation the amount of time spent sucking reaches a peak of about 300 sec. per half hour, and shows no further major increase although the male may obtain more clutches. As a result of the courtship activities of the male, the nest complex contains eggs in various stages of development, and the male directs the bulk of his sucking activity towards the clutches in the most advanced stage of development. He pulls holes in the nest so that his mouth is in close contact with the eggs while he is sucking. Usually there are at least two holes in a nest and this presumably eases the ventilation. After the young hatch the male may remove the empty egg cases from the nest, but he does not build a nursery nor does he take any more care of the young though he does not attack them. At about 18°C, the eggs hatch in about eight days. When the male has only one or two clutches, the cycle of sucking activity is very similar to the fanning cycles of *Culaea*, *Pungitius* or *Gasterosteus*, for the male shows a peak of sucking activity just before the eggs hatch and then sucking declines rapidly. So that although sucking is a distinctly different activity from fanning, their temporal pattern during the parental cycle is similar except that the male *Apeltes* continues to acquire fresh clutches for a far longer period during the cycle (Hall, 1956; Rowland, 1974a).

A male may build a nest at a new site even before all the eggs in the first nest complex have hatched. He leads gravid females to this new nest site and the eggs are laid in the new nest. If the male has eggs at both nest sites, he shows the duration of sucking at each site that is appropriate to the stage of development of the eggs at that site; the male behaves as though the other nest complex does not exist except of course he is regularly visiting both sites. This observation, and the observation that even at one nest complex the male spends the appropriate amount of time sucking at each level suggests that simuli from the eggs are primarily responsible for regulating the amount of sucking and that changes internal to the male are less important (cf. Chapter 13) (Hall, 1956).

The sexual and parental phases of the male *Apeltes* overlap to a considerable extent, with the male retaining the ability to court and spawn with gravid females for two to three weeks after the first fertilisation. This organisation of the reproductive cycle is significantly different from that in *Culaea, Pungitius* and *Gasterosteus* where the development of the parental cycle is accompanied by a decline in the sexual responsiveness of the male. The peculiar temporal organisation of the reproductive behaviour of *Apeltes* is correlated with the very small size of the nest and the substitution of sucking for fanning as the behaviour that ventilates the nest. Given the small size of the nest, it may be that fanning would cause too strong a current of water over the eggs and would dislodge them from the nest, and so fanning is replaced by sucking. The small size of the nest inevitably means that relatively few eggs can be laid in it, but the male ensures that he fertilises many eggs by having a tiered nest complex and retaining the ability to court gravid females even while caring for several clutches of eggs. Also in contrast to the other three species, the male *Apeltes* does not care for the young once they have hatched. The fry fall or jump out of the nest and come to rest on the bottom or in vegetation where they remain motionless for some time. About two days after hatching the young swim to the surface, fill their air bladders and assume an active, free-swimming life. Thus in *Apeltes*, parental care is sacrificed to some extent and sexual behaviour is more prominent than in the other sticklebacks (Hall, 1956).

There is considerably more to be learnt about the biology of *Apeltes* before a full comparison with the other genera of sticklebacks can be made. But it is clear that at least in its reproductive behaviour *Apeltes* is distinctly different from the others and quite unique.

19. *Spinachia spinachia:*
The Fifteen-Spined or Sea Stickleback
(Synonyms: *Spinachia vulgaris* Fleming; *Gasterosteus spinachia* L.)

All the Gasterosteids described so far are morphologically similar, but *Spinachia spinachia* is completely distinctive for it is a very elongated fish. While the other sticklebacks have a length to depth ratio that varies between about 4 : 1 and 5 : 1, for *Spinachia* this ratio is about 11 : 1. It is by far the largest of the sticklebacks; mature *Spinachia* are 10 to 15 cm long although specimens up to 20 cm long have been recorded. Another distinctive feature is that it is the only stickleback never found in inland waters. Unfortunately this beautiful and unusual fish is the least wellknown of the sticklebacks (Fig. 70).

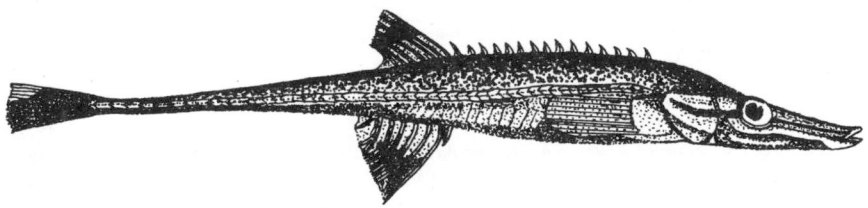

Fig. 70. *Spinachia spinachia* (L.).

The snout of *Spinachia* is long, but the mouth itself is relatively small so that the anterior margin of the orbit of the eye lies well behind the jaw articulation. In the other sticklebacks, the jaw articulation lies under or almost under the anterior margin of the eye orbit. *Spinachia* has fifteen small dorsal spines which are inclined alternately to the left and to the right as in *Apeltes* and *Pungitius*. The two pelvic spines are very small and each is paired with two soft rays to form a pelvic fin. These pelvic fins are set relatively far back along the body. The dorsal and anal fins are small and triangular,

313

with the anal fin inserted slightly behind the dorsal fin. Both fins contain six or seven fin rays. Behind the fins there is a long, slender caudal peduncle which terminates with the rounded caudal fin. Along the length of the body, there are about forty-one small, overlapping lateral plates. In the caudal region these lateral plates

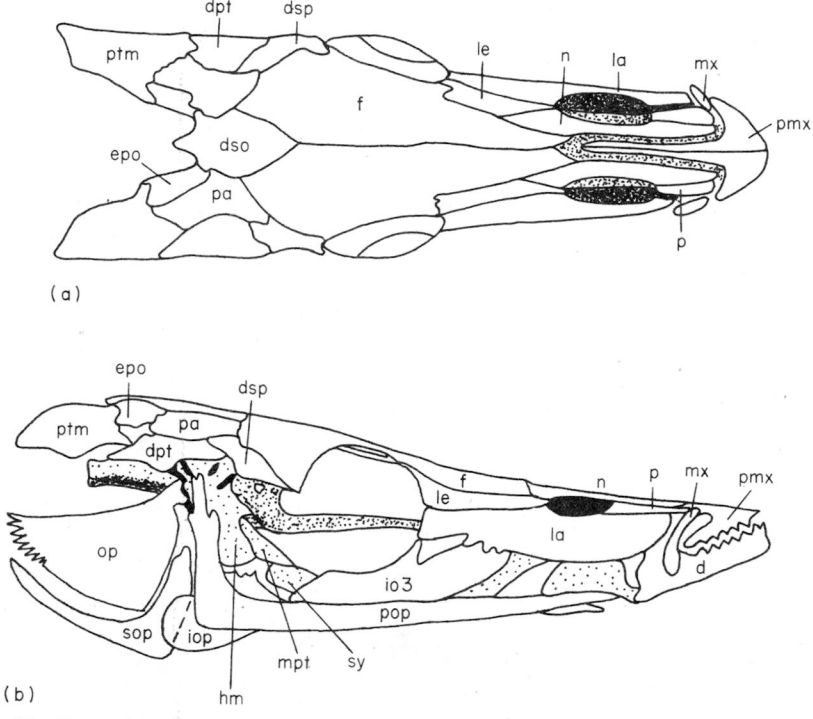

Fig. 71. Skull of *Spinachia spinachia* (after Banister, 1967). (a) Dorsal view; (b) lateral view. Note the elongation of the pre-orbital bones compared with the arrangement in *Gasterosteus aculeatus* (Fig. 2). Key to lettering: d, dentary; dpt, dermoterotic; dso, dermosupraoccipital; dsp, dermosphenotic; epo, epiotic; f, frontal; hm, hyomandibular; io, infraorbital; iop, interopercular; la, lachrymal; le, lateral ethmoid; mpt, metapterygoid; mx, maxilla; n, nasal; op, opercular; p, autopalatine; pa, parietal; pmx, premaxilla; pop, preopercular; ptm, posttemporal; sop, subopercular; sy, symplectic.

meet and sometimes fuse with the median plates so that part of the caudal peduncle is enclosed by this bony armour. There are between forty and forty-two vertebrae, usually with eighteen precaudals and twenty-three caudals (Nelson, 1971a).

A study of the bones of the head region showed that the elongation of the snout reflects an elongation in the pre-orbital region. Compared with *Gasterosteus* (Chapter 1), *Spinachia* has very elongated nasal and lachrymal bones on the dorsal surface of the skull, while in the suspensorium the symplectic and the posterior process of the tri-radiate pterygoid are elongated compared with the condition in the short snouted sticklebacks (Fig. 71) (Kampf, 1962; Banister, 1967; Mural, 1973).

Spinachia is entirely restricted to the seas of western Europe (Fig. 72). It ranges from the Bay of Biscay in the south (45° N) to

Fig. 72. Distribution of *Spinachia spinachia*.

northern Norway (71° N). These limits approximately correspond to the yearly surface water isotherms of 14°C and 4°C. It is found around the coast of Great Britain, the Shetlands, Orkneys and the Faeroes, but is absent from the coast of Iceland. Although found exclusively in the sea, *Spinachia* can tolerate salinities as low as 5 ‰ (full seawater is 35 ‰), and so is able to penetrate into estuaries and is found in regions of the Baltic Sea where the salinity is low (Bertin, 1925). However, it cannot survive in fresh water even when the salinity is lowered gradually (Raffy, 1954). Although a marine fish, it is confined to shallow water and is not found in the open sea or at depths greater than 20 m. Typical habitats are beds of *Zostera* the marine grass, along the bottoms of rocks covered in sea-weed, among the stems of fucoid sea-weeds on the sea floor and sometimes in rock pools.

Over sandy or muddy substrates, *Spinachia* tends to be brownish with dark bars and a silverish belly, but when living amongst algae it assumes an olive colour with dark, greenish blotches (Wheeler, 1969). Differences in the colour of the fish can be obtained by keeping them over either a dark or light substrate (Baker, 1963).

Small crustacea such as copepods, amphipods and isopods form the diet of *Spinachia* (Blegvad, 1917). When taking food, the fish either swims up to the prey and sucks it into the mouth, or draws itself into a sigmoid position and then suddenly launches itself at the prey (Hall, 1956). In captivity, *Spinachia* will take *Tubifex*, chopped mussels and chopped meat and will soon learn to come to the surface to take food.

Spinachia probably lives for only one year, although some very large specimens may be more than a year old. Studies of the ear otoliths have not found any annual rings. Breeding takes place in late spring or early summer. By the August after birth, the young fish are 3 to 8 cm long but then show little growth over the winter months. This represents a far faster growth rate than occurs in the other sticklebacks but there have been no studies on the rate of food consumption or the growth efficiency of *Spinachia* (Jones and Hynes, 1950).

Both field studies and observations on fish in aquaria suggest that *Spinachia* is a solitary fish which does not form large schools. Even outside the breeding season it is rare to find many individuals close together. With the onset of the reproductive maturity in spring, the males become territorial. The territories of the males are in spots sheltered from excessive wave action, and on occasions are in rock pools that may be uncovered for a few hours when the tide ebbs. Descriptions of the aggressive behaviour of the male *Spinachia* indicate that it consists of little more than simple, direct attacks on any intruders into the territory of the male. Biting is often directed at the slender caudal peduncle, which is of course well protected by the lateral and median plates. When attacked, the intruder will flee, erecting both dorsal and pelvic spines as it does so (Sevenster, 1951; Hall, 1956).

Within the territory of the male *Spinachia* there are patches of seaweed such as *Halidrys* or *Fucus*, and it is in such a patch that the male builds his nest. He repeatedly pushes his way through the weed and eventually starts laying down a network of glue in the weed. Each bout of glueing may last as long as fifteen minutes with bouts repeated at intervals of one to five hours. Both the length of each bout and the interval between successive bouts are far longer than in the other stickleback species. The glue, which is secreted by the kidneys, is deposited in thick threads more than 0.1 mm thick, each thread made up of a number of parallel, fine threads. Only after the initial bouts of glueing have laid down a matrix of glue does the male begin to bring material to the nest site. He tears off or picks up bits of seaweed and thrusts them into the network of glue. With the repetition of glueing and collecting, the male accumulates a large spherical mass of material in the seaweed which he consolidates by pushing and glueing. The nest is 5 to 8 cm in diameter, but it lacks a distinct entrance or exit tunnel. The male starts fanning the nest towards the end of the nest building phase; this fanning is similar both in form and orientation to the fanning of *Pungitius* and *Culaea*. It is distinct from the sucking of *Apeltes* (Leiner, 1934; Sevenster, 1951; Hall, 1956).

Neither the male nor the female adopt any distinctive breeding coloration. Gravid females can be distinguished by their distended bellies. A male with a completed nest approaches a gravid female, nudging or biting her on the caudal peduncle or fins. If the female flees, the male continues to attack her, chasing her out of his territory. But a ripe female responds to the initial attack of the male by turning towards him. He then swims directly to his nest and shows it to the female by placing his snout in the nest then jerking his snout from side to side. If the female has not followed the male to the nest, the sequence of approach and bite is repeated. Eventually, the female follows the male when he swims back to the nest, and in response to his showing pushes her way into the nest. Once the female is in the nest, the male takes up horizontal position at right angles to her and starts to bite at her caudal peduncle (Fig. 73). This is similar to the behaviour of *Apeltes* at the equivalent stage in courtship. After the female has spawned, the male pushes his way through the nest, fertilising the eggs. The male does not always push through the nest in the same direction as the female, but may go through at right angles to her path, which indicates that the nest of *Spinachia* does not have the polarity of the nests of *Pungitius* and *Gasterosteus* with their distinct tunnels. Once he has fertilised the eggs, the male starts to attack the female, becoming more and more aggressive and finally chasing the female away (Sevenster, 1951). Leiner (1934) had claimed that the female *Spinachia* helps to position the eggs in the nest, but this was not confirmed by Sevenster (1951); Leiner's report is the only instance in which it has been claimed that a female stickleback shows some parental behaviour.

A male will spawn with several females accumulating several hundred eggs in his nest. The amber-coloured eggs are about 2 mm in diameter.

In the parental phase of the male, fanning becomes the predominant activity, reaching a peak of 300 or 400 seconds per half hour shortly before the eggs hatch. The development of the embryos follows a pattern comparable to that described for *G. aculeatus* in Chapter 3, but spread out over a longer period of time. Hatching

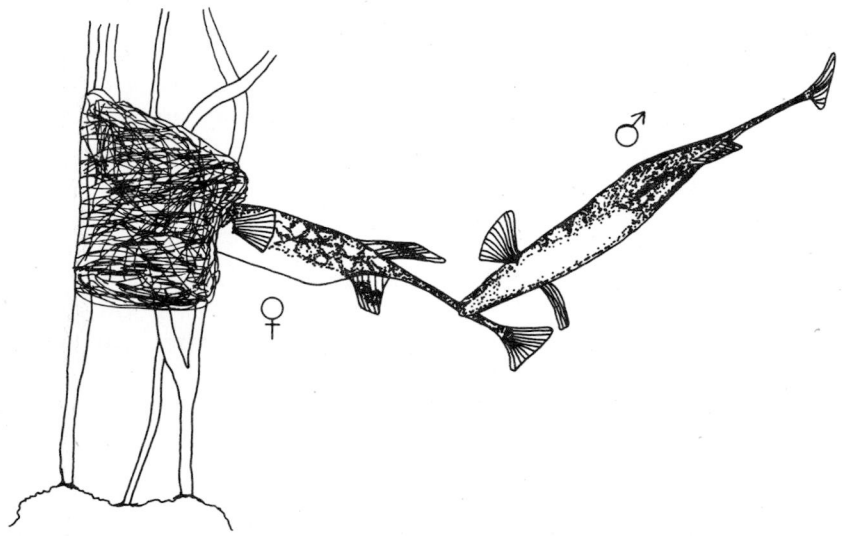

Fig. 73. Tail biting during the courtship of *Spinachia spinachia* (after Sevenster, 1951).

takes place from the eighteenth day after fertilisation onwards and the rate of development probably depends on the water temperature. Prince (1885) kept eggs in water that ranged from 5° to about 10°C and found that the eggs hatched between twenty-five and forty days after fertilisation. Eggs in the middle of the mass of eggs in the nest developed at a slower rate than those towards the outside. Soon after hatching the young begin to escape from the nest. At this stage, the larvae are about 6 mm long, they have rounded heads and blunt snouts which is very unlike the elongated shape of their parents. But within a few months they are several centimetres long and have assumed the adult shape (Leiner, 1934; Sevenster, 1951; Hall, 1956; Wheeler, 1969).

Although relatively little is known about the biology of *Spinachia*, in addition to its intrinsic interest, *Spinachia* is important for it provides a clue to the phylogenetic relationships of the stickleback family within the huge class of bony fishes, the Teleosts. This topic, the evolution and phylogeny of the sticklebacks, will be considered in the next chapter.

20. The Evolutionary Relationships of the Sticklebacks

The sticklebacks pose two problems for biologists interested in the evolution of this family. Firstly, there is the problem of the evolutionary relationships within the Gasterosteidae. Can any of the genera be regarded as more primitive than the others, and can a phylogenetic tree be deduced for the family? Secondly, there is the problem of the evolutionary relationship of the Gasterosteidae to the other teleosts. Which other families of the higher bony fishes have the closest affinities to the stickleback?

As yet no definitive answer can be given to either of these questions, although important pieces of evidence have accumulated. Unfortunately the fossil record of the sticklebacks is as yet poorly studied and relates primarily to *Gasterosteus* (see Chapter 14), and so provides no clues as to the evolution of the whole family. This means that all the evidence comes from studies on living genera and so there is the problem of distinguishing between likenesses which are due to common ancestry and those that are due to evolutionary convergence because similar biological problems are being solved in similar ways. This problem becomes particularly acute when the relationship of the sticklebacks to other families of the teleosts is considered. The bulk of the relevant evidence comes from comparative studies of morphology, anatomy, behaviour and chromosomes. On the basis of this sort of information the relationships within the Gasterosteidae can be discussed.

Morphologically, a primary division is between the slender and very elongated *Spinachia* and the other genera which are deeper bodied. The length to depth ratio for *Spinachia* is of the order of 11:1, whereas for the other sticklebacks this ratio lies between about 4:1 and 5:1 (Hall, 1956). Not only is *Spinachia* the most elongated stickleback, but it also has the most dorsal spines, although these spines are relatively short. *Pungitius* also has a relatively high number of dorsal spines, which like those of *Spinachia* and *Apeltes* are inclined to the right or left of the midline. The dorsal spines of *Culaea* and *Gasterosteus* lie directly behind each other along the midline. All the genera have a pair of pelvic fins with each fin formed by a spine and one or two soft rays, although there are populations of *G. aculeatus*, *P. pungitius* and *Culaea* in which all or a high proportion of the individuals lack the pelvic skeleton. *Spinachia* and *Apeltes* have two soft rays in a pelvic fin as does *G. wheatlandi*, *Pungitius* has one or two while *Culaea* and *G. aculeatus* have only one.

Spinachia has the most numerous lateral plates, perhaps because it is by far the longest of the sticklebacks. In *Spinachia*, these plates form a complete row along the length of the body from the pectoral fin to the caudal fin, as they do in some forms of *Pungitius* and *G. aculeatus*, but these two species also have forms that lack lateral plates altogether. *Apeltes* always lacks lateral plates and although *Culaea* has thirty to thirty-six, these are very small and are unlikely to function as protective armour (Nelson, 1971a).

Pungitius, Culaea and *Spinachia* have branchial membranes which are united so that these membranes, which enclose the gill chambers on each side of the body, are linked as one continuous membrane. In *Apeltes* and *Gasterosteus* the branchial membranes from each gill cavity fuse to the isthmus of the throat and do not form one membrane (Nelson, 1971a).

On the basis of these external characters it is not possible to detect any particular grouping of the five genera, nor any clear cut pattern of relationships between them. Rather they present a mosaic of characters with no particular set of characters seeming more primitive or less specialised than another set. Does an examination of the skeletal anatomy help to clarify this situation?

The caudal fin of teleost fishes is supported by hypural bones, which represent enlarged haemal arches of the vertebrae. In three of the five genera of sticklebacks, *Culaea, Pungitius* and *Apeltes*, the hypural bones are fused to form a single plate. In the two species of *Gasterosteus*, *G. aculeatus* and *G. wheatlandi*, the hypural plate is incompletely fused and is split into an upper and lower plate. This division of the hypural plate into an upper and lower segment is diagnostic of the genus *Gasterosteus* (Nelson, 1971a). A description of the ontogeny of the hypural plate in *G. aculeatus* based on Huxley (1859) is provided in Chapter 3. The hypural plate of *Spinachia* is usually described as a single fused plate (Nelson, 1971a; Banister, 1967), but there is some evidence that it consists of ten to twelve incompletely fused hypurals (Mural, 1973). A description of the ontogeny of the hypural plate in this genus would be valuable. Other elements of the caudal suspension also vary between the genera. In *G. aculeatus* there is usually only one epural, although during ontogeny two epural cartilages appear. The two epurals of *Pungitius* are often in close contact and appear as a single bone. *Culaea* and *G. wheatlandi* have separated epurals with the anterior of the pair in close contact with the neural spine immediately in front. *Spinachia* also has two epurals which are separated with a narrow anterior and an expanded posterior bone. *Apeltes* has only a single expanded epural which resembles a neural spine (Mural, 1973). On the evidence from the caudal skeleton, *Apeltes* seems most distinct from the other sticklebacks with *Spinachia* also rather different.

Gasterosteus, *Pungitius* and *Culaea* have somewhat similar pelvic skeletons supporting the pelvic fins. The pelvic bone on each side has an anterior process, a posterior process and an ascending process together with the spine and one or two soft rays. The pelvic bones are sutured in the ventral midline to form the ventral shield. This junction between the two halves of the skeleton is most strongly sutured in *Gasterosteus* and least strongly in *Culaea*. In *G. aculeatus* the anterior margin of the ventral shield is straight, in *G. wheatlandi* slightly concave, while in *Pungitius* and *Culaea* the margin is deeply concave (Fig. 74). The ventral plate tapers posteriorly in all three genera but this posterior section is longest and most well developed in *Gasterosteus*. This genus also has the most well-developed ascending process which in *G. aculeatus* tilts slightly forward, but in *G. wheatlandi* is vertical, and the dorsal margin of the ascending process is notched. *Pungitius* has an ascending process that tilts slightly backwards and has a rounded or straight dorsal margin, as does *Culaea* which has the least well-developed ascending process.

The pelvic skeletons of *Spinachia* and *Apeltes* lack an ascending process, but apart from this they are distinctly different. Each half of the pelvic skeleton of *Apeltes* consists of a broad anterior plate, strongly sutured to its partner in the ventral midline, and a posterior prong which lies lateral to the pelvic spine and is widely separated from its partner. Since these posterior prongs lie lateral to the pelvic spines, they do not seem to be equivalent to the sutured posterior processes in the pelvic skeleton of *Gasterosteus*, *Pungitius* and *Culaea*. In *Spinachia*, the pelvic skeleton is located much further back along the body than in the other sticklebacks with the entire skeleton forming an H. Each half has an elongated anterior and posterior prong which are well separated from their partners. The two halves

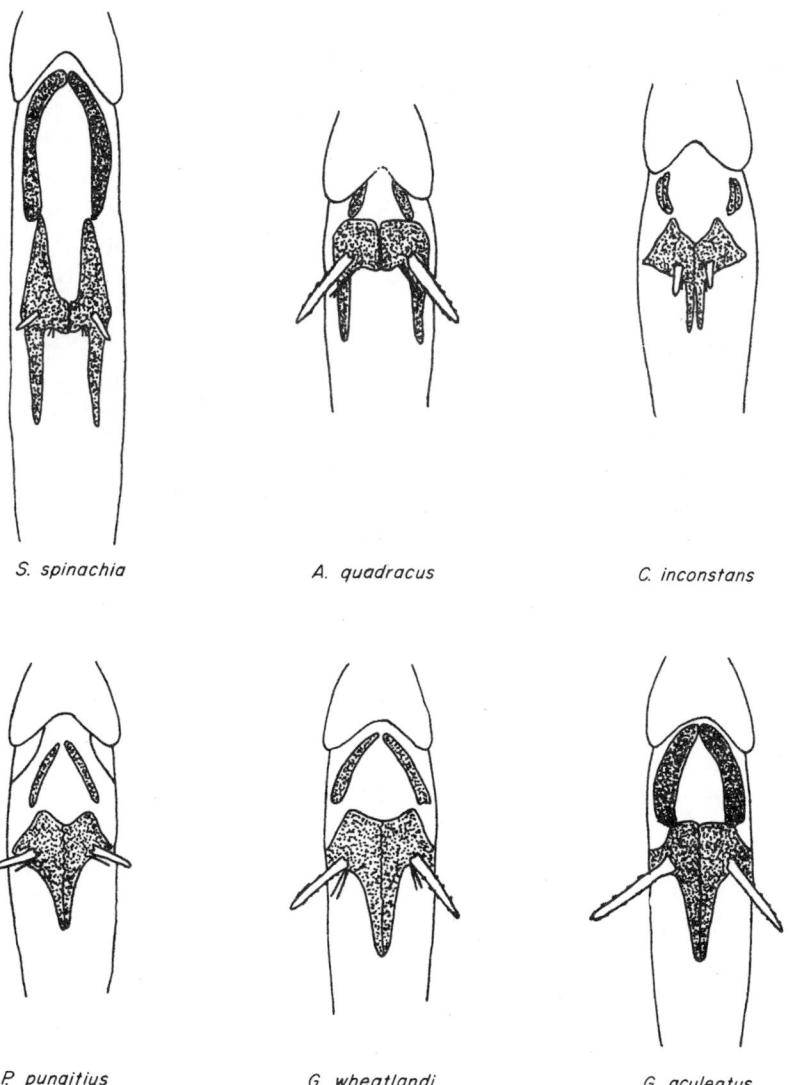

S. spinachia   A. quadracus   C. inconstans

P. pungitius   G. wheatlandi   G. aculeatus

Fig. 74. The ventral shields of the Gasterosteidae (after Bertin and Arambourg, 1958, and Nelson, 1971a).

are weakly sutured together through a pair of transverse processes which meet in the ventral midline (Nelson, 1971a; Mural, 1973).

On the evidence from the pelvic bones, *Gasterosteus*, *Pungitius* and *Culaea* seem to form one group, while *Apeltes* and *Spinachia*, although similar in one respect in that both lack the ascending process of the pelvic bone, are distinct both from each other and from the group of three genera.

Each half of the pectoral skeleton of the Gasterosteidae usually consists of a posttemporal bone, a supracleithrum, a cleithrum, scapula, coracoid and ectocoracoid and the actinosts on which all but the most dorsal of the pectoral fin rays articulate. The posttemporal, the most dorsal of these bones, abuts onto the skull and indeed is a bone of the head region (see Table III, p. 9). This association with the skull is loosest in *Culaea*, most firm in *G. aculeatus* and intermediate in the other genera. *G. wheatlandi* is curious in that it lacks the posttemporal altogether. When present, it is a forked bone with an upper and lower lobe. In *G. aculeatus* it is rhombic, while in *Culaea* and *Pungitius* it is elongated. *Apeltes* has a triangular shaped posttemporal in which the lower lobe is long and pointed. The posttemporal of *Spinachia* is broad, elongated and the two lobes are of roughly equal size. The supracleithrum is a small, narrow bone which connects the posttemporal and the cleithrum. In *G. wheatlandi* it is absent while in *Spinachia* it is either absent or very much reduced. The functional significance of the absence of a posttemporal and supracleithrum in *G. wheatlandi* is not understood. One suggestion is that this characteristic reflects the lower level of parental fanning seen in *G. wheatlandi* compared with *G. aculeatus* (McInerney, 1969), but the levels are not lower than those seen in *Pungitius* and *Culaea* both of which retain these bones. All five genera have cleithra of a similar basic shape. There is a long straight shaft which forms the ventral segment of the bone and a broad triangular head which forms the dorsal segment. *Pungitius* and *Gasterosteus* have very similar cleithra, both have a broad flange on the posterior edge of the shaft and a posterior projection on the head. *Spinachia* also has a posterior projection on the head of the cleithrum, but the shaft resembles those of *Apeltes* and *Culaea*. These two species have a rounded posterior margin to the head segment. The scapula fits under the head of the cleithrum and has a foramen on its anterior margin. This foramen is relatively large except in *Apeltes*. *Pungitius* and *Gasterosteus* have a flange on the posterior edge of the scapular underlying several of the actinosts. Ventral to the scapula lies the coracoid. The anterior edge of the coracoid lacks a foramen although a trace of a coracoid foramen occurs in *Apeltes* and *Culaea* and often in *Pungitius*. In the Aulorhynchidae which, as will be described below, are the family of teleosts most closely related to the Gasterosteidae, there is a well-developed coracoid foramen. The most ventral bone of the pectoral skeleton is the ectocoracoid (= infracleithrum) which partially overlaps and in adults fuses with the ventral portion of the coracoid. In *Gasterosteus*, *Pungitius* and *Spinachia* the ectocoracoid extends anteriorly and towards the ventral midline where it meets its partner from the other half of the pectoral skeleton. The ectocoracoid of *Gasterosteus* is a heavy triangle and in *Pungitius platygaster* this condition is approached, but in most forms of *Pungitius* and in *Spinachia* it is a long, slender bone, that of *Spinachia* overlapping with the anterior process of the pelvic skeleton. *Apeltes* lacks the anterior projection of the ectocoracoid; indeed the bone does not reach the end of the cleithrum, but meets the shaft of the cleithrum at right angles. A grooved posterior margin of the ectocoracoid of *Apeltes* surrounds part of the pelvic skeleton which in this genus lies far forward along the body. Both *Apeltes* and *Culaea* have ectocoracoids that are firmly fused to the coracoids except for the short posterior projection overlapping the pelvic skeleton.

Overall, the pectoral skeletons of *Pungitius* and *Gasterosteus* are very similar, while *Pungitius* and *Spinachia* have similar ectocoracoids and scapulas. *Apeltes* and *Culaea* have relatively similar ectocoracoids, cleithra and scapulas, and *Apeltes*, *Culaea* and to a lesser extent *Pungitius* have traces of a coracoid foramen. However, there is still no clear cut pattern of primitive and advanced characters which would allow the deduction of evolutionary relationships (Nelson, 1971a).

The operculum which covers the gills consists of four dermal bones, the opercular, subopercular, interopercular and preopercular. In *Gasterosteus* and *Culaea* the opercular is a rectangular bone with a well-developed process at the antero-dorsal corner. *Pungitius* and *Spinachia* have a triangular opercular, again with a well-developed process on the corner. The opercular of *Apeltes* is triangular but with a markedly concave dorsal margin and a less well-developed process. All the sticklebacks have a sickle-shaped subopercular, with those of *Gasterosteus*, *Culaea* and *Spinachia* showing some similarities and those of *Apeltes* and *Pungitius* also somewhat alike. The interopercular, a bone that has a sharply pointed anterior section and a broadened posterior segment, is alike in all genera. Finally the opercular series is completed by the preopercular. This bone has a vertical segment and a horizontal arm, forming a reversed L-shape. In *Culaea* and *Gasterosteus* the angle between the vertical and horizontal arms is a right angle (slightly more than 90 degrees in *G. wheatlandi*), but in *Pungitius*, *Spinachia* and to a lesser extent *Apeltes* the angle between the two arms is greater than 90 degrees. On the basis of the opercular series, there seem to be resemblances between *Gasterosteus* and *Culaea* and between *Spinachia* and *Pungitius*, but again no unambiguous set of relationships emerges (Mural, 1973).

Although the bones of the head region of *Gasterosteus* have been described by Swinnerton (1902), Kampf (1962) and Banister (1967), a complete comparative account for the stickleback family has still to be given. Consequently, only fragmentary evidence on the relationships between the genera is available from the bones of the hyoid region, the jaw and the skull.

The hyomandibular forms the posterior element in the jaw suspensorium, articulating with the neurocranium. It consists of a central shaft which divides at its dorsal end into three heads, so that the bone is shaped roughly like a cross. The most anterior of the three heads articulates with the sphenotic region of the neurocranium, fitting into a cavity at the junction of the autosphenotic and prootic bones. The next head, that directly in line with the shaft, also articulates with the neurocranium for it fits into a depression in the autopterotic, but the posterior head articulates with the opercular of the opercular series. A flange of bone on the anterior edge of the hyomandibular articulates with the metapterygoid, the next bone in the sequence of the suspensorium. In *Gasterosteus*, the hyomandibular forms an angle of about 80 degrees with the body axis and the sphenotic and opercular heads meet the shaft at an acute angle, whereas in *Pungitius* the angle to the body axis is about 65 degrees and the sphenotic and opercular heads meet the shaft almost at right angles. *Culaea* has a hyomandibular that is intermediate in form and orientation between those of *Gasterosteus* and *Pungitius*. The hyomandibular of *Apeltes* is like that of *Gasterosteus* or *Culaea* but has a particularly well-developed articulation with the metapterygoid. Perhaps this is because *Apeltes* ventilates its nest by sucking rather than the fanning used by the other genera and so requires a more robust connection between these two elements of the suspensorium. In *Spinachia* the hyomandibular makes a markedly acute angle with the body axis, an orientation related to the elongation of the head in this species (Mural, 1973).

A metapterygoid extends from the anterior edge of the hyomandibular down to the symplectic, adhering to the lateral face of the symplectic. In turn, the anterior end of the symplectic articulates with the quadrate, the bone which forms part of the jaw articulation. The symplectic of *Gasterosteus* tapers anteriorly from a relatively broad posterior end. Both the ventral and dorsal portions bear a bony flange with the dorsal flange being rather broad. *Culaea* has a similar symplectic although the dorsal flange is weaker, while

Pungitius has a long, narrow symplectic with even weaker ventral and dorsal flanges. In *Apeltes*, the dorsal flange on the symplectic interdigitates with a process of the pterygoid, the bone that lies anterior to the symplectic and dorsal to the quadrate. *Spinachia* has an elongated, poorly ossified symplectic, but the dorsal flange is expanded compared to that of the other species and as in *Apeltes* it interdigitates with pterygoid (Banister, 1967; Mural, 1973).

Articulating with the anterior end of the symplectic is the quadrate, and it is this bone that together with the articular bone forms the jaw articulation. The quadrate is a fan-shaped bone with a long, thin, ventral process that is attached to the anterior end of the preopercular. In *Spinachia*, the ventral process is both long and deep while only a shallow groove marks the division of the quadrate into two segments. Dorsal to the quadrate there is the pterygoid bone. Teleost usually have a pterygoid series that consists of three bones, the meta-, endo- and ectopterygoid, but in the Gasterosteidae there are only two bones in the series, a metapterygoid and a tri-radiate ptyergoid. Banister (1967) has argued, partly on the basis of Swinnerton's (1902) embryological evidence, that the tri-radiate pterygoid of the sticklebacks represents a fused ecto- and endo-pterygoid, serving the functions of both bones. Mural (1973) believes that the endopterygoid is missing in the sticklebacks and that the tri-radiate bone is an ectopterygoid. The posterior process of the pterygoid is a broad sheet of bone that makes contact with the symplectic, the small middle process adheres to the quadrate, and the most anterior process, the palatine process, is contiguous with the autopalatine bone. *Gasterosteus* has broad pterygoid bones, those of *Pungitius* are narrow, with those of *Culaea* intermediate. *Apeltes* has broad pterygoids but also has a dorsal flange on the edge of the posterior process. This posterior process in *Spinachia* is very long and deep (Banister, 1967; Mural, 1973).

This evidence from the bones of the head region suggests that *Gasterosteus*, *Pungitius* and *Culaea* are a group of similar forms, with *Apeltes* and *Spinachia* somewhat distinct. *Spinachia* is particularly set apart from the others because of the marked elongation of the snout.

Taking the morphological evidence as a whole, a grouping of *Culaea*, *Pungitius* and *Gasterosteus* seems justified with *Apeltes* and *Spinachia* distinct from that grouping but also distinct from each other. Nevertheless, there are affinities between *Pungitius* and *Spinachia*, for example in the high number of dorsal spines which incline away from the midline and in some aspects of the pectoral skeleton and the opercular series; between *Spinachia* and *Apeltes* in the lack of an ascending process in the pelvic skeleton and the symplectic-pterygoid interdigitation; and between *Culaea* and *Apeltes* in the shape of the pectoral skeleton. Given these ambiguities in the affinities between the species, evidence from fields other than comparative morphology and anatomy is required. But it must be remembered that apart from *Gasterosteus aculeatus* knowledge of the anatomy and morphology and the morphogenesis of the stickle-backs is extremely restricted.

An aspect of the biology of the stickleback that has received considerable attention is the reproductive behaviour of the males of the various species. From such studies a number of points relevant to the evolutionary relationships between the genera emerge (Hall, 1956; Reisman and Cade, 1967).

In the phase of courtship that precedes the entry of the gravid female into the nest of the male, *Apeltes* and *Culaea* males show bouts of pummelling the female, whereas in *Gasterosteus* and *Pungitius* the zig-zagging or jumping of the male is the most conspicuous component of this phase of courtship. Rowland (1974a) showed that in the spiralling shown by the *Apeltes* male after he has pummelled the female, there is a zig-zag component, but this component was detected only during an analysis of movie film and is not obvious to the naked eye. The courtship of *Spinachia* has not been described in detail, but it seems to be relatively unspecialised with the approach of the male to the female direct and aggressive. Once the female is in the nest, the males of *Apeltes* and *Spinachia* induce her to spawn by tail biting, whereas *Culaea*, *Pungitius* and *Gasterosteus* all show quivering.

Gasterosteus, always, and *Pungitius* in some North American populations have nests on the substrate, the other genera and probably most populations of *Pungitius* have nests that are built in weed off the substrate, though *Apeltes* will build a ground nest if vegetation is not available (Rowland, 1974b). *Gasterosteus* and *Pungitius* are also the two genera in which the nest has a complete tunnel with both an entrance and an exit; this tunnel is formed when the male creeps through the nest. In *G. aculeatus*, nest-directed activities such as creeping through, fanning and glueing play an important, though not completely understood role in courtship, and correlated with this is the performance of dorsal pricking by the male during courtship, a behaviour that has not been described in any other species of stickleback.

Apeltes is unique for its builds a multi-tiered nest, which it ventilates by sucking and not by the fanning so characteristic of all the other stickleback species. Another aspect of the reproductive behaviour of *Apeltes* that may also be unique is that the male remains willing to court and mate with gravid females during his parental phase.

Pungitius and *Culaea* males become dark coloured or black during the breeding season, as do males of a few unusual populations of *G. aculeatus*. Since colour is a character particularly likely to be affected by selection pressures imposed by predation, it is not at all clear that this character provides any evidence of a close evolutionary relationship between *Culaea* and *Pungitius*. These two genera also share the characteristics that they show insertion glueing during nest building or repair and build nurseries for the young when they hatch. But again these similarities may be a result of convergent evolution reflecting similar selection pressures operating on both *Pungitius* and *Culaea*. The apparent similarities in the ecology of these two genera makes it particularly difficult to judge whether similarities between the two are a reflection of their ecology or represent a particularly close evolutionary relationship that is reflected in their ecology, behaviour and morphology. A study of populations of *Culaea* and *Pungitius* that are sympatric would be of interest from both an ecological and an evolutionary point of view.

Gasterosteus, Culaea and *Pungitius* have the most complex and highly organised patterns of aggressive, courtship and parental behaviour, while *Spinachia* has the least complex repertoire, though this interpretation may have to be changed as more becomes known about the behaviour of this last species. *Apeltes*, although it has a relatively simple pattern of aggressive behaviour, shows such peculiarities of nest construction and parental behaviour and indeed of the temporal organisation of the reproductive period that it resembles neither *Spinachia* nor the other three genera.

Comparative studies on the chromosomes of the sticklebacks provide further evidence of the affinities between the species (Chen and Reisman, 1970; Muramoto and Igarashi, 1969; Muramoto *et al.*, 1969). In *Apeltes* and *Culaea* the diploid number of chromosomes is forty-six, while in *Gasterosteus* and *Pungitius* the diploid number is forty-two. Although *Apeltes* and *Culaea* have the same number of chromosomes, there are distinct differences between the two genera in chromosome morphology. The species that have a diploid number of forty-two all have four pairs of large biarmed chromosomes but apart from this there is a marked difference in the morphology of the chromosomes between *Pungitius* and *Gasterosteus*. There are only slight differences in the morphology of chromosomes between *G. aculeatus* and *G. wheatlandi* and the same is true for the chromosomes of *P. pungitius pungitius* and *P. p. sinensis* while no difference could be detected between the chromosomes *P. pungitius pungitius* and *P. p. tymensis*. All the species so far studied have a pair of distinctive chromosomes, a large submetacentric pair, which indicates a monophyletic origin for the sticklebacks, although the number and morphology of the chromosomes of *Spinachia* have not yet been studied (Table XV).

Amongst teleosts there is some evidence for a trend towards a decrease in chromosome number and in the DNA content of the nuclei with increasing specialisation. This implies that the evolutionarily more advanced fish will have a lower number of chromosomes and less DNA than evolutionarily less advanced fish (Chen and

TABLE XV

Karyotypes of the Gasterosteidae (after Muromoto *et al.*, 1969 and Chen and Reisman, 1970).

Species	Chromosome number (diploid)	Morphology of chromosomes			
		M	SM	A	AN
Apeltes quadracus	46	12	20	14	78
Culaea inconstans	46	0	8	38	54
Gasterosteus aculeatus	42	6	6	30	54
Gasterosteus wheatlandi	42	4	6	32	52
Pungitius pungitius	42	16	12	14	70

M metacentric chromosomes, SM submetacentric chromosomes, A acentric chromosomes, AN arm numbers.

Reisman, 1970; Hinegardner, 1968). If there is a trend towards a reduction in chromosome number, then it suggests that the chromosome number of *Apeltes* and *Culaea* represents the more primitive condition. It is more plausible to derive the *Gasterosteus* chromosome number and morphology from the *Culaea* karyotype than from the *Apeltes* karyotype, which is morphologically distinct. A provisional scheme of the relationships based on karyotypes was given by Chen and Reisman (1970), although it is recognised that the scheme may have to be drastically revised when the karyotype of *Spinachia* becomes known. *Culaea* represents a conservative derivative of the common ancestor, with *Apeltes* a distinct offshoot, so it is *Culaea* which forms the bridge to the *Gasterosteus* and *Pungitius* groups. This scheme is partially compatible with the morphological, anatomical and behavioural evidence which also suggests that *Culaea*, *Pungitius* and *Gasterosteus* are more closely related to each other than to either *Spinachia* or *Apeltes*, and that this latter genus, although having some affinities with *Spinachia* and *Culaea*, is relatively isolated. It is perhaps unfortunate for this scheme that *Culaea* has a lower DNA content per cell than *G. aculeatus*, for, on the second criterion given above, this implies that *Culaea* is more specialised than *Gasterosteus*. A haploid cell of *Culaea* contains 0.67×10^{-12} g of DNA whereas a haploid cell of *G. aculeatus* contains 0.70×10^{-12} g (Hinegardner, 1968).

Physiologically, *Culaea* is also more specialised than *Gasterosteus*, *Pungitius* or *Apeltes*. It is the only stickleback that is entirely restricted to fresh water and it has the lowest salinity tolerance of the five genera (Nelson, 1968a). *Spinachia* is restricted to marine or brackish water and is never found in fresh water and so represents the other end of the spectrum of salinity tolerance of the stickle-backs. If, as some evidence discussed below suggests, the sticklebacks have evolved from a group of marine fishes, *Culaea* must be regarded as the most specialised although much of the other evidence argues that it represents a conservative stickleback.

Evidence from the geographical distribution of the sticklebacks does not help to clarify their evolutionary relationships. *Apeltes* and *Culaea* are entirely restricted to North America, and *Spinachia* to western Europe, while *Gasterosteus* and *Pungitius* are widely dis-tributed in America, Asia and Europe. No obvious centre of origin for the sticklebacks can be detected. In America there are four genera represented by five species, and in Eurasia there are three genera represented by four species (this is assuming that *G. aculeatus* and *P. pungitius* are not split into several species). Although the euryhalinity of the sticklebacks argues that they originated in the sea and have colonised fresh water, this is only conjecture, whose tentative nature is only underscored by the absence of a good fossil record of the sticklebacks.

Modern biochemical and chemical methods of investigating phylo-genetic relationships such as immunological techniques, electro-phoretic techniques and the analysis of the amino acid sequences of proteins (Avise, 1974) or DNA hybridisation experiments (Shields and Straus, 1975) have not been used on the Gasterosteidae, with the exception of a comparison of the immunological characteristics of the blood of *G. aculeatus* and *P. pungitius* (Penczak, 1961b). Another approach that might prove profitable would be the use of more objective measures of the similarities between species. As yet no one has attempted to apply the techniques of numerical taxonomy to the Gasterosteidae.

A difficulty that becomes more and more apparent as the relationships of the sticklebacks to each other are considered is that for most of the characters analysed there is no understanding of the adaptive significance of these characters. It is not known what biological problems are being solved by particular characters and so it is not possible to define the environmental conditions under which the characters might have evolved. For example, the hypural plate in the caudal skeleton of *Gasterosteus* is divided into an upper and lower segment, yet in *Culaea*, *Pungitius* and *Apeltes* the hypural plate is undivided, but the functional significance of a divided hypural plate is not known. *Apeltes* ventilates its nest by sucking, all other sticklebacks ventilate the nest by fanning, but the functional significance of this difference is not clearly understood. In *Gasterosteus* and *Culaea*, the dorsal spines lie along the midline whereas in the other genera they are inclined alternately to one side or the other, but the significance of these two arrangements is not known. Perhaps it will never be known.

Although the phylogenetic relationships within the stickleback family remain unclear, there is no doubt that the Gasterosteidae is a natural family with all the members having a common ancestory. The question now arises as to which other teleosts have affinities with the Gasterosteidae and which of the modern sticklebacks comes closest to forming a link to other families of teleosts.

In 1866, a fish was collected from waters of the north-west Pacific off British Columbia and was identified as *Gasterosteus spinachia*, a synonym of *S. spinachia*. It is now known that *Spinachia* is restricted to western Europe, while the fish from the Pacific was a tubesnout *Aulorhynchus flavidus* (Clemens and Wilby, 1961). *Aulorhynchus* is a member of the family Aulorhynchidae which contains only two genera each of which contains a single species, *Aulorhynchus flavidus* Gill and *Aulichthys japonicus* Brevoort. Both species have limited distributions and both are entirely marine. *Aulorhynchus* occurs along the Pacific coast from Sitka, Alaska as far south as Punta Banta, California, whilst *Aulichthys* is found only in the seas around Korea and Japan.

Morphologically, the superficial resemblence between the Aulorhynchidae and *Spinachia* is very close, for the Aulorhynchidae are very elongate with a long, tapering caudal peduncle and a long snout. Along the back, there are twenty-four to twenty-six short, isolated, fixed spines in front of a triangular dorsal fin with nine or ten rays. The anal fin is also triangular, again with nine or ten rays preceded by a minute spine. As in *Spinachia*, the pectoral fins are broad with eleven rays, but the pelvic fins are far more distinct than in *Spinachia* for each contains a spine and four rays. The caudal fin is distinctly forked, a characteristic not seen in any of the sticklebacks. Tubesnouts, like the sticklebacks, have a row of lateral plates and lack the normal teleost scales. *Aulichthys* has about fifty-two plates in the lateral row, the plates overlap and each bears a small, posteriorly directed spine. *Aulorhynchus* has between fifty-three and fifty-seven overlapping lateral plates but these lack spines although plates three to six have a unique dorso-posteriorly directed wing. Both species have plates along the dorsal and ventral midlines, but these do not meet the lateral plates in the way they do along the caudal peduncle of *Spinachia* (Banister, 1967; Nelson, 1971a).

These resemblances between the Aulorhynchidae and the Gasterosteidae extend to details of the skeletal anatomy. In the bones of the head region the Aulorhynchidae show a number of features that are found in the Gasterosteidae yet are relatively unusual in the teleosts as a whole. These features include the tri-radiate pterygoid which probably consists of a fused endo- and ectopterygoid, a ventrally directed projection of the frontal which contacts a dorsal projection of the parasphenoid (see description in Chapter 1), the absence of the supraethmoid, and also of jaw ligaments although the jaw is protrusible. The symplectic of the Aulorhynchidae resembles that of *Spinachia* more than that of *Gasterosteus* and the other short-snouted sticklebacks, for it has an expanded dorsal flange. The branchial skeleton is similar in the two families, and the caudal skeleton of the Aulorhynchidae, which consists of a single hypural plate and a single epural, is rather similar to the caudal skeleton in *Culaea, Pungitius, Apeltes* and perhaps *Spinachia* (Banister, 1967).

Some of the differences between the Aulorhynchidae and Gasterosteidae suggest that the former are less specialised than the sticklebacks, and may represent an evolutionary line that has diverged less from the basic teleost stock. If this is so, it provides support for the hypothesis that *Spinachia* is the most primitive of the Gasterosteidae, a position supported by the relatively simple reproductive behaviour of *Spinachia* and its restriction to a marine environment. The Aulorhynchidae have pelvic fins which consist of a short spine and four soft fin rays, so that the spine does not dominate the pelvic fin as it does in the sticklebacks. The pelvic skeleton of the tubesnouts consists of an enlarged anterior process and a reduced posterior process, and there is no ascending process so that the pelvic skeleton resembles those of *Spinachia* and *Apeltes* rather than of *Gasterosteus*, *Culaea* and *Pungitius*. In the tubesnouts, the two halves of the pelvic skeleton are only weakly sutured together to form a ventral plate. The pectoral skeleton has a coracoid with a large foramen that opens anteriorly. Only *Apeltes* and *Culaea* regularly show traces of a coracoid foramen. Further less specialised features are found in the skull of the Aulorhynchidae. There is a complete series of infra-orbital bones bordering the eye, whereas in the Gasterosteidae there is a gap in the infraorbital series (see Chapter 1), a gap that is largest in *Apeltes*. The tubesnouts retain the pterosphenoid bone which is lost in the Gasterosteidae, and they have a cephalic lateral line system which in the sticklebacks is very much reduced. The tubesnouts have a higher number of branchiostegal rays, four compared with the three of the sticklebacks (Banister, 1967; Nelson, 1971a). Another difference between the two families is in the ribs. All the sticklebacks have both epipleural and pleural ribs, but *Aulichthys* has only pleural ribs while *Aulorhynchus* appears to lack all ribs; the lateral plates in the abdominal region have internal transverse processes which make contact with the transverse process of the vertebrae and so resemble ribs (Nelson, 1971a).

Although the evidence that indicates the close phylogenetic relationship between the Aulorhynchidae and the Gasterosteidae is morphological and anatomical, some observations on the repro-ductive behaviour of *Aulorhynchus* are also pertinent. In contrast to *Spinachia*, a solitary fish, *Aulorhynchus* normally lives in schools which may contain several thousand individuals. But in the breeding season males start to defend territories often around plants of the giant kelp, *Macrocystis*. The male secretes glue over a stipe of the plant, bending the top part of the stipe downwards, so that the pneumatocysts of the stipe form a sort of umbrella. The eggs are laid so that each egg mass rings the stipe, at the junction of the stipe and the branch that bears a pneumatocyst. A series of these egg masses may be laid down the length of the stipe so that each pneumatocyst on a section of the stipe bears a ring of eggs at its lower junction. The male then defends this egg-laden stipe, driving away intruders by charging directly at them (Limbaugh, 1962). This reproductive pattern of *Aulorhynchus* could be interpreted as a primitive form of the pattern that reaches its evolutionary peak with the sticklebacks. The male *Aulorhynchus* does not seem to bring material to the glued area, but the addition of this behavioural element might result in a nest similar to that of *Spinachia*. More reminiscent of the multi-tiered nest of *Apeltes* is the way in which the egg masses are strung out along the length of the stipe. It must be added that Breder and Rosen (1966) in their review of the modes of reproduction in fishes interpreted the glueing and spawning behaviour of *Aulorhynchus* as deriving from a former nest-building habit and not as being more primitive.

Aulichthys deposits its eggs in the peribranchial cavity of the ascidian *Cynthia roretzi*, a behaviour that has no parallel in the Gasterosteidae (Uchida, 1934).

If, on the basis of the anatomical and behavioural evidence, it is assumed that the Aulorhynchidae are less specialised than the Gasterosteidae and so represent a phylogenetically more conservative group closely related to the sticklebacks, then this suggests that *Spinachia* can be regarded as the most primitive of the modern sticklebacks. The mosaic pattern of characters in the Gasterosteidae argues against any of the modern sticklebacks being ancestral to the family. This thesis implies that the stock that gave rise to both the Aulorhynchidae and Gasterosteidae were long-snouted forms. The contemporary restricted distribution of *Aulorhynchus*, *Aulichthys* and *Spinachia* could then be interpreted as an indication of the relative lack of success of the more primitive long-snouted forms when compared with the evolutionarily more advanced forms such as *Gasterosteus*. The evolution of the short-snouted forms would have taken place within the Gasterosteidae after they had become distinct from the Aulorhynchidae. An alternative hypothesis would be to argue that the ancestral stock of both families consisted of short-snouted forms, but these had the evolutionary potential of giving rise to long-snouted forms, a potential manifested independently in the Aulorhynchidae and *Spinachia*. On this hypothesis, the restricted distribution of these forms is a measure of their specialisation and the wide-spread distribution of *Gasterosteus* and *Pungitius* is because they are less specialised and more adaptable. *Apeltes*, being both short-snouted and having a restricted distribution, falls neatly into neither hypothesis. It is curious that the four genera that are wholly or largely restricted to the sea have non-overlapping geographical distributions. *Aulichthys* is found around Japan, *Aulorhynchus* along the Pacific coast of North America, *Apeltes* along the Atlantic coast of North America and *Spinachia* along the Atlantic coast of Europe. Such a mutually exclusive distribution is not found in the sticklebacks that have a wide distribution in fresh water, where *Pungitius* and *Gasterosteus* are frequently sympatric, as are *Culaea* and *Pungitius* in North America.

A tentative phylogenetic tree for the sticklebacks and tubesnouts is shown in Fig. 75. In this scheme it is accepted that the ancestral stock of both families consisted of long-snouted forms. This scheme is provided more as a target for informed criticism than as a definitive statement, and alternative schemes given by Bertin (1925) and Leiner (1934) are provided for comparison. A series of studies making use of modern techniques for studying phylogenetic relation-

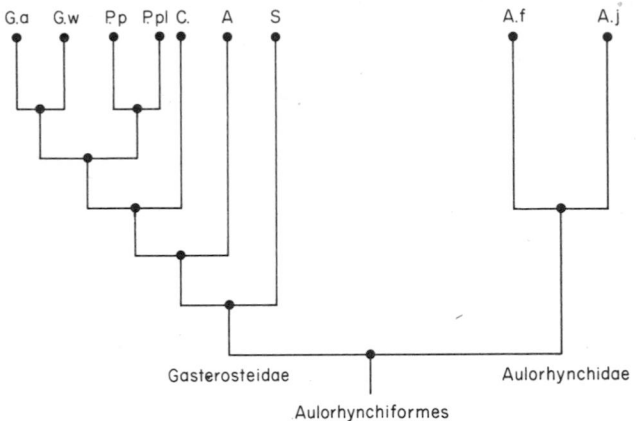

Wootton (this chapter)

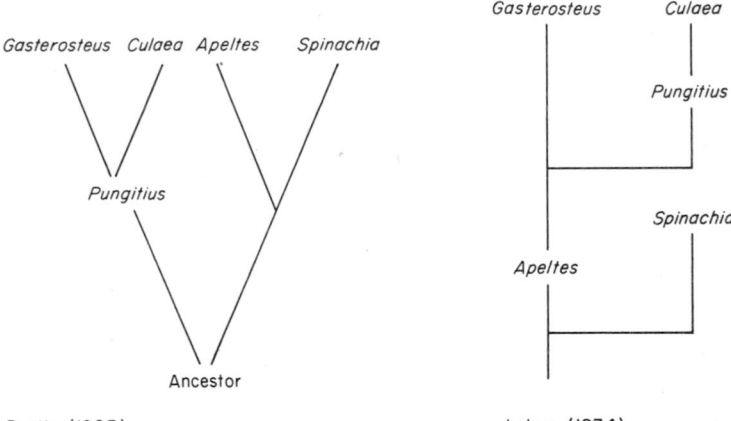

Bertin (1925)   Leiner (1934)

Fig. 75. Three phylogenetic schemes for the Gasterosteidae. Key to lettering: A, *A. quadracus*; A.f, *Aulorhynchus flavidus*; A.j, *Aulichthys japonicus*; C, *C. inconstans*; G. a, *G. aculeatus*; G.w, *G. wheatlandi*; P.p, *P. pungitius*; P.pl, *P. platygaster*; S, S. *spinachia.*

ships and which embrace both the Gasterosteidae and the Aulorhynchidae are required to clarify the situation.

There is no doubt that the Gasterosteidae and the Aulorhynchidae form a natural group that has descended from a common ancestor; indeed sometimes it is suggested that they should be combined as one family. There is considerable doubt as to the phylogenetic relationship of these families to the teleosts as a whole.

In most classifications of the teleosts, the two families have been

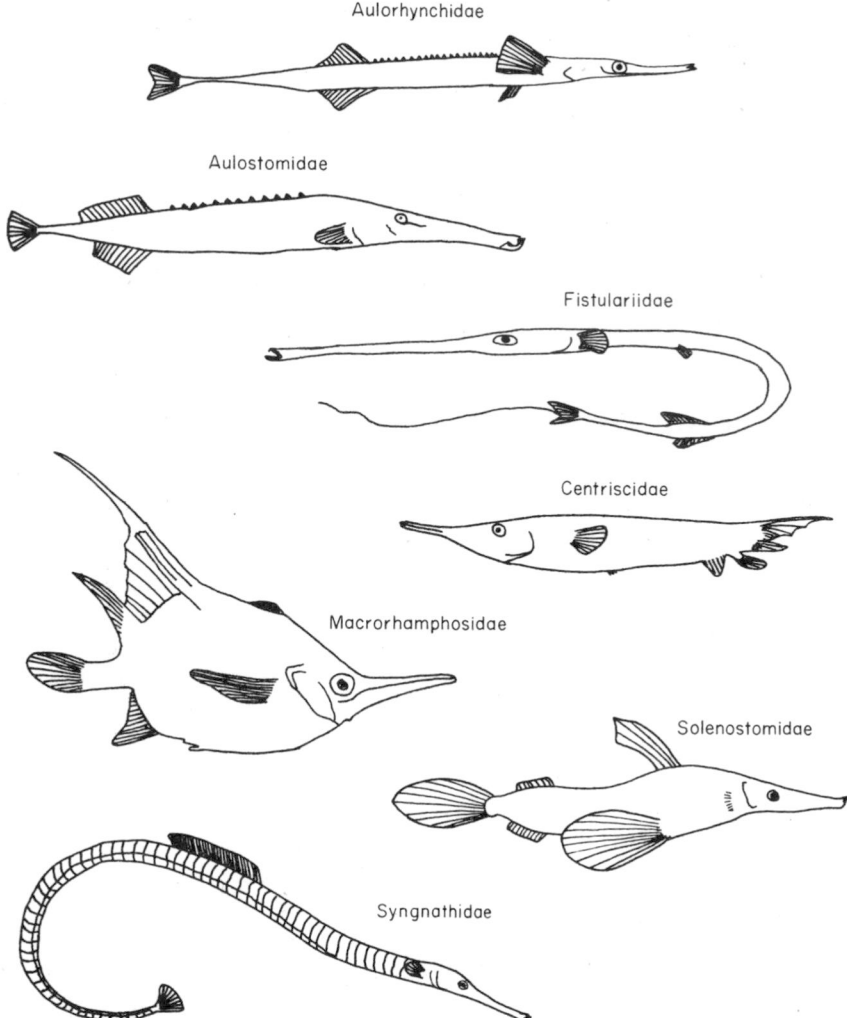

Fig. 76. The Gasterosteiformes, excluding the sticklebacks.

placed close to the Aulostomidae, Fistulariidae, Centriscidae, Macro-rhamphosidae, Solenostomidae and Syngnathidae (Cope, 1870; Smith Woodward, 1901; Swinnerton, 1902; Boulenger, 1904; Goodrich, 1909; Gregory, 1933; Berg, 1940; Bertin and Arambourg, 1958). All these families consist of somewhat odd-looking fish, often with an elongated snout and a body protected with bony plates rather than scales (Fig. 76). All are marine.

Aulostoma is an elongated fish, with a long snout. In front of the dorsal fin there is a series of isolated dorsal fin spines, but the pelvic fins are devoid of spines. The body is covered with small ctenoid scales rather than bony plates. It occurs in the Atlantic along the coasts of tropical America where it grows to a length of about 60 cm. Nothing is known about its reproductive behaviour.

Fistularia is a very elongated fish; *F. tabaccaria* has been reported to reach a length of nearly 2 m. The snout forms a long tube terminating in a narrow mouth with minute teeth. Both scales and bony plates are absent so the body is entirely naked. One peculiarity is that the caudal fin has a long filament supported by the middle fin rays. The genus, which one author described as "gigantic marine sticklebacks", lives in tropical and sub-tropical waters of the Atlantic and Indo-Pacific Oceans. One species, *F. petimba*, is known to produce pelagic eggs, but nothing is known of reproductive behaviour of this family.

Centriscus and *Macrorhamphosus* are both moderately elongated fish with a long snout forming a tube. They have two dorsal fins, the first of which is unusual because the supports are formed primarily by inter-neurals of the vertebral column and not by fin rays. The fifth element in this first dorsal fin is a large spine. *Centricus* has a body protected by bony plates, whereas *Macrorhamphosus* is protected by "scales" and this armour consists only of rows of thoracic plates and three rows of plates along the ventral keel. It is not clear whether the "scales" of *Macrorhamphosus* are homologous with the bony plates of *Centricus*. They are found in the Atlantic, Indian and Pacific Oceans.

Solenostomus is an elongated, laterally compressed fish from the Indian and Pacific Oceans. Again the snout is tube-like. The body is partially covered with star-shaped bony plates. In *Solenostomus*, the female has pelvic fins that are modified to form a brood pouch, so that in this family it is the female that assumes the parental role.

The Syngnathidae are the pipefishes and seahorses. These usually have an elongate body, with a tubiform snout, and the body is protected by bony rings. Both the Syngnathidae and the Solenostomidae have gill lamellae in the form of tufted lobes, and so there has been a tendency to group the two families as the Lophobranchii. In the Syngnathidae the males assume a parental role, for they have a brood pouch into which the fertilised eggs are transferred and kept until they hatch. There are complex courtship and mating behaviour patterns to ensure that the transfer of eggs from the female to the male is achieved. Of the families considered in this list, the Syngnathidae is represented by the most species and has the widest distribution.

What are the characters that link these families to the Aulorhynchidae and Gasterosteidae and led Swinnerton (1902) to unite all the families in the order Thoracostei and Goodrich (1909) to place them all in the order Gasterosteiformes? A list of the characters is given in Table XVI, they include the possession of bony plates rather than scales, a tendency for the snout to be elongated, the large size of supraoccipital bone which prevents the parietals from meeting, the elongation of the symplectic, the reduction or complete

TABLE XVI

Characters of the Gasterosteiformes (Thoracostei).

1. Abdominal position of pelvic fins.
2. Tendency for a reduction in the pharyngeal apparatus.
3. Presence of "interclavicles" (= ectocoracoids).
4. Simple posttemporals.
5. Body plates.
6. Elongation of the snout.
7. Absence of the opisthotic and basisphenoid bones.
8. Sculpturing of roofing bones of the skull.
9. Large size of supraoccipital which separates the parietals widely.
10. Forwards slant of the hyomandibular.
11. Elongation of sympletic and presence of flange on its dorsal margin.
12. Reduction or suppression of metapterygoid.
13. Shape of the ethmoid.
14. Acrartete condition (single articulation between palato-quadrate and ethmoid).

absence of the metapterygoid, the tendency for a reduction in the branchial apparatus, and the presence of "interclavicles" or ectocoracoids in the pectoral skeleton.

A recent classification of the teleosts by Greenwood *et al.* (1966) attempts to provide a phyletic rather than a typological classification, that is a classification that deliberately attempts to provide a picture of the evolutionary relationships rather than simply reflecting similarities in body structure. This classification continues the tradition of linking all the families in a single order:

Order : Gasterosteiformes
(a) Suborder : Gasterosteoidei (Thoracostei)
    Family : Gasterosteidae
    Family : Aulorhynchidae
    Family : Indostomidae

(b)   Suborder : Aulostomoidei
        Family : Aulostomidae
        Family : Fistulariidae
        Family : Macrorhamphosidae
        Family : Centriscidae
(c)   Suborder : Syngnathoidei
        Family : Solenostomidae
        Family : Syngnathidae.

This classification does not conform to the tradition that the Gasterosteiformes are at a lower evolutionary level than the Acanthopterygii, the evolutionarily most advanced of the teleosts. Greenwood *et al.* (1966) place the Gasterosteiformes within the Superorder Acanthopterygii though they place the order off the main trend of acanthopterygian evolution and suggest that a detailed analysis of the order may show that it is polyphyletic and therefore not a natural grouping.

The evidence linking the Gasterosteoidei with the other two suborders is not so over-whelming that this grouping has invariably been made. Regan (1929) placed the sticklebacks and tube-snouts in the suborder Gasteroidea, which formed part of the order Scleroparei. Other members of this order were the Scorpaenoidei (fish such as the redfish, *Sebastes marinus*) and the Cottidoidea (fish such as the bullhead, *Cottus gobio*). Quite separate from the Scleroparei was the order Solenichthyes which contained two suborders:

Suborder I
        A. Aulostomidae, Fistulariidae
        B. Centriscidae, Macrorhamphosidae
Suborder II
        A. Solenostomidae
        B. Syngnathidae

A recent revision of the Gasterosteiformes (*sensu* Greenwood *et al.*) is that of Banister (1967), who argues three theses. The first of these is not of major significance in the context of this chapter; it concerns the position of the Indostomidae. This family is represented by one species, *Indostomus paradoxus* Prashad and Mukerji, a perculiar little fish from fresh water in Burma. Its inclusion in the Gasterosteiformes was based on superficial characters and it is probably completely unrelated to the sticklebacks and the others (Banister, 1970) though Fraser (1972) has pointed out that nearly all the reasons that Banister cites for removing the Indostomidae from the Gasterosteiformes are negative characters, that is characters have been lost rather than new characters evolved. The second thesis is that Gasterosteiformes retain a number of features which argue against their incorporation in the Acanthopterygii. A mixture of relatively primitive and relatively advanced characters suggests that the Gasterosteiformes have approached the acanthopterygian grade of evolution independently of the main line of teleost evolution. This placement of the Gasterosteiformes below the Acanthopterygii follows a tradition established by Cope (1870) and reinforced by Swinnerton (1902), Goodrich (1909) and Berg (1940). Banister's third thesis is that while the Aulorhynchidae and Gasterosteidae are clearly related, it is much less clear that they are related to the other two suborders, the Aulostomoidei and the Syngnathoidei. Gregory (1933) thought that the Gasterosteidae and Aulorhynchidae probably had a separate origin from the other families, though he included them with the other families in the order Thoracostei.

There are several characters which suggest that the Gasterosteiformes are not part of the Acanthopterygii, though it must be added that there are more than 7000 species of fish in the Acanthopterygii, most of which have not been studied in detail so that this superorder still has to be defined in a relatively precise way (Rosen, 1973). In the Gasterosteiformes, the pelvic fins are in an abdominal position, whereas in the acanthopterygians the pelvic fins take up a more anterior position in the thoracic or jugular region. Another primitive feature of the Gasterosteiformes is that the occipital condyle, the skull component of the articulation between the skull and vertebral column, is formed entirely by the basioccipital with the exoccipitals taking no part. The branchial skeleton of the non-gasterosteid Gasterosteiformes is also relatively primitive. *Aulostoma* has a cartilaginous suprapharyngobranchial and lacks a dorsal retractor muscle connecting the third pharyngobranchial to the vertebral column. In *Fistularia*, there are three large, toothed pharyngobranchials arranged in a line. *Gasterosteus* has a "percid" type of branchial skeleton, so that in this character it reaches the acanthopterygian grade of evolution. In most acanthopterygians and in many teleosts that are evolutionarily more primitive such as the Salmonidae and the Esocidae, the ethmoid in the olfactory region of the skull articulates with the palatine-pterygoid at two points (the disartete condition). But in the Gasterosteiformes, there is only one point of articulation between the ethmoid and palatine-pterygoid (the acrartete condition). The metapterygoid in the Gasterosteiformes tends to be reduced or

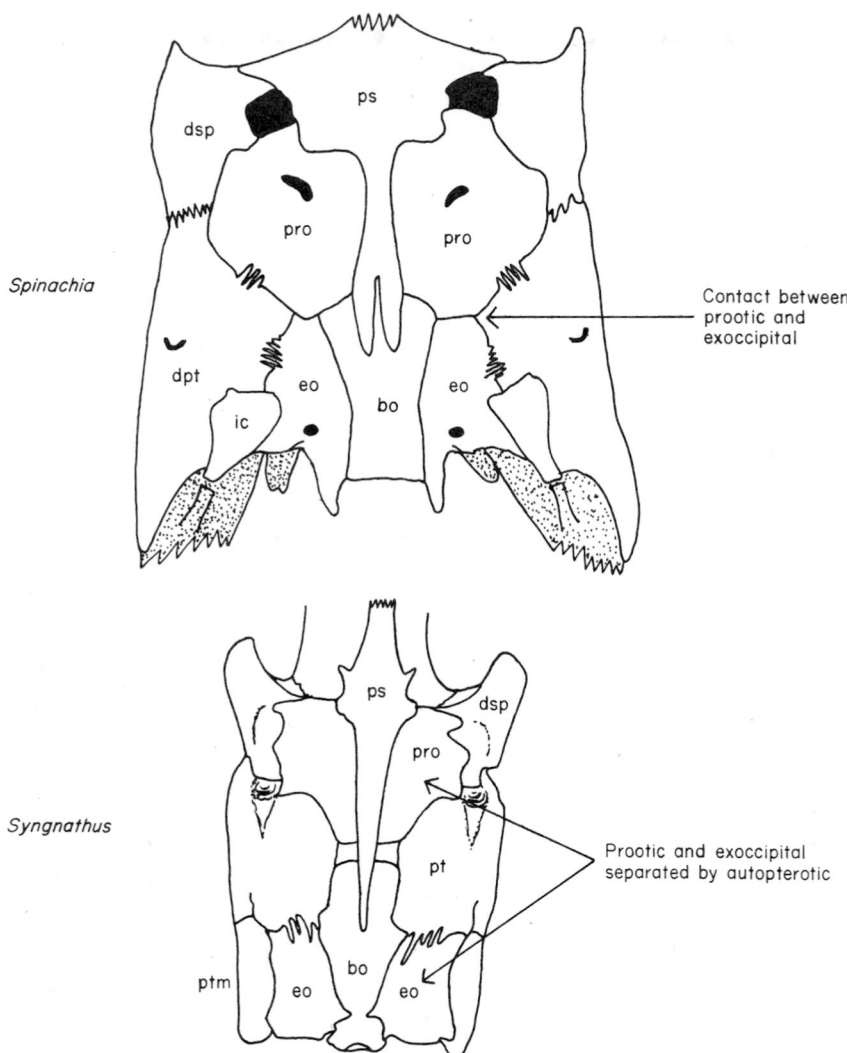

Fig. 77. Comparison of floor of brain case of *Spinachia* and *Syngnathus* (after Banister, 1967). Key to lettering: bo, basioccipital; dpt, dermopterotic; dsp, dermosphenotic; eo, exoccipital; ic, intercalary; pro, prootic; ps, parasphenoid; pt, autopterotic.

absent, but the symplectic is elongated with an expanded dorsal flange (Swinnerton, 1902; Banister, 1967).

While the presence of the dorsal lamina on the symplectic is one of the characters that sets the Gasterosteiformes off from the Acanthopterygii, the fate of metapterygoid helps to subdivide the Gasterosteiformes. This bone is retained in the Gasterosteidae and

Aulorhynchidae but absent in the Aulostomidae, Fistulariidae, Syngnathidae and Solenostomidae. Another important feature separating the sticklebacks and tubesnouts from the other families in the Gasterosteiformes is the arrangement of the floor of the brain case. In the Gasterosteidae and Aulorhynchidae, the exoccipitals make contact with the prootics, an arrangement that is common in the teleosts, but in the the other families of the Gasterosteiformes the exoccipitals do not meet the prootics (Fig. 77). In *Solenostoma*, the basioccipital is expanded laterally and these lateral expansions lie between the exoccipitals and prootics. In the other familes, the autopterotics are expanded medially and contact the basioccipital so that the autopterotic lies between the exoccipital and prootic. The pre-maxilla of the Gasterosteidae and Aulorhynchidae has an ascending process, a feature associated with protrusible jaws (Chapter 1), but none of the other Gasterosteiformes has a pre-maxilla with an ascending process. With the exception of the Aulostomidae, the Gasterosteiformes that lack this ascending process have a vomer that appears on the dorsal surface of the snout, an unusual condition in teleosts. In the snout region all the Gasterosteiformes except the Gasterosteidae and Aulorhynchidae have a dermal bone, the supra-ethmoid, that covers the endochondral ethmoid. A further feature that can be used to subdivide the Gasterosteiformes is the condition of the anterior vertebrae. The Gasterosteidae and the Aulorhynchidae have anterior vertebrae that are not enlarged, but the other families have anterior vertebrae that are enlarged and firmly sutured together (Banister, 1967).

From this and other evidence Banister argued that the Gasterosteiformes is not a natural group, but contains two groups that have independently approached the acanthopterygian grade of organisation. These two groups may have orginated from myctophoid-like fish of the Cretaceous era, but the fossil record is too sketchy to substantiate this hypothesis. The Gasterosteiformes should be divided into two distinct orders:

      Order : Aulorhynchiformes
        Family : Aulorhynchidae
        Family : Gasterosteidae

      Order : Aulostomiformes
(a) Suborder : Aulostomoidei
        Family : Aulostomidae
        Family : Fistulariidae
        Family : Solenostomidae
        Family : Syngnathidae

(b)   Suborder : Centriscoidei
          Family : Centriscidae
          Family : Macrorhamphosidae

The characters of these two orders are listed in Tables XVII and XVIII. Though neither of the orders falls unambiguously into the

TABLE XVII

Characters of the Aulorhynchiformes (from Banister, 1967).

1. A tri-radiate fused ecto- and endopterygoid.
2. Jaws protrusible and the ascending process of the pre-maxilla large, but articular process is absent.
3. Jaw ligaments absent.
4. Three or more infraorbitals are present and at least one contacts the pre-opercular.
5. Postcleithrum absent.
6. Dorsal fin preceded by a row of isolated spines.
7. Caudal skeleton shows reduction and fusion of caudal fin elements, with a single hypural plate emanating from a single half centrum.
8. Scales absent, but body protected by bony plates.
9. Lateral line system shows tendency towards reduction.
10. Ramus lateralis accessorius of the facial nerve is absent.
11. Parietals and nasals present.
12. Normal metapterygoid present.
13. The autopterotic does not contact the basioccipital.
14. Basiphenoids and orbitosphenoids absent.
15. Supraethmoid absent.
16. Intercalaries present although small.

Items 1 to 10 are relatively advanced or unusual characteristics, 11 to 15 occur commonly throughout the teleosts.

TABLE XVIII

Characters of the Aulostomiformes (from Banister, 1967).

1. Trend towards a modification of the anterior vertebrae.
2. Basioccipital sutures with the autopterotic.
3. Intercalaries absent.
4. Ptersophenoid generally present.
5. Ectopterygoid and endopterygoid are present and may be toothed.
6. Infraorbital series greatly modified or absent.
7. Tendency towards the development of unorthodox "scales" or bony plates.
8. Elongated snout with the vomer appearing on the dorsum of the snout.
9. Supraethmoid present.
10. Trigemino-facialis chamber primitive or reduced.
11. Postcleithrum present.
12. Tendency to reduce caudal skeleton.
13. Development of dorsal lamina of the symplectic.

Acanthopterygii, the Aulorhynchiformes are probably evolutionarily more advanced than the Aulostomiformes. The relatively primitive characters of this latter order include toothed endo- and ecto-pterygoids, the absence of the ascending process in the pre-maxilla, and the structure of the pharyngeal skeleton (Banister, 1967).

Clearly, the reconstruction of the phylogeny of the sticklebacks remains a tantalising puzzle; as one of the authorities on the morphology of these fishes has written:

> The evidence for evolution is overwhelming; the problems that beset us in reconstructing its pathway however are immense. Nelson (1971a).

Bibliography

Abdel'-Malek, S. A. (1963). (Diurnal rhythm of feeding of the three-spined stickleback (*Gasterosteus aculeatus* L.) of the Kandalakshskogo Bay of the White Sea.) *Vopr. Ikhtiol.* 3, 326–335. (In Russian.)

Abdel'-Malek, S. A. (1968). Feeding of young three-spined sticklebacks (*Gasterosteus aculeatus* L.) in Kandalaksha Bay in the White Sea. *Probl. Ichthyol.* 8, 74–80.

Ahsan, S. N. and Hoar, W. S. (1963). Some effects of gonadotropic hormones on the three-spined stickleback, *Gasterosteus aculeatus*. *Can. J. Zool.* 41, 1045–1053.

Alexander, McN. R. (1967). The functions and mechanisms of the protrusible upper jaws of some acanthopterygian fish. *J. Zool., Lond.* 151, 43–64.

Amaoka, K. and Haruta, C. (1972). Three-spined stickleback *Gasterosteus aculeatus aculeatus*, new record from Shimonoseki. *Jap. J. Ichthyol.* 19, 128–131.

Aneer, G. (1973). Biometric characteristics of the three-spined stickleback (*Gasterosteus aculeatus* L.) from the Northern Baltic proper. *Zool. Scr.* 2, 157–162.

Anker, G. C. (1974). Morphology and kinetics of the head of the stickleback *Gasteroseus aculeatus* L. *Trans. Zool. Soc. Lond.* 32, 311–416.

Anthouard, M. (1967). Activite et dominance chez l'epinoche (*Gasterosteus aculeatus* L.). *C.R. Acad. Sc. Paris* (D) 256, 1235–1239.

Arme, C. and Owen, R. W. (1967). Infections of the three-spined stickleback, *Gasterosteus aculeatus* L., with the plerocercoid larvae of *Schistocephalus solidus* (Müller, 1776), with special reference to pathological effects. *Parasitology* 57, 301–314.

Armitage, K. B. and Olund, L. J. (1962). Salt tolerance of the brook stickleback. *Amer. Midl. Nat.* 68, 274–277.

Assem, J. van den (1967). Territory in the three-spined stickleback, *Gasterosteus aculeatus* L. An experimental study in intra-specific competition. *Behaviour Suppl.* 16, 1–164.

Assem, J. van den and Molen, J. N. van der (1969). Waning of the aggressive response in the three-spined stickleback upon constant exposure to a conspecific. I. A preliminary analysis of phenomenon. *Behaviour,* 36, 286–334.

Avise, J. C. (1974). Systematic value of electrophoretic data. *Syst. Zool.* 23, 465–481.

Bacescu, M. and Mayer, R. (1956). Certari Asupra Ghidrinilor (*Gasterosteus aculeatus* L.) Din Apele Rominestri. *Bul. Inst. Cerc. Piscicole* 15, 19–36.

Baerends, G. P. (1971). The ethological analysis of fish behaviour. *In* "Fish Physiology" (W. S. Hoar and D. J. Randall, eds.), Vol. 6, pp. 279–370. Academic Press, London, New York.

Baggerman, B. (1957). An experimental study on the timing of breeding and migration in the three-spined stickleback (*Gasterosteus aculeatus* L.). *Arch. néerl. Zool.* 12, 105–317.

Baggerman, B. (1964). On the endocrine background of stickleback behaviour. *Arch. néerl. Zool.* 16, 159–163.

Baggerman, B. (1966). On the endocrine control of reproductive behaviour in the male three-spined stickleback (*Gasterosteus aculeatus* L.). *Symp. Soc. Exp. Biol.* 20, 427–456.

Baggerman, B. (1968). Hormonal control of reproductive and parental behaviour in fishes. *In* "Perspectives in Endocrinology: Hormones in the Lives of Lower Vertebrates" (E. J. W. Barrington and C. Barker Jørgensen, eds.), pp. 351–404. Academic Press, London, New York.

Baggerman, B. (1969). Influence of photoperiod and temperature on the timing of the breeding season in the stickleback, *Gasterosteus aculeatus. Gen. Comp. Endocrinol.* 13, 491.

Baggerman, B. (1972). Photoperiod responses in the stickleback and their control by a daily rhythm of photosensitivity. *Gen. Comp. Endocrinol. Suppl.* 3, 466–476.

Baker, B. I. (1963). Effect of adaptation to black and white backgrounds on the teleost pituitary. *Nature, Lond.* 198, 404.

Ball, J. N. (1969). Prolactin (fish prolactin or paralactin) and growth hormone. In "Fish Physiology" (W. S. Hoar and D. J. Randall, eds.), Vol. 2, pp. 207–240. Academic Press, London, New York.

Banister, K. E. (1967). The anatomy and classification of the order Gasterosteiformes. Ph.D. thesis, Department of Zoology, University of Newcastle upon Tyne.

Banister, K. E. (1970). The anatomy and taxonomy of *Indostomus paradoxus* Prashad and Mukerji. *Bull. Br. Mus. nat. hist. (Zool.)* 19, 181–209.

Bannister, L. H. (1965). The fine structure of the olfactory surface of teleostean fishes. *Quart. J. Microscop. Sci.* 106, 333–342.

Baron, H. (1934). Insel-und Zymogengewebe in ihren gegenseiten Bezehungen bei *Gasterosteus aculeatus* und einigen Teleostiern. *Z. wiss. Zool.* 146, 1–40.

Barr, W. A. (1968). Patterns of ovarian activity. *In* "Perspectives in Endocrinology" (E. J. W. Barrington and C. Barker Jørgensen, eds.), pp. 164–237. Academic Press, London, New York.

Barraud, E. M. (1955). Notes on the territorial behaviour of captive ten-spined sticklebacks (*Pygosteus pungitius*). *Brit. J. Anim. Behav.* 3, 134–136.

Bartmann, W. (1973). Eine Putzsymbiose swischen Stichling (*Gasterosteus aculeatus* L.) und Hecht (*Esox lucius* L.) im Aquarium. *Z. Tierpsychol.* 33, 153–162.

Baudelot, M. E. (1864). Recherches experimentales sur les fonctions de l'encephale des poissons. *Ann. sci. nat. Zool.* 1, 105–112.

de Beer, G. R. (1937). "The Development of the Vertebrate Skull" Clarendon Press, Oxford.

Bell, M. A. (1973a). Pleistocene three-spined sticklebacks, *Gasterosteus aculeatus*, (Pisces) from Southern California. *J. Palaentol.* 47, 479–483.

Bell, M. A. (1973b). The pliocene stickleback, *Pungitius haynesi*, a junior synonym of *Gasterosteus aculeatus*. *Copeia* 1973, 588–590.

Bell, M. A. (1974). Reduction and loss of the pelvic girdle in *Gasterosteus* (Pisces): a case of parallel evolution. *Nat. Hist. Mus. Los. Ang. Cty. Contrib. Sci.* 257. 1–36.

Bengston, S. (1971). Food and feeding of diving ducks breeding at Lake Myvatn, Iceland. *Ornis Fenn.* 48, 77–92.

Benjamin, M. (1973). Studies on the pituitary gland and saccus vasculosus of teleost fishes. Ph.D. thesis, Department of Zoology, University College of Wales, Aberystwyth.

Benjamin, M. (1974a). A morphometric study of the pituitary cell types in the freshwater stickleback, *Gasterosteus aculeatus* form *leiurus*. *Cell Tiss. Res.* 152, 69–92.

Benjamin, M. (1974b). Seasonal changes in the prolactin cell of the pituitary gland of the freshwater stickleback, *Gasterosteus aculeatus* form *leiurus*. *Cell Tiss. Res.* 152, 93–102.

Benjamin, M. (1974c). Ultrastructural studies on the coronet cells of the saccus vasculosus of the freshwater stickleback, *Gasterosteus aculeatus* form *leiurus*. *Z. Zellforsch.* 147, 551–565.

Benjamin, M. and Ireland, M. P. (1974). The ACTH-interrenal axis in the freshwater stickleback, *Gasterosteus aculeatus* form *leiurus*. *Cell Tiss. Res.* 155, 105–115.

Benzie, V. L. (1965). Some aspects of the anti-predator responses of two species of stickleback. D. Phil. Thesis, Department of Zoology, University of Oxford.

Berg, L. S. (1940). Classification of fishes, both recent and fossil. *Trav. Inst. Zool. Acad. Sci. U.S.S.R.* 5, 1–517.

Berg, L. S. (1949). "Freshwater Fishes of the U.S.S.R. and Adjacent Countries" Israel Program for Scientific Translations, Jerusalem (1965).

Berrie, A. D. (1960). Two *Diplostomum* larvae in the eyes of sticklebacks (*Gasterosteus aculeatus* L.). *J. Helminth.* 34, 211–216.

Bertin, L. (1925). Recherches bionomiques, biométriques et systématiques sur les Epinoches (Gastérostéides). *Ann. Inst. Oceanogr. Monaco* 2, 1–204.

Bertin, L. and Arambourg, C. (1958). Super-ordre des teleosteens (Teleostei). *In* "Traite de Zoologie" (P. Grasse, ed.), Vol. 13, fasc. 3, pp. 2204–2500. Masson, Paris.

Beukema, J. J. (1968). Predation by the three-spined stickleback (*Gasterosteus aculeatus* L.): the influence of hunger and experience. *Behaviour* 31, 1–126.

Biether, M. (1970). Die Chloridzellen des Stichlings. *Z. Zellforsch.* 107, 421–446.

Bijtel, J. H. (1949). The structure and the mechanism of movement of the gill filaments in Teleostei. *Arch. néerl. Zool.* 8, 267–288.

Black, R. (1971). Hatching success in the three-spined stickleback (*Gasterosteus aculeatus*) in relation to changes in behaviour during the parental phase. *Anim. Behav.* 19, 532–541.

Black, R. and Wootton, R. J. (1970). Dispersion in a natural population of three-spined sticklebacks. *Can. J. Zool.* 48, 1133–1135.

Blegvad, H. (1917). On the food of fish in the Danish waters within the Skaw. *Rep. Danish Biol. Sta.* 24, 19–72.

Bock, F. (1928). Die Hypophyse des Stichlings (*Gasterosteus aculeatus* L.) unter besonderer Berücksichtigung der jahrescyklischen Veränderungen. *Z. wiss. Zool.* 131, 645–710.

Bock, F. (1930). Die Epidermis des Stichlings. *Z. Zellforsch.* 10, 394–400.

Bol, A. C. A. (1959). A consummatory situation. The effect of eggs on the sexual behaviour of the male three-spined stickleback (*Gasterosteus aculeatus* L.). *Experientia* 15, 115–116.

Boulenger, G. A. (1904). Fishes (Systematic account of Teleostei). *In* "The Cambridge Natural History" (S. F. Harmer and A. E. Shipley, eds.), Vol. 7, pp. 539–727. McMillan, London.

Braekevelt, C. R. and McMillan, D. B. (1967). Cyclic changes in the ovary of the brook stickleback *Eucalia inconstans* (Kirtland). *J. Morph.* 123, 373–396.

Breder, C. M. Jr. (1936). "All modern conveniences". A note on the nest architecture of the four-spined stickleback. *Bull. New York Zool. Soc.* 39, 72–76.

Breder, C. M. Jr. and Rosen, D. E. (1966). "Modes of Reproduction in Fishes" Natur. Hist. Press, New York.

Brett, J. R. (1944). Some lethal temperature relations of Algonquin Park fishes. *Univ. Toronto Biol. Ser.* 52, 1–49.

Brock, V. E. and Riffenburgh, R. H. (1960). Fish schooling: a possible factor in reducing predation. *J. Cons. int. Explor. Mer* 25, 307–317.

Brush, A. H. and Reisman, H. M. (1965). The carotenoid pigments in the three-spined stickleback, *Gasterosteus aculeatus. Comp. Biochem. Physiol.* 14, 121–125.

Burton, D. (1975). The integumentary melanophore patterns of two teleost species *Gasterosteus aculeatus* and *Pseudopleuronectes americanus. Can. J. Zool.* 53, 507–515.

Bykhovskaya-Pavlovskaya, I. E. *et al.* (1964). "Key to Parasites of Freshwater Fish of the U.S.S.R." Israel Program for Scientific Translations, Jerusalem.

Cameron, J. N., Kostoris, J. and Penhale, P. A. (1973). Preliminary energy budget of the nine-spine stickleback (*Pungitius pungitius*) in an Arctic Lake. *J. Fish. Res. Bd. Canada* 30, 1179–1189.

Campos, H. (1969). Die Geschmacksknospen im vorderdam von susswasser-flüschen, zahl, verteilung und Entwicklung (*Phoxinus phoxinus* L., *Gasterosteus aculeatus* L., *Hemigrammus caudorittatus* Ahl., *Anoptichthys fordani* Hubbs et Innes und *Salmo gairdneri* Rich.). *Z. wiss. Zool.* 179, 253–299.

Cane, V. (1961). Some ways of describing behaviour. *In* "Current Problems in Animal Behaviour" (W. H. Thorpe and O. L. Zangwill, eds.), pp. 361–388. Cambridge University Press, Cambridge.

Carew, B. A. M. (1968). Some effects of methallibure (I.C.I. 33,828) on the stickleback *Gasterosteus aculeatus* L. M.Sc. Thesis, Department of Zoology, University of British Columbia.

Chappell, L. H. (1969a). The parasites of the three-spined stickleback *Gasterosteus aculeatus* L. from a Yorkshire pond I. Seasonal variation of parasitic fauna. *J. Fish Biol.* 1, 137–152.

Chappell, L. H. (1969b). The parasites of the three-spined stickleback *Gasterosteus aculeatus* L. from a Yorkshire pond II. Variation of the parasite fauna with sex and size of fish. *J. Fish Biol.* 1, 339–347.

Chappell, L. H. (1969c). Competitive exclusion between two intestinal parasites of the three-spined stickleback, *Gasterosteus aculeatus. J. Parasitol.* 55, 775–778.

Chappell, L. H. and Owen, R. W. (1969). A reference list of parasite species recorded in freshwater fish from Great Britain and Ireland. *J. nat. Hist.* 3, 197–216.

Chen, T. R. and Reisman, H. M. (1970). A comparative chromosome study of the North American species of sticklebacks (Teleostei: Gasterosteidae). *Cytogenetics* 9, 321–332.

Clarke, A. S. (1954). Studies on the life history of the pseudophyllidean cestode *Schistocephalus solidus*. *Proc. zool. Soc. Lond.* 124, 257–302.

Clemens, W. A. and Wilby, G. V. (1961). Fishes of the Pacific Coast of Canada. *Bull. Fish. Res. Bd. Canada* 68.

Coad, B. W. (1973). Modifications of the pelvic complex in nine-spine sticklebacks, *Pungitius pungitius* (L), of eastern Canada and North-west Territories. *Le Naturaliste Canadien* 100, 315–316.

Coad, B. W. (1974). Vertebral frequencies with notes on anomalies in samples of three-spine sticklebacks (*Gasterosteus aculeatus* L.) from eastern North America. *Can. Field-Nat.* 88, 220–223.

Coad, B. W. and Power, G. (1973a). Life history notes and meristic variation in the freshwater four-spine stickleback, *Apeltes quadracus* (Mitchill) near Sept-Iles, Quebec, *Nat. Can. (Que.).* 100, 247–251.

Coad, B. W. and Power, G. (1973b). Observations on the ecology of lacustrine population of the three-spine stickleback (*Gasterosteus aculeatus* L. 1758) in the Matamek River system. Quebec. *Le Naturaliste Canadien* 100, 437–445.

Coad, B. W. and Power, G. (1973c). Observations on the ecology and phenotypic variation of the three-spine stickleback *Gasterosteus aculeatus* L. 1758, and the blackspotted stickleback, *G. wheatlandi* Putnam 1867 (Osteichthyes: Gasterosteidae) in Amory Cove, Quebec. *Can. Field Nat.* 87, 113–122.

Coad, B. W. and Power, G. (1973d). Observations on the ecology and meristic variation of the nine-spine stickleback, *Pungitius pungitius* (L. 1758) of the Matamek River system, Quebec. *Am. Midl. Nat.* 90, 498–503.

Coad, B. W. and Power, G. (1974). Meristic variation in the three-spined stickleback, *Gasterosteus aculeatus*, in the Matamek River system, Quebec. *J. Fish. Res. Bd. Canada* 31, 1155–1157.

Cope, E. D. (1870). Contributions to the ichthyology of the Lesser Antilles. *Trans. Americ. Phil. Soc.* 14, 445–483.

Courrier, R. (1921). Glande interstitielle du testicule et caracteres sexuels secondaires chez les Poissons. *C.R. Acad. Sc. Paris* 172, 1316–1317.

Courrier, R. (1922). Sur l'independence de la glande seminale et des caracteres sexuels secondaires chez les Poissons. Etude experimentale. *C.R. Acad. Sc. Paris* 174, 70–72.

Cox, P. (1923). Regional variation of the four-spined stickleback, *Apeltes quadracus* Mitchill. *Can. Field. Nat.* 37, 146–147.

Craig-Bennett, A. (1931). The reproductive cycle of the three-spined stickleback, *Gasterosteus aculeatus* L., *Phil. Trans. Roy. Lond., B* 219, 197–279.

Creutz, G. (1963). Stichlinge als Vogelnahurung. *Orn. Beob.* 62, 24–26.

Cronly-Dillon, J. and Sharma, S. C. (1968). Effect of season and sex on the photopic spectral sensitivity of the three-spined stickleback. *J. Exp. Biol.* 49, 679–687.

Cullen, E. (1960). Experiment on the effect of social isolation on reproductive behaviour in the three-spined stickleback. *Anim. Behav.* 8, 235.

Dadswell, M. J. (1972a). New records of freshwater fishes from the northwestern coast of insular Newfoundland. *Can. Field. Nat.* 86, 289–290.

Dadswell, M. J. (1972b). Postglacial dispersal of four deep-water fishes on the basis of new distribution records in Eastern Ontario and Western Quebec. *J. Fish. Res. Bd. Canada* 29, 545–553.

Daniel, W. (1965). Beitrage zur Biologie des Dreistachligen Stichlings (*Gasterosteus aculeatus* L.). *Faun. Mitt. Nord-deutsch* 2, 289-307.

Dartnall, H. J. G. (1973). Parasites of the nine-spined stickleback *Pungitius pungitius* (L). *J. Fish Biol.* 5, 505-509.

David, L. R. (1945). A Neogene stickleback from the Ridge Formation of California. *J. Palaentol.* 19, 315-318.

Davis, G. E. and Warren, C. E. (1971). Estimation of food consumption rates. *In* "Methods of Assessment of Fish Production in Fresh Waters" (W. E. Ricker, ed.), pp. 227-248. Blackwell Scientific Publications, Oxford.

Degraeve, G. M. (1970). Three types of burrowing behaviour of the brook stickleback, *Culaea inconstans. Trans. Amer. Fish. Soc.* 99, 433.

Dodd, J. M. and Kerr, T. (1963). Comparative morphology and histology of the hypothalamo-neurohypophysial system. *Symp. Zool. Soc. London* 9, 5-27.

Eekhoudt, J. P. van den (1946). Recherches sur l'influence de la lumiere sur le cycle sexuel de l'Epinoche (*Gasterosteus aculeatus* L.). *Ann. Soc. Zool. Belg.* 77, 83-89.

Elkan, E. (1962). *Dermocystidium gasterostei* n. sp., a parasite of *Gasterosteus aculeatus* L. and *G. pungitius* L. *Nature, Lond.* 196, 958-960.

Evans, D. H. (1969). Studies on the permeability to water of selected marine, freshwater and euryhaline teleosts. *J. Exp. Biol.* 50, 689-703.

Falk, M. R. (1972). Unusual occurrence of the brook stickleback (*Culaea inconstans*) in the MacKenzie River, Northwest Territories. *J. Fish. Res. Bd. Canada* 29, 1655-1656.

Fange, R. (1953). The mechanism of gas transport in the euphysoclist swimbladder. *Acta Physiol. Scand.* 23, *Suppl. 110*, 1-133.

Follenius, E. (1965). Cytologie fine des spermatocytes de l'Epinoche (*Gasterosteus aculeatus*) echanges nucleo-cytoplasmiques et formation d'amas de mitochondries. *C.R. Acad. Sc. Paris* (D) 261, 4849-4852.

Follenius, E. (1967). Marquage selectif des cellules acidophiles de la mesoadenohypophyse de *Gasterosteus aculeatus* apres injection de DL-noradrenaline-[3] H-7; etude autoradiographe au microscope electronique. *C.R. Acad. Sc. Paris* (D) 265, 358-361.

Follenius, E. (1968a). Innervation adrenergique de la meta-adenohypophyse de l'epinoche (*Gasterosteus aculeatus* L.): mise en evidence par autoradiographie au microscope electrique. *C.R. Acad. Sc. Paris* (D) 267, 1208-1211.

Follenius, E. (1968b). Cytologie et cytophysiologie des cellules interstitielles de l'epinoche: *Gasterosteus aculeatus* L. Etude au microscope electronique. *Gen. Comp. Endocrinol.* 11, 198-219.

Follenius, E. (1968c). Analyse de la structure fine des differents types cellules hypophysaire des poissons teleosteens. *Pathol. Biol.* 16, 619-632.

Follenius, E. (1971). Intergration de la dopamine dans les terminaisons aminergiques de la meta-adenohypophyse de l'epinoche (*Gasterosteus aculeatus* L.). *C.R. Acad. Sc. Paris* (D) 273, 1039-1040.

Follenius, E. (1972a). Cytologie fine de la degenerescence des fibres aminergiques intra hypophysaire chez le poisson teleosteen *Gasterosteus aculeatus* apres traitement par la 6-hydroxydopamine. *Z. Zellforsch.* 128, 69-82.

Follenius, E. (1972b). Integration selective du GABA-H[3] dans la neurohypophyse du poisson teleosteen *Gasterosteus aculeatus* L. *C.R. Acad. Sc. Paris* (D) 275, 1435-1438.

Follenius, E. and Dubois, M. P. (1974). Immunocytological localisation and identification of the MSH-producing cells in the pituitary of the stickleback (*Gasterosteus aculeatus* L.). *Gen. Comp. Endocrinol.* 24, 203–207.

Ford, E. B. (1964). "Ecological Genetics" Methuen, London.

Fraser, T. H. (1972). Some thoughts about the teleostean fish concept the Paracanthopterygii. *Jap. J. Ichthyol.* 19, 232–242.

Fridberg, G. and Olsson, R. (1959). The praeopticohypophysial system, nucleus tuberislateris and the subcommissural organ of *Gasterosteus aculeatus* after changes in osmotic stimuli. *Z. Zellforsch.* 49, 431–440.

Frost, W. E. (1954). The food of pike *Esox lucius* L. in Windermere. *J. Anim. Ecol.* 23, 339–360.

Frost, W. E. and Brown, M. E. (1967). "The Trout" Collins, London.

Garside, E. T. and Hamor, T. (1973). Meristic variation in the three-spine stickleback, *Gasterosteus aculeatus* L., in eastern Canadian waters. *Can. J. Zool.* 51, 547–551.

Garside, E. T. and Kerekes, J. J. (1969). Eastern extension of the range of the black-spotted stickleback, *Gasterosteus wheatlandi*, in Newfoundland. *J. Fish. Res. Bd. Canada* 26, 460–461.

Gerell, R. (1968). Food habits of the mink, *Mustela vison* Schreb. in Sweden. *Viltrevy* 5, 120–194.

Glaser, D. (1966). Untersuchungen über die absoluten Geschmacksswellen von Fischen. *Z. vergl. Physiol.* 52, 1–25.

Goodrich, E. S. (1909). Cyclostomes and fishes. *In* "A Treatise on Zoology" (R. Lankester, ed.), Pt. 7. Adams and Charles, London.

Gottfried, H. and Mullem, P. J. van (1967). On the histology of the interstitium and the occurrence of steroids in the stickleback (*Gasterosteus aculeatus* L.) testis. *Acta Endocrinol.* 56. 1–15.

Greenbank, J. and Nelson, P. (1959). Life History of the three-spine stickleback *Gasterosteus aculeatus* Linnaeus in Karluk Lake and Bare Lake Kodiak Island, Alaska. *U.S. Fish Wildlife Serv. Bull.* 153, 537–559.

Greenwood, P. H., Rosen, D. E., Weitzman, S. and Myers, G. (1966). Phyletic studies of teleostean fishes, with a provisional classification of living forms. *Bull. Amer. Mus. Nat. Hist.* 131, 339–455.

Gregory, W. K. (1933). Fish skulls: a study of the evolution of natural mechanisms. *Trans. Amer. Phil. Soc.* 17, 75–481.

Griswold, B. L. and Smith, L. L. Jr. (1972). Early survival and growth of the nine-spine stickleback, *Pungitius pungitius*. *Trans. Am. Fish. Soc.* 101, 350–352.

Griswold, B. L. and Smith, L. L. Jr. (1973). The life history and trophic relationship of the nine-spine stickleback, *Pungitius pungitius*, in the Apostle Islands area of Lake Superior. *Fishery Bulletin* 71, 1039–1060.

Gueylard, F. (1924). De l'adaptation aux changements de salinite. Recherches biologiques et physicochimiques sur l'Epinoche (*Gasterosteus leiurus*, Cuv. et Val.). *Arch. Phys. Biol.* 3, 79–197.

Guiton, P. (1960). On the control of behaviour during the reproductive cycle of *Gasterosteus aculeatus*. *Behaviour* 15, 163–184.

Gutz, M. (1970). Experimentelle Untersuchungen zur Salzadaptation verschiedener Rassen des Dreistachligen Stichlings (*Gasterosteus aculeatus* L.). *Int. Rev. ges. Hydrobiol.* 55, 845–894.

Hagen, D. W. (1967). Isolating mechanisms in three-spine sticklebacks (*Gasterosteus*). *J. Fish. Res. Bd. Canada* 24, 1637–1692.

Hagen, D. W. (1973). Inheritance of numbers of lateral plates and gill rakers in *Gasterosteus aculeatus. Hereditary* 30, 303–312.

Hagen, D. W. and Gilbertson, L. G. (1972). Geographic variation and environmental selection in *Gasterosteus aculeatus* L. in the Pacific northwest, America. *Evolution* 26, 32–51.

Hagen, D. W. and Gilbertson, L. G. (1973a). Selective predation and the intensity of selection acting upon the lateral plates of three-spine sticklebacks. *Hereditary* 30, 273–287.

Hagen, D. W. and Gilbertson, L. G. (1973b). The genetics of plate morphs in freshwater three-spine sticklebacks. *Hereditary* 31, 75–84.

Hagen, D. W. and McPhail, J. D. (1970). The species problem within *Gasterosteus aculeatus* on the Pacific coast of North America. *J. Fish. Res. Bd. Canada* 27, 147–155.

Hagen, D. W., Moodie, G. E. E. and Moodie, P. F. (1972). Territoriality and courtship in the Olympic mud-minnow (*Novumbra hubbsi*). *Can. J. Zool.* 50, 1111–1115.

Hale, P. A. (1965). The morphology and histology of the digestive systems of two freshwater teleosts, *Poecilia reticulata* and *Gasterosteus aculeatus. J. Zool., Lond.* 146, 132–149.

Hall, M. F. (1956). A comparative study of the reproductive behaviour of the sticklebacks (Gasterosteidae). D. Phil. Thesis, Department of Zoology, University of Oxford.

Hamada, K. (1975). Excessively enlarged thyroid follicles of the three-spined stickleback, *Gasterosteus aculeatus aculeatus* reared in freshwater. *Jpn. J. Ichthyol.* 24, 183–190.

Hanek, G. and Threlfall, W. (1969a). *Thersitina gasterostei* (Pagenstecher, 1861) (Copepoda: Ergasilidae) from *Gasterosteus wheatlandi* Putnam, 1867. *Can. J.* 627–629.

Hanek, G. and Threlfall, W. (1969b). Digenetic trematodes from Newfoundland, Canada. I. Three species from *Gasterosteus aculeatus* Linnaeus, 1758. *Can. J. Zool.* 47, 793–794.

Hanek, G. and Threlfall, W. (1969c). Monogenetic trematodes from Newfoundland, Canada. I. New species of the genus *Gyrodactylus* Nordmann, 1832. *Can. J. Zool.* 47, 951–955.

Hanek, G. and Threlfall, W. (1969d). Digenetic trematodes from Newfoundland, Canada. 2. Two species from *Gasterosteus aculeatus* Linnaeus, 1758. *Can. J. Zool.* 47, 1086–1087.

Hanek, G. and Threlfall, W. (1970a). *Ergasilus auritis* Markewitsch, 1940 (Copepoda: Ergasilidae) from *Gasterosteus aculeatus* Linnaeus, 1758 in Newfoundland. *Can. J. Zool.* 48, 185–187.

Hanek, G. and Threlfall, W. (1970b). Helminth parasites of the four-spine stickleback (*Apeltes quadracus* (Mitchill)) in Newfoundland. *Can. J. Zool.* 48, 404–406.

Hanek, G. and Threlfall, W. (1970c). Parasites of the nine-spine stickleback *Pungitius pungitius* in Newfoundland and Labrador. *Can. J. Zool.* 48, 600–602.

Harden Jones, F. R. (1968). "Fish Migration" Edward Arnold, London.

Harris, C. J. (1968). "Otters" Weidenfeld and Nicolson, London.

Hartley, P. H. T. (1948). Food and feeding relationships in a community of fresh-water fishes. *J. Anim. Ecol.* 17, 1–14.

Hay, D. E. (1974). Ecological genetics of three-spine sticklebacks (*Gasterosteus*). Ph.D. thesis, Department of Zoology, University of British Columbia.

Hay, D. E. and McPhail, J. D. (1975). Mate selection in three-spine sticklebacks (*Gasterosteus*). *Can. J. Zool.* 53, 441-450.

Hay, O. P. (1907). A new fossil stickleback from Nevada. *Proc. U.S. Nat. Mus.* 32, 271-273.

Hazel, C. R., Thomsen, W. and Meith, S. J. (1971). Sensitivity of striped bass and stickleback to ammonia in relation to temperature and salinity. *Calif. Fish Game* 57, 138-153.

Healy, A. (1954). Perch (*Perca fluviatilis* L.) in three Irish Lakes. *Sci. Proc. R. Dublin Soc.* 26, 397-407.

Healy, A. (1956). Pike (*Esox lucius* L.) in three Irish Lakes. *Sci. Proc. R. Dublin Soc.* 27, 51-67.

Healy, E. G. (1957). The nervous system. *In* "The Physiology of Fishes" (M. E. Brown, ed.), Vol. 2, pp. 1-119. Academic Press, London, New York.

Henderson, I. W., Chan, D. K. O., Sandor, T. and Chester Jones, I. (1970). The adrenal cortex and osmo-regulation in teleosts. *In* "Hormones and the Environment" *Mem. Soc. Endocrinol. No. 18* (G. K. Benson and J. G. Phillips, eds.), pp. 31-53. University Press, Cambridge.

Hentschel, H. (1973). Vergleichend histologisch-histochemische Untersuchungen an den Harnorganen von Stichlingen (Gasterosteidae, Pisces). Dr. rer. nat. Thesis, Technischen Universität, Hannover.

Hess, W. N. (1918). A seasonal study of the kidney of the five-spined stickleback *Eucalia inconstans cayuga* Jordan. *Anat. Rec.* 14, 141-163.

Heuts, M. J. (1943). La regulation osmotique chez l'Epinochette (*Pygosteus pungitius* L.). *Ann. Soc. Zool. Belg.* 74, 99-105.

Heuts, M. J. (1945). La regulation minerale en fonction de la temperature chez *Gasterosteus aculeatus* L. *Ann. Soc. Zool. Belg.* 76, 88-99.

Heuts, M. J. (1946). Physiological isolating mechanisms and selection within the species *Gasterosteus aculeatus* L. *Nature, Lond.* 158, 839.

Heuts, M. J. (1947a). The phenotypic variability of *Gasterosteus aculeatus* L. populations in Belgium. *Meded. Kon. Vl. Akad. Wetensch.* 9 (*25*), 1-63.

Heuts, M. J. (1947b). Experimental studies on adaptive evolution in *Gasterosteus aculeatus* L. *Evolution* 1, 89-102.

Heuts, M. J. (1949). Racial divergence in fin ray variation patterns in *Gasterosteus aculeatus*. *J. Genet.* 49, 183-191.

Heuts, M. J. (1956). Temperature adaption in *Gasterosteus aculeatus* L. *Publ. Staz. Zool. Napoli* 28, 44-61.

Hickman, C. P. Jr. and Trump, B. F. (1969). The kidney. *In* "Fish Physiology" (W. S. Hoar and D. J. Randall, eds.), Vol. 1, pp. 91-239. Academic Press, London, New York.

Hinegardner, R. (1968). Evolution of cellular DNA content in teleost fishes. *Amer. Nat.* 102, 517-523.

Hoar, W. S. (1962a). Reproductive behaviour of fish. *Gen. Comp. Endocrinol. Suppl.* 1, 206-216.

Hoar, W. S. (1962b). Hormones and the reproductive behaviour of the male three-spined stickleback (*Gasterosteus aculeatus*). *Anim. Behav.* 10, 247-266.

Hoar, W. S. (1965). The endocrine system as a chemical link between the organism and its environment. *Trans. Roy. Soc. Can.* 3, 175-200.

Hoar, W. S. (1969). Reproduction. *In* "Fish Physiology" (W. S. Hoar and D. J. Randall, eds.), Vol. 3, pp. 1-72. Academic Press, London, New York.

Hoffman, G. L. (1967). "Parasites of North American Freshwater Fishes" University of California Press, Berkley.

Hoogland, R. D. (1951). On the fixing-mechanism in the spines of *Gasterosteus aculeatus* L. *Konink, Neder. Akad. weten. Proc. ser. C.* **54**, 171–180.

Hoogland, R. D., Morris, D. and Tinbergen, N. (1957). The spines of sticklebacks (*Gasterosteus* and *Pygosteus*) as means of defence against predators (*Perca* and *Esox*). *Behaviour* **10**, 205–237.

Hopkins, C. A. (1959). Seasonal variation in the incidence and development of the cestode *Proteocephalus filicollis* (Rud. 1810) in *Gasterosteus aculeatus* (L. 1766). *Parasitology* **49**, 529–542.

Hopkins, C. A. and Smyth, J. D. (1951). Notes on the morphology and life history of *Schistocephalus solidus* (Cestoda: Diphyllobothriidae). *Parasitology* **41**, 283–291.

Hopkirk, J. D. (1973). Endemism in fishes of the Clear Lake region of central California. *Univ. Calif. Publ. Zool.* **96**, 1–135.

Hubbs, C. L. (1929). The Atlantic American species of the fish genus *Gasterosteus*. *Occ. Pap. Mus. Zool., Univ. Michigan* **200**, 1–9.

Hughes, G. M. (1963). "Comparative Physiology of Vertebrate Respiration" Heinemann, London.

Hunt, B. P. and Carbine, W. F. (1951). Food of young pike, *Esox lucius* L. and associated fishes in Peterson's Ditches, Houghton Lake, Michigan. *Trans. Amer. Fish. Soc.* **80**, 67–83.

Hunt, P. C. and Jones, J. W. (1972). The food of brown trout in Llyn Alaw, Anglesey, North Wales. *J. Fish Biol.* **4**, 333–352.

Huntingford, F. A. (1974). A comparison of anti-predator behaviour and aggression towards conspecifics in the three-spined stickleback, *Gasterosteus aculeatus*. D. Phil. Thesis, Department Experimental Psychology, University of Oxford.

Huxley, T. H. (1859). Observations on the development of some parts of the skeleton of fishes. *Quart. J. Microscop. Sci.* **7**, 33–46.

Hynes, H. B. N. (1950). The food of fresh-water sticklebacks (*Gasterosteus aculeatus* and *Pygosteus pungitius*), with a review of methods used in studies of the food of fishes. *J. Anim. Ecol.* **19**, 36–58.

Iersel, J. J. A. van (1953). An analysis of the parental behaviour of the male three-spined stickleback (*Gasterosteus aculeatus* L.). *Behaviour Suppl.* **3**, 1–159.

Iersel, J. J. A. van (1958). Some aspects of territorial behaviour of the male three-spined stickleback. *Arch. néerl. Zool.* **13**, Suppl. 1, 381–400.

Igarashi, K. (1969). On the distribution and variation of *Pungitius pungitius* in the Mogami Basin with particular regard to its scutes. *Zool. Mag. Tokyo* **78**, 340–350.

Igarishi, K. (1970a). Formation of the scutes in the marine form of the three-spined stickleback, *Gasterosteus aculeatus aculeatus* (L.). *Annot. Zool. Jap.* **43**, 34–42.

Igarishi, K. (1970b). On the variation of the scute in the three-spined stickleback, *Gasterosteus aculeatus* (Linnaeus) from Nasu Area, Tochigi-Ken. *Annat. Zool. Jap.* **43**, 43–49.

Ikeda, K. (1933). Effect of castration on the secondary sexual characters of anadromous three-spined stickleback, *Gasterosteus aculeatus aculeatus* (L.). *Japan J. Zool.* **5**, 135–157.

Immers, J. (1953). The influence of the sexual cycle on the metabolism of glycogen in the liver, gonads and skin of the stickleback (*Gasterosteus aculeatus* L.) and minnow (*Phoxinus laevis* Ag.). *Arkiv. Zool.* 4, 327–339.

Ireland, M. P. (1969). Effect of urophysectomy in *Gasterosteus aculeatus* on survival in freshwater and sea-water. *J. Endocrinol.* 43, 133–134.

Jenni, D. A. (1972). Effects of conspecifics and vegetation on nest site selection in *Gasterosteus aculeatus* L. *Behaviour* 42, 97–118.

Jenni, D. A., Iersel, J. J. A. van and Assem, J. van den (1969). Effects of pre-experimental conditions on nest site selection and aggression in *Gasterosteus aculeatus* L. *Behaviour* 35, 61–76.

Jones, J. R. E. (1935). The toxic action of heavy metal salts on the three-spined stickleback (*Gasterosteus aculeatus*). *J. Exp. Biol.* 12, 165–173.

Jones, J. R. E. (1938). The relative toxicity of salts of lead, zinc and copper to the stickleback (*Gasterosteus aculeatus* L.) and the effect of calcium on the toxicity of lead and zinc salts. *J. Exp. Biol.* 15, 394–407.

Jones, J. R. E. (1939). The relationship between the electrolytic solution pressure of the metals and their toxicity to the stickleback (*Gasterosteus aculeatus* L.). *J. Exp. Biol.* 16, 425–437.

Jones, J. R. E. (1947a). The oxygen consumption of *Gasterosteus aculeatus* L. in toxic solutions. *J. Exp. Biol.* 23, 298–311.

Jones, J. R. E. (1947b). The reactions of *Pygosteus pungitius* L. to toxic solutions. *J. Exp. Biol.* 24, 110–122.

Jones, J. R. E. (1948). A further study of the reactions of fish to toxic solutions. *J. Exp. Biol.* 25, 22–34.

Jones, J. R. E. (1952). The reactions of fish to water of low oxygen concentration. *J. Exp. Biol.* 29, 403–415.

Jones, J. R. E. (1964). "Fish and River Pollution" Butterworths, London.

Jones, J. W. and Hynes, H. B. N. (1950). The age and growth of *Gasterosteus aculeatus, Pygosteus pungitius* and *Spinachia vulgaris*, as shown by their otoliths. *J. Anim. Ecol.* 19, 59–73.

Jordan, C. M. and Garside, E. T. (1972). Upper lethal temperatures of three-spine stickleback, *Gasterosteus aculeatus* (L.), in relation to thermal and osmotic acclimation, ambient salinity and size. *Can. J. Zool.* 50, 1405–1411.

Jordan, D. S. and Hubbs, C. L. (1925). Record of fishes obtained by D. S. Jordan in Japan, 1922. *Mem. Carnegie Mus.* 10, 93–346.

Kampf, W. D. (1962). Vergleichende funktionsmorphologische Untersuchungen anden Viscerocranien einiger räuberisch lebender Knochenfische. *Zool. Beitr.* (*N.F.*) 6, 391–496.

Keenlyside, M. H. A. (1955). Some aspects of the schooling behaviour of fish. *Behaviour* 8, 183–248.

Kennedy, C. R. (1974). A checklist of British and Irish freshwater parasites with notes on their distribution. *J. Fish Biol.* 6, 613–644.

Koch, H. J. A. (1968). Migration. *In* "Perspectives in Endocrinology: Hormones in the Lives of Lower Vertebrates" (E. J. W. Barrington and C. Barker Jørgensen, eds.), pp. 305–349. Academic Press, London, New York.

Koch, H. J. and Heuts, M. J. (1942). Influence de l'hormone thyroidienne sur la regulation osmotique chez *Gasterosteus aculeatus* L. forme *gymnurus*. *Ann. Soc. Roy. Zool. Belg.* 73, 165–172.

Koch, H. J. and Heuts, M. J. (1943). Regulation osmotique, cycle sexuel et migration de reproduction chez les Epinoches. *Arch. int. Physiol.* 53, 253–266.

Kreuger, W. H. (1961). Meristic variation in the fourspine stickleback, *Apeltes quadracus. Copeia 1961*, 442–450.

Krogius, F. V. (1973). Population dynamics of growth of young sockeye salmon in Lake Dalnee. *Hydrobiologia* 43, 45–51.

Krokhin, E. M. (1957). Determining the diurnal amount of food consumed by the young of sockeye salmon and the three-spined stickleback by use of the respiration method. *Izvestiya Tikhookeanskogo nauchno-issledovatel' skogo instituta rybnogo khozyaistva i okeanografii 44*, 97–110. (Published for the National Science Foundation and the Department of Commerce, Washington, D.C., U.S.A. by the Israel Program for Scientific Translations).

Krokhin, Ye. M. (1970). Estimation of the biomass and abundance of the threespine stickleback (*Gasterosteus aculeatus* L.) in Lake Dan'neye based on the food consumption of plankton-feeding fishes. *J. Ichthyol.* 10, 471–475.

Kühlmann, D. H. (1963). Beobachtungen zur Biologie von *Gasterosteus aculeatus* L. und Gedanken zus einer Bekampfung als Schadling. *Z. Fisch. N.F.* 11, 301–309.

Lagler, K. F. and Ostenson, B. T. (1942). Early spring food of the otter in Michigan. *J. Wildl. Manag.* 6, 244–254.

Lam, T. J. (1968). Effect of prolactin on plasma electrolytes of the early-winter marine threespine stickleback, *Gasterosteus aculeatus*, form trachurus, following the transfer from sea- to freshwater. *Can. J. Zool.* 46, 1095–1097.

Lam, T. J. (1969a). A new technique for the collection of urine of small fishes and for the study of exchanges of materials via the head region. *Can. J. Zool.* 47, 225–228.

Lam, T. J. (1969b). Effect of prolactin on loss of solutes via the head region of the early-winter marine threespine stickleback (*Gasterosteus aculeatus* L., form trachurus) in freshwater. *Can. J. Zool.* 47, 865–869.

Lam, T. J. (1969c). The effect of prolactin on osmotic influx of water in isolated gills of the marine threespine stickleback *Gasterosteus aculeatus* L. form trachurus. *Comp. Biochem. Physiol.* 31, 909–913.

Lam, T. J. (1972). Prolactin and hydromineral regulation in fishes. *Gen. Comp. Endocrinol. Suppl.* 3, 328–338.

Lam, T. J. and Hoar, W. S. (1967). Seasonal effects of prolactin on freshwater osmoregulation of the marine form (trachurus) of the stickleback *Gasterosteus aculeatus. Can. J. Zool.* 45, 509–516.

Lam, T. J. and Leatherland, J. F. (1969a). Effect of prolactin on freshwater survival of the marine form (trachurus) of the threespine stickleback, *Gasterosteus aculeatus* in early winter. *Gen. Comp. Endocrinol.* 12, 385–387.

Lam, T. J. and Leatherland, J. F. (1969b). Effects of prolactin on the glomerulus of the marine threespine stickleback *Gasterosteus aculeatus* L., form trachurus, after transfer from seawater to freshwater, during the late autumn and early winter. *Can. J. Zool.* 47, 245–250.

Lam, T. J. and Leatherland, J. F. (1970). Effect of hormones on survival of the marine form (trachurus) of the threespine stickleback (*Gasterosteus aculeatus* L.) in deionised water. *Comp. Biochem. Physiol.* 33, 295–303.

Lamsa, A. (1963). Downstream movements of brook sticklebacks, *Eucalia inconstans* (Kirtland), in a small southern Ontario stream. *J. Fish. Res. Bd. Canada* 20, 587–589.

Lange, R. and Fugelli, K. (1965). The osmotic adjustment in the euryhaline teleosts, the founder, *Pleuronectes flesus* L. and the three-spined stickleback, *Gasterosteus aculeatus* L., *Comp. Biochem. Physiol.* 15, 283–292.

Laurent, P. J. (1972). Lac Leman: effects of exploitation, eutrophication, and introductions on the salmonic community. *J. Fish. Res. Bd. Canada* 29, 867-875.

Lawler, G. H. (1958). Variation in number of dorsal spines in the brook stickleback, *Eucalia inconstans. Can. J. Zool.* 36, 127-129.

Lawler, G. H. (1965). The food of the pike, *Esox lucius*, in Heming Lake, Manitoba. *J. Fish. Res. Bd. Canada* 22, 1357-1377.

Lea, G. R. (1968). Lateral plates in the three-spined stickleback (*Gasterosteus aculeatus* L.) as a defence against predators. B.Sc. Thesis, Department of Zoology, University of British Columbia.

Leatherland, J. F. (1970a). Seasonal variation in the structure and ultrastructure of the pituitary in the marine form (trachurus) of the threespine stickleback, *Gasterosteus aculeatus* L. I. Rostral pars distalis. *Z. Zellforsch.* 104, 301-317.

Leatherland, J. F. (1970b). Seasonal variation in the structure and ultrastructure of the pituitary in the marine form (trachurus) of the threespine stickleback, *Gasterosteus aculeatus* L. II. Proximal pars distalis. *Z. Zellforsch.* 104, 318-336.

Leatherland, J. F. (1970c). Histological investigations of pituitary homotransplants in the marine form (trachurus) of the threespine stickleback, *Gasterosteus aculeatus* L. *Z. Zellforsch.* 104, 337-344.

Leatherland, J. F. and Lam, T. J. (1969a). Prolactin and survival in deionised water of the marine form (trachurus) of the threespine stickleback, *Gasterosteus aculeatus* L. *Can. J. Zool.* 47, 989-995.

Leatherland, J. F. and Lam, T. J. (1969b). Effect of prolactin on the density of mucus cells of the gill filaments of the marine form (trachurus) of the threespine stickleback, *Gasterosteus aculeatus* L. *Can. J. Zool.* 47, 787-792.

Leatherland, J. F. and Lam, T. J. (1971). Effects of prolactin, corticotrophin and cortisol on the adenohypophysis and interrenal gland of anadromous threespine sticklebacks, *Gasterosteus aculeatus* form *trachurus* in winter and summer. *J. Endocrinol.* 51, 425-436.

Le Cren, E. D. (1947). The determination of the age and growth of the perch (*Perca fluviatilis*) from the opercular bone. *J. Anim. Ecol.* 16, 188-204.

Le Cren, E. D. (1951). The length-weight relationship and seasonal cycle in gonad weight and condition in the perch (*Perca fluviatilis*). *J. Anim. Ecol.* 20, 201-219.

Leim, A. H. and Scott, W. B. (1966). Fishes of the Atlantic Coast of Canada. *Bull. Fish. Res. Bd. Canada* 155.

Leiner, M. (1929). Ökologische Studien an *Gasterosteus aculeatus. Z. Morph. Ökol. Tiere* 14, 360-399.

Leiner, M. (1930). Fortsetzung der ökologischen studien an *Gasterosteus aculeatus. Z. Morph. Ökol. Tiere* 16, 499-540.

Leiner, M. (1931a). Oekologisches von *Gasterosteus aculeatus* L. *Zool. Anz.* 93, 317-333.

Leiner, M. (1931b). Der Laich- und Brutflegeinstinkt des Zwergstichlings *Gasterosteus (Pygosteus) pungitius* L. *Z. Morph. Ökol. Tiere* 21, 765-788.

Leiner, M. (1934). Die drei europäischen Stichlinge (*Gasterosteus aculeatus* L., *Gasterosteus pungitius* L. und *Gasterosteus spinachia* L) und ihre Kreuzungsprodukte. *Z. Morph. Ökol. Tiere* 28, 107-154.

Leiner, M. (1940). Kurze Mitteilung uber den Brutpflegeinstinkt von Stichlingsbastarden. *Z. Tierpsychol.* 4, 167-169.

Leiner, M. (1957). Stichlingsbastarde. *Nature u. Volk* 87, 299-300.

Lemmetyinen, R. (1973). Feeding ecology of *Sterna paradisea* Pontopp. and *S. hirundo* L. in the archipeligo of southwest Finland. *Ann. Zool. Fenn.* **10**, 507–525.

Lester, R. J. G. (1971). The influence of *Schistocephalus* plerocercoids on the respiration of *Gasterosteus* and a possible resulting effect on the behaviour of the fish. *Can. J. Zool.* **49**, 361–366.

Lester, R. J. G. (1972). Attachment of *Gyrodactylus* to *Gasterosteus* and host response. *J. Parasitol.* **58**, 717–722.

Lester, R. J. G. (1974). Parasites of *Gasterosteus aculeatus* near Vancouver, British Columbia. *Syesis* **7**, 195–200.

Lester, R. J. G. and Adams, J. R. (1974a). *Gyrodactylus alexanderi*: reproduction, mortality and effect on its host *Gasterosteus aculeatus*. *Can. J. Zool.* **52**, 827–833.

Lester, R. J. G. and Adams, J. R. (1974b). A simple model of a *Gyrodactylus* population. *Int. J. Parasitol.* **4**, 497–506.

Levins, R. (1968). "Evolution in Changing Environments" Princeton University Press, Princeton.

Lewis, D. B., Walkey, M. and Dartnall, H. J. G. (1972). Some effects of low oxygen tensions on the distribution of the three-spined stickleback *Gasterosteus aculeatus* L. and the nine-spined stickleback *Pungitius pungitius* (L). *J. Fish Biol.* **4**, 103–108.

Liley, N. R. (1969). Hormones and reproductive behaviour in fishes. *In* "Fish Physiology" (W. S. Hoar and D. J. Randall, eds.), Vol. 3, pp. 73–116. Academic Press, London, New York.

Limbaugh, C. (1962). Life history and ecological notes on the tubenose, *Aulorhynchus flavidus*, a hemibranch fish of western North America. *Copeia* **1962**, 549–555.

Lindsey, C. C. (1962a). Experimental study of meristic variation in a population of threespine sticklebacks, *Gasterosteus aculeatus*. *Can. J. Zool.* **40**, 271–312.

Lindsey, C. C. (1962b). Observations on meristic variation in ninespine sticklebacks, *Pungitius pungitius*, reared at different temperatures. *Can. J. Zool.* **40**, 1237–1247.

Liu Hsien-T'Ing and Wang Nien-Chung (1974). A new *Pungitius* from the Nihowan formation of North China. *Vertebr. Palasiat.* **12**, 89–98.

McAllister, D. E. (1960). The twospine stickleback *Gasterosteus wheatlandi* new to Canadian freshwater fish fauna. *Can. Field Nat.* **74**, 177–178.

McFarland, D. J. (1974). Time-sharing as a behavioural phenomenon. *In* "Advances in the Study of Behaviour" (D. S. Lehrman, J. S. Rosenblatt, R. A. Hinde and E. Shaw, eds.), pp. 201–225. Academic Press, London, New York.

McInerney, J. E. (1969). Reproductive behaviour of the blackspotted stickleback *Gasterosteus wheatlandi*. *J. Fish. Res. Bd. Canada* **26**, 2061–2075.

McInerney, J. E. and Evans, D. O. (1970). Action spectrum of the photoperiod mechanism controlling sexual maturation in the threespine stickleback, *Gasterosteus aculeatus*. *J. Fish. Res. Bd. Canada* **27**, 749–763.

McKenzie, J. A. (1969a). A descriptive analysis of the aggressive behaviour of the male brook stickleback, *Culaea inconstans*. *Can. J. Zool.* **47**, 1275–1279.

McKenzie, J. A. (1969b). The courtship behaviour of the male brook stickleback, *Culaea inconstans* (Kirkland). *Can. J. Zool.* **47**, 1281–1286.

McKenzie, J. A. (1974). The parental behaviour of the male brook stickleback *Culaea inconstans* (Kirkland). *Can. J. Zool.* **52**, 649–652.

McKenzie, J. A. and Keenlyside, M. H. A. (1970). Reproductive behaviour of ninespine sticklebacks (*Pungitius pungitius* (L)) in South Bay, Manitoulin, Ontario. *Can. J. Zool.* 48, 55-61.

MacLean, J. A. and Gee, J. H. (1971). Effects of temperature on movements of prespawning brook sticklebacks, *Culaea inconstans*, in the Roseau River, Manitoba. *J. Fish. Res. Bd. Canada* 28, 919-23.

McPhail, J. D. (1963). Geographic variation in North American ninespine sticklebacks, *Pungitius pungitius*. *J. Fish. Res. Bd. Canada* 20, 27-44.

McPhail, J. D. (1969). Predation and the evolution of a stickleback (*Gasterosteus*). *J. Fish. Res. Bd. Canada* 26, 3183-3208.

McPhail, J. D. and Lindsey, C. C. (1970). Freshwater fishes of northwestern Canada and Alaska. *Bull. Fish. Res. Bd. Canada* 173, 1-373.

Maitland, P. S. (1965). The feeding relationships of salmon, trout, minnows, stone loach and three-spined sticklebacks in the River Endrick, Scotland. *J. Anim. Ecol.* 34, 109-133.

Mann, R. H. K. (1971). The populations, growth and production of fish in the four small streams in southern England. *J. Anim. Ecol.* 40, 155-190.

Mann, R. H. K. and Orr, D. R. O. (1969). A preliminary study of the feeding relationships of fish in a hard-water and a soft-water stream in southern England. *J. Fish Biol.* 1, 31-44.

Markley, M. H. (1940). Notes on the food habits and parasites of the stickleback *Gasterosteus aculeatus* Linn. in the Sacramento River, California. *Copeia 1940*, 223-225.

Marshall, N. B. (1971). "Explorations in the Life of Fishes" Oxford University Press, London.

Matthiessen, P. and Brafield, A. E. (1973). The effects of dissolved zinc on the gills of the stickleback *Gasterosteus aculeatus* L. *J. Fish Biol.* 5, 607-613.

Mayr, E. (1963). "Animal Species and Evolution" Harvard University Press, Cambridge, Mass.

Meakins, R. H. (1974). A quantitative approach to the effects of the plerocercoid of *Schistocephalus solidus* Müller 1776 on the ovarian maturation of the three-spined stickleback *Gasterosteus aculeatus* L. *Z. Parasitenkd.* 44, 73-79.

Meakins, R. H. (1975). The effects of activity and season on the respiration of the three-spined stickleback, *Gasterosteus aculeatus* L. *Comp. Biochem. Physiol.* 51A, 155-157.

Meesters, A. (1940). Über die Organization des Gesichsfeldes der Fische. *Z. Tierpsychol.* 4, 84-149.

Merriman, D. and Schedl, H. P. (1941). Gametogenesis in sticklebacks. *J. Exp. Zool.* 88, 413-449.

Metz, H. (1974). Stochastic models for the temporal fine structure of behaviour sequences. *In* "Motivational Control Systems Analysis" (D. J. McFarland, ed.). pp. 5-86. Academic Press, London, New York.

Miller, R. R. (1960). The type locality of *Gasterosteus aculeatus williamsoni* and its significance in the taxonomy of Californian sticklebacks. *Copeia 1960*, 348-350.

Miller, R. R. (1961). Speciation rates in some freshwater fishes of Western North America. *In* "Vertebrate Speciation" (W. F. Blair, ed.), pp. 537-560. University of Texas Press, Austin.

Miller, R. R. and Hubbs, C. L. (1969). Systematics of *Gasterosteus aculeatus* with particular reference to integradation and introgression along the Pacific coast of North America: a commentary on a recent contribution. *Copeia 1969*, 52-69.

Molenda, E. and Fiedler, K. (1971). Die Wirkung von Prolaktin auf das Verhalten von Stichlingsmannen (*Gasterosteus aculeatus* L.). *Z. Tierpsychol.* 28, 463-474.

Moodie, G. E. E. (1972a). Predation, natural selection and adaptation in an unusual threespine stickleback. *Hereditary* 28, 155-167.

Moodie, G. E. E. (1972b). Morphology, life history and ecology of an unusual stickleback (*Gasterosteus aculeatus*) in the Queen Charlotte Islands, Canada. *Can. J. Zool.* 50, 721-732.

Moodie, G. E. E. and Reimchen, T. E. (1973). Endemism and conservation of sticklebacks in the Queen Charlotte Islands. *Can. Field Nat.* 87, 173-175.

Moodie, G. E. E., McPhail, J. D., and Hagen, D. W. (1973). Experimental demonstration of selective predation on *Gasterosteus aculeatus*. *Behaviour* 47, 95-105.

Morris, D. (1952). Homosexuality in the ten-spined stickleback. *Behaviour* 4, 233-261.

Morris, D. (1958). The reproductive behaviour of the ten-spined stickleback (*Pygosteus pungitius* L.). *Behaviour Suppl.* 6, 1-154.

Morris, D. (1970). "Patterns of Reproductive Behaviour" Jonathan Cape, London.

Mourier, J.-P. (1970). Structure fine du rein de l'epinoche (*Gasterosteus aculeatus* L.) au cours de sa transformation muqueuse. *Z. Zellforsch.* 106, 232-250.

Mourier, J.-P. (1972). Etude de la cytodifferentiation du rein de l'Epinoche femelle apres traitement par la methyltestosterone. *Z. Zellforsch.* 123, 96-111.

Muckensturm, B. (1965). Possibilites inattendues de manipulation chez l'epinoche (*Gasterosteus aculeatus*). *C.R. Acad. Sc. Paris* (D) 260, 3183-3184.

Muckensturm, B. (1967). L'epinoche et les leurres, complexite de la reaction. *C.R. Acad. Sc. Paris* (D) 264, 745-748.

Muckensturm, B. (1968). La reaction des Epinoches aux leurres ne provient pas d'une confusion avec un congenere. *C.R. Acad. Sc. Paris* (D) 266, 2114-2116.

Mullem, P. J. van (1959). A histo- and cytochemical study on the pituitary of the stickleback, *Gasterosteus aculeatus* L. forma *trachura* Cuv. partly based on a new fixation procedure after freeze drying. *Arch. néerl. Zool.* 13, 149-195.

Mullem, P. J. van (1967). On synchronisation in the reproduction of the stickleback (*Gasterosteus aculeatus* L. Forma *Leiura* Cuv.). *Arch. néerl. Zool.* 17, 258-274.

Mullem, P. van and Vlugt, J. van der (1964). On the age, growth and migration of the anadromous stickleback *Gasterosteus aculeatus* L. investigated in mixed populations. *Arch néerl. Zool.* 16, 111-139.

Mullins, L. J. (1950). Osmotic regulation in fish as studied with radioisotopes. *Acta. physiol. scand.* 21, 303-314.

Münzing, J. (1959). Biologie, variabilität und genetik von *Gasterosteus aculeatus* L. (Pisces). Untersuchungen im Elbegebiet. *Int. Rev. Ges. Hydrobiol.* 44, 317-382.

Münzing, J. (1961). *Gasterosteus aculeatus* L. (Pisces) im Ostseeraum. *Mitt, Hamburg, Zool. Mus. Inst.* 59, 61-72.

Münzing, J. (1962a). Ein neuer semiarmatus-Typ von *Gasterosteus aculeatus* L. (Pisces) aus dem Izniksee. *Mitt. Hamburg. Zool. Mus.* 60, 181-194.

Münzing, J. (1962b). Die Populationen der marinen Wanderform von *Gasterosteus aculeatus* L. (Pisces) an den holländischen und deutschen Nordseeküsten *Neth. J. Sea Res.* 1, 508–525.

Münzing, J. (1963a). The evolution of variation and distributional patterns in European populations of the three-spined stickleback, *Gasterosteus aculeatus*. *Evolution*, 17, 320–332.

Münzing, J. (1963b). Die Verbreitung des Dreistachligen Stichlings in Europa. *Natur u. Mus.* 93, 284–290.

Münzing, J. (1964). Variabilität und Verbreitung von *Gasterosteus aculeatus* L. (Pisces) in Europa. *Verh. Ver. naturw. Unternh. Heimatforsch. Hamb.* 36, 1–22.

Münzing, J. (1969). Variabilität, Verbreitung und Systematik der Arten und Unterarten in der Gattung *Pungitius* Coste, 1848 (Pisces, Gasterosteidae). *Z. Zool. Syst. Evol. Forsch.* 7, 208–233.

Münzing, J. (1972). Polymorphe populationen von *Gasterosteus aculeatus* L. (Pisces, Gasterosteidae) in sekundären intergradionszonen der Deutschen Bucht und benachbarter Gebiete. *Faun. Okol. Mitt.* 4, 69–84.

Mural, R. J. (1973). The Pliocene sticklebakcs of Nevada with a partial osteology of the Gasterosteidae. *Copeia 1973*, 721–734.

Muramoto, J. and Igarashi, K. (1969). A preliminary note on the chromosomes and enzymatic patterns of three forms of sticklebacks. *J. Fac. Sci. Hokkaido Univ. (Ser. Zool.)* 17, 266–270.

Muramoto, J. K., Igarashi, K., Itoh, M. and Makino, S. (1969). A study of the chromosomes and enzymatic patterns of sticklebacks of Japan. *Proc. Jap. Acad.* 65, 803–807.

Narver, D. W. (1969). Phenotypic variation in three-spine sticklebacks (*Gasterosteus aculeatus*) of the Chignik River system, Alaska. *J. Fish. Res. Bd. Canada* 26, 405–412.

Neill, S. R. St J. and Cullen, J. M. (1974). Experiments on whether schooling by their prey affects the hunting behaviour of cephalopods and fish predators. *J. Zool., Lond.* 172, 549–569.

Nelson, J. S. (1968a). Salinity tolerance of brook sticklebacks, *Culaea inconstans*, freshwater ninespine sticklebacks, *Pungitius pungitius*, and freshwater fourspine sticklebacks, *Apeltes quadracus*. *Can. J. Zool.* 46, 663–667.

Nelson, J. S. (1968b). Deep-water ninespine sticklebacks, *Pungitius pungitius*, in the Mississippi drainage, Crooked Lake, Indiana. *Copeia 1968*, 326–334.

Nelson, J. S. (1969a). Geographical variation in the brook stickleback, *Culaea inconstans*, and notes on nomenclature and distribution. *J. Fish. Res. Bd. Canada* 26, 2431–2447.

Nelson, J. S. (1969b). Ecology of the southernmost sympatric population of the brook stickleback, *Culaea inconstans*, and the ninespine stickleback, *Pungitius pungitius*, in Crooked Lake, Indiana. *Proc. Indiana Acad. Sci.* 77, 185–192.

Nelson, J. S. (1971a). Comparison of the pectoral and pelvic skeletons and of some other bones and their phylogenetic implications in the Aulorhynchidae and Gasterosteidae (Pisces). *J. Fish. Res. Bd. Canada* 28, 427–442.

Nelson, J. S. (1971b). Absence of the pelvic complex in ninespine sticklebacks, *Pungitius pungitius*, collected in Ireland and Wood Buffalow National Park Region, Canada, with notes on meristic variation. *Copeia 1971*, 707–711.

Nelson, J. S. and Atton, F. M. (1971). Geographical and morphological variation in the presence and absence of the pelvic skeleton in the brook stickleback, *Culaea inconstans* (Kirkland), in Alberta and Saskatchewan. *Can. J. Zool.* 49, 343–352.

Nelson, K. (1965). After effects of courtship in the male three-spined stickle-back. *Z. vergl. Physiol.* 50, 569–597.

Nikolskii, G. V. (1969). "Fish Population Dynamics" Oliver and Boyd, Edinburgh.

Nieuwenhuys, R. (1959). The structure of the telencephalon of the teleost *Gasterosteus aculeatus. Konink. Neder. Akad. Weten. ser C.* 62, 341–361.

Nolte, W. (1933). Experimentelle Untersuchungen zum Problem der lokalisation des Assoziationsvermögens im Fischgehirn, *Z. verg. Physiol.* 18, 255–279.

O'Donald, P. (1973). Models of sexual and natural selection in polygamous species. *Hereditary* 31, 145–156.

Ogawa, M. (1968). Seasonal difference of glomerular change of the marine form of the stickleback, *Gasterosteus aculeatus* L. after transferred into freshwater. *Sci. Rep. Saitama Univ.* 5 (*Ser. B*)., 117–123.

Oguro, C. (1956). Some observations on the effect of oestrogen upon the liver of the three-spined stickleback, *Gasterosteus aculeatus aculeatus* L. *Ann. Zool. Jap.* 29, 19–23.

Oguro, C. (1957). Notes on the change in the kidney of *Gasterosteus aculeatus* L. caused by oestrogen administration. *J. Fac. Sci. Hokkaido Univ., Ser. VI,* 13, 404–407.

Oguro, C. (1958). Effects of sex hormones on the kidneys of the three-spined stickleback, *Gasterosteus aculeatus. J. Fac. Sci. Hokkaido Univ., Ser. VI.* 14, 45–50.

Okada, Y. (1959/1960). Studies on the freshwater fishes of Japan. *J. Fac. Fish. Pref. Univ. Mie* 4, 1–860.

Oordt, G. J. van (1923). Secondary sex characters and the testis of the ten-spined stickleback (*Gasterosteus pungitius* L.). *K. Akad. Wetens Amst.* 26, 309–314.

Oordt, G. J. van (1924). Die Veränderungen des Hodens während des Auftretens ser sekundären Geschlechtsmerkmale bei Fischen. I. *Gasterosteus pungitius. Arch. Mikr. Anat. Entw. Berlin,* 102, 379–405.

Opperman, G. (1973). Ueber Schleimzellen im Nephron von Teleostiern: Enzymhistochemische und elecktronenmikroskopische Beobachtungen an der Niere des dreistachligen Stichlings (*Gasterosteus aculeatus* L.) und des neunstachligen Stichlings (*Pungitius pungitius* L.) waehrend der Fort-pflanzungsperiode. *Arch. Hydrobiol.* 72, 384–406.

Orr, T. S. C. and Hopkins, C. A. (1969). Maintenance of *Schistocephalus solidus* in the laboratory with observations on the rate of growth of, and proglottid formation in, the plerocercoid. *J. Fish. Res. Bd. Canada* 26, 741–752.

Orr, T. S. C., Hopkins, C. A. and Charles, G. H. (1969). Host specificity and rejection of *Schistocephalus solidus. Parasitology* 59, 683–690.

Oshima, K. and Gorbman, A. (1969). Effects of sex hormones on photically evoked potentials in frog brain. *Gen. Comp. Endocrinol.* 12, 397–404.

Overbeeke, A. P. van (1960). "Histological Studies on the Interrenal Tissue and the Phaerochromis Tissue in Teleosti" Munsters Drukkerijen, Amsterdam.

Owen, D. F. (1960). The nesting success of the heron *Ardea cinerea* in relation to the availability of food. *Proc. zool. soc. Lond.* 133, 597–617.

Paepke, H. (1970). Studien zur Ökologie, Variabilität und Populationsstruktur des Dreistachligen und Neunstachligen Stichlings. *Veroff. Bez-Muz., Potsdam* 21, 5–48.

Peeke, H. V. S. (1969). Habituation of conspecific aggression in the three-spined stickleback (*Gasterosteus aculeatus* L.). *Behaviour* 35, 137–156.

Peeke, H. V. S. and Peeke, S. C. (1973). Habituation in fish with special reference to intraspecific aggressive behaviour. *In* "Habituation" (H. V. S. Peeke and M. J. Herz, eds.), Vol. 1, pp. 59–83. Academic Press, London, New York.

Peeke, H. V. S. and Veno, A. (1973). Stimulus specificity of habituated aggression in the stickleback (*Gasterosteus aculeatus*). *Behav. Biol.* 8, 427–432.

Peeke, H. V. S., Wyers, E. J. and Herz, M. J. (1969). Waning of the aggressive response to male models in the three-spined stickleback (*Gasterosteus aculeatus* L.). *Anim. Behav.* 17, 224–228.

Pelkwijk, J. J. ter and Tinbergen, N. (1937). Eine reizbiologische Analyse einiger Verhaltenswiesen von *Gasterosteus aculeatus* L. *Z. Tierpsychol.* 1, 193–200.

Penczak, T. (1959). The resistance of stickleback (*Gasterosteus aculeatus* L.) to changes of osmotic pressure and the action of various salts in ambient surrounding. *Przegl. Zool.* 3, 100–105.

Penczak, T. (1960a). Studies on the stickleback (*Gasterosteus aculeatus* L.) in Poland. Pt. 1. *Fragm. Faun. Warsaw* 8, 367–400.

Penczak, T. (1960b). New cases of variability of the stickleback *Gasterosteus aculeatus* L. *Fragm. Faun. Warsaw* 8, 403–410.

Penczak, T. (1961a). Significance of the regeneration of lateral plates of the stickleback (*Gasterosteus aculeatus* L.). *Nature, Lond.*, 191, 621.

Penczak, T. (1961b). Serological relationships between the nine-spined and three-spined stickleback. *Nature, Lond.*, 192, 673–674.

Penczak, T. (1962). The biometry of the threespine stickleback *Gasterosteus aculeatus* L. from the Ner River. *Fragm. Faun, Warsaw* 10, 137–161.

Penczak, T. (1964). Three-spined stickleback from Iceland *Gasterosteus aculeatus islandicus*. *Ann. Zool.* 22, 441–448.

Penczak, T. (1965). Morphological variation of the stickleback (*Gasterosteus aculeatus* L.) in Poland. *Zool. Pol.* 15, 3–49.

Penczak, T. (1966). Comments on the taxonomy of the three-spined stickleback, *Gasterosteus aculeatus* Linnaeus. *Ohio J. Sci.* 66, 81–87.

Penczak, T. (1968). *Gasterosteus aculeatus* L. as food of *Mergus merganser* L. *Przegl. zool.* 12, 357–358. (Original in Polish).

Pennycuik, L. (1971a). Quantitative effects of three species of parasites on a population of three-spined sticklebacks, *Gasterosteus aculeatus*. *J. Zool., Lond.* 165, 143–162.

Pennycuik, L. (1971b). Seasonal variations in the parasite infections in a population of three spined sticklebacks, *Gasterosteus aculeatus* L. *Parasitology* 63, 373–388.

Pennycuik, L. (1971c). Frequency distributions of parasites in a population of three-spined sticklebacks, *Gasterosteus aculeatus* L., with particular reference to the negative binomial distribution. *Parasitology* 63, 389–406.

Pennycuik, L. (1971d). Difference in the parasite infections in three-spined sticklebacks (*Gasterosteus aculeatus* L.) of different sex, age and size. *Parasitology* 63, 407–418.

Perlmutter, A. (1963). Observations on fishes of the genus *Gasterosteus* in the waters of Long Island, New York. *Copiea 1963*, 168–173.

Phillips, G. C. (1962). Survival value of the white colouration of gulls and other seabirds. D. Phil. Thesis, Dept. Zoology, University of Oxford.

Pipping, M. (1926). Der Geruchssiunn der Fische mit besonderer Berücksichtigung seiner Bedeutung für das Aufsuchen des Futters. *Soc. Sci. Fennica, Commentariones Biol.* 2, 1–28.

Popham, E. J. (1966). An ecological study on the predatory action of the three-spined stickleback (*Gasterosteus aculeatus* L.). *Arch. Hydrobiol.* 62, 70-81.

Potapova, T. L. (1972). The intraspecies variability of threespine stickleback *Gasterosteus aculeatus* L. *Vopr. Ikhtiol.* 12, 25-40.

Potapova, T. L., Legedeva, T. V. and Shatunovkiy, M. I. (1968). Differences in the condition of females and eggs of the three-spined stickleback, *Gasterosteus aculeatus*. *Probl. Ichthyol.* 8, 143-146.

Prince, E. E. (1885). On the nest and development of *Gasterosteus spinachia* at the St. Andrew's Marine laboratory. *Ann. Mag. Nat. Hist. Ser. 5*, 16, 487-496.

Raffy, A. (1954). Pouvoir d'adaptation de *Spinachia vulgaris* Flem. aux changement de salinite. *C.R. Soc. Biol. Paris* 147, 2005-2007.

Raunich, L., Callergarini, C. and Cucchi, C. (1972). Ecological aspects of haemoglobin polymorphism in *Gasterosteus aculeatus* (Teleostea). *Vth European Marine Biology Symposium* 153-162.

Regan, C. T. (1909). The species of thee-spined sticklebacks (*Gasterosteus*). *Ann. Mag. Nat. Hist. Ser. 8*, 4, 435-437.

Regan, C. Tate (1911). "The Freshwater Fishes of the British Isles" Methuen, London.

Regan, C. Tate (1929). Fishes. *In* "Encyclopaedia Britannica" 14th Edition, Vol. 9, pp. 305-329. London.

Reisman, H. M. (1963). Reproductive behaviour of *Apeltes quadracus*, including some comparisons with other gasterosteid fishes. *Copeia 1963*, 191-192.

Reisman, H. M. (1968a). Effects of social stimuli on the secondary sex characters of male three-spined sticklebacks, *Gasterosteus aculeatus*. *Copeia 1968*, 816-826.

Reisman, H. M. (1968b). Reproductive isolating mechanisms of the blackspotted stickleback, *Gasterosteus wheatlandi*. *J. Fish. Res. Bd. Canada* 25, 2703-2706.

Reisman, H. M. and Cade, T. J. (1967). Physiological and behavioural aspects of reproduction in the brook stickleback, *Culaea inconstans*. *Amer. Midl. Nat.* 77, 257-295.

Rinkel, G. L. and Hirsch, G. C. (1940). Die Restitution des Eiweiss-Sekretes zum Nestbau beim Stichling *Gasterosteus* in Verbindung mit dem Arbeitsrhythmus der Niere. *Z. Zellforsch.* 64, 649-688.

Rogers, D. E. (1968). A comparison of the food of sockeye salmon fry and threespine sticklebacks in Wood River Lakes. *Univ. Wash. Publs.* 3 (N.S.), 1-43.

Rogers, D. E. (1973). Abundance and size of juvenile sockeye salmon, *Oncorhynchus nerka*, and associated species in Lake Aleknagik, Alaska in relation to their environment. *Fishery Bulletin* 71, 1061-1075.

Rosen, D. E. (1973). Interrelationships of higher euteleostean fishes. *In* "Interrelationships of Fishes" (P. H. Greenwood, R. S. Miles and C. Patterson, eds.), pp. 397-513. Academic Press, London, New York.

Ross, S. T. (1973). The systematics of *Gasterosteus aculeatus* (Pisces: Gasterosteidae) in central and southern California. *Nat. Hist. Mus. Los. Ang. Cty. Contrib. Sci.* 243, 1-20.

Rowland, W. J. (1974a). Reproductive behaviour of the four-spine stickleback *Apeltes quadracus*. *Copeia 1974*, 183-194.

Rowland, W. J. (1974b). Ground nest construction in the four-spine stickleback *Apeltes quadracus*. *Copeia 1974*, 788-789.

Ruby, S. M. and McMillan, D. B. (1970). Cyclic changes in the testis of the brook stickleback *Eucalia inconstans* (Kirtland). *J. Morphol.* 131, 447–465.

Ruby, S. M. and McMillan, D. B. (1975). The interstitial origin of germinal cells in the testis of the stickleback. *J. Morph.* 145, 295–318.

Ryder, J. A. (1882). Notes on the development of the spinning habits and structure of the four-spined stickleback *Apeltes quadracus. Bull. U.S. Fish. Comm.* 1, 24–29.

Saunders, J. T. (1914). A note on the food of freshwater fish. *Proc. Camb. Phil. Soc.* 17, 236–239.

Schneider, L. (1969). Experimentelle Untersuchungen über den Einfluss von Tägeslange und Temperatur auf die Gonadenreifung beim Dreistachligen stichling (*Gasterosteus aculeatus*). *Oecologia* 3, 249–265.

Schönherr, J. (1955). Ueber die Abhängigkeit der Instinkthandlungen vom Voderhirn und Zwischenhirn (Epiphyse) bei *Gasterosteus aculeatus. Zool. Jahrb. Abt. Allg. Zool. Physiol. Tiere* 65, 358–386.

Schütz, E. and Tschanz, B. (1971). Die Wirkung von Nestmaterial auf das Nestbauverhalten des dreistachligen Stichlings (*Gasterosteus aculeatus*). *Rev. Suisse. Zool.* 78, 793–805.

Schwartz, F. J. (1965). Age, growth and egg complement of the stickleback *Apeltes quadracus* at Solomons, Maryland. *Chesapeake Sci.* 6, 116–118.

Scott, W. B. and Crossman, E. J. (1964). Fishes occurring in the fresh waters of insular Newfoundland. Dept. Fish. Canada, Ottawa.

Scott, W. B. and Crossman, E. J. (1973). Freshwater Fishes of Canada. *Bull. Fish. Res. Bd. Canada 184.*

Segaar, J. (1956). Brain and instinct with *Gasterosteus aculeatus. Konink. Neder, Akad. Weten. Proc. Ser. C.* 59, 738–749.

Segaar, J. (1961). Telencephalon and behaviour in *Gasterosteus aculeatus* males. *Behaviour* 18, 256–287.

Segaar, J. (1966). Wie "weiss" der Stichling das Alter seiner Embryonen? *Umschau* 66, 333.

Segaar, J. and Nieuwenhuys, R. (1963). New etho-physiological experiments with male *Gasterosteus aculeatus* with anatomical comment. *Anim. Behav.* 11, 331–344.

Semler, D. E. (1971). Some aspects of adaptation in a polymorphism for breeding colours in the threespine stickleback (*Gasterosteus aculeatus*). *J. Zool., Lond.* 165, 291–302.

Sevenster, P. (1949). Modderbaarsjes. *Lev. Nat.* 52, 161–168, 184–189.

Sevenster, P. (1951). The mating of the sea stickleback. *Discovery* 12, 52–56.

Sevenster, P. (1961). A causal study of a displacement acitvity (Fanning in *Gasterosteus aculeatus* L.). *Behaviour Suppl.* 9, 1–170.

Sevenster, P. (1968). Motivation and learning in sticklebacks. *In* "The Central Nervous System and Fish Behaviour" (D. Ingle, ed.), pp. 233–245. University of Chicago Press, London.

Sevenster, P. (1973). Incompatibility of response and reward. *In* "Constraints on Learning" (R. A. Hinde and J. Stevenson-Hinde, eds.), pp. 265–283. Academic Press, London, New York.

Sevenster, P. and 't Hart, M. (1974). A behavioural variant in the three-spined stickleback. *In* "The Genetics of Behaviour" (J. H. F. van Abeelen, ed.), pp. 141–165. North-Holland Publishing Company, Amsterdam.

Sevenster-Bol, A. C. A. (1962). On the causation of drive reduction after a consummatory act (in *Gasterosteus aculeatus*). *Arch. néerl. Zool.* 15, 175–236.

Shields, G. F. and Straus, N. A. (1975). DNA-DNA hybridization studies of birds. *Evolution* 29, 159-166.

Smith, R. F. J. (1970). Effects of food availability on aggression and nest building in brook stickleback (*Culaea inconstans*). *J. Fish. Res. Bd. Canada* 27, 2350-2355.

Smith, R. J. F. and Hoar, W. S. (1967). The effects of prolactin and testosterone on the parental behaviour of the male stickleback *Gasterosteus aculeatus*. *Anim. Behav.* 15, 342-352.

Stanworth, P. (1953). A study of reproduction in the threespined stickleback, *Gasterosteus aculeatus* L., with some reference to endocrine control Ph.D. Thesis, Dept. of Zoology, Sheffield University.

Stenger, A. H. (1963). An apparent error in a report of structural hermaphroditism in an Alaskan threespine stickleback, *Gasterosteus aculeatus*. *Copeia* 1963, 454-455.

Svärdson, G. (1961). Young sibling fish species in Northwestern Europe. *In* "Vertebrate Speciation" (W. F. Blair, ed.), pp. 498-513. University of Texas Press, Austin.

Swarup, H. (1956). Production of heteroploidy in the three-spined stickleback, *Gasterosteus aculeatus* (L.). *Nature, Lond.* 178, 1124-1125.

Swarup, H. (1958a). Stages in the development of the stickleback *Gasterosteus aculeatus* L. *J. Embryol. exp. Morph.* 6, 373-383.

Swarup, H. (1958b). Abnormal development in the temperature-treated eggs of *Gasterosteus aculeatus* (L.); I. Cleavage abnormalities. *J. Zool. Soc. India* 19, 108-113.

Swarup, H. (1958c). The reproductive cycle and development of gonads in *Gasterosteus aculeatus*. *Proc. Zool. Soc. Bengal* 11, 47-61.

Swarup, H. (1959a). Production of triploidy in *Gasterosteus aculeatus* (L.). *J. Genet.* 56, 129-142.

Swarup, H. (1959b). Effect of triploidy on body size, general organisation and cellular structure in *Gasterosteus aculeatus* (L.). *J. Genet.* 56, 143-155.

Swarup, H. (1959c). The oxygen consumption of diploid and triploid *Gasterosteus aculeatus* (L.). *J. Genet.* 56, 156-160.

Swarup, H. (1959d). Independent origin and development of the crystalline lens in *Gasterosteus aculeatus* L. *Curr. Sci.* 28, 118-119.

Swarup, H. (1959e). Abnormal development in temperature treated eggs of *Gasterosteus aculeatus* (L.); II. Gastrulation abnormalities. *J. zool. Soc. India* 11, 1-6.

Swarup, H. (1959f). Abnormal development in the temperature treated eggs of *Gasterosteus aculeatus* (L.); III. Twinning. *J. zool. Soc. India* 11, 7-10.

Swarup, H. (1959g). Abnormal development in the temperature treated eggs of *Gasterosteus aculeatus* (L.); IV. Microcephaly. *J. zool. Soc. India* 11, 102-108.

Swinnerton, H. H. (1902). A contribution to the morphology of the teleostean head skeleton based upon a study of the developing skull of the three-spined stickleback (*Gasterosteus aculeatus*). *Quart. J. Microscop. Sci.* 45, 503-593.

Swinnerton, H. H. (1905). A contribution to the morphology and development of the pectoral skeleton of teleosteans. *Quart. J. Microscop. Sci.* 49, 363-382.

Symons, P. E. K. (1965). Analysis of spine-raising in the male three-spined stickleback. *Behaviour* 26, 1-74.

Symons, P. E. K. (1971). Spacing and density in schooling threespine sticklebacks (*Gasterosteus aculeatus*) and mummichog (*Fundulus heteroclitus*). *J. Fish. Res. Bd. Canada* 28, 999-1004.

Teichmann, H. (1954). Vergleichende Untersuchungen an der Nase der Fische. *Z. Morphol. Oekol. Tiere* 43, 171–212.

Thomas, G. (1974). The influences of encountering a food object on subsequent searching behaviour in *Gasterosteus aculeatus* L. *Anim. Behav.* 22, 941–952.

Thomopoulos, A. (1953). Sur l'oeuf de l'epinoche (*Gasterosteus aculeatus*). *Bull. soc. zool. France* 78, 142–149.

Threlfall, W. (1968). A mass die-off of three-spined sticklebacks (*Gasterosteus aculeatus* L.) caused by parasites. *Can. J. Zool.* 46, 105–106.

Tinbergen, N. (1939). On the analysis of social organisation among vertebrates with special reference to birds. *Am. Midl. Nat.* 21, 210–234.

Tinbergen, N. (1940). Die Übersprungbewegung. *Z. Tierpsychol.* 4, 1–40.

Tinbergen, N. (1942). An objectivistic study of the innate behaviour of animals. *Biblioth. biotheor.* 1, 39–98.

Tinbergen, N. (1948). Social releasers and the experimental method required for their study. *Wilson Bull.* 60, 6–52.

Tinbergen, N. (1951). "The Study of Instinct" Clarendon Press, Oxford.

Tinbergen, N. (1952). Derived activities; their causation, function and origin. *Quart. Rev. Biol.* 27, 1–32.

Tinbergen, N. (1953). "Social Behaviour in Animals" Methuen, London.

Tinbergen, N. and Iersel, J. J. A. van (1947). "Displacement reactions" in the three-spined stickleback. *Behaviour* 1, 56–63.

Titschack, E. (1922). Die sekundären Geschlechtsmerkmale von *Gasterosteus aculeatus* L. *Zool. Jahrb. Physiol.* 39, 83–148.

Tromp-Blom, N. (1959). The ovaries of *Gasterosteus aculeatus* (L.) before, during and after the reproductive period. *Proc. K. ned. Akad. Wet.* (C) 62, 225–237.

Tschanz, B. and Schärf, M. (1971). Nestortwahl und Orienteirung zum Nestort beim Dreistachligen Stichling. *Rev. Suisse Zool.* 78, 717–721.

Tugendhat, B. (1960a). The normal feeding behaviour of the three-spined stickleback (*Gasterosteus aculeatus* L.). *Behaviour* 15, 284–318.

Tugendhat, B. (1960b). The disturbed feeding behaviour of the three-spined stickleback: I. Electric shock is administered in the food area. *Behaviour* 16, 159–187.

Tyler, A. V. (1963). A cleaning symbiosis between rainwater fish, *Lucania parva*, and the stickleback, *Apeltes quadracus*. *Chesapeake Sci.* 4, 105–106.

Uchida, K. (1934). Life history of *Aulichthys japonicus* Brevoort (Hemibranchii, Pisces). *Jap. J. Zool.* 5, 4–5.

Valdez, R. A. (1974). Two parasites of threespine stickleback from Amchitka, Aleutian Islands, Alaska. *Trans. Am. Fish. Soc.* 103, 632–635.

Valdez, R. A. and Helm, W. T. (1971). Ecology of threespine stickleback *Gasterosteus aculeatus* Linnaeus on Amchitka Island, Alaska. *Bioscience* 21, 641–645.

Voronin, V. N. (1974). (Some microsporidians (Microsporidia, Nosematidae) from sticklebacks *Pungitius pungitius* and *Gasterosteus aculeatus* of the Finish Bay.) *Acta Protozool.* 13, 221–220 (In Russian).

Vrat, V. (1949). Reproductive behaviour and development of eggs of the three-spined stickleback (*Gasterosteus aculeatus*) of California. *Copeia 1949*, 252–260.

Wai, E. H. and Hoar, W. S. (1963). The secondary sex characters and reproductive behaviour of gonadectomised sticklebacks treated with methyl testosterone. *Can. J. Zool.* 41, 611–628.

Walkey, M. (1967). The ecology of *Neoechinorynchus rutili* (Müller). *J. Parasit.* 53, 795-801.

Walkey, M. and Meakins, R. H. (1970). An attempt to balance the energy budget of a host-parasite system. *J. Fish Biol.* 2, 361-372.

Wendelaar Bonga, S. E. (1973a). Morphometrical analysis with the light and electron microscope of the kidney of the anadromous three-spined stickleback *Gasterosteus aculeatus*, form trachurus from freshwater and from seawater. *Z. Zellforsch.* 137, 563-588.

Wendelaar Bonga, S. E. (1973b). The effect of prolactin on kidney structure in the anadromous teleost *Gasterosteus aculeatus* (form trachurus) during transfer from the sea to freshwater. A morphometrical study with light and electron microscope. *J. Endocrinol.* 57, xii-xiii.

Wendelaar Bonga, S. E. and Greven, J. A. A. (1975). A second cell type in Stannius Bodies of two euryhaline teleost species. *Cell. Tiss. Res.* 159, 287-290.

Wendelaar Bonga, S. E. and Veenhuis, M. (1974). The membranes of the basal labyrinth in kidney cells of the stickleback, *Gasterosteus aculeatus*, studied in ultrathin sections and freeze-etch replicas. *J. Cell Sci.* 14, 587-609.

Wheeler, A. (1969). "The Fishes of the British Isles and North-west Europe" MacMillan, London.

Whitear, M. (1970). The skin surface of bony fishes. *J. Zool., Lond.* 160, 437-454.

Whitear, M. (1971a). The free nerve endings in fish epidermis. *J. Zool., Lond.* 163, 231-236.

Whitear, M. (1971b). Cell specialization and sensory function in fish epidermis. *J. Zool., Lond.* 163, 237-264.

Whitley, G. P. (1950). New fish names. *Proc. Roy. Zoo. Soc. New S. Wales* 1948-49, 44.

Wiles, M. (1975). The glochidia of certain Unionidae (Mollusca) in Nova Scotia and their fish hosts. *Can. J. Zool.* 53. 33-41.

Wilz, K. J. (1967). The organization of courtship behaviour in sticklebacks. D. Phil. Thesis, Department of Zoology, University of Oxford.

Wilz, K. J. (1970a). Self-regulation of motivation in the three-spined stickleback (*Gasterosteus aculeatus* L.). *Nature, Lond.* 266, 465-466.

Wilz, K. J. (1970b). Causal and functional analysis of dorsal pricking and nest activity in the courtship of the three-spined stickleback *Gasterosteus aculeatus*. *Anim. Behav.* 18, 115-124.

Wilz, K J. (1970c). The disinhibition interpretation of the "displacement" activities during courtship in the three-spined stickleback, *Gasterosteus aculeatus*. *Anim. Behav.* 18, 682-687.

Wilz, K. J. (1970d). Reproductive isolation in two species of stickleback (Gasterosteidae). *Copeia 1970*, 587-590.

Wilz, K. J. (1971). Comparative aspects of courtship behaviour in the ten-spined stickleback, *Pygosteus pungitius* (L.). *Z. Tierpsychol.* 29, 1-10.

Wilz, K. J. (1972). Causal relationships between aggression and the sexual and nest behaviours in the three-spined stickleback (*Gasterosteus aculeatus*). *Anim. Behav.* 20, 335-340.

Wilz, K. J. (1973). Quantitative differences in the courtship of two populations of three-spined sticklebacks, *Gasterosteus aculeatus*. *Z. Tierpsychol.* 33, 141-146.

Winn, H. E. (1960). Biology of the brook stickleback, *Eucalia inconstans* (Kirtland). *Amer. Midl. Nat.* 63, 424-438.

Woodward, A. Smith (1901). Catalogue of the fossil fishes in the British Museum, London, Pt. 4.

Wootton, R. J. (1970). Aggression in the early phases of the reproductive cycle of the male three-spined stickleback (*Gasterosteus aculeatus*). *Anim. Behav.* 18, 740–746.

Wootton, R. J. (1971a). Measures of the aggression of parental male three-spined sticklebacks. *Behaviour* 40, 228–262.

Wootton, R. J. (1971b). A note on the nest-raiding behaviour of male sticklebacks. *Can. J. Zool.* 49, 960–962.

Wootton, R. J. (1972a). The behaviour of the male three-spined stickleback in a natural situation: a quantitative description. *Behaviour* 41, 232–241.

Wootton, R. J. (1972b). Changes in the aggression of the male three-spined stickleback after fertilization of eggs. *Can. J. Zool.* 50, 537–541.

Wootton, R. J. (1973a). The effect of size of food ration on egg production in the female three-spined stickleback, *Gasterosteus aculeatus* L. *J. Fish Biol.* 5, 89–96.

Wootton, R. J. (1973b). Fecundity of the three-spined stickleback, *Gasterosteus aculeatus* (L.). *J. Fish Biol.* 5, 683–688.

Wootton, R. J. (1974a). The inter-spawning interval of the female three-spined stickleback, *Gasterosteus aculeatus*. *J. Zool., Lond.* 172, 331–342.

Wootton, R. J. (1974b). Changes in the courtship behaviour of female three-spined sticklebacks between spawnings. *Anim. Behav.* 22, 850–855.

Wooton, R. J. and Evans, G. W. (1976). Cost of egg production in the three-spined stickleback (*Gasterosteus aculeatus* L.). *J. Fish Biol.* 8, 385–395.

Wourms, J. P. (1973). Stickleback nest cement: an extracellular matrix secreted by kidney tubule cells. *J. Cell Biol.* 59, 370.

Wunder, W. (1928). Experimentelle Untersuchungen an Stichlingen (Kämpfe, Nestbau, Laichen, Brutpflege). *Zool. Anz. Suppl.* 3, 115–127.

Wunder, W. (1930). Experimentelle Untersuchungen an dreistachligen Stichling (*Gasterosteus aculeatus* L.) während der Laichzeit. *Z. Morph. Ökol. Tiere* 16, 453–498.

Yamamoto, T. (1961). Physiology of fertilization in fish eggs. *Int. Rev. Cytol.* 12, 361–405.

Yamamoto, T. S. (1963). Eggs and ovaries of the stickleback *Pungitius tymensis*, with a note on the formation of a jelly-like substance surrounding the egg. *J. Fac. Sci. Hokkaido Univ.* (*IV*) *Zool.* 15, 190–201.

Zhiteneva, L. D. (1971). Composition of the blood of the ninespine stickleback (*Pungitius pungitius* L.) under conditions of adverse oxygen regime. *Vopr. Ikhtiol.* (Eng. Ed.) 11, 409–417.

AUTHOR INDEX

SUBJECT INDEX

Page references to figures in italics

A

Acanthopterygii, 340, 341, 342, 343, 345
Algae, 58, 60, 62, 63, 274, 293, 316
  Diatoms, 57, 60, 62
    Nitzschia sigmoidea, 60
  Fucus, 316
  Halidrys, 316
  Macrocystis, 334
  Nitella, 281
  Spirogyra, 279
Ammonia, 102
Amphibia, 123
Annelida, 62, 79
  Hirundinea, 79
    Haemopsis marmorata, 90
  Oligochaeta, 57, 58, 59, 60, 293
    Enchytraeids, 55, 72
    Tubifex, 55, 57, 64, 68, 69, 70, 71, 72, 73, 144, 145, 316
Apeltes quadracus, 97, 108, 243, 261, 266
  age, 305
  aggression, 308, 310, 329
  colour, 306, 308, 309
  courtship, 309–310, 311, 312, 328
  cryptic behaviour, 306–307
  distribution, 305, *306*, 331, 335
  fecundity, 308
  food, 306
  glue and glueing, 308–309
  morphology, 304–305, *304*
  nest-building, 308–309, 310–311, 328, 329, 334
  ovaries, 308
  parasites, 307

  parental behaviour, 311–312, 329
  reproductive biology, 308–312, 328–329
  salinity tolerance, 304, 331
  spawning, 310
  spines, 305, 308, 309, 310, 313, 321
  sucking, 309, 311, 317, 326, 328, 332
  tail-biting, 310, 317, 328
  territory, 308
  testes, 308
Aulorhynchidae, 332–335, *337*, 339, 341, 343
  axial skeleton, 334, 343
  caudal skeleton, 333
  lateral line system, 334
  lateral plates, 333
  morphology, 332–334
  pectoral skeleton, 333
  pelvic skeleton, 333
  phylogenetic relationships, 335–336, *336*
  syncranium, 333, 334, 343
Aulichthys japonicus, 332, 333, 334, 335
  distribution, 332, 335
  reproductive biology, 334–335
Aulorhynchus flavidus, 332, 333, 334, 335
  distribution, 332, 335
  reproductive biology, 334
Aulorhynchiformes (see also Gasterosteiformes), 343–345
Aulostomiformes (see also Gasterosteiformes), 343–345

376

382   SUBJECT INDEX

Gasterosteus aculeatus—contd.

secondary sexual characters, 150, 183, 184

semiarmatus form, 93–94, 231, 232, 243, 244, 268

distribution,
European, 25, 26, 241–243
North American, 243

fecundity, 146, *147*

growth, 51

morphology, *5*, 6, 232–233

osmo-regulation, 117, 120, 121, 123

reproductive behaviour, 108

systematic status and evolution, 255

sexual behaviour (see *G. aculeatus—*courtship)

sexual maturation, female (see ovaries)

sexual maturation, male (see testes)

skin, 24

skull, *10*, 11, 14, 42

spines (see also *G. aculeatus—*predation), 3, 4, 14, 90–91, 96, 105, 188, 190, 224, 235, 236, 248, 250, 256, 321, 332
conspecific fighting, 168, 169, 171–172, 207–208

Stannius, corpuscle of, 23

stomach, 23, 65, 67, 70, 72

suspensorium, 9, *10*, 326–327

swim bladder, *23*, 24, 107

syncranium, 9

systematics, 252–257

taste receptors, 20, 64, 213

territory (see also *G. aculeatus—*aggression), 106, 107, 168, 177, 182, 199, 229
determinants of size, 177–179, 192, 223

territorial behaviour (see also *G. aculeatus—*aggression), 158, 168–171

testes, 23, *155*, 183
hormones, effect on, 153
interstitial cells, 151, *152*, 153, 156
photoperiod, effect on, 153, 157
spermatogenesis, 86, 151
structure, 150–151, *152*

temperature, effect on, 153

thermal tolerance, 33–34, 255

thyroid, 23, 122, 123, 126–127

trachurus form, *5*, 93–94, 231, 232, 233, 234, 238, 243, 252, 256, 264, 268
blood serum, 112
colour, 5
distribution,
European, 25, 26, 28, 29, 242–243
North American, 30–32, 243
fecundity, 7, 146, *147*
food, 61–62, 241
growth, 51–52
habitat preferences, 127–128, 159, 160, 240–241
maximum age, 53, 54
migration, 5, 46–47, 110, 126
morphology, 4–6, *5*, 7, 8, 235, 254
osmoregulation, 117, 118–119, 120, 121, 123, 125, 126
reproductive behaviour, 108, 127
salinity preference, 121, 127
salinity tolerance, 120, 123, 124–125, 237–238
systematic status and evolution, 231, 254–255

triploids, 43

Type A (see also leiurus), 232, 237

Type B (see also trachurus), 232, 237

urinary bladder, *23*, 112, 154, *155*

urohypophysis, 19, 127

vertebrae, 14, *15*, 232, 235, 245, 250

vision, 19, 64
colour sensitivity, 19, 141, 142, 175–176

Gasterosteus aculeatus aculeatus, 256

Gasterosteus aculeatus islandicus, 257

Gasterosteus aculeatus microcephalus, 32, 256

Gasterosteus aculeatus williamsoni, 32, 256

Gasterosteus pungitius (see *Pungitius pungitius*)

Gasterosteus trachurus, 231

Gasterosteus wheatlandi, 243, 261, 262, 305